First World War
and Army of Occupation
War Diary
France, Belgium and Germany

32 DIVISION
14 Infantry Brigade
Dorsetshire Regiment
1st Battalion
1 January 1916 - 31 March 1919

WO95/2392/1

The Naval & Military Press Ltd
www.nmarchive.com
Published in association with The National Archives

Published by

The Naval & Military Press Ltd

Unit 10 Ridgewood Industrial Park,
Uckfield, East Sussex,
TN22 5QE England
Tel: +44 (0) 1825 749494

www.naval-military-press.com
www.nmarchive.com

This diary has been reprinted in facsimile from the original. Any imperfections are inevitably reproduced and the quality may fall short of modern type and cartographic standards.

Contents

Document type	Place/Title	Date From	Date To
Heading	WO95/2392/1		
Heading	32nd Division 14th Infy Bde 1st Bn Dorset Regt Jan 1916 1917 March		
Heading	14th Brigade. 32nd Division. 1st Battalion The Dorset Regiment January 1916		
War Diary	Sailly Lorette	01/01/1916	02/01/1916
War Diary	Millencourt	03/01/1916	10/01/1916
War Diary	G.I. Subsector	11/01/1916	14/01/1916
War Diary	Authville	15/01/1916	18/01/1916
War Diary	Millencourt	19/01/1916	26/01/1916
War Diary	G.I. Subsector	27/01/1916	27/01/1916
War Diary	G.I	28/01/1916	31/01/1916
Miscellaneous	To 14th Inf. Brig. Intelligence Report.	11/01/1916	11/01/1916
Miscellaneous	A Form. Messages And Signals.		
Miscellaneous	Intelligence Report GI Subsector.	12/01/1915	12/01/1915
Miscellaneous	A Form. Messages And Signals.		
Miscellaneous	GI Intelligence Report	13/01/1916	13/01/1916
Miscellaneous	A Form. Messages And Signals.		
Miscellaneous	Intelligence Report.	14/01/1916	14/01/1916
Miscellaneous	A Form. Messages And Signals.		
Miscellaneous	Intelligence.	27/01/1916	27/01/1916
Miscellaneous	A Form. Messages And Signals.		
Miscellaneous	Intelligence Report.	23/01/1916	23/01/1916
Miscellaneous	14th Infantry Bde.	28/01/1916	28/01/1916
Miscellaneous	Intelligence Report.	29/01/1916	29/01/1916
Miscellaneous	Situation Report.	29/01/1916	29/01/1916
Miscellaneous	Intelligence.	30/01/1916	30/01/1916
Miscellaneous	Situation Report	30/01/1916	30/01/1916
Miscellaneous	Intelligence Report.	31/01/1916	31/01/1916
Miscellaneous	Situation Report	31/01/1916	31/01/1916
Miscellaneous	In The Field	07/01/1916	07/01/1916
Miscellaneous	In The Field	13/01/1916	13/01/1916
Miscellaneous	In The Field	20/01/1916	20/01/1916
Miscellaneous	In The Field	27/01/1916	27/01/1916
Heading	14th Brigade. 32nd Division. 1st Battalion The Dorset Regiment February 1916		
War Diary	Martinsart	02/02/1916	06/02/1916
War Diary	Millencourt	07/02/1916	11/02/1916
War Diary	Baikeux	12/02/1916	12/02/1916
War Diary	Rainneville	13/02/1916	14/02/1916
War Diary	Frechencourt	15/02/1916	29/02/1916
Miscellaneous	In The Field	03/02/1916	03/02/1916
Miscellaneous	In The Field	10/02/1916	10/02/1916
Miscellaneous	In The Field	17/02/1916	17/02/1916
Miscellaneous	In The Field.	24/02/1916	24/02/1916
Miscellaneous	In The Field	01/03/1916	01/03/1916
Heading	14th Brigade. 32nd Division.1st Battalion The Dorset Regiment March 1916		
War Diary	Millencourt	05/03/1916	09/03/1916
War Diary	E3 Sub Sector	09/03/1916	09/03/1916

War Diary	E3	10/03/1916	10/03/1916
War Diary	E3 Subsector	11/03/1916	11/03/1916
War Diary	E3	12/03/1916	15/03/1916
War Diary	Albert Aveluy	16/03/1916	21/03/1916
War Diary	E3 Subsector	21/03/1916	21/03/1916
War Diary	E3	22/03/1916	22/03/1916
War Diary	E3 Subsector	22/03/1916	27/03/1916
War Diary	Millencourt	28/03/1916	31/03/1916
Miscellaneous	In The Field	09/03/1916	09/03/1916
Miscellaneous			
Miscellaneous	In The Field	16/03/1916	16/03/1916
Miscellaneous			
Miscellaneous	In The Field	23/03/1916	23/03/1916
Miscellaneous			
Miscellaneous	In The Field	30/03/1916	30/03/1916
Miscellaneous			
Heading	14th Brigade. 32nd Division. 1st Battalion The Dorset Regiment April 1916 Field States Attached.		
War Diary	E.3. Subsector	27/03/1916	27/03/1916
War Diary	Millencourt	28/03/1916	03/04/1916
War Diary	G.I. Subsector (to be called henceforth Thiepval Subsector)	03/04/1916	06/04/1916
War Diary	Thiepval Subsector	07/04/1916	08/04/1916
War Diary	Authville	09/04/1916	12/04/1916
War Diary	Senlis	12/04/1916	16/04/1916
War Diary	Bouzincourt	17/04/1916	22/04/1916
War Diary	Bouzincourt & Pierrgot	23/04/1916	23/04/1916
War Diary	Pierrgot	24/04/1916	30/04/1916
Miscellaneous	In The Field	06/04/1916	06/04/1916
Miscellaneous			
Miscellaneous	In The Field	13/04/1916	13/04/1916
Miscellaneous			
Miscellaneous	In The Field	20/04/1916	20/04/1916
Miscellaneous			
Miscellaneous	In The Field	27/04/1916	27/04/1916
Miscellaneous			
Heading	14th Brigade. 32nd Division. 1st Battalion Dorsetshire Regiment May 1916		
War Diary	Contay	01/05/1916	04/05/1916
War Diary	Contay & Bouzincourt	05/05/1916	05/05/1916
War Diary	Bouzincourt Thiepval Subsector	06/05/1916	08/05/1916
War Diary	Thiepval Subsector	08/05/1916	10/05/1916
War Diary	Blackhorse Shelters Authville	11/05/1916	14/05/1916
War Diary	Thiepval Subsector	15/05/1916	18/05/1916
War Diary	Bouzincourt	19/05/1916	22/05/1916
War Diary	Bouzincourt & Aveluy Wood	23/05/1916	25/05/1916
War Diary	Warloy	25/05/1916	28/05/1916
War Diary	Warloy & Mirvaux	29/05/1916	29/05/1916
War Diary	Mirvaux	30/05/1916	04/06/1916
Miscellaneous	In The Field	04/05/1916	04/05/1916
Miscellaneous		05/05/1916	05/05/1916
Miscellaneous	In The Field	11/05/1916	11/05/1916
Miscellaneous			
Miscellaneous	In The Field	18/05/1916	18/05/1916
Miscellaneous	In The Field	25/05/1916	25/05/1916
Miscellaneous	Situation Report to 4 pm 8th Apl 1916 1st Dorset Rgt.	07/05/1916	07/05/1916

Miscellaneous	1st Dorset Regt.	09/05/1916	09/05/1916
Miscellaneous	1st Dorset Rgt.	07/05/1916	07/05/1916
Miscellaneous	Intelligence.	08/05/1916	08/05/1916
Miscellaneous	Intelligence Report Thiepval Subsector	09/05/1916	09/05/1916
Miscellaneous	1st Dorset Rgt.	10/05/1916	10/05/1916
Miscellaneous	Intelligence.	10/05/1916	10/05/1916
Miscellaneous	Plan Of armoured plate from German Sniping Post.	10/05/1916	10/05/1916
Miscellaneous	1st Dorset Rgt.	15/05/1916	15/05/1916
Miscellaneous	Intelligence Report.	15/05/1916	15/05/1916
Miscellaneous	Intelligence Report	16/05/1916	16/05/1916
Miscellaneous	1st Dorset Rgt.	16/05/1916	16/05/1916
Miscellaneous	1st Dorset Rgt.	17/05/1916	17/05/1916
Miscellaneous	Intelligence Report.	17/05/1916	17/05/1916
Miscellaneous	1st Dorset Rgt.	18/05/1916	18/05/1916
Miscellaneous	Intelligence Report. Thiepval Subsector.	17/05/1916	17/05/1916
Heading	14th Brigade. 32nd Division. 1st Battalion Dorsetshire Regiment June 1916		
War Diary	Mirvaux	01/06/1916	11/06/1916
War Diary	Warloy	12/06/1916	13/06/1916
War Diary	Blackhorse Shelters	13/06/1916	15/06/1916
War Diary	Blackhorse Shelters And Thiepval Subsector	16/06/1916	17/06/1916
War Diary	Thiepval Subsector	17/06/1916	21/06/1916
War Diary	Blackhorse Shelters	22/06/1916	23/06/1916
War Diary	Camp W. Of Senlis	24/06/1916	30/06/1916
Miscellaneous	In The Field	01/06/1916	01/06/1916
Miscellaneous	In The Field	05/06/1916	05/06/1916
Miscellaneous	In The Field	15/06/1916	15/06/1916
Miscellaneous	In The Field	22/06/1916	22/06/1916
Miscellaneous	In The Field	29/06/1916	29/06/1916
Heading	14th Brigade. 32nd Div. War Diary 1st Battalion The Dorset Regiment. July 1916		
War Diary	Camp W. Of Senlis	30/06/1916	01/07/1916
War Diary	Outer Defences Of Authville	02/07/1916	03/07/1916
War Diary	Senlis	04/07/1916	04/07/1916
War Diary	Senlis And Forceville	05/07/1916	05/07/1916
War Diary	Forceville	06/07/1916	06/07/1916
War Diary	Bouzincourt	07/07/1916	07/07/1916
War Diary	Bouzincourt & Ovillers	08/07/1916	08/07/1916
War Diary	Ovillers	08/07/1916	11/07/1916
War Diary	Bouzincourt	12/07/1916	14/07/1916
War Diary	Ovillers	15/07/1916	15/07/1916
War Diary	Senlis	16/07/1916	16/07/1916
War Diary	Senlis & Halloy	17/07/1916	17/07/1916
War Diary	Halloy & Brevillers	18/07/1916	18/07/1916
War Diary	Brevillers & Sibiville	19/07/1916	19/07/1916
War Diary	Sibiville & Orlencourt	20/07/1916	20/07/1916
War Diary	Orlencourt & Floringhem	21/07/1916	21/07/1916
War Diary	Floringhem	22/07/1916	25/07/1916
War Diary	Floringhem & Houchin	26/07/1916	26/07/1916
War Diary	Houchin	27/07/1916	28/07/1916
War Diary	Houchin & Annezin	29/07/1916	29/07/1916
War Diary	Annezin	30/07/1916	31/07/1916
Operation(al) Order(s)	Operation Order No. 15 By Major J.V. Shute Comdg 1st Bn Dorset Regt	25/06/1916	25/06/1916
Map	Appendix "A"		
Miscellaneous	In The Field	06/07/1916	06/07/1916

Miscellaneous	In The Field	13/07/1916	13/07/1916
Miscellaneous	In The Field	20/07/1916	20/07/1916
Miscellaneous			
Miscellaneous	In The Field	27/07/1916	27/07/1916
Miscellaneous			
Heading	14th Brigade. 32nd Division. 1st Battalion The Dorset Regiment August 1916		
Miscellaneous	H.Q. 14th Bde.	01/09/1916	01/09/1916
War Diary	Annezin	01/08/1916	04/08/1916
War Diary	Le Quesnoy	05/08/1916	05/08/1916
War Diary	Cuinchy Right Subsector	06/08/1916	11/08/1916
War Diary	In Close Support To Cuinchy Sector	12/08/1916	16/08/1916
War Diary	And Cuinchy Right Subsector	17/08/1916	25/08/1916
War Diary	Le Quesnoy	24/08/1916	29/08/1916
War Diary	Cuinchy Right Subsector	30/08/1916	31/08/1916
Miscellaneous	In The Field	03/08/1916	03/08/1916
Miscellaneous	In The Field	10/08/1916	10/08/1916
Miscellaneous	In The Field	17/08/1916	17/08/1916
Miscellaneous	In The Field	24/08/1916	24/08/1916
Miscellaneous	In The Field	31/08/1916	31/08/1916
Heading	14th Brigade. 32nd Division. 1st Battalion The Dorsetshire Regiment September 1916		
War Diary	Cuinchy Right Subsection	01/09/1916	04/09/1916
War Diary	In Bde. Support Keep & Harley St.	05/09/1916	08/09/1916
War Diary	Bethune	09/09/1916	17/09/1916
War Diary	Ecoivres	18/09/1916	20/09/1916
War Diary	Annequin	21/09/1916	22/09/1916
War Diary	Cambrin Right Sub Sector	23/09/1916	26/09/1916
War Diary	Village Line In Bde Reserve	27/09/1916	30/09/1916
Miscellaneous	In The Field	07/09/1916	07/09/1916
Miscellaneous	In The Field	14/09/1916	14/09/1916
Miscellaneous	In The Field	21/09/1916	21/09/1916
Miscellaneous	In The Field	28/09/1916	28/09/1916
Heading	14th Brigade. 32nd Division. 1st Battalion The Dorsetshire Regiment October 1916		
War Diary	Cambrin St Sub-Sector	01/10/1916	04/10/1916
War Diary	Annezin	05/10/1916	09/10/1916
War Diary	La Perriere	10/10/1916	15/10/1916
War Diary	Floringhem	16/10/1916	16/10/1916
War Diary	Averdoingt	17/10/1916	17/10/1916
War Diary	Rebruviette	18/10/1916	18/10/1916
War Diary	Beauval	19/10/1916	21/10/1916
War Diary	Warloy	22/10/1916	23/10/1916
War Diary	Albert Bouzincourt Brick Fields Area	24/10/1916	25/10/1916
War Diary	Brick Fields Area	26/10/1916	26/10/1916
War Diary	Contay Wood	27/10/1916	31/10/1916
Miscellaneous	In The Field	06/10/1916	06/10/1916
Miscellaneous	In The Field	12/10/1916	12/10/1916
Miscellaneous	In The Field	19/10/1916	19/10/1916
Miscellaneous	In The Field	26/10/1916	26/10/1916
Heading	14th Brigade. 32nd Division. 1st Battalion The Dorsetshire Regiment November 1916		
War Diary	Contay Wood	01/11/1916	09/11/1916
War Diary	Harponville	10/11/1916	13/11/1916
War Diary	Bouzincourt	11/11/1916	15/11/1916
War Diary	Mailly-Maillet	15/11/1916	24/11/1916

War Diary	Terramesnil And Doullens	25/11/1916	25/11/1916
War Diary	Berteaucourt	26/11/1916	30/11/1916
Miscellaneous	1st Dorset Regt.	01/12/1916	01/12/1916
Miscellaneous	In The Field	02/11/1916	02/11/1916
Miscellaneous	In The Field	09/11/1916	09/11/1916
Miscellaneous	In The Field	16/11/1916	16/11/1916
Miscellaneous	In The Field	23/11/1916	23/11/1916
Miscellaneous	In The Field	30/11/1916	30/11/1916
Heading	14th Brigade. 32nd Division. 1st Battalion The Dorsetshire Regiment December 1916		
War Diary	Berteaucourt	01/12/1916	31/12/1916
Miscellaneous	In The Field	08/12/1916	08/12/1916
Miscellaneous	In The Field	15/12/1916	15/12/1916
Miscellaneous	In The Field	22/12/1916	22/12/1916
Miscellaneous	In The Field	29/12/1916	29/12/1916
War Diary	Berteaucourt	01/01/1917	06/01/1917
War Diary	Bus	07/01/1917	08/01/1917
War Diary	Trenches	09/01/1917	12/01/1917
War Diary	Bus	13/01/1917	15/01/1917
War Diary	Trenches	16/01/1917	17/01/1917
War Diary	Bus	18/01/1917	23/01/1917
War Diary	Bertrancourt	24/01/1917	27/01/1917
War Diary	Mailly Maillet	28/01/1917	29/01/1917
War Diary	Trenches	30/01/1917	31/01/1917
Miscellaneous	In The Field	05/01/1917	05/01/1917
Miscellaneous	In The Field	12/01/1917	12/01/1917
Miscellaneous	In The Field	19/01/1917	19/01/1917
Miscellaneous	In The Field	28/01/1917	28/01/1917
War Diary	Mailley-Maillet	01/02/1917	04/02/1917
War Diary	Trenches	04/02/1917	08/02/1917
War Diary	Mailley-Maillet	09/02/1917	11/02/1917
War Diary	Trenches	12/02/1917	13/02/1917
War Diary	Mailley-Maillet-Forceviller Rd	14/02/1917	15/02/1917
War Diary	Bus	16/02/1917	16/02/1917
War Diary	Warloy	17/02/1917	21/02/1917
War Diary	Mullens-Au-Bois	22/02/1917	22/02/1917
War Diary	Camon	23/02/1917	23/02/1917
War Diary	Hangard	23/02/1917	24/02/1917
War Diary	Le Quesnel	25/02/1917	25/02/1917
War Diary	Trenches	26/02/1917	28/02/1917
Miscellaneous	In The Field	03/02/1917	03/02/1917
Miscellaneous	In The Field	10/02/1917	10/02/1917
Miscellaneous			
Miscellaneous	In The Field	17/02/1917	17/02/1917
Miscellaneous			
Miscellaneous	In The Field	24/02/1917	24/02/1917
War Diary	Trenches	01/03/1917	08/03/1917
War Diary	Le Quesnel	09/03/1917	14/03/1917
War Diary	Rouvroy Tech	14/03/1917	16/03/1917
War Diary	Rouvroy And Kouropakin Trench	17/03/1917	19/03/1917
War Diary	Rouy Le Petit	19/03/1917	21/03/1917
War Diary	Matigny	22/03/1917	31/03/1917
Miscellaneous	In The Field	03/03/1917	03/03/1917
Miscellaneous			
Miscellaneous	In The Field	12/03/1917	12/03/1917
Miscellaneous			

Miscellaneous	In The Field	16/03/1917	16/03/1917
Miscellaneous			
Miscellaneous	In The Field	13/03/1917	13/03/1917
Miscellaneous			
Miscellaneous	In The Field	30/03/1917	30/03/1917
Miscellaneous			
War Diary	Lanchy	01/04/1917	01/04/1917
War Diary	Holnon	02/04/1917	07/04/1917
War Diary	Germaine	08/04/1917	12/04/1917
War Diary	Near St Quentin	13/04/1917	14/04/1917
War Diary	Cepy Farm	14/04/1917	15/04/1917
War Diary	Savy	16/04/1917	30/04/1917
Miscellaneous	O.C., 1st Dorset Regt.	17/04/1917	17/04/1917
Miscellaneous	G.O.C. 14th Bn.	17/04/1917	17/04/1917
Miscellaneous	C Coy A.S.H. B. Coy. J.A.B. A. Coy D. Coy.		
Miscellaneous	In The Field	06/04/1917	06/04/1917
Miscellaneous			
Miscellaneous	In The Field	13/04/1917	13/04/1917
Miscellaneous			
Miscellaneous	In The Field	20/04/1917	20/04/1917
Miscellaneous			
Miscellaneous	In The Field	27/04/1917	27/04/1917
Miscellaneous			
War Diary	Ugny And Lanchy	01/05/1917	14/05/1917
War Diary	Offoy	15/05/1917	15/05/1917
War Diary	Curchy & Puzeaux	16/05/1917	17/05/1917
War Diary	Beaufort	18/05/1917	29/05/1917
War Diary	Ignaucourt	30/05/1917	31/05/1917
Miscellaneous	In The Field	04/05/1917	04/05/1917
Miscellaneous			
Miscellaneous	In The Field	11/05/1917	11/05/1917
Miscellaneous	In The Field	18/05/1917	18/05/1917
Miscellaneous			
Miscellaneous	In The Field	25/05/1917	25/05/1917
Miscellaneous			
War Diary	Ignaucourt	01/06/1917	02/06/1917
War Diary	Steenwerck Area	03/06/1917	13/06/1917
War Diary	Eecke	13/06/1917	15/06/1917
War Diary	Teteghem	16/06/1917	16/07/1917
War Diary	Juniac Camp Dost Dunkerque		
War Diary	Nieuport	17/05/1917	30/05/1917
War Diary	Ribaillet Camp	01/07/1917	01/07/1917
War Diary	D Subsector	02/07/1917	06/07/1917
War Diary	Jeanniot Camp	06/07/1917	10/07/1917
War Diary	Ribaillet Camp	11/07/1917	13/07/1917
War Diary	Nieuport	13/07/1917	17/07/1917
War Diary	C Subsector	17/07/1917	18/07/1917
War Diary	C.16.C.	19/07/1917	02/08/1917
War Diary	Coxyde	03/08/1917	03/08/1917
War Diary	Lapanne	04/08/1917	27/08/1917
War Diary	Redan	28/08/1917	31/08/1917
War Diary	In The Line	01/09/1917	12/09/1917
War Diary	Lapanne	13/09/1917	20/09/1917
War Diary	Wulpen	21/09/1917	24/09/1917
War Diary	In The Line	25/09/1917	18/10/1917
War Diary	St Pol	19/10/1917	26/10/1917

War Diary	Arneke	27/10/1917	10/11/1917
War Diary	Winnezeele Area	11/11/1917	11/11/1917
War Diary	Poperinghe	12/11/1917	24/11/1917
War Diary	Dambre Camp Irish Camp	25/11/1917	27/11/1917
War Diary	Brake Camp	28/11/1917	30/11/1917
War Diary	Wurst Farm	01/12/1917	09/12/1917
War Diary	Hilltop Farm	10/12/1917	10/12/1917
War Diary	Siege Camp	11/12/1917	27/12/1917
War Diary	Hilltop Farm	28/12/1917	31/12/1917
War Diary	Nielles Les Ardres	01/01/1918	13/01/1918
War Diary	Nielles Les Ardres	14/01/1918	21/01/1918
War Diary	Dirty Bucket Camp	22/01/1918	29/01/1918
War Diary	Boesinghe Camp	30/01/1918	01/02/1918
War Diary	Left Subsector	02/02/1918	03/02/1918
War Diary	Boesinghe Camp	04/02/1918	04/02/1918
War Diary	Right Subsector	05/02/1918	07/02/1918
War Diary	Support Battalion Gruyterzale Farm	08/02/1918	10/02/1918
War Diary	Camp-T256 D	11/02/1918	19/02/1918
War Diary	Left Subsector	19/02/1918	22/02/1918
War Diary	In The Line	23/02/1918	28/02/1918
Heading	32nd Division. 14th Infantry Brigade. 1st Battalion The Dorset Regiment March 1918		
War Diary	Battalion In Support Line Subsector	01/03/1918	04/03/1918
War Diary	Battalion In Reserve	05/03/1918	31/03/1918
Heading	14th Inf. Bde. 32nd Div. War Diary 1st Battn. The Dorsetshire Regiment. April 1918		
War Diary		01/04/1918	31/05/1918
Miscellaneous	32nd Division.	26/05/1918	26/05/1918
War Diary		01/06/1918	31/07/1918
Map	Damery Ordnance Survey. (O.B.).		
War Diary		01/08/1918	31/08/1918
War Diary	Gaby Trench N 24 & Sheet 62c S.W.	01/09/1918	02/09/1918
War Diary	Ac For 2nd	03/09/1918	03/09/1918
War Diary	Trench System N 29 A.S.C. Sheet 6 C. S.W.	04/09/1918	05/09/1918
War Diary	Bn HQ. Quarry At P 31 C 00.45 Coys. Along the Line P 27 B. 6.0 P 27 D. 6.0	06/09/1918	06/09/1918
War Diary	Sheet 62c S.E.	06/09/1918	07/09/1918
War Diary	Q 32 B.	08/09/1918	11/09/1918
War Diary	Squares W 8 And 14	12/09/1918	14/09/1918
War Diary	Sheet 62d. N6d. 1/40000 Daours.	15/09/1918	17/09/1918
War Diary	Sheet 62 C S.W. U 23b. Leighton Park	18/09/1918	23/09/1918
War Diary	Larris Woods 62.C. S.E.	24/09/1918	30/09/1918
Miscellaneous	A Form. Messages And Signals.		
Miscellaneous	32nd Div. No. G.S. 1882/18/2	06/09/1918	06/09/1918
Miscellaneous			
Miscellaneous	32nd Divisional Routine Orders.	06/09/1918	06/09/1918
Miscellaneous	The following remarks have been received by the Divisional Commander, also the Brigade. General 14th Bde.	07/09/1918	07/09/1918
Miscellaneous	C.R.A., 32nd Divn.	13/09/1918	13/09/1918
Miscellaneous			
Miscellaneous	A Form. Messages And Signals.		
Miscellaneous	32nd. Div. No. G.S. 1882/18/4	14/09/1918	14/09/1918
Miscellaneous	32nd Divisional Routine Orders.	18/09/1918	18/09/1918
Miscellaneous	5/6th Royal Scots.	24/09/1918	24/09/1918
Miscellaneous	Australian Corps.	12/09/1918	12/09/1918

War Diary	Fleche Wood	01/10/1918	01/10/1918
War Diary	Infants Alley	02/10/1918	02/10/1918
War Diary	H 33d	03/10/1918	03/10/1918
War Diary	Sequehart	04/10/1918	04/10/1918
War Diary	Lehaucourt	05/10/1918	05/10/1918
War Diary	Vendelles	06/10/1918	06/10/1918
War Diary	Bouvincourt	07/10/1918	22/10/1918
War Diary	Bohain	23/10/1918	31/10/1918
War Diary	6 R S	01/11/1918	05/11/1918
War Diary	Favril	06/11/1918	07/11/1918
War Diary	Go Fayt	08/11/1918	09/11/1918
War Diary	Avesnes	10/11/1918	13/11/1918
War Diary	Sains	14/11/1918	19/11/1918
War Diary	Sivry	20/11/1918	20/11/1918
War Diary	Froidchapelle	21/11/1918	24/11/1918
War Diary	Daussois	25/11/1918	27/11/1918
War Diary	Villers-Deux-Eglises	28/11/1918	30/11/1918
War Diary	Villers-Deux-Eglises.	01/12/1918	12/12/1918
War Diary	Mettet	13/12/1918	13/12/1918
War Diary	Anhee	14/12/1918	31/12/1918
Heading	Lancashire Division (Late 32nd Divn) 14th Infy Bde (1st Lancs Infy Bde) 1st Bn Dorset Regt. Jan-March		
War Diary	Anhee	01/01/1919	19/01/1919
War Diary	Namur	20/01/1919	28/01/1919
War Diary	Beuel	29/01/1919	29/01/1919
War Diary	Bonn	30/01/1919	30/01/1919
War Diary	Obercassel	31/01/1919	18/03/1919
War Diary	Romlinghoven	19/03/1919	23/03/1919
War Diary	Grenau	24/03/1919	31/03/1919

32ND DIVISION

14TH INFY BDE

1ST BN DORSET REGT

JAN ~~1916 DEC 1916~~

1916 1917 MAR

FROM 5 JULY 15 BDE

14th Brigade.

32nd Division.

1st BATTALION

THE DORSET REGIMENT

JANUARY 1 9 1 6

Appendices attached:-

Situation Reports.

Field States.

Instructions regarding War Diaries and Intelligence Summaries are contained in F. S. Regs., Part II. and the Staff Manual respectively. Title Pages will be prepared in manuscript.

WAR DIARY
or
INTELLIGENCE SUMMARY

(Erase heading not required.)

1st Dorset Regt

Army Form C. 2118.

Vol 15

Sheet 1

Place	Date 1916	Hour	Summary of Events and Information	Remarks and references to Appendices
SAILLY LORETTE.	Jan 1st	–	Battalion in billets in SAILLY LORETTE.	AMIENS Map, Sheet 12 1/250,000
"	" 2nd	–	do.	
MILLENCOURT	" 3rd	12.30pm	Battalion moved to billets in MILLENCOURT.	H.D.T.
"	" 4	–	In billets in MILLENCOURT	H.D.T.
"	" 5		do	H.D.T.
"	" 6		do	H.D.T.
"	" 7		do.	H.D.T.
"	" 8		do. (95th Infantry Bde. now called 14th Infantry Bde.)	H.D.T.
"	" 9		do.	H.D.T.
"	" 10	7.20pm	do. Battalion relieved 15th Lancashire Fusiliers in trenches in G.1. subsector. Reinforcement draft of 25 O.R. arrived. Quartermasters stores remaining in MILLENCOURT with advanced depot at MARTINSART.	H.D.T.
G.1. Subsector.	" 11.		Situation normal. Slight activity by trench mortars and artillery on both sides.	H.D.T.
"	" 12		" Both sides somewhat active with artillery, trench mortars + grenades.	H.D.T.
"	" 13.		" 2/Lieut COUSINS wounded. A very quiet day. Enemy fired a few trench mortars and rifle grenades. Which were replied to by our trench mortars and silenced.	H.D.T.
"	14		Situation normal. 2/Lieut K. Brodie slightly wounded by rifle grenade also 1 man killed and 3 Other ranks wounded. Enemy active in morning with rifle grenades we replied with WEST SPRING GUN and Catapult.	H.D.T.

2449 Wt. W14957/M90 750,000 1/16 J.B.C. & A. Forms/C.2118/12.

1st Dorset Regt

Army Form C. 2118.

VOL III
Sheet 2

WAR DIARY
or
INTELLIGENCE SUMMARY

(Erase heading not required.)

Instructions regarding War Diaries and Intelligence Summaries are contained in F. S. Regs., Part II. and the Staff Manual respectively. Title Pages will be prepared in manuscript.

Place	Date	Hour	Summary of Events and Information	Remarks and references to Appendices
G1 Subsector	14		Relieved by 2nd Manchester regt. in the trenches at 3.50 pm and withdrawn to billets in AUTHUILLE – Nos. 1 and 2 Platoons at GORDON CASTLE	HDT
AUTHUILLE	15		In billets at AUTHUILLE	HDT
AUTHUILLE	16		In billets AUTHUILLE	HDT
AUTHUILLE	17		In billets AUTHUILLE	HDT
AUTHUILLE	18		Relieved in AUTHUILLE by 2nd R. Inniskilling Fusiliers at 7 pm. In billets at MILLENCOURT at 9.15 pm.	HDT
MILLENCOURT	19		In billets at MILLENCOURT	HDT
"	20		" " " MILLENCOURT	HDT
"	21		" " " MILLENCOURT –	HDT
"	22		" " " MILLENCOURT – C.O. inspected draft	HDT
"	23		In billets at MILLENCOURT	HDT
"	24		In billets at MILLENCOURT	HDT
"	25		In billets at MILLENCOURT	HDT
"	26	9.15 pm	In billets at MILLENCOURT. The Battalion relieved 16th Lancashire Fusiliers in G1 Subsector at 9.15 pm. A very quiet night. Enemy's working parties opposite 150 trench dispersed by our rifle fire. KOYLI on our right 15 HLI on our left	HDT

2449 Wt. W14957/M90 750,000 1/16 J.B.C. & A. Forms/C.2118/12.

Instructions regarding War Diaries and Intelligence Summaries are contained in F. S. Regs., Part II. and the Staff Manual respectively. Title Pages will be prepared in manuscript.

WAR DIARY
or
~~INTELLIGENCE SUMMARY~~
(Erase heading not required.)

1st Dorset Regt.

Army Form C. 2118.

VOL III

Sheet 3

Place	Date	Hour	Summary of Events and Information	Remarks and references to Appendices
G.1 Subsector	27		At 3.45 pm enemy sent over volleys of "Oil cans" at intervals till 4.30 pm on 148 and 149 trenches – Our artillery retaliated with 18 pounders. A quiet night	H.B.
G. 1.	28		One man killed by rifle grenade in the morning. Our trenches were lightly shelled by enemy's field guns. No damage was done. Our trench mortars fired on enemy trenches in reply to their oil cans and rifle grenades. The enemy fired several shells into AUTHUILLE about 6.20 pm. A quiet night	H.B.
G. 1.	29		Two other ranks wounded by rifle grenades. A very quiet day and night.	H.B.
G. 1	30.		Very misty day. A German newspaper was found in front of our wire. (Very heavy bombardment of G2 with oil cans, high explosives and field guns, but very little damage reported) – Two other ranks wounded – A quiet night.	H.B.
G. 1.	31		No casualties. A very quiet day and night.	H.B.
G. 1.	February 1	11 pm	No casualties. With the exception of a few oil cans a very quiet day relieved by 2/Manchester Regt. at 8.30 pm, and retired to billets at MARTINSART. and one company in AUTHUILLE. In billets at 11 pm.	H.B.

2449 Wt. W14957/M90 750,000 1/16 J.B.C. & A. Forms/C.2118/12.

TO 14TH INF. BRIG

Intelligence Report. 11-1-16

Artillery – Enemy sent over seven or eight salvoes of four 77 mm. between our support and reserve trenches. Our field guns fired 8 rounds retaliation and the Hows fired a few rounds.

Trench Mortars. The enemy fired two rounds about 11.30 AM one landed in our trench 146 and did considerable damage. Our mortar fired two rounds back.

Patrols A patrol from [illegible] the German wire opposite is strong – in [illegible] lines – first line is coiled barbed wire on iron stakes. Two gaps were found (Lieut MAINHOOD)
Patrols from 147 have nothing to report.
Patrol from 149 came across two German patrols advancing & keeping in touch by means of whistling. ~~Another patrol later~~ Our patrol threw two bombs at one of the parties and then retreated. A later patrol from same place reported German wire only 4 or 5 yards thick

GREEN LIGHT observed on our left at 11·30 PM and [illegible] 1/45 at 12·05 AM (midnight)
A single waggon was heard to enter THIEPVAL at 11· and left about 11·15 PM.

SNIPING ETC very quiet.

H Mansel-Pleydell

2·20 PM

[illegible] 1/4 DORSETS

G 1.

"A" Form. Army Form C. 2121.

MESSAGES AND SIGNALS. No. of Message

Prefix ... Code ... m. | Words | Charge | This message is on a/c of ... Service. (Signature of "Franking Officer.") | Recd. at ... Date ... From ... By ...

Office of Origin and Service Instructions.

Sent At ... m. To ... By ...

TO 14th Infantry Bde

Sender's Number.	Day of Month	In reply to Number	AAA
* R97	11	—	

Daily Situation Report

Three patrols went out from the left, right and center of this sector last night with the object of examining our own and the German wire AAA The German wire was strong but has weak places and 2 gaps were found opposite 145 by Lieut MAINHOOD's patrol AAA A patrol of one officer (Lieut Mansel-Pleydell) and one man, that left 149 about 10.30 pm came across two German patrols AAA Our men threw two bombs and retreated AAA The enemy shelled our front trenches in different places with light shells between 11.30 am & noon to-day AAA No damage of consequence was done; we retaliated with 8 rounds from field guns.

From DORSETS.

Place

Time

The above may be forwarded as now corrected. (Z)

Censor. Signature of Addressor or person authorised to telegraph in his name.

* This line should be erased if not required.

(774-5) —McC. & Co. Ltd., London.— W 1789/1402. 150,000. 8/15 Forms C2121/10.

"A" Form. Army Form C. 2121.

MESSAGES AND SIGNALS. No. of Message

Prefix Code m. Office of Origin and Service Instructions.	Words	Charge	This message is on a/c of ... Service. (Signature of "Franking Officer.")	Recd. at m. Date From By
	Sent At m. To By			

TO (Cont)

Sender's Number.	Day of Month	In reply to Number	AAA
R 47			

Shortly after 11.30 am the enemy fired a few rounds from trench-mortar into our 146 AAA. The trench and wire netting were considerable damaged and are being repaired AAA An N.C.O and man of the 2nd Manchesters who were working in the trench are suffering from shock and superficial wounds AAA Our trench-mortar retaliated with two rounds, the effect of which is not known.

The condition of trenches and wire is very fair; work on the former — especially pumping & cleaning in the centre — has been carried on all day; work on the latter will be continued tonight AAA

At 12.05 am. last night a green

From
Place
Time

The above may be forwarded as now corrected. (Z)

Censor. Signature of Addressor or person authorised to telegraph in his name.

* This line should be erased if not required.

(774-5) —McC. & Co. Ltd., London.— W 1789/1402. 150,000. 8/15. Forms C 2121/10.

"A" Form. Army Form C. 2121.

MESSAGES AND SIGNALS.

No. of Message

Prefix Code m. Office of Origin and Service Instructions.	Words	Charge	This message is on a/c of ... Service. (Signature of "Franking Officer.")	Recd. at m. Date From By
	Sent At m. To By			

TO

Sender's Number.	Day of Month	In reply to Number	AAA
R97			

light was observed to go up from German trench opposite our 145 AAA.

H Cecil Butcher
Lieut for Lieut Col
Comdg. 1st Dorset Regt

From Dorsets
Place
Time 11.30 pm

The above may be forwarded as now corrected. (Z)

Censor. Signature of Addressor or person authorised to telegraph in his name.

* This line should be erased if not required.

(774-5) —McC. & Co. Ltd., London.— W 1789/1402. 150,000. 8/15. Forms C 2121/10.

INTELLIGENCE REPORT 12-1-15

G1 Subsector.

AERIAL – no German machines have been over this morning. Our machines were shelled – but not heavily.

NEW WORK. None has been noticed except a little digging opposite 145 fire trench.

MORTARS. A big trench howitzer fired two shells into G2 subsector at 7.5 PM. The mortar was 66° Magnetic from a point ten yards NORTH of AUTHUILE–THIEPVAL road about half way between British and German lines.

GENERAL. It appears that Germans blow a horn similar to that used by FRENCH railway men as a warning to their men that our big mortar has fired.

Germans do practically no sniping.

PATROLS. A patrol at 7.15 PM going along S. side of hedge from 145 F.T. heard two German patrols whistling to one another. They lay in wait with bombs but the hostile patrol retired apparently as they did not come on

PATROLS (cont) Patrol from 14q took bearing of trench mortar reported above & reported everything quiet & patrols from centre company made a similar report.

TRANSPORT was heard in THIEPVAL between 8 & 9 PM

Patrols Pte Kitchen
Pte Embury
2 Lieut Drayton
Sergt Webb
Coy Sergt Maj Fox
Sergt Stevens
2 Lieut Mansel-Pleydell

Patrols on night of 10-11 Jan
Sergt Webb
Coy S.M. Fox
Pte Perry
2 Lt Mainwood
2 Lt Blakeway
2 Lt Mansel-Pleydell

ARTILLERY:

The 77 mms shelled Bn HQ at 7:30 last night and then shortened onto the front-line. All our guns have been active today Germans sent over several light bombs and some rifle grenades we retaliated with 40 rifle grenades 80 Mills grenades and 40 or 5 "gas-pipe" trench mortar bombs.

H G M Mansel-Pleydell
2 Lieut
1st Dorset

G1 subsector.

"A" Form. Army Form C. 2121.

MESSAGES AND SIGNALS. No. of Message

Prefix Code m.	Words	Charge	This message is on a/c of	Recd. at m.
Office of Origin and Service Instructions.	Sent		Service.	Date
	At m.			From
	To			
	By		(Signature of "Franking Officer.")	By

TO 14 Infantry Bde

Sender's Number.	Day of Month	In reply to Number	AAA
* K 129	12	—	

Situation report AAA. Enemy replied very feebly to our artillery activity this morning aaa Between 11 am & 1 pm Germans fired a considerable number of rifle grenades & bombs about the centre of this sector aaa We replied with 12 grenades from the WEST bomb-thrower — all of which were good shots and landed on enemy's parapet or in his trench aaa We also fired 20 rifle grenades and a few mortar bombs aaa Early this afternoon enemy fired some light shells around Bn. H.Q. without doing any damage aaa Our artillery retaliated aaa

From the following patrols report
Place that enemy were heard to blow
Time a horn in trenches when our

The above may be forwarded as now corrected. (Z)

artillery opens fire aaa

Censor. Signature of Addressor or person authorised to telegraph in his name.

* This line should be erased if not required.

(774-5) —McC. & Co. Ltd., London.— W 1789/1402. 150,000. 8/15. Forms C 2121/10.

"A" Form. Army Form C. 2121.

MESSAGES AND SIGNALS.

No. of Message

Prefix Code m.	Words	Charge	This message is on a/c of	Recd. at m.
Office of Origin and Service Instructions.	Sent		Service.	Date
	At m.			From
	To			
	By		(Signature of "Franking Officer.")	By

TO

Sender's Number.	Day of Month	In reply to Number	AAA
*			

Sgt WEBB and Pte BRYON went out on patrol last night from 148 trench but have no further information about German wire or patrols to report aaa They were able to get up to enemies wire aaa Two other patrols — (1) Sgt LANE and Cpl GROVES — and (2) Sgt STEVENS and Pte Smith also went out from left and right respectively aaa
There is little sniping aaa
Our wire has been improved by addition of 6 extra coils and repairs to damaged knife rests aaa

From Dorsets.
Place
Time 5.20 pm

H. Cecil Butcher
Lieut a/adjt
for O.C. 1st Dorset

The above may be forwarded as now corrected. (Z)

Censor. Signature of Addressor or person authorised to telegraph in his name.

* This line should be erased if not required.

(774-5) —McC. & Co. Ltd., London.— W 1789/1402. 150,000. 8/15. Forms C 2121/10.

G1 INTELLIGENCE REPORT 13-1-16

ARTILLERY: No activity at all
AERIAL Also no activity – wind seems too high.

TRENCH MORTAR – Two "oil cans" were
fired behind our left sector doing no
damage – we retaliated with four big
mortar bombs and about 20 small
bombs from the West-bomb-thrower. No
further steps were taken by the Germans

PATROLS Capt ALGEO and 2nd Lieut MAINHOOD
went on patrol to a point just NORTH of
GERMAN MOUND – they walked up to
the German line and the Germans did not
notice them so they fired ten rounds
each at the German trench. Still no
signs from the Germans so they returned.
2 LIEUT MAINHOOD SERGT CHARLES and
PTE JAMES then went out to find out
if there were any gaps through which an
entry might be made into German trench
They reported three rows of wire the first
composed of strong barbed "concertina"
wire, the middle one of knife rests,
the third of mixed wire. The officer
did not consider an entry could be
made – He also heard one German

fire a shot then walk up the trench lightly his pipe, and then fire another shot some 20 yards further up the trench.

2 Lieut CHAMBERS and Sergt ~~[illegible]~~ SULLIVAN from 149 report German type "patchy" and snipers active

2 Lieut CLARKE L/Cpl BARTER + Pte BLAKE patrolled neighbourhood of hedge in front of 145 - nothing to report.

Sergt PLENTY Pte LEWIS and Pte SIMS patrolled in front of 146 heard tapping in German lines.

H Mansel-Pleydell

G1. 1 D. 1st DORSET

[illegible]

"A" Form. Army Form C. 2121.

MESSAGES AND SIGNALS. No. of Message

Prefix Code m. | Words | Charge | This message is on a/c of ... Service. (Signature of "Franking Officer.") | Recd. at m. Date From By

Office of Origin and Service Instructions. Sent At m. To By

TO 14th Infantry Bde

Sender's Number.	Day of Month	In reply to Number	AAA
* K 157	13	—	

Situation report aaa Enemy very quiet. We retaliated for two "oil-cans" with trench mortars and West Bombthrower.
Lieut Clarke L/Cpl Barter and Pte Blake patrolled from 100 yds in front of 144 trench to hedge in front of 145 trench. No evidence of hostile patrols or working parties observed.
Sergt Plenty, Pte Lewis & Pte Sims patrolled in front of 146 trench. They heard sounds of tapping from the German lines.
A patrol composed of Capt. Algeo, Lieut Mainhood Sgt. Charles & Pte James went out in front of 148 trench with a view to bombing operations

From
Place
Time

The above may be forwarded as now corrected. (Z)
Censor. Signature of Addressor or person authorised to telegraph in his name.

* This line should be erased if not required.

(774-5) —McC. & Co. Ltd., London.— W 1780/1402. 150,000. 8/15. Forms C 2121/10.

"A" Form. Army Form C. 2121.

MESSAGES AND SIGNALS.

No. of Message

Prefix ... Code ... m.	Words	Charge	This message is on a/c of	Recd. at ... m.
Office of Origin and Service Instructions.	Sent		... Service.	Date
	At ... m.			From
	To			
	By		(Signature of "Franking Officer.")	By

TO (2)

Sender's Number.	Day of Month	In reply to Number	AAA
*			

The German trench was found to be held very weakly – only one man being located, who walked up and down the trench and occasionally fired a shot – and 10 rounds rapid was fired into German trench without any activity resulting on the part of the enemy. The wire was too far out for patrol to throw bombs into the trench and no gaps could be located.

At midnight Lieut Chambers and Sgt Sullivan visited German wire in front of 149 trench but were prevented by an active sniper from making too close an inspection. No German patrols were seen

From

Place

Time

The above may be forwarded as now corrected. (Z)

Censor. Signature of Addressor or person authorised to telegraph in his name.

* This line should be erased if not required.

(774-5) —McC. & Co. Ltd., London.— W 1780/1402. 150,000. 8/15. Forms C 2121/10.

"A" Form. Army Form C. 2121.

MESSAGES AND SIGNALS. No. of Message

Prefix Code m. | Words | Charge | This message is on a/c of Service. (Signature of "Franking Officer.") | Recd. at m. Date From By

Office of Origin and Service Instructions.

Sent At m. To By

TO (3)

Sender's Number. Day of Month In reply to Number AAA

by any of our parties.

Wire was put out in front of 144. 145 & 148 Trenches and 60 yds, 6 yds deep in front of 149 trench.

State of trenches fair. Work of upkeep of trenches carried on by all available men. West bomberthrower emplacements made & machines got into position.

H. Cecil Butcher
Lieut & Adjutant
for O.C. 1 Dorset Regt.

From Dorsets
Place
Time 4.20 pm

The above may be forwarded as now corrected. (Z)

Censor. Signature of Addressor or person authorised to telegraph in his name.

* This line should be erased if not required.

(774-5) —McC. & Co. Ltd., London.— W 1789/1402. 150,000. 8/15. Forms C 2121/10.

INTELLIGENCE REPORT 14-1-16

ARTILLERY: Germans fired two or three salvos yesterday evening at Bn HQ. our guns retaliated with 12 rounds enemy also fired one 77 shell at 149 trench and wounded 2 men

AERIAL Several of our machines have been over this morning – one was chased by a hostile machine & it was brought very low – it could not be seen long enough to say whether it was brought down or not.

GENERAL Germans put up a notice-board yesterday afternoon for an hour or so – the writing was too small to be legible

PATROLS 2 Lieut BLAKEWAY and Corpl MATTHEWS went out by sap 15 in 149 trench & leaving an unwired sap on their left were approaching German wire when two men were seen to leave the German trench and approach them. They had no rifles & seemed to be loaded with bombs. Our men went back a bit and the Germans did not follow up. It was very light

2 Lieut MANSEL-PLEYDELL & Pte RYAN searched sunken road in front of

1415 trench for traces of a 'snipers rest' reported there – no empty cartridge cases or other indications were found)

TRENCH MORTAR Germans sent over one "oil can" yesterday evening – we retaliated with two 2" mortar bombs and a considerable number of mills grenades from the WEST BOMBER and the CATAPULTS.

W J Mansel Pleydell

10 DORSET.

G.1.

"A" Form. Army Form C. 2121.

MESSAGES AND SIGNALS. No. of Message

Prefix ... Code ... m. Office of Origin and Service Instructions.	Words / Charge / Sent At ... m. To ... By ...	This message is on a/c of ... Service. (Signature of "Franking Officer.")	Recd. at ... Date ... From ... By ...

TO 14th Infantry Bde.

Sender's Number.	Day of Month	In reply to Number	
* R 186	14	—	AAA

Situation report aaa.

Battalion relieved by 2nd Manchester Rgt. There is nothing further to add to the report sent in by Intelligence Officer. Enemy quiet. Work on wire and trenches was continued aaa

H Cecil Butcher
Lieut & Adjutant
for O.C. 1st Dorset Rgt

From Dorsets
Place
Time 4.20 pm

The above may be forwarded as now corrected.

Censor.

(Z)

Signature of Addressor or person authorised to telegraph in his name.

* This line should be erased if not required.

(774-5) —McC. & Co. Ltd., London.— W 1789/1402. 150,000. 8/15. Forms C 2121/10.

"A" Form
MESSAGES AND SIGNALS.

INTELLIGENCE 27-1-16

ARTILLERY: Two howitzers and a few 77 mm: shells only have landed in our sector to day. No damage done at all.

WORK. Enemy were heard wiring opposite 150 trench and were dispersed by rifle fire.

Where (?) New work is also apparent in German MOUND.

A new trench is being dug from SOUTH WEST of MOUND salient towards junction of ~~F2~~ Gun Right and G1 subsector.

RIFLE GRENADES. Germans sent over 3 rifle grenades near 148 trench – We retaliated with WEST SPRING GUN

PATROLS. Two patrols only went out last night under CAPT ALGEO and 2 LIEUT BLAKEWAY to examine damage done yesterday to our wire. Damage reported not considerable. One of these was fired on by enemy from new trench reported above. I should like to suggest that a reconnaissance could be made of this spot by aeroplane with less risk and more result than by infantry patrol in the dark.

G1

[illegible] Plewdell [illegible]

"A" Form. Army Form C. 2121.

MESSAGES AND SIGNALS. No. of Message

Prefix Code m.	Words	Charge	This message is on a/c of:	Recd. at m.
Office of Origin and Service Instructions.	Sent		Service.	Date
	At m.			From
	To			
	By		(Signature of "Franking Officer.")	By

TO 14th Infantry Bde.

* Sender's Number.	Day of Month	In reply to Number	AAA
R 296	27	—	

Situation report AAA
Very quiet night and quiet day till 3.45 pm when enemy commenced sending over volleys of "oil cans" around 148 and 149 trenches. This continued at intervals till 4.30pm. Rifle grenades accompanied this bombardment. The damage caused was not serious. Our artillery retaliated. 4.5's have been called upon but have not fired yet.
The trenches are in good condition and work has been confined to cleaning and clearing and repairing parapet in right sector. Battles

From
Place
Time

The above may be forwarded as now corrected. (Z)

Censor. Signature of Addressor or person authorised to telegraph in his name.

* This line should be erased if not required.

(774-5) —McC. & Co. Ltd., London.— W 1780/1402. 150,000. 8/15. Forms C 2121/10.

"A" Form. Army Form C. 2121.

MESSAGES AND SIGNALS. No. of Message

Prefix Code m. | Words | Charge | This message is on a/c of: ... Service. (Signature of "Franking Officer.") | Recd. at m. Date From By

Office of Origin and Service Instructions. Sent At m. To By

TO

Sender's Number. | Day of Month | In reply to Number | AAA

from 19th Lancs. Fusiliers worked on shelters and BURY Avenue.
Wire has been damaged in places by enemy 'oil cans'. This has not yet been fully repaired but will be completed tonight. Material was not available earlier.
Patrols went out only to examine our own wire.
An enemy working party was heard last night in vicinity of trenches opposite 150 & 151 and was dispersed by our fire.

H. Cecil Butcher
Lieut for Lt. Col
Comdg Dorset Regt

From Dorsets
Place
Time 5 pm

The above may be forwarded as now corrected. (Z)
Censor. Signature of Addressor or person authorised to telegraph in his name.

* This line should be erased if not required.

(774-5) —McC. & Co. Ltd., London.— W 1789/1402. 150,000. 8/15. Forms C 2121/10.

Intelligence Report 28-1-16

1 Enemy's Artillery:

a	1 am	11.30 am	1 pm	2.45 pm
b	Trench 146	[illegible] 14	Bn HQ	[illegible] 143
c	NE	NE	NE	NE
d	77 mm	[illegible] 77 mm	[illegible]	77 mm
e	slight	nil	nil	slight
f	nil	nil	nil	nil [illegible]

2. Enemy lights and Signals — Nil
3 Enemy Transport — Normal
4. Movement of hostile troops: None observed
5. Enemy working parties
a) 8-30 a m
b) six
c) Listening post about X 1a 5/5
d) Party X 1a 4/8 Occupation souvenir hunting

6 Patrols
a) 6.30 pm from 143 | 9.15 pm from [illegible]
b) To harass new work near X 1a 10/8 | To examine saps about X 1a 4/8
c) 2 Lieut FRASER Sergt CHARLES | L/Cpl WOOD Pte WELLS
d) were forestalled by K.O.Y.L.I. patrol | examining the saps
e) Reported no saps running out from this work | Reported saps well wired [illegible]

7 General: Trench Mortars

At 11.30 AM Germans sent over about 10 rifle grenades or small grenades. They later sent over 3 3in oil cans, dud at the trench end of KILMUN STREET. We retaliated with 6 2" trench howitzers 10 2 lb trench mortars & the enemy did not reply again.

H. Mansel-Pleydell
1st Dorset.

28.1.16.

B.38. 14th Infantry Bde.

Situation Report.

(a) Patrols. Lieut. FRASER and No 7456. Sgt. CHARLES left 143 trench at 6.30 pm with the object of examining and bombing enemy work at X. 1. a. 10/8. A patrol of the K.O.Y.L.I. arrived first and bombed the same place. Our patrol reports no saps running out from this work in our direction. Returned to 143 trench about 8pm.

A second patrol (No 9397 L/cpl. WOOD and No 6245 Pte WELLS) left 143 trench about 9.15 pm to find out if enemy trench opposite was strongly held. They report it well wired & strongly held. They returned at 10.20 by same trench.

(b) Artillery. At 1am enemy fired 6. 77mm. shells at 144 trench doing very slight damage which is repaired.

At 11.30 am 7. 77mm shells

were fired near left of 143 trench without doing any damage.

At 1pm one shell was fired at Battn H.Q. without doing any damage.

At 2.30 pm 4 light shells were fired at 143 trench. Damage very slight. Repaired.

Retaliation by our artillery: NIL.

Trench mortar batteries. Our 2inch trench howitzers fired 6 rounds and the 4lb. trench mortars 10 rounds at enemy trenches opposite our 148 and 149. This was in reply to rifle grenades and oil cans fired into KILMUN Street near fire trench. Our shooting was good and enemy were silenced.

Spring guns & catapults. NIL.

State of trenches & work done. Fair.

143 trench. 30 yards French wire put out.

144 trench. 40 yds. French wire put out. fire platform improved, floorboards taken up & trench drained.

3/

145 trench. 20 yds fire step constructed. Trench cleared of mud. 30 yds French wire put out.

146. 147 and 148 trenches. Cleared of debris. 148 trench parapet revetted with sandbags for 5 yards.

149 & 150 trenches. 60 yds double row barbed wire erected in front of existing weak wire.

Tobermary St. deepened 2 ft. for 75 yards. Avenues & streets cleaned and cleared.

State of Wire. Fair. Work done: See above.

Working parties. 19th Lancs. Fusiliers. 60 men worked on shelters.

Materials. Sandbags are very urgently required. An infinitesimal portion of those demanded have been supplied. Floorboards are also needed in large quantities. None have been supplied. More rifle grenades required.

1st Dorset Rgt.
28. 1. 16

H Cecil Butcher.
Lieut. & Adjutant

Intelligence Report 24-1-16

1) Enemy Artillery fire

a At 6PM enemy shelled AUTHUILLE WOOD, HORSE ROAD and AVELUY ROAD and battery positions round AVELUY. © Enemy fire seemed to come from three directions. For two of them it is impossible to give more accurate description than right front and front (i.e. about due EAST and SOUTH EAST). Bearing was taken of a howitzer which was 84° from point R 31 a 1/5 (d) The guns appeared to be 77 mm and 4'9" howitzers (e) damage done is unknown. (f) In this sector artillery replied by firing a salvo of two 18 pounder shells - which burst very short

2) Enemy Lights and Signals

At 7 pm from about point 4088 a red light was sent up shortly followed by a green one - Result - nil apparent This was observed from point R 31 C-1/9.

3) At about 6·30 pm - from trench 149 enemy HORSE transport was heard moving in THIEPVAL Action taken reported to 14TH INF Brig - Result - no result observed

4) Movements of hostile troops - none observed

5) Enemy's working parties

At about 7 a.m. two men were observed working on German wire about [illegible]19 a 4/8. They were observed from about [illegible]19 a 4/7. Action taken by ourselves — shot at them [illegible] — both were seen to fall and it is certain that one was hit.

6) Patrols 2 LIEUT HUNT, Sgt AVEY and CORP MATTHEWS went out from 143 trench at 6.30 pm — Object to find out if any work was proceeding at night. On getting near German trench the patrol became aware of presence of two German patrols — one on each flank. Patrol went back & 15 rounds rapid were fired in supposed direction of hostile patrols.

This patrol later went out on each side of Hedge cutting trench 144 — Reported some sandbagging in progress — no digging.

2 LIEUT BLAKEWAY & CORP MATTHEWS went out about 7.15 pm from trench 147 — Object of patrol — general reconnaissance — Reported usual trench noises heard & no patrols met.

2 LIEUT MANSEL-PLEYDELL - Pte RYAN and Pte HEMBURY went out about 10.30 PM from 149 trench to ~~[illegible]~~ throw grenades at [illegible] in R31a 4.5/8.2

6) Patrols (cont)

When about 100 yards out the patrol suspected the presence of an enemy patrol some distance to the NORTH. This suspicion was strengthened by the fact that when four bombs were thrown at the sap – the enemy sent up no lights and fired no shots – nor were any shots fired during the time the patrol was out although the sentries could be distinctly heard talking + walking about.

7) General – One "oil can" fell in front of 143 trench at 12.40 p.m. As we had no mortar or howitzer near we were unable to retaliate. No damage was done – The position of this weapon is being located.

H Mansel-Pleydell
1st Dorset
10.1
G1

Situation Report. 29. 1. 16.

Patrols. Lieut HUNT, 8197 Sgt. AVEY and 14672 Cpl. HUGHES went out from the right of 143 trench at 6.30 pm. to find out if there was any work proceeding in enemy's lines opposite. When about 40 yards from the German wire they found there was a hostile patrol on either flank. They withdrew and we opened rapid fire in direction of hostile patrols. No work was in progress in German lines.

At 9 pm and 11.30 pm this and 2 other patrols (Sgt. DOWNES, + 6245 Pte WELLS 9397 L/cpl WOODS, + 14699 Pte LUCKWELL) went out on either side of hedge in front of 144 trench and came to German wire, where they lay and listened. Enemy were found to be doing some sandbagging. Patrols returned at 12.30 am by 144 trench.

At 7.15 pm Lieut BLAKEWAY and Corpl. MATTHEWS went out from right of 147 trench with the object of making a general reconnaissance. No enemy patrols were seen or heard; coughing was heard in German trench and men located

2/ walking up and down.

Lieut MANSEL-PLEYDELL with Ptes. RYAN and HEMBURY left 149 trench at 10.30pm to bomb German sap at R 31. a 5/6. Four grenades were thrown at the sap without bringing a reply of any kind from the enemy. As sentries were heard talking in German trench it is thought a hostile patrol was also out in this locality, thus preventing enemy from firing.

Artillery. At 6pm enemy shelled AUTHUILLE, AVELUY Road and battery positions in AVELUY with 4.9 howitzers and 77mm guns. Probably about 80 shells were fired. No damage was done in G.1 subsector.

Trench Mortar Batteries. Not active

Spring guns & catapults. Nothing of importance to report.

State of trenches. Good.

Work done:

143. Trench cleared, traverse repaired.

144. Mud cleared from beneath floorboards.

145 12 yds. firestep made; parapet improved.
147 mud cleared from beneath boards.
148 6 yards of trench cleared where completely blocked by fall of earth.
149 10 yards of parados revetted.
150 parapet revetted. 2 sump pits dug.

Tobermory St deepened for 50 yds. Shelters improved. Work cleaning & clearing communication trenches.

State of Wire Fair.
Work done: 45 yds concertina wire from 143.
40 yards from 144.
60 yds double concertina wire from and 30 yds single from 145.
80 yds barbed wire in front of 147 repaired.
60 yds barbed wire erected in front of 149.
2 rows of barbed wire erected for 60 yds in front of 150.

Working parties. 60 men 19th L. F. on shelters in 91.

Materials. Sandbags & floorboards very urgently needed.

H Cecil Butcher Lt. & Adjutant
1st Dorset Regt

INTELLIGENCE 30-1-16

1 Enemy's Artillery

Between 4 & 6 pm during the bombardment of G 2 about 50 6" howitzer shells fell around the junction of THIEPVAL AVENUE and TOBERMORY STREET — about 10 were blind — slight material damage.

Action taken by our artillery — our 18 pounders fired.

2 Enemy's lights and Signals — nil

3 Enemy's Transport — none reported

4 Movement of hostile troops At 7.45 pm from 144 trench — a fife and drum band was heard behind the German lines in an easterly direction. Action Taken — nil.

5 Enemy's Working Parties

1) at 7.30 am a German working party strength about 6 was seen from X 1 a 4/6 working in front of their trench. We machine gunned them & dispersed them — it was too misty to see result clearly

2) at 8 am a similar party was seen from 144 trench — they were about point 6382 — they were also dispersed with M G fire

3) At 11 am a similar party was seen opposite 145 from 145. Similar action was taken

(d) Patrols – At 2.30 a.m. CAPT THWAYTES and 2 LIEUT BLAKEWAY went out from 147. They went to examine German wire & found it very strong. They were in the wire when two German patrols came & searched for them – they escaped – and reached trench 147 again at 3.30 a.m. The Germans were wearing great coats and PICKELHAUBEN without spikes on them.

Two sniping patrols (a) Corp FRANCIS & L. CORP ADLAM (b) L. CORP WELLS & Pte WITTAKER) ~~but had from~~ went out from 144 & 148 but had no success.

L Corp Hughes – Ptes Fowler, Bell, [illegible] Bull – Carson – Boughton, Sergt Fineham, Corp Gallop – L. Corp Webb L. Corp Sperling Ptes Hill, James, Thomas, Beehan, Foley, Farmer and Miller – patrolled at various times in the night in front of trenches 143 to 146. They reported nothing unusual.

H. Mansel Pleydell
10 Dorsets

The "Kolnische Volkszeitung" was found in front of 146 last night

[illegible]

Situation Report
from 3pm 29th Jan to 3pm 30th Jan. 1916
1st Dorset Rgt.

Patrols

Capt. Thwaytes and Lieut BLAKEWAY went out from 147 trench at 2.30am to examine German wire and make a general reconnaissance. Wire very strong. While they were in the German wire two hostile patrols came out and searched for them, passing within 15 yds. Our patrol escaped and entered 147 trench again at 3.30 am. Enemy were wearing greatcoats and helmets without spikes.

Two patrols (Corp FRANCIS and L/Cpl ADLAM) & L/Cpl WELLS & Pte WHITTAKER went out from 144 and 148 trenches with object of sniping any of the enemy that might be walking on the top in the mist. They saw no one.

20 NCO's & men patrolled during the night from 143/4/5/6 trenches. They went out in two's & threes at different times and all report nothing unusual occurring.

Artillery. During bombardment of G.2 between 4 & 6 pm about 50 heavy howitzer

2/ shells fell near junction of THIEPVAL Avenue & TOBERMORY St, doing slight damage. Many of the shells were blind.
Our 18pounders retaliated; effect not known to us.

Trench Mortars. Quiet.

Spring guns & catapults. Quiet.

State of trenches. Good.
Work done: 143. trench cleared of fallen earth. Fire step made
144. 50yds of mud beneath floorboards cleared.
145. 17yds. firestep made. West Gun emplacement improved.
146/7/8. Mud cleared from beneath floorboards. 148 deepened.
149. Fire step repaired.
Tobermory st. deepened 18inches for a distance of 70yds. Parapet revetted with hurdles and expanded metal.
Places damaged by shelling repaired.
Shelters improved.
Street & avenues kept clear.

State of wire. Fair. 150yds concertina wire erected in front of 143./4./5. 30yds. of wire

3/

entanglement 4yds deep erected in front of 149.

Working parties. 60 men from 19th Lancs. Fusiliers worked on shelters.

Materials. Floorboards required. All sandbags asked for to-day have been promised us. Large numbers will be required every day for a considerable time. Reserve of MILLS grenades needs building up.

Dorset Rgt.
30.1.18

A. Cecil Butcher.
Lieut. & Adjutant.

INTELLIGENCE REPORT

31-1-16

1. Enemy's artillery - nil. mortars - one came over behind 148 at about 5.30 PM. It was of the [illegible] type and came from about R 31 A 55
2. Enemy's lights and signals, nil.
3. Enemy's Transport. Nil reported.
4. Movements of Hostile Troops - nil observed.
5. Enemy's working parties.
   At 2 pm two Germans were seen about point 65 82 from 148 trench. They were thought to be mending the roof of a shelter as sawing and hammering were heard. They were fired on by M G & dispersed.
6. Patrols. Between 10 pm and midnight and also between 1 am and 3 am, each company had 2 listening patrols out of 4 men each. These patrols were placed in front of our wire. Patrol leaders were Sergt DAVIS, Corpl BROWN Corp MAYHEW & Lce CORP LEGG Corpl MATTHEWS Lce CORPS, MASSEY, DARLEY, WELLS, DENNER & RAWLINSON.

   The patrol from 150, under CORP MAYHEW reported that at 11 pm he observed two Germans patrolling their trench about point R 31 a 55 between wire & parapet. They were out of bombing distance.
   2 LIEUT MANSEL-PLEYDELL, going out

5) Patrols (cont'd)

from 149 trench at 4 pm with Pte RYDAL found a German SAUSAGE hung on to a cross bar nailed to a telegraph pole about point R31 a 37

7) General. At 9.15 pm a German patrol approached our trench 147 [illegible]. They were challenged by a sentry group and threw a grenade and fired two pistol shots. The group immediately threw back two MILLS grenades both of which were blind. The group then opened rapid fire but the German patrol ~~etc~~ was then out of sight. They left no trace behind them.

Rifle grenades fell about 2 pm and 10 a m around the EAST ENDS of KILBERRY and INVERARY STREETS We retaliated

H G M Mansel-Pleydell

I.O. 1st Dorset

Situation Report
from 3pm 30 Jan. to 3pm 31st Jan.
1st Dorset Rgt.

Patrols. Between 10pm & midnight and between 1. and 3am each company sent out two watching patrols of four men each. They had orders to conceal themselves in front of our wire with the object of capturing any hostile patrols that might be out. No hostile patrols were reported, with the exception of two men observed at 11am (from 150 trench) between the German wire & their parapet.

Lieut MANSEL-PLEYDELL & Pte RYDAL left 149 trench at 4pm for a general reconnaissance. They found a German sausage nailed to a cross bar on a telegraph post. Nothing to report.

At 9.15pm a German patrol approached ~~at~~ 147 trench. On being challenged by our sentry group they threw a bomb and fired two shots. Our sentry threw two MILLS grenades, both of which failed to explode, and then opened fire. The hostile patrol disappeared in the darkness.

Artillery. NIL

Trench Mortars. Small T.M. fired 5 or 6 rounds during the morning at trench opposite 148/9.

Spring guns & catapults. Between 11 am & 1pm we fired about 30 grenades from WEST gun & catapult at German trench opposite 148. We also fired a few rifle grenades. Enemy did not retaliate.

State of trenches. Good.
Work done: Removing mud from beneath floorboards in all fire trenches. Large latrine dug in 150. Fire step built in 148 and 150. 20 yds BURY Ave. cleared. Streets & Avenues kept in repair as usual.

State of Wire. Fair. 150 yds put out in front of 144/5. 5 coils put out from 147.

Working parties. 60 men of 19th Lancs. Fus. worked on G.I. shelters.

Materials. Floorboards urgently needed. Tubular metal for headquarters shelters has not been available so far.

1/Dorset Rgt.
31. 1. 16.

H. Cecil Butcher
Lieut & Adjutant

Unit 1 Battalion The Dorsetshire Regiment.

Place In the Field

Date 7. 1. 16

FIELD STATE.

Army Form B 231.

To be rendered in accordance with Field Service Regulations, Part II.

FIGHTING STRENGTH — This should *not* include details attached to unit, or personnel detailed to march with the Train, or any men unfit to go into action with unit

RATION STRENGTH — To include Fighting Strength, Personnel detailed to march with the Train, and all Personnel and animals attached for Rations and Forage

UNIT	Personnel		Horses and Mules		Other Animals		Guns and Ammunition Wagons (stating nature)	Machine Guns	Ambulances	Tool Carts, Technical Carts (stating nature)	Remarks	Personnel	Horses and Mules		Other Animals		Mechanically Propelled Vehicles					Remarks
	Officers	Other Ranks	Riding	Draught and Pack								Total, all Ranks entitled to Rations.	Heavy Horses	Other Horses and Mules			Motor Cars	Motor Bicycles.	Lorries. 3 Ton	Lorries. 30 Cwt.	Tractors	
(1)	(2)	(3)	(4)	(5)	(6)	(7)	(8)	(9)	(10)	(11)	(12)	(13)	(14)	(15)	(16)	(17)	(18)	(19)	(20)	(21)	(22)	(23)
1 Battalion The Dorsetshire Regiment.	26	906	11	45			4 Lewis M.G.	4		17		556		54								7 officers 56 O.R. detached from [illegible]
TOTALS ...	26	906	11	45				4		7		556		54								

Ammunition with Unit:—

·303 inch; approximate number of rounds per Man ______

·303 inch; „ „ „ per Machine Gun ______

Gun or Howitzer; approximate number of rounds per Gun or Howitzer ______

Supplies with Unit:—

Approximate number of days' rations for men of ration strength ______

„ „ „ forage for Animals „ „ ______

„ „ „ fuel and lubricants for Mechanically Propelled Vehicles ______

(90988.) Wt.W. 5216—2140. 900,000 7/15. J. P. & Co. Ltd. Forms B 231 / 3

C. O.

Signature of Commander Sd. L. [illegible] Jones Bateman Lt Col. Comdg. 1st The Dorsetshire Regt.

Unit 1st Bn The Dorsetshire Regt

Place In the Field

Date 13. 1. 16.

FIELD STATE.

Army Form B 231.

To be rendered in accordance with Field Service Regulations, Part II.

UNIT	FIGHTING STRENGTH — This should *not* include details attached to unit, or personnel detailed to march with the Train, or any men unfit to go into action with unit											RATION STRENGTH — To include Fighting Strength, Personnel detailed to march with the Train, and all Personnel and animals attached for Rations and Forage										
	Personnel		Horses and Mules		Other Animals		Guns and Ammunition Wagons (stating nature)	Machine Guns	Ambulances	Tool Carts, Technical Carts (stating nature)	Remarks	Personnel	Horses and Mules		Other Animals		Mechanically Propelled Vehicles					Remarks
	Officers	Other Ranks	Riding	Draught and Pack								Total, all Ranks entitled to Rations.	Heavy Horses	Other Horses and Mules			Motor Cars	Motor Bicycles.	Lorries. 3 Ton	Lorries. 30 Cwt.	Tractors	
(1)	(2)	(3)	(4)	(5)	(6)	(7)	(8)	(9)	(10)	(11)	(12)	(13)	(14)	(15)	(16)	(17)	(18)	(19)	(20)	(21)	(22)	(23)
	26.	913	10	45.			4 Lewis	4		14		884		56								6 officers 67 O.R. detached from Bn
TOTALS ...	26.	913	10	45.				4		14		884		56								

Ammunition with Unit:—

·303 inch; approximate number of rounds per Man

·303 inch; " " " per Machine Gun

Gun or Howitzer; approximate number of rounds per Gun or Howitzer

Supplies with Unit:—

Approximate number of days' rations for men of ration strength

" " " forage for Animals " "

" " " fuel and lubricants for Mechanically Propelled Vehicles

P.T.O.

(90988.) Wt. W. 5216—2140. 900,000 7/15. J. P. & Co. Ltd. Forms B 231 / 3

Signature of Commander (Sd) [illegible] Lt Col
Comdg 1st Bn The Dorsetshire Regiment

Unit 1st Bn The Dorsetshire Regt

Place In the Field

Date 20. 1. 16

FIELD STATE.

Army Form B 231.

To be rendered in accordance with Field Service Regulations, Part II.

UNIT	FIGHTING STRENGTH — This should *not* include details attached to unit, or personnel detailed to march with the Train, or any men unfit to go into action with unit											RATION STRENGTH — To include Fighting Strength, Personnel detailed to march with the Train, and all Personnel and animals attached for Rations and Forage										
	Personnel		Horses and Mules		Other Animals		Guns and Ammunition Wagons (stating nature)	Machine Guns	Ambulances	Tool Carts, Technical Carts (stating nature)	Remarks	Personnel	Horses and Mules		Other Animals		Mechanically Propelled Vehicles					Remarks
	Officers	Other Ranks	Riding	Draught and Pack								Total, all Ranks entitled to Rations.	Heavy Horses	Other Horses and Mules			Motor Cars	Motor Bicycles.	Lorries. 3 Ton	Lorries. 30 Cwt.	Tractors	
(1)	(2)	(3)	(4)	(5)	(6)	(7)	(8)	(9)	(10)	(11)	(12)	(13)	(14)	(15)	(16)	(17)	(18)	(19)	(20)	(21)	(22)	(23)
	25	926	10	46			4 Lewis M.G.	4		14		890		54								4 officers 46 Ranks detached from Bn
TOTALS ...	25	926	10	46				4		14		890		54								

Ammunition with Unit:—

·303 inch; approximate number of rounds per Man

·303 inch; " " " per Machine Gun

Gun or Howitzer; approximate number of rounds per Gun or Howitzer

Supplies with Unit:—

Approximate number of days' rations for men of ration strength

" " " forage for Animals " "

" " " fuel and lubricants for Mechanically Propelled Vehicles

P.T.O.

Signature of Commander Sd/ J. R. Jones Bateman Lt Col
Comdg 1st Bn The Dorsetshire Regiment

(90988.) Wt.W. 5216—2140. 900,000 7/15. J. P. & Co. Ltd. Forms B 231 / 3

Unit 1/4th The Dorsetshire Regt

Place In the Field

Date 27.1.16

FIELD STATE.

Army Form B 231.

To be rendered in accordance with Field Service Regulations, Part II.

UNIT	FIGHTING STRENGTH — This should *not* include details attached to unit, or personnel detailed to march with the Train, or any men unfit to go into action with unit											RATION STRENGTH — To include Fighting Strength, Personnel detailed to march with the Train, and all Personnel and animals attached for Rations and Forage										
	Personnel		Horses and Mules		Other Animals		Guns and Ammunition Wagons (stating nature)	Machine Guns	Ambulances	Tool Carts, Technical Carts (stating nature)	Remarks	Personnel	Horses and Mules		Other Animals		Mechanically Propelled Vehicles					Remarks
	Officers	Other Ranks	Riding	Draught and Pack								Total, all Ranks entitled to Rations.	Heavy Horses	Other Horses and Mules			Motor Cars	Motor Bicycles.	Lorries. 3 Ton	Lorries. 30 Cwt.	Tractors	
(1)	(2)	(3)	(4)	(5)	(6)	(7)	(8)	(9)	(10)	(11)	(12)	(13)	(14)	(15)	(16)	(17)	(18)	(19)	(20)	(21)	(22)	(23)
	25	965	10	46			4 Lewis M.G.	4		14		964		37								6 officers 14 1/6 Ranks detached from Bn
TOTALS ...	25	965	10	46				4		14		964		37								

Ammunition with Unit:—

·303 inch; approximate number of rounds per Man ______

·303 inch; " " " per Machine Gun ______

Gun or Howitzer; approximate number of rounds per Gun or Howitzer ______

Supplies with Unit:—

Approximate number of days' rations for men of ration strength ______

" " " forage for Animals " " ______

" " " fuel and lubricants for Mechanically Propelled Vehicles ______

P.T.O.

Signature of Commander (Sd.) [illegible] Bateman Lt Col

Comdg 1/4th The Dorsetshire Regiment

(90988.) Wt.W. 5216—2140. 900,000 7/15. J. P. & Co. Ltd. Forms B 231 / 3

14th Brigade.

32nd Division.

1st BATTALION

THE DORSET REGIMENT

FEBRUARY 1 9 1 6

Appendices attached:-

Field States.

Instructions regarding War Diaries and Intelligence Summaries are contained in F. S. Regs., Part II. and the Staff Manual respectively. Title Pages will be prepared in manuscript.

WAR DIARY
or
INTELLIGENCE SUMMARY
(Erase heading not required.)

Army Form C. 2118.

VOL III
Sheet 4

Place	Date	Hour	Summary of Events and Information	Remarks and references to Appendices
MARTINSART	Feb. 2		In billets at MARTINSART and AUTHUILLE (A Company Garrisoning the Keeps)	HBT
	3		In billets at MARTINSART and AUTHUILLE (A Company Garrisoning the Keeps)	HBT
	4		In billets at MARTINSART and AUTHUILLE (A Coy Garrisoning the Keeps)	HBT
	5		In billets at MARTINSART and AUTHUILLE. Battalion went to MARTINSART wood between 11 am and 2.45 pm while our artillery bombarded THIEPVAL and trenches in case of counter bombardment.	HBT
	6		Companies relieved in MARTINSART at 5.45 pm and withdrew to MILLENCOURT	HBT
		8.10 pm	B.C & D Coys in MILLENCOURT. 8.10 pm A Company arrived at 10.25 pm	
MILLENCOURT	7		In billets MILLENCOURT	HBT
	8		In billets MILLENCOURT	HBT
	9		In billets MILLENCOURT	HBT
	10		In billets MILLENCOURT	HBT
	11		In billets MILLENCOURT	HBT
BAIKEUX	12	11.5 am	Moved to BAIKEUX arriving there at 11.5 am	HBT
RAINNEVILLE	13	12.5 pm	Moved to RAINNEVILLE. In billets 12.5 pm	HBT
	14		In billets RAINNEVILLE.	HBT
FRECHENCOURT	15		Battalion moved to FRECHENCOURT - in billets 3.40 pm	HBT
				HBT

2449 Wt. W14957/M90 750,000 1/16 J.B.C. & A. Forms/C.2118/12.

9. 19

Army Form C. 2118.

Instructions regarding War Diaries and Intelligence Summaries are contained in F. S. Regs., Part II. and the Staff Manual respectively. Title Pages will be prepared in manuscript.

WAR DIARY
or
INTELLIGENCE SUMMARY
(Erase heading not required.)

VOL III
Sheet 5

Place	Date	Hour	Summary of Events and Information	Remarks and references to Appendices
	Feb.			
FRECHENCOURT	15		Battalion in billets at FRECHENCOURT commenced company training.	HBT
	16–20		In billets at FRECHENCOURT	HBT
	21		School for young officers and NCO's for 32nd Div opened - Each course to last a fortnight under Lt Col Jones-Bateman CMG - The Battalion continued company training and a certain number of officers & NCO's were attached each day to the Companies.	HBT
	22–26		Battalion in billets at FRECHENCOURT carrying out ~~scheme of~~ company training, also musketry - and obstacle course. (The range and musketry course were built by the regiment.)	HBT
	27		In the afternoon there was an inter Battalion Cross Country run for the Brigade The Regiment got the first 13 men home and so won a cup presented by Br. General Compton CB	HBT

2449 Wt. W14957/M90 750,000 1/16 J.B.C. & A. Forms/C.2118/12.

Army Form C. 2118.

Instructions regarding War Diaries and Intelligence Summaries are contained in F. S. Regs., Part II. and the Staff Manual respectively. Title Pages will be prepared in manuscript.

WAR DIARY
or
INTELLIGENCE SUMMARY

(Erase heading not required.)

VOL III
Sheet 6.

Place	Date	Hour	Summary of Events and Information	Remarks and references to Appendices
FRECHENCOURT	Feb 28		Battalion took part in a Brigade (Skeleton) attack scheme on imaginary trenches which were traced out on the ground at the URT in BEHENCOURT (Amiens map, sheet 17). The C.O., Adjutant and Company Commanders present also Platoon Sergeants two men a platoon as flankers and one man as Grenadier (Also officers of class). The scheme was carried out in skeleton with the idea of repeating the next day.	HDT
FRECHENCOURT	29		Battalion scheme cancelled as the Brigade with the exception of 1/Dorset Regt. moved into billets at MILLENCOURT etc. prior to going into the trenches. Parades carried on as usual	HDT
"	March 1		In billets at FRECHENCOURT. Usual parades carried on. Draft of 16 OR arrived	HDT
"	2		In billets at FRECHENCOURT, parades as usual. Officers of class carried out a scheme under Commanding Officer at SEPTENVILLE. Draft of 25 arrived	HDT
"	3		In billets at FRECHENCOURT. Parades as usual.	HDT
"	4		Battalion moved to billets at MILLENCOURT	HDT

2449 Wt. W14957/M90 750,000 1/16 J.B.C. & A. Forms/C.2118/12.

Unit 1st Bn The Dorsetshire Regt

Place In the Field

Date 3. 2. 16

FIELD STATE.

Army Form B 231.

To be rendered in accordance with Field Service Regulations, Part II.

Attd Sheet 4 Vol III

UNIT	FIGHTING STRENGTH. This should *not* include details attached to unit, or personnel detailed to march with the Train, or any men unfit to go into action with unit											RATION STRENGTH. To include Fighting Strength, Personnel detailed to march with the Train, and all Personnel and animals attached for Rations and Forage										
	Personnel		Horses and Mules		Other Animals		Guns and Ammunition Wagons (stating nature)	Machine Guns	Ambulances	Tool Carts, Technical Carts (stating nature)	Remarks	Personnel	Horses and Mules		Other Animals		Mechanically Propelled Vehicles					Remarks
	Officers	Other Ranks	Riding	Draught and Pack								Total, all Ranks entitled to Rations.	Heavy Horses	Other Horses and Mules			Motor Cars	Motor Bicycles.	Lorries. 3 Ton	Lorries. 30 Cwt.	Tractors	
(1)	(2)	(3)	(4)	(5)	(6)	(7)	(8)	(9)	(10)	(11)	(12)	(13)	(14)	(15)	(16)	(17)	(18)	(19)	(20)	(21)	(22)	(23)
	25	953	11	46			4 Lewis M. Gun	4		16		850		58								9 officers 139 OR detached from Bn
TOTALS ...	25	953	11	46				4		16		850		58								

Ammunition with Unit:—

·303 inch; approximate number of rounds per Man ______

·303 inch; " " " per Machine Gun ______

Gun or Howitzer; approximate number of rounds per Gun or Howitzer ______

Supplies with Unit:—

Approximate number of days' rations for men of ration strength ______

" " " forage for Animals " " ______

" " " fuel and lubricants for Mechanically Propelled Vehicles ______

P.T.O.

Signature of Commander (Sd) L. H. Jones Bateman Lt Col

Comdg 1st Bn The Dorsetshire Regiment

(79269.) Wt. W. 5870—621. 900,000 10/14. J. P. & Co. Ltd. Forms B 231 / 3

Unit 1 Bn The Dorsetshire Regt.
Place In the Field
Date 10. 2. 16

FIELD STATE.

Army Form B 231.

To be rendered in accordance with Field Service Regulations, Part II.

Attd Sheet 4 VOL VII

UNIT	FIGHTING STRENGTH — This should *not* include details attached to unit, or personnel detailed to march with the Train, or any men unfit to go into action with unit											RATION STRENGTH — To include Fighting Strength, Personnel detailed to march with the Train, and all Personnel and animals attached for Rations and Forage										
	Personnel		Horses and Mules		Other Animals		Guns and Ammunition Wagons (stating nature)	Machine Guns	Ambulances	Tool Carts, Technical Carts (stating nature)	Remarks	Personnel	Horses and Mules		Other Animals		Mechanically Propelled Vehicles					Remarks
	Officers	Other Ranks	Riding	Draught and Pack								Total, all Ranks entitled to Rations.	Heavy Horses	Other Horses and Mules			Motor Cars	Motor Bicycles.	Lorries. 3 Ton	Lorries. 30 Cwt.	Tractors	
(1)	(2)	(3)	(4)	(5)	(6)	(7)	(8)	(9)	(10)	(11)	(12)	(13)	(14)	(15)	(16)	(17)	(18)	(19)	(20)	(21)	(22)	(23)
	25	955	11	45			4 Lewis M.G.	4		16		834		47								7 officer 14 O.R. detached from Battn.
Totals ...	25	955	11	45				4		16		834		47								

Ammunition with Unit:—

·303 inch; approximate number of rounds per Man

·303 inch; " " " per Machine Gun

Gun or Howitzer; approximate number of rounds per Gun or Howitzer

Supplies with Unit:—

Approximate number of days' rations for men of ration strength

" " " forage for Animals " "

" " " fuel and lubricants for Mechanically Propelled Vehicles

P.T.O.

Signature of Commander (Sd) J. R. Jones Bateman Lt Col
Comdg 1 Bn The Dorsetshire Regt

(79269.) Wt. W. 5870—621. 900,000 10/14. J. P. & Co. Ltd. Forms B 231 / 3

Army Form B 231.

FIELD STATE.

Unit 1 Bn the Dorsetshire Regt

Place In the Field

Date 14.2.16.

To be rendered in accordance with Field Service Regulations, Part II.

Att'd Sheet 5 Vol III

UNIT	FIGHTING STRENGTH — This should *not* include details attached to unit, or personnel detailed to march with the Train, or any men unfit to go into action with unit											RATION STRENGTH — To include Fighting Strength, Personnel detailed to march with the Train, and all Personnel and animals attached for Rations and Forage										
	Personnel		Horses and Mules		Other Animals		Guns and Ammunition Wagons (stating nature)	Machine Guns	Ambulances	Tool Carts, Technical Carts (stating nature)	Remarks	Personnel	Horses and Mules		Other Animals		Mechanically Propelled Vehicles					Remarks
	Officers	Other Ranks	Riding	Draught and Pack								Total, all Ranks entitled to Rations.	Heavy Horses	Other Horses and Mules			Motor Cars	Motor Bicycles.	Lorries. 3 Ton	Lorries. 30 Cwt.	Tractors	
(1)	(2)	(3)	(4)	(5)	(6)	(7)	(8)	(9)	(10)	(11)	(12)	(13)	(14)	(15)	(16)	(17)	(18)	(19)	(20)	(21)	(22)	(23)
	29	937	11	45			4 Lewis M.G.	4		14		921		57								4 officers 96 O.R. detached from Bn
TOTALS ...	29	937	11	45				4		14		921		57								

Ammunition with Unit:—

·303 inch; approximate number of rounds per Man ______

·303 inch; " " " per Machine Gun ______

Gun or Howitzer; approximate number of rounds per Gun or Howitzer ______

Supplies with Unit:—

Approximate number of days' rations for men of ration strength ______

" " " forage for Animals " " ______

" " " fuel and lubricants for Mechanically Propelled Vehicles ______

P.T.O.

Signature of Commander (Sd) J.H. Jones Bateman Lt Col
Comdg 1 Bn the Dorsetshire Regt

(79269.) Wt.W. 5870—621. 900,000 10/14. J. P. & Co. Ltd. Forms B 231 / 3

Unit 1/Bn The Dorsetshire Regiment

Place In the Field

Date 24. 2. 16.

FIELD STATE.

Army Form B 231.

To be rendered in accordance with Field Service Regulations, Part II.

Attd sheet 5 vol III

FIGHTING STRENGTH — This should *not* include details attached to unit, or personnel detailed to march with the Train, or any men unfit to go into action with unit

RATION STRENGTH — To include Fighting Strength, Personnel detailed to march with the Train, and all Personnel and animals attached for Rations and Forage

UNIT	Fighting Strength: Personnel		Horses and Mules		Other Animals		Guns and Ammunition Wagons (stating nature)	Machine Guns	Ambulances	Tool Carts, Technical Carts (stating nature)	Remarks	Ration Strength: Personnel	Horses and Mules		Other Animals		Mechanically Propelled Vehicles					Remarks
	Officers	Other Ranks	Riding	Draught and Pack								Total, all Ranks entitled to Rations.	Heavy Horses	Other Horses and Mules			Motor Cars	Motor Bicycles.	Lorries. 3 Ton	Lorries. 30 Cwt.	Tractors	
(1)	(2)	(3)	(4)	(5)	(6)	(7)	(8)	(9)	(10)	(11)	(12)	(13)	(14)	(15)	(16)	(17)	(18)	(19)	(20)	(21)	(22)	(23)
	27.	934	11	45			4 Lewis M.G.	4		14		938		54								4 officers 99 O.R. detached from Bn. 12 officers 50 O.R. attd Bn.
TOTALS ...	27.	934.	11	45.				4		14		938		54								

Ammunition with Unit:—

·303 inch; approximate number of rounds per Man ____

·303 inch; " " " per Machine Gun ____

Gun or Howitzer; approximate number of rounds per Gun or Howitzer ____

Supplies with Unit:—

Approximate number of days' rations for men of ration strength ____

" " " forage for Animals " " ____

" " " fuel and lubricants for Mechanically Propelled Vehicles ____

P.T.O.

Signature of Commander (Sd) J. H. Jones Bateman Lieut Col
Comdg 1/Bn The Dorsetshire Regt

(79269.) Wt. W. 5870—621. 900,000 10/14. J. P. & Co. Ltd. Forms B 231/3

Unit 1/Bn The Dorsetshire Regt

Place In the Field

Date 1.3.16

FIELD STATE.

Army Form B 231.

Attd sheet 6 Vol III

To be rendered in accordance with Field Service Regulations, Part II.

UNIT	FIGHTING STRENGTH. This should *not* include details attached to unit, or personnel detailed to march with the Train, or any men unfit to go into action with unit											RATION STRENGTH. To include Fighting Strength, Personnel detailed to march with the Train, and all Personnel and animals attached for Rations and Forage										
	Personnel		Horses and Mules		Other Animals		Guns and Ammunition Wagons (stating nature)	Machine Guns	Ambulances	Tool Carts, Technical Carts (stating nature)	Remarks	Personnel	Horses and Mules		Other Animals		Mechanically Propelled Vehicles					Remarks
	Officers	Other Ranks	Riding	Draught and Pack								Total, all Ranks entitled to Rations.	Heavy Horses	Other Horses and Mules			Motor Cars	Motor Bicycles.	Lorries. 3 Ton	Lorries. 30 Cwt.	Tractors	
(1)	(2)	(3)	(4)	(5)	(6)	(7)	(8)	(9)	(10)	(11)	(12)	(13)	(14)	(15)	(16)	(17)	(18)	(19)	(20)	(21)	(22)	(23)
	30	935	11	45			4 Lewis M.G.	4		17		942		57								4 officers 5 O.R. detached from Bn. 12 officers 50 O.R. attd to Bn
TOTALS ...	30.	935	11	45.			4 Lewis M.G.	4		17		942		57								

Ammunition with Unit:—

·303 inch; approximate number of rounds per Man

·303 inch; " " " per Machine Gun

Gun or Howitzer; approximate number of rounds per Gun or Howitzer

Supplies with Unit:—

Approximate number of days' rations for men of ration strength

" " " forage for Animals " "

" " " fuel and lubricants for Mechanically Propelled Vehicles

P.T.O.

(79269.) Wt.W. 5870—621. 900,000 10/14. J. P. & Co. Ltd. Forms B 231/3

Signature of Commander (Sd) A. A. Jones Bateman Lt Col Comdg 1/Bn The Dorsetshire Regiment

14th Brigade.

32nd Division.

1st BATTALION

THE DORSET REGIMENT

MARCH 1 9 1 6

Field states attached.

Army Form C. 2118. 32

1 Dorset Regt
Vol 19420 VOL III

Instructions regarding War Diaries and Intelligence Summaries are contained in F. S. Regs., Part II. and the Staff Manual respectively. Title Pages will be prepared in manuscript.

WAR DIARY
or
INTELLIGENCE SUMMARY
(Erase heading not required.)

Place	Date	Hour	Summary of Events and Information	Remarks and references to Appendices
MILLENCOURT	March 5		Battalion in billets at MILLENCOURT – Received orders that we would probably return to trenches on 8th inst. and that the school was cancelled.	HCB
"	6		In billets at MILLENCOURT	HCB
"	7		In billets at MILLENCOURT – Orders to proceed to trenches on the 9th.	HCB
"	8		In billets at MILLENCOURT – 2nd in Command, Company Commanders and M.G. officer visited the trenches in E3. Subsector.	HCB
MILLENCOURT	9		In billets at MILLENCOURT – Relieved 2/Manchester Regt in E3. Subsector	2/KOYLI on right
E3 Sub Sector		5.40pm	relief complete. German machine gun opened fire at 6pm otherwise spent an abnormally quiet night – Trenches were in a very bad state owing to recent fall of snow and consequently a large number of men were required for working parties – Casualties NIL.	19/Lancs Fus left. HCB
E3	10		A quiet day, with the exception of a little intermittent shelling, which our artillery replied to. A trench mortar emplacement was located near Y sap. and our 4.5 guns did some good shooting at this about 4.15pm. A quiet night on our front – Enemy bombarded F2 and G1 Subsectors & made a successful raid. Work was continued on trenches and wire. No casualties. (Lieut Mansel-Pleydell + 8 engl grenadiers went out to reconnoitre Y Sap – They encountered 4 Germans in their wire and dispersed them by throwing 8 grenades + returned)	HCB

G.20

2449 Wt. W14957/M90 750,000 1/16 J.B.C. & A. Forms/C.2118/12.

Instructions regarding War Diaries and Intelligence Summaries are contained in F. S. Regs., Part II. and the Staff Manual respectively. Title Pages will be prepared in manuscript.

WAR DIARY
or
INTELLIGENCE SUMMARY
(Erase heading not required.)

Army Form C. 2118.

VOL III
Sheet 8.

Place	Date	Hour	Summary of Events and Information	Remarks and references to Appendices
E3 Subsector	March 11		Very little activity during the day. At 10.30 pm the enemy sent over a volley of about 8 'oil cans' and some rifle grenades which blew in about 15 yds of 121 trench. Our trench mortars replied. Work continued improving trenches and wire. No casualties	HGB
E3	12		A little artillery activity on both sides. An exceptionally quiet night. No casualties. (Enemy sent over a number of light shells behind USNA Redoubt about 5 pm. which wounded one pack pony.)	HGB
E3.	13.		Enemy rather more active on our right with 'oil cans' and rifle grenades. One fell at the head of DUMFERMLINE ST. about 4 pm killing one officer (Lt. McKay) 15/HLI. and killing 2 other ranks and wounding 3 other ranks of the RE working party. Our 18 pounders did some very good shooting cutting wire around Y Sap in the afternoon. The enemy were very jumpy during the night sending over volleys of 'oil cans' and light shells at intervals. Our artillery were active. Enemy were also active with machine guns. We had one man wounded by Shrapnel.	HGB
E 3	14		An exceptionally quiet day a little artillery activity on both sides. In the morning the enemy shelled ALBERT and AVELUY. Our 4.5 guns fired on enemy's trench mortar positions, ~~tcd~~ in LA BOISSELLE between 3.15 and 4.15 pm. Enemy's trench mortars active during the night our 18 pounders replied to them and one of the enemy's mortars was reported put out of action. No casualties.	HGB

2449 Wt. W14957/M90 750,000 1/16 J.B.C. & A. Forms/C.2118/12.

Army Form C. 2118.

Instructions regarding War Diaries and Intelligence Summaries are contained in F. S. Regs., Part II. and the Staff Manual respectively. Title Pages will be prepared in manuscript.

WAR DIARY
or
INTELLIGENCE SUMMARY

(Erase heading not required.)

VOL III
Sheet 9

Place	Date	Hour	Summary of Events and Information	Remarks and references to Appendices
E3	March 15		Enemy's trench mortars active about 10 am. Replied to by our 18 pounders and silenced. Between 10.30 and 11 am enemy sent about a dozen howitzer shells close to headquarters (ST. ANDREWS AV. and DUMFERMLINE ST.) which damaged B. Battery observation station. At 6.30 pm the enemy concentrated very heavy artillery on DUMFERMLINE ST and ST. ANDREWS AVENUE. for about 5 minutes. At 6.50 pm they again concentrated their artillery fire on these places. Killing one other rank and wounding four.	H.B.
		9.50 pm	Were relieved by 2/Manchester Regt. at 9.50 pm and withdrew to billets. Headquarters A & B Companies to ALBERT and C & D. Companies to AVELUY. Battalion in billets at 11.15 P.M.	
ALBERT-AVELUY	16		Battalion in billets - Found working parties. A peaceful day until 10 pm when enemy fired several heavy shells into ALBERT. doing no damage. No casualties. (The CO. went on leave.)	H.B.
ALBERT-AVELUY	17		In billets at ALBERT and AVELUY: a party of 80 men under CAPT. ALGEO. & 2/Lieuts MANSEL-PLEYDELL, BLAKEWAY and CLARKE proceeded to MILLENCOURT to dig fac-simile of German lines and practice a bombing raid. All troops and transport were ordered to evacuate ALBERT and AVELUY between the hours of 11 am and 1 pm. - Enemy shelled the Town with about a dozen H.E. shells and shrapnel doing no damage. The Town was also shelled by the enemy	H.B.

2449 Wt. W14957/M90 750,000 1/16 J.B.C. & A. Forms/C.2118/12.

Army Form C. 2118.

VOL III
Sheet 10

Instructions regarding War Diaries and Intelligence Summaries are contained in F. S. Regs., Part II. and the Staff Manual respectively. Title Pages will be prepared in manuscript.

WAR DIARY
or
INTELLIGENCE SUMMARY
(Erase heading not required.)

Place	Date	Hour	Summary of Events and Information	Remarks and references to Appendices
ALBERT – AVELUY	March 17		at 6.30 pm. 7.30 pm and 10.30 pm. – No damage was done except two riding horses were wounded. One NCO. was wounded at AVELUY on a working party.	HCB
"	18		Battn. in billets at ALBERT and AVELUY – ALBERT was shelled about 12.50 pm 5 men were wounded and 2 horses killed and two wounded. Otherwise a quiet day. A draft of 8 men arrived	HCB
"	19		In billets at ALBERT and AVELUY. Quiet day. At 3.30 pm the enemy dropped about eight heavy shells into ~~the~~ ALBERT but did no damage. No casualties	HCB
"	20		In billets ALBERT – AVELUY. A quiet day. About a dozen shells fired into ALBERT wounding one man about 3.30 pm. Received orders re. relief of trenches.	HCB
ALBERT – AVELUY	21		In billets ALBERT – AVELUY. A peaceful day till about 3.30 pm when the enemy sent over about 8 Howitzer (5.9) in ALBERT. which did no damage.	HCB
E3 Subsector		9.5pm	Relief commenced at 7 pm and reported complete at 9.5 pm. no casualties	2/KOYLI on our right 19/Lancs. Fus on left
E3 "	22		The morning was much quieter than usual but about 2.30 pm the enemy started sending 'oil cans' into BURNT ISLAND and 77 mm shells at KEATS REDAN – Our 18 pounder batteries were called upon and fired very effectively on the enemy trenches and LA BOISSELLE – The enemy also	HCB

2449 Wt. W14957/M90 750,000 1/16 J.B.C. & A. Forms/C.2118/12.

Instructions regarding War Diaries and Intelligence Summaries are contained in F. S. Regs., Part II. and the Staff Manual respectively. Title Pages will be prepared in manuscript.

WAR DIARY
or
~~INTELLIGENCE SUMMARY~~

(Erase heading not required.)

Army Form C. 2118.

VOL III
Sheet 11

Place	Date 1916	Hour	Summary of Events and Information	Remarks and references to Appendices
E 3 Subsector	22 contd		fired on BURNT ISLAND and DUMFERMLINE ST. and KEATS REDAN and both sides artillery fire was kept up till 4 pm. At 10.30 pm the enemy fired on KEATS REDAN our 18 pounder batteries replied with 67 rounds. At 11 pm the enemy fired 'oil cans' into BURNT ISLAND they were immediately silenced with with 36 rounds from our 18 pounders. and no further activity took place during the night. During the afternoon one man of the 2/Manchester Regt was killed; two wounded, one 15/HLI wounded and 2 1/Dorset men wounded - about BURNT Island.	HB
E3 Subsector	23		An exceptionally quiet day - About 3.30 pm the enemy fired two Salvos of 77 mm shells into KEATS REDAN and also a number of trench Mortar bombs into BURNT ISLAND. Our 18 pounders were active - At 12.10 am the enemy fired 9 'oil cans' into BURNT ISLAND our guns immediately retaliated and the night was quiet from then onwards - No casualties.	HB
E 3 Subsector	24.		Very quiet day and night. No casualties.	16th H.L.I. on our right. 19th Lancs on our left.
do	25.		Quiet day. Patrols went out at 7.30 pm to examine enemy wire and find out if gaps made by artillery are still open. Capt. ALGEO and party of 80 men who were left behind in MILLENCOURT on 21st inst. to practice a raid on German trench, arrived in trenches during the afternoon. No casualties.	HB

Army Form C. 2118.

WAR DIARY
or
INTELLIGENCE SUMMARY
(Erase heading not required.)

Instructions regarding War Diaries and Intelligence Summaries are contained in F. S. Regs., Part II. and the Staff Manual respectively. Title Pages will be prepared in manuscript.

VOL III
Sheet 12

Place	Date 1916	Hour	Summary of Events and Information	Remarks and references to Appendices
E3. Subsector	26th March	-	Situation normal till 1.30 pm when enemy began firing 5.9 shells at various points in the subsector, continuing all the afternoon. Little damage was done though BURNT Island was damaged by "oil-cans". Enemy activity died down at 8 pm. Patrols were sent out soon after dark and reported at 10.45 pm that Germans were repairing the gaps in wire in front of "Y" sap through which raiding parties are to go on the enterprise during to-night. Bursts of machine gun fire were opened to stop this work. At 12.27 am a mine was exploded opposite LA BOISELLE. This was a pre-arranged signal for a raid to be made on "Y" sap and the enemy's trenches to the right of it for the purpose of taking prisoners. The raiding party (86 men) led by Lieut. MANSEL-PLEYDELL, Lieut. BLAKEWAY and Lieut. CLARKE, all under the direction of Capt. ALGEO, then went forward in two parties. One party went to the left to enter the front trench of "Y" sap and the other to the right to enter the front GERMAN trench on the right of the BAPAUME Road. Both parties managed to get through the gaps already cut for them in the German wire although a considerable amount of loose wire had been put out, and the majority of the men got into the German trenches. Immediately they came under heavy fire from grenades, bombs, "oil-cans", ~~and~~ artillery & machine guns. The "Y" sap appears to have been empty, and only one or two Germans	HCD

2449 Wt. W14957/M90 750,000 1/16 J.B.C. & A. Forms/C.2118/12.

Army Form C. 2118.

VOL III

Sheet 13

WAR DIARY
or
INTELLIGENCE SUMMARY
(Erase heading not required.)

Instructions regarding War Diaries and Intelligence Summaries are contained in F. S. Regs., Part II. and the Staff Manual respectively. Title Pages will be prepared in manuscript.

Place	Date 1916	Hour	Summary of Events and Information	Remarks and references to Appendices
E.3 subsector	26th March		were seen running away. One was shot. The bombing was so heavy that when the signal to retire was given at 12.35 am as arranged the left party had not got as far as had been anticipated. Our casualties were 2 killed, 14 wounded, and 2nd Lieut BLAKEWAY wounded and missing. The latter was seen lying on the German parapet, and though every possible effort was made to remove him, this was found impossible. Parties were at work assisting to get in the wounded until dawn, a task that was rendered extremely difficult and dangerous by German machine gun fire. To assist the raiding party while in the enemy trenches, artillery barrages were kept up, nearly 1000 rounds being fired. The enemy's artillery retaliation was intense but did not cause much damage. 32nd Divisional report on this raid + a special routine order by Br. General C.W. COMPTON. C.M.G. commanding 14th Infantry Bde, are attached to this diary. Total casualties: one officer wounded and missing, 3 O.R. killed, 17. O.R. wounded	HB
E.3 subsector	27th		Our 8 inch guns fired about 50 rounds at enemy machine gun and other emplacements in LA BOISSELLE. Enemy replied by firing 5.9's intermittently all the afternoon at St. ANDREWS Avenue and Counter Attack Coy's headquarters.	HB

Instructions regarding War Diaries and Intelligence Summaries are contained in F. S. Regs., Part II. and the Staff Manual respectively. Title pages will be prepared in manuscript.

WAR DIARY
or
INTELLIGENCE SUMMARY.

(Erase heading not required.)

Army Form C. 2118.

Place	Date	Hour	Summary of Events and Information	Remarks and references to Appendices
			Copied from first page of War Diary for April 1916.	
E.3 Subsector	March 1916 27th.	10.20.p.m.	Relief by 2nd Manchester Regiment completed. Battalion withdraws to billets in Millencourt.	
MILLENCOURT	28th		In billets in MILLENCOURT in Divisional Reserve.	
do.	29th		do.	
do.	30th		do.	
do.	31st		do.	

D. D. & L., London, E.C.
(A8004) Wt. W1771/M2 31 750,000 5/17 Sch. 52 Forms/C2118/14

Unit 1st Bn Dorset Regt.
Place In the Field
Date 9 3 1916

FIELD STATE.

Army Form B 231.

To be rendered in accordance with Field Service Regulations, Part II.

FIGHTING STRENGTH — This should *not* include details attached to unit, or personnel detailed to march with the Train, or any men unfit to go into action with unit (columns 2–12)

RATION STRENGTH — To include Fighting Strength, Personnel detailed to march with the Train, and all Personnel and animals attached for Rations and Forage (columns 13–23)

UNIT	Personnel		Horses and Mules		Other Animals		Guns and Ammunition Wagons (stating nature)	Machine Guns	Ambulances	Tool Carts, Technical Carts (stating nature)	Remarks	Personnel	Horses and Mules		Other Animals		Mechanically Propelled Vehicles					Remarks
	Officers	Other Ranks	Riding	Draught and Pack								Total, all Ranks entitled to Rations.	Heavy Horses	Other Horses and Mules			Motor Cars	Motor Bicycles	Lorries. 3 Ton	Lorries. 30 Cwt.	Tractors	
(1)	(2)	(3)	(4)	(5)	(6)	(7)	(8)	(9)	(10)	(11)	(12)	(13)	(14)	(15)	(16)	(17)	(18)	(19)	(20)	(21)	(22)	(23)
	30	965	11	45			Lewis M.G. 6.	6		17		938		58								8 Officers 67 O.R. detached from Battn. 1 Officer 3 O.R. attached to Bn.
TOTALS ...	30	965	11	45				6		17		938		58								

Ammunition with Unit:—

·303 inch; approximate number of rounds per Man ______

·303 inch; " " " per Machine Gun ______

Gun or Howitzer; approximate number of rounds per Gun or Howitzer ______

Supplies with Unit:—

Approximate number of days' rations for men of ration strength ______

" " " forage for Animals " " ______

" " " fuel and lubricants for Mechanically Propelled Vehicles ______

Signature of Commander (Sd) L. V. Jones-Bateman Lt Col
Commanding 1st Dorset Regt

(90988.) Wt.W. 5216—2140. 900,000 7/15. J. P. & Co. Ltd. Forms B 231/3

Capt R. V. Kestell-Cornish	1st Dorsets	To F Amb	7. 3. 16
Lieut J. H. Butlin	3rd –"–	–"–	6. 3. 16
–"– S. A. Gomez	3rd –"–	–"–	4. 3. 16
–"– M. A. Fraser	3rd –"–	–"–	6. 3. 16
–"– A. E. Hainwood	1st –"–	–"–	3. 3. 16
–"– H. K. J. Statham	3rd –"–	To 19th Lanc Fus.	
Lieut J. Hewitt	19th Lanc. Fus.	Ceased to be attached to Battn	6. 3. 16
–"– G. W. Douglas	17th H. F.		
Lieut R. J. Sharratt	16th L. F.		
–"– J. S. Marr	17th H. L. I.		
–"– D. R. Macdermid	16th H. L. I.		
–"– F. A. A. Hewson	10th Border Rgt.		
–"– J. A. Thompson	15th H. L. I.		
–"– R. Reed.	16th H. L.		
– C. A. L. Walker.	2nd Royal Innis. Fus.		
–"– C. Crossley.	15th Lanc. Fus.		
–"– D. F. G. Johnson	2nd Manchester Regt.		

Unit 1st Bn Dorset Regt.

Place In the Field

Date 16 · 3 · 1916.

Yol III Army Form B 231.

Sheet 9.

FIELD STATE.

To be rendered in accordance with Field Service Regulations, Part II.

UNIT	FIGHTING STRENGTH — This should *not* include details attached to unit, or personnel detailed to march with the Train, or any men unfit to go into action with unit											RATION STRENGTH — To include Fighting Strength, Personnel detailed to march with the Train, and all Personnel and animals attached for Rations and Forage										
	Personnel		Horses and Mules		Other Animals		Guns and Ammunition Wagons (stating nature)	Machine Guns	Ambulances	Tool Carts, Technical Carts (stating nature)	Remarks	Personnel	Horses and Mules		Other Animals		Mechanically Propelled Vehicles					Remarks
	Officers	Other Ranks	Riding	Draught and Pack								Total, all Ranks entitled to Rations.	Heavy Horses	Other Horses and Mules			Motor Cars	Motor Bicycles.	Lorries. 3 Ton	Lorries. 30 Cwt.	Tractors	
(1)	(2)	(3)	(4)	(5)	(6)	(7)	(8)	(9)	(10)	(11)	(12)	(13)	(14)	(15)	(16)	(17)	(18)	(19)	(20)	(21)	(22)	(23)
	30	956	11	48.			Lewis M.G. 6.	6		18		924		61								8 officers 130 R. detached to Bn
																						1 offr 3 O.R. attached to Bn.
TOTALS ...	30	956	11	48				6		18		924		61								

Ammunition with Unit:—

·303 inch; approximate number of rounds per Man

·303 inch; " " " per Machine Gun

Gun or Howitzer; approximate number of rounds per Gun or Howitzer

Supplies with Unit:—

Approximate number of days' rations for men of ration strength

" " " forage for Animals " "

" " " fuel and lubricants for Mechanically Propelled Vehicles

P.T.O.

Signature of Commander (Sd) C. H. Jones-Bateman Lt Col
Commanding 1st Dorset Regt.

(90988.) Wt.W. 5216—2140. 900,000 7/15. J. P. & Co. Ltd. Forms B 231 / 3

Lieut H. C. Butcher	R. Lanc Regt	To F. Amb	9.	3.	16
" K. Brodie	3rd Dorsets	Rejoined	15.	3.	16
Lt & Q.M. W. Alderman	1st Dorsets	To Leave	11.	3.	16
		Rejoined	16.	3.	16

Army Form B 231.

VOL III
Sheet 11.

FIELD STATE.

Unit 1st Dorset Regt

Place In the Field

Date 23. 3. 1916.

To be rendered in accordance with Field Service Regulations, Part II.

UNIT	FIGHTING STRENGTH — This should *not* include details attached to unit, or personnel detailed to march with the Train, or any men unfit to go into action with unit											RATION STRENGTH — To include Fighting Strength, Personnel detailed to march with the Train, and all Personnel and animals attached for Rations and Forage										
	Personnel		Horses and Mules		Other Animals		Guns and Ammunition Wagons (stating nature)	Machine Guns	Ambulances	Tool Carts, Technical Carts (stating nature)	Remarks	Personnel	Horses and Mules		Other Animals		Mechanically Propelled Vehicles					Remarks
	Officers	Other Ranks	Riding	Draught and Pack								Total, all Ranks entitled to Rations.	Heavy Horses	Other Horses and Mules			Motor Cars	Motor Bicycles.	Lorries. 3 Ton	Lorries. 30 Cwt.	Tractors	
(1)	(2)	(3)	(4)	(5)	(6)	(7)	(8)	(9)	(10)	(11)	(12)	(13)	(14)	(15)	(16)	(17)	(18)	(19)	(20)	(21)	(22)	(23)
	30	992	9	47			Lewis M.G. 6	6		18		920		58								9 officers 94 OR. detached from Battn. 1 officer 3 OR attached to Bn
TOTALS ...	30	992	9	47				6		18		920		58								

Ammunition with Unit:—

·303 inch; approximate number of rounds per Man

·303 inch; " " " per Machine Gun

Gun or Howitzer; approximate number of rounds per Gun or Howitzer

Supplies with Unit:—

Approximate number of days' rations for men of ration strength

" " " forage for Animals " "

" " " fuel and lubricants for Mechanically Propelled Vehicles

Signature of Commander (Sd) L H Jones-Bateman Lieut Col
Commanding 1st Dorset Regt

(90988.) Wt.W. 5216—2140. 900,000 7/15. J. P. & Co. Ltd. Forms B 231 / 3

Lt. Col.	L. N. Jones-Bateman CMG.	1st Norfolks	To Leave	17. 3. 16
Capt	O.W. White	1st Dorsets	Joined Bn	16. 3. 16.
Capt.	R.V. Kestell-Cornish	-"-	Rejoined Unit	18. 3. 16
2/Lieut	W.P. Lipscomb	1st Dorsets	To Leave	21. 3. 16.
-"-	W.G. Ball.	1st Dorsets.	-do-	20. 3. 16.

Unit 1st Bn Dorset Regt.
Place In the Field
Date 30 3. 1916.

FIELD STATE.

VOL III Army Form B 231.
Sheet 14

To be rendered in accordance with Field Service Regulations, Part II.

UNIT	FIGHTING STRENGTH — This should *not* include details attached to unit, or personnel detailed to march with the Train, or any men unfit to go into action with unit											RATION STRENGTH — To include Fighting Strength, Personnel detailed to march with the Train, and all Personnel and animals attached for Rations and Forage										
	Personnel		Horses and Mules		Other Animals		Guns and Ammunition Wagons (stating nature)	Machine Guns	Ambulances	Tool Carts, Technical Carts (stating nature)	Remarks	Personnel	Horses and Mules		Other Animals		Mechanically Propelled Vehicles					Remarks
	Officers	Other Ranks	Riding	Draught and Pack								Total, all Ranks entitled to Rations.	Heavy Horses	Other Horses and Mules			Motor Cars	Motor Bicycles.	Lorries. 3 Ton	Lorries. 30 Cwt.	Tractors	
(1)	(2)	(3)	(4)	(5)	(6)	(7)	(8)	(9)	(10)	(11)	(12)	(13)	(14)	(15)	(16)	(17)	(18)	(19)	(20)	(21)	(22)	(23)
	28	954	9	45			Lewis M.G. 6	6		17		900		56								7 officers 93 O.R. detached from Battn. 1 officer 3 O.R. attached to Bn.
TOTALS ...	28	954	9	45				6		17		900		56								

Ammunition with Unit:—

·303 inch; approximate number of rounds per Man ______

·303 inch; „ „ „ per Machine Gun ______

Gun or Howitzer; approximate number of rounds per Gun or Howitzer ______

Supplies with Unit:—

Approximate number of days' rations for men of ration strength ______

„ „ „ forage for Animals „ „ ______

„ „ „ fuel and lubricants for Mechanically Propelled Vehicles ______

R.O.

Signature of Commander (Sd) L. H. Jones-Bateman Lieut. Col.
Comdg 1st Dorset Regt.

(90988.) Wt. W. 5216—2140. 900,000 7/15. J. P. & Co. Ltd. Forms B 231/3

2/Lieut W A Smellie	3rd Dorsets	To F. Amb.	13. 3. 16
		Rejoined	29. 3. 16.
2/Lieut M A Fraser	-"-	From F. Amb.	29. 3. 16
-"- W. G. Ball	1st Dorsets	From Leave	27. 3. 16.
-"- H. C. Butcher	R. Lancaster Regt	From F. A	24. 3. 16
Capt O. W. White	1st Dorsets	To 14th Bde H.Q.	27. 3. 16.
-"- W. B. Algeo	-"-	-"-	30. 3. 16.

14th Brigade.

32nd Division.

1st BATTALION

THE DORSET REGIMENT

APRIL 1 9 1 6

Field States attached.

14th Brigade.

32nd Division.

1st BATTALION

THE DORSET REGIMENT

APRIL 1 9 1 6

Field States attached.

Army Form C. 2118.

VOL III
Sheet 14

Instructions regarding War Diaries and Intelligence Summaries are contained in F. S. Regs., Part II. and the Staff Manual respectively. Title Pages will be prepared in manuscript.

WAR DIARY
or
INTELLIGENCE SUMMARY
(Erase heading not required.)

Place	Date 1916	Hour	Summary of Events and Information	Remarks and references to Appendices
E.3. Subsector	Mch. 27th	10.20pm	Relief by 2nd Manchester Regiment completed. Battalion withdraws to billets in MILLENCOURT.	ALBERT (Combined Sheet) 57D. S.E. 57.C. S.W. 62.D. N.E. 62.C. N.W. 1/40.000
MILLENCOURT	28		In Billets in MILLENCOURT in Divisional reserve.	
do	29		do	
do	30		do	
do	31		do	
do	Apl. 1st		do	
do	" 2nd		do	
do	" 3rd		do	
G.1. Subsector (to be called henceforth THIEPVAL subsector)	3rd	11.40pm	Battalion relieved 15th Lancashire Fusiliers (96th Inf. Bde.) in trenches in G.1 subsector (now known as THIEPVAL subsector.) (Refce. R.25 and R.31). Battalion comes under orders of 96th Infantry Bde. till to-morrow, 4th inst.	Refce. R.25. and R.31. 19th Lancs. Fus on our right. 10th Ryl. Inniskilling Fus. on our left
do	4th	–	Situation quiet generally. One man wounded.	
do	5th	–	do. No casualties.	
do	6th	–	Quiet during the day. No casualties. The Brigade front being extended, the 19th Lancs. Fusiliers took over half our subsector (as far as KILMUN St) and Dorsets moved up to the left as far as GEORGE St. taking over front held by two coys. of 10th Inniskillin Fusiliers. THIEPVAL subsector, as held by battalion, extends now from KILMUN St. on the right to GEORGE St. on the left. In the evening very heavy artillery fire was heard and observed for some hours about two miles to our left (1 mile North of HAMEL) on the front occupied by 36th Division.	

2449 Wt. W14957/M90 750,000 1/16 J.B.C. & A. Forms/C.2118/12.

WAR DIARY
or
INTELLIGENCE SUMMARY
(Erase heading not required.)

Army Form C. 2118.

VOL III

Sheet 15.

Instructions regarding War Diaries and Intelligence Summaries are contained in F. S. Regs., Part II. and the Staff Manual respectively. Title Pages will be prepared in manuscript.

Place	Date 1916	Hour	Summary of Events and Information	Remarks and references to Appendices
THIEPVAL subsector	Apl. 7th	-	Quiet day. Three men wounded.	HGB
"	" 8	-	Situation very quiet. No casualties. Battalion relieved in the evening by 15th H.L.I and withdrew to shelters in AUTHUILLE SOUTH, with two platoons at CRUCIFIX corner, two platoons in JOHNSTONE POST in support to 15th H.L.I., and two platoons manning the keeps in AUTHUILLE village. Battalion in Brigade reserve.	HGB
AUTHUILLE	" 9	-	D^o. D^o. 7. slight casualties.	
do	" 10	-	D^o. D^o	HGB
do	" 11	-	D^o. D^o.	
do	" 12	-	D^o. D^o. One man on working party wounded.	
SENLIS	" 12	-	Battalion relieved by 2nd K.O.Y.L.I. at 11.30 pm.	HGB
do	" 13	-	Battalion in billets in SENLIS at 2 am.	HGB
do	" 14	-	Battalion in billets in SENLIS; Brigade being in Divisional reserve. All men on leave recalled by wire.	HGB
do	" 15	-	In billets in SENLIS	
do	" 16	-	do . One company moved to billets in AVELUY arriving 11.55 am.	
BOUZINCOURT.	17	-	Battalion moved from SENLIS to billets in BOUZINCOURT.	HGB
do	18	-	Battalion in billets in BOUZINCOURT. Majority of men employed every day on working parties.	HGB
do	19	-	D^o D^o	HGB
do	20	-	D^o D^o	
do	21	-	D^o D^o.	HGB
do	22	-	D^o D^o	

2449 Wt. W14957/M90 750,000 1/16 J.B.C. & A. Forms/C.2118/12.

Army Form C. 2118.

Instructions regarding War Diaries and Intelligence Summaries are contained in F. S. Regs., Part II. and the Staff Manual respectively. Title Pages will be prepared in manuscript.

WAR DIARY
or
~~INTELLIGENCE SUMMARY~~
(Erase heading not required.)

1st Dorset. Regt

VOL III
Sheet 16.

Place	Date 1916	Hour	Summary of Events and Information	Remarks and references to Appendices
BOUZINCOURT and PIERRGOT	Apl 23	–	Battalion marched from billets in BOUZINCOURT and AVELUY to billets in PIERRGOT at 1.30 pm, arriving at latter place at 8.30 pm.	[illegible]
PIERRGOT	" 24	–	Battalion in billets in PIERRGOT, and undergoing training.	
"	" 25	–	Do. Do	
"	" 26	–	Do. Do.	[illegible]
"	" 27	–	Do. Do. Battalion took part in Divisional tactical scheme for an attack.	
"	" 28	–	In billets in PIERRGOT, training.	
"	" 29	–	Do. ← Lieut.-Col. JONES-BATEMAN left for England.	[illegible]
"	" 30	–	Do. MAJOR. SHUTE assumed command.	

2449 Wt. W14957/M90 750,000 1/16 J.B.C. & A. Forms/C.2118/12.

Unit 1st Battn Dorset Regt
Place In the Field
Date 6. 4. 16.

Vol III Army Form B 231.
Sheet 14.

FIELD STATE.

To be rendered in accordance with Field Service Regulations, Part II.

FIGHTING STRENGTH — This should *not* include details attached to unit, or personnel detailed to march with the Train, or any men unfit to go into action with unit

RATION STRENGTH — To include Fighting Strength, Personnel detailed to march with the Train, and all Personnel and animals attached for Rations and Forage

UNIT	Personnel		Horses and Mules		Other Animals		Guns and Ammunition Wagons (stating nature)	Machine Guns	Ambulances	Tool Carts, Technical Carts (stating nature)	Remarks	Personnel	Horses and Mules		Other Animals		Mechanically Propelled Vehicles					Remarks
	Officers	Other Ranks	Riding	Draught and Pack								Total, all Ranks entitled to Rations.	Heavy Horses	Other Horses and Mules			Motor Cars	Motor Bicycles.	Lorries. 3 Ton	Lorries. 30 Cwt.	Tractors	
(1)	(2)	(3)	(4)	(5)	(6)	(7)	(8)	(9)	(10)	(11)	(12)	(13)	(14)	(15)	(16)	(17)	(18)	(19)	(20)	(21)	(22)	(23)
	27	944	10	45			Lewis M.G. 8	8		17		884		57								8 officers 91 O.R. detached from Bn / 1 officer 3 O.R. attached to Bn.
TOTALS ...	27	944	10	45				8		17		884		57								

Ammunition with Unit:—

·303 inch; approximate number of rounds per Man

·303 inch; " " " per Machine Gun

Gun or Howitzer; approximate number of rounds per Gun or Howitzer

Supplies with Unit:—

Approximate number of days' rations for men of ration strength

" " " forage for Animals " "

" " " fuel and lubricants for Mechanically Propelled Vehicles

R.O.

Signature of Commander (Sd) L. H. Jones Bateman Lt. Col.
Comdg 1st Dorset Regt

(90988.) Wt.W. 5216—2140. 900,000 7/15. J. P. & Co. Ltd. Forms B 231/3

2/Lieut G. C. N. Webb. 3rd Dorsets To Leave 1. 4. 16.
2/Lieut W. H. Clark 1st Dorsets. To 32nd Divnl Base Depot 4. 4. 16
2/Lieut W. P. Lipscombe 7th Dorsets Telescopic Sight Course 2. 4. 16

Unit 1st Bn Dorset Regt
Place In the Field
Date 13. 4. 16.

FIELD STATE.

VOL III
Sheet 15

Army Form B 231.

To be rendered in accordance with Field Service Regulations, Part II.

FIGHTING STRENGTH — This should *not* include details attached to unit, or personnel detailed to march with the Train, or any men unfit to go into action with unit

RATION STRENGTH — To include Fighting Strength, Personnel detailed to march with the Train, and all Personnel and animals attached for Rations and Forage

UNIT	Fighting Strength: Personnel		Horses and Mules		Other Animals		Guns and Ammunition Wagons (stating nature)	Machine Guns	Ambulances	Tool Carts, Technical Carts (stating nature)	Remarks	Ration Strength: Personnel	Horses and Mules		Other Animals		Mechanically Propelled Vehicles					Remarks
	Officers	Other Ranks	Riding	Draught and Pack								Total, all Ranks entitled to Rations.	Heavy Horses	Other Horses and Mules			Motor Cars	Motor Bicycles.	Lorries. 3 Ton	Lorries. 30 Cwt.	Tractors	
(1)	(2)	(3)	(4)	(5)	(6)	(7)	(8)	(9)	(10)	(11)	(12)	(13)	(14)	(15)	(16)	(17)	(18)	(19)	(20)	(21)	(22)	(23)
	28	935	11	44			Lewis M. G. 8	8		17		880		57								10 Officers 91 O.R. detached from Battn.
																						1 Officer 3 O.R. attached to Bn.
TOTALS ...	28	935	11	44				8		17		880		57								

Ammunition with Unit:—

·303 inch; approximate number of rounds per Man ____________

·303 inch; " " " per Machine Gun ____________

Gun or Howitzer; approximate number of rounds per Gun or Howitzer ____________

Supplies with Unit:—

Approximate number of days' rations for men of ration strength ____________

" " " forage for Animals " " ____________

" " " fuel and lubricants for Mechanically Propelled Vehicles ____________

K.O.

(Sd)

Signature of Commander L. H. Jones-Bateman Lt. Col.
Comdg 1st Dorset Regt

(90988.) Wt.W. 5216—2140. 900,000 7/15. J. P. & Co. Ltd. Forms B 231 / 3

Lieut W. C. Green	3rd Dorsets	To Leave	12. 4. 16
2/Lieut G. C. R. Webb	-"-	From Leave	8. 4. 16
-"-	-"-	To Bayonet Fty Course	13. 4. 16
2/Lieut M. K. Clift	-"-	Joined Battn.	7. 4. 16
-"- W. P. Lipscombe	7th Dorsets	From Telescopic sight Course	9. 4. 16

Unit 1st Bn Dorset Regt

Place In the Field

Date 20. 4. 16

FIELD STATE.

Army Form B 231.

VOL III
Sheet 15.

To be rendered in accordance with Field Service Regulations, Part II.

FIGHTING STRENGTH — This should *not* include details attached to unit, or personnel detailed to march with the Train, or any men unfit to go into action with unit

UNIT	Personnel		Horses and Mules		Other Animals		Guns and Ammunition Wagons (stating nature)	Machine Guns	Ambulances	Tool Carts, Technical Carts (stating nature)	Remarks
	Officers	Other Ranks	Riding	Draught and Pack							
(1)	(2)	(3)	(4)	(5)	(6)	(7)	(8)	(9)	(10)	(11)	(12)
	28	930	11	44			Lewis MG 8	8		17	
TOTALS ...	28	930	11	44				8		17	

RATION STRENGTH — To include Fighting Strength, Personnel detailed to march with the Train, and all Personnel and animals attached for Rations and Forage

UNIT	Personnel	Horses and Mules		Other Animals		Mechanically Propelled Vehicles					Remarks
	Total, all Ranks entitled to Rations.	Heavy Horses	Other Horses and Mules			Motor Cars	Motor Bicycles.	Lorries. 3 Ton	Lorries. 30 Cwt.	Tractors	
(1)	(13)	(14)	(15)	(16)	(17)	(18)	(19)	(20)	(21)	(22)	(23)
	891		57								5 officers 83 OR detached from Battn 1 officer 3 OR attached to Bn
TOTALS ...	891		57								

Ammunition with Unit:—

·303 inch; approximate number of rounds per Man

·303 inch; " " " per Machine Gun

Gun or Howitzer; approximate number of rounds per Gun or Howitzer

Supplies with Unit:—

Approximate number of days' rations for men of ration strength

" " " forage for Animals " "

" " " fuel and lubricants for Mechanically Propelled Vehicles

P.T.O.

Signature of Commander (Sd) L. H. Jones-Bateman Lt Col Comdg 1st Dorset Regt

(79269.) Wt.W. 5870—621. 900,000 10/14. J. P. & Co. Ltd. Forms B 231 / 3

1. 2/Lieut Webb G. C. W. 3/Dorsets from B. T. Course 19.4.16

Lieut Dawe G. H. " to T.M. Course 8.4.16

Unit 1st Dorset Regt
Place In the Field
Date 27. 4. 16.

FIELD STATE.

Army Form B 231.

VOL III
Sheet 16.

To be rendered in accordance with Field Service Regulations, Part II.

UNIT	FIGHTING STRENGTH — This should *not* include details attached to unit, or personnel detailed to march with the Train, or any men unfit to go into action with unit											RATION STRENGTH — To include Fighting Strength, Personnel detailed to march with the Train, and all Personnel and animals attached for Rations and Forage										
	Personnel		Horses and Mules		Other Animals		Guns and Ammunition Wagons (stating nature)	Machine Guns	Ambulances	Tool Carts, Technical Carts (stating nature)	Remarks	Personnel	Horses and Mules		Other Animals		Mechanically Propelled Vehicles					Remarks
	Officers	Other Ranks	Riding	Draught and Pack								Total, all Ranks entitled to Rations.	Heavy Horses	Other Horses and Mules			Motor Cars	Motor Bicycles.	Lorries. 3 Ton	Lorries. 30 Cwt.	Tractors	
(1)	(2)	(3)	(4)	(5)	(6)	(7)	(8)	(9)	(10)	(11)	(12)	(13)	(14)	(15)	(16)	(17)	(18)	(19)	(20)	(21)	(22)	(23)
	35	973	11	44			Lewis Gun 8	8		17		917		57								8 Officers 101 O.R. detached from Battn 1 off + 3 O.R. attached to Bn
TOTALS ...	35	973	11	44				8		17		917		57								

Ammunition with Unit:—

·303 inch; approximate number of rounds per Man

·303 inch; " " " per Machine Gun

Gun or Howitzer; approximate number of rounds per Gun or Howitzer

Supplies with Unit:—

Approximate number of days' rations for men of ration strength

" " " forage for Animals " "

" " " fuel and lubricants for Mechanically Propelled Vehicles

Signature of Commander (Sd) L. R. Jones-Bateman for Col
Comdg 1st Dorset Regt

(90988.) Wt.W. 5216—2140. 900,000 7/15. J. P. & Co. Ltd. Forms B 231 / 3

Capt D. B. Algeo. 1st Dorsets To Leave 26-4-16
Lieut. A. E. Mainwood. — " — " 28 4.16

14th Brigade.

32nd Division.

1st BATTALION

DORSETSHIRE REGIMENT

M A Y 1 9 1 6

{Field States
{Intelligence Summaries attached.

MAY. 1 Dorset Regt 32 Vol 21 & 22 14/32

Army Form C. 2118.

WAR DIARY
or
~~INTELLIGENCE SUMMARY~~

(Erase heading not required.)

Instructions regarding War Diaries and Intelligence Summaries are contained in F. S. Regs., Part II. and the Staff Manual respectively. Title Pages will be prepared in manuscript.

Place	Date 1916	Hour	Summary of Events and Information	Remarks and references to Appendices
CONTAY	May 1st	✓	Battalion in billets in CONTAY. One company training, remainder providing working parties	57.D.S.W. 1/20.000 + 62.D 1/20.000
"	" 2nd	✓	Ditto. Ditto.	
"	" 3rd	✓	Ditto. Ditto.	
"	" 4th	✓	Ditto. Ditto.	
CONTAY & BOUZINCOURT	" 5	✓	Battalion moved from CONTAY to BOUZINCOURT in the afternoon, taking over huts from 2nd K.O.Y.L.I.	
BOUZINCOURT	" 6	8pm	Left BOUZINCOURT.	
THIEPVAL subsector	" 6	11.30pm	Relieved 16th Lancs. Fus. (96th Inf. Bde) in THIEPVAL subsector.	1/10.000 BEAUMONT and OVILLERS
do	" 7	✓	Situation quiet. No casualties up till 3pm.	
	" 7/8		At 11pm Germans opened very heavy bombardment on the whole of our sector. This became intense at 11.15pm and at 11.30pm three parties of the enemy (each about 35 strong) attacked the left of the sector; two parties entered 'D' Companies trenches; third party attempted to enter trenches occupied by 'C' Company but was repulsed by Lewis gun & rifle fire. The whole of that portion of the line occupied by D Coy (extreme left of the Battn.) was practically demolished by trench mortar bombs & artillery fire before the enemy raided. Germans were eventually driven out leaving one of their dead and one prisoner in our hands. At 1.45am 8th May the situation again became normal. Our casualties were: 2/Lieut BAYLY killed, 2/Lieut DRAYTON wounded, 12 other ranks killed, 28 other ranks wounded, 23 other ranks missing, 1 other rank wounded & missing and 8 other ranks suffering from shell shock and effect of gas shells. 2/Lieut CLIFT was slightly wounded in the afternoon. A supporting company of the 9th (?) Inniskilling Fus	19th L.F. on our left. 10th Inniskilling Fus. on our right.

2449 Wt. W14957/M90 750,000 1/16 J.B.C. & A. Forms/C.2118/12.

Army Form C. 2118.

Instructions regarding War Diaries and Intelligence Summaries are contained in F. S. Regs., Part II. and the Staff Manual respectively. Title Pages will be prepared in manuscript.

WAR DIARY
or
~~INTELLIGENCE SUMMARY~~
(Erase heading not required.)

Place	Date 1916	Hour	Summary of Events and Information	Remarks and references to Appendices
THIEPVAL subsector	May 8th		moved up and assisted in holding the left of our subsector during the night; platoon from A. Company relieved this company during the morning of 8 May.	
"	8th		Situation normal.	
"	9th		do. No casualties. 13th Ryl Irish Rifles relieved 10th Inniskillings on our left on night of 8/9th May.	
"	10th		Situation quiet. 2 O.R. wounded. Battn relieved by 15th H.L.I. and withdrew to dugouts at BLACKHORSE BRIDGE (less D Coy. manning KEEPS in AUTHUILLE village and 2 platoons of A.Coy at shelters at CRUCIFIX CORNER). Relief complete at 10.15 pm. At 2.30 pm our 8" Howitzers commenced registering on enemy trenches.	
BLACKHORSE SHELTERS AUTHUILLE	11th		Battalion in close support in shelters at BLACKHORSE BRIDGE (SOUTH of AUTHUILLE). Situation normal. One man wounded.	
do	12th		Ditto. No casualties.	
do	13th		Ditto. Do	
do and THIEPVAL subsector	14th		Ditto. Do. Battalion relieved 15th H.L.I. in THIEPVAL subsector at 10.15 pm. During the night enemy machine guns very active.	
do	15		Situation normal. Two other ranks wounded. Heavy bombardment on our left at night.	
do	16		Situation quiet. 3 O.R. wounded (including 2 S.I.W.)	

2449 Wt. W14957/M90 750,000 1/16 J.B.C. & A. Forms/C.2118/12.

Instructions regarding War Diaries and Intelligence Summaries are contained in F. S. Regs., Part II. and the Staff Manual respectively. Title pages will be prepared in manuscript.

WAR DIARY
or
INTELLIGENCE SUMMARY.
(Erase heading not required.)

Army Form C. 2118.

Hour, Date, Place	Summary of Events and Information	Remarks and references to Appendices
1916		
THIEPVAL subsector. 17th May.	Situation normal during night of 16/17 May. 3 O.R. wounded. Capt. W. B. ALGEO & Lieut. H. G. M. MANSEL-PLEYDELL left the HAMMERHEAD SAP (extreme left of subsector) during the morning to patrol "No man's land" and locate enemy M.G. emplacements in front of THIEPVAL. Neither of these officers returned. Sgt. ROGERS and Sgt. GOODWILLIE went out in the afternoon to attempt to find these officers. Sgt. GOODWILLIE did not return. At 10.45 pm our artillery dispersed a large enemy working party in wood just W. of THIEPVAL. Our Lewis guns also dispersed enemy working parties. Later heavy transport was heard in THIEPVAL, and on our artillery opening fire great confusion ensued.	(Both since reported by enemy "found dead near THIEPVAL") HGB
do. 18th May.	Situation normal. Battalion relieved at 11.55 pm by 2nd K.O.Y.L.I., withdrawing to billets in BOUZINCOURT. No casualties.	HGB
BOUZINCOURT. 19th May.	Battalion reached billets in BOUZINCOURT at 1.40 am.	HGB
do. 20th May.	Battalion in billets in BOUZINCOURT. Majority of men employed on working parties.	HGB
do. 21st May	Ditto.	HGB
do 22nd May.	A & D Coys moved to bivouacs in AVELUY WOOD in order to be nearer work. B & C. Coys. remained in billets in BOUZINCOURT.	HGB
BOUZINCOURT & AVELUY WOOD 23rd May	Half Battn in BOUZINCOURT, half in AVELUY WOOD.	

(73989) W4141—463. 400,000. 9/14. H.&J.Ltd. Forms/C. 2118/10.

Instructions regarding War Diaries and Intelligence Summaries are contained in F. S. Regs., Part II. and the Staff Manual respectively. Title pages will be prepared in manuscript.

WAR DIARY
or
INTELLIGENCE SUMMARY.
(Erase heading not required.)

Army Form C. 2118.

Hour, Date, Place 1916	Summary of Events and Information	Remarks and references to Appendices
BOUZINCOURT and AVELUY WOOD. May 24th.	A & D Coys in AVELUY WOOD, B & C in BOUZINCOURT. All men employed on working parties.	H.G.
May 24th/May 25th.	Battalion moved to billets in WARLOY arriving there at 12.25am 25/5/16. Bde. in Divisional reserve.	H.G.
WARLOY. May 25th	Battalion in billets in WARLOY training.	H.G.
do " 26	Ditto.	
do " 27	Ditto.	
do " 28	Ditto.	
WARLOY & MIRVAUX May 29.	Battalion moved from billets in WARLOY to billets in MIRVAUX arriving MIRVAUX 8.20pm.	H.G.
MIRVAUX. May 30th.	In Billets in MIRVAUX training	H.G.
do. May 31st.	Battalion moved to bivouacs in BAVELINCOURT WOOD at 7.10pm, this move being part of the Divisional tactical training scheme.	H.G.
do June 1st.	Battalion in billets in MIRVAUX training. All ranks re-inoculated.	H.G.
do " 2nd	In Billets in MIRVAUX.	H.G.
do " 3rd	do	
do " 4th.	do.	

(73989) W4141—463. 400,000. 9/14. H.&J.Ltd. Forms/C. 2118/10.

Unit 1/Bn The Dorset Regt

Place In the Field

Date 4. 5. 16

FIELD STATE.

Army Form B 231.

To be rendered in accordance with Field Service Regulations, Part II.

UNIT	FIGHTING STRENGTH This should *not* include details attached to unit, or personnel detailed to march with the Train, or any men unfit to go into action with unit											RATION STRENGTH To include Fighting Strength, Personnel detailed to march with the Train, and all Personnel and animals attached for Rations and Forage										
	Personnel		Horses and Mules		Other Animals		Guns and Ammunition Wagons (stating nature)	Machine Guns	Ambulances	Tool Carts, Technical Carts (stating nature)	Remarks	Personnel	Horses and Mules		Other Animals		Mechanically Propelled Vehicles					Remarks
	Officers	Other Ranks	Riding	Draught and Pack								Total, all Ranks entitled to Rations.	Heavy Horses	Other Horses and Mules			Motor Cars	Motor Bicycles.	Lorries. 3 Ton	Lorries. 30 Cwt.	Tractors	
(1)	(2)	(3)	(4)	(5)	(6)	(7)	(8)	(9)	(10)	(11)	(12)	(13)	(14)	(15)	(16)	(17)	(18)	(19)	(20)	(21)	(22)	(23)
	34	964	11	44			8 Lewis Guns	8		14		898		56								8 Officers 126 OR detached from Battalion
TOTALS ...	34	964	11					8		14		898		56								

Ammunition with Unit:—

·303 inch; approximate number of rounds per Man ______

·303 inch; " " " per Machine Gun ______

Gun or Howitzer; approximate number of rounds per Gun or Howitzer ______

Supplies with Unit:—

Approximate number of days' rations for men of ration strength ______

" " " forage for Animals " " ______

" " " fuel and lubricants for Mechanically Propelled Vehicles ______

P.10

Signature of Commander (Sd) J. H. Shute Major
Comdg 1/Bn The Dorsetshire Regt

(90988.) Wt.W. 5216—2140. 900,000 7/15. J. P. & Co. Ltd. Forms B 231 / 3

Capt. H.R. Thwayte To Leave 5. 5. 16.
2/Lieut. J.H. Hart " 3. 5. 16

Unit 1st Bn The Dorsetshire Regt

Place In the Field

Date 11. 5. 16

FIELD STATE.

Army Form B 231.

To be rendered in accordance with Field Service Regulations, Part II.

UNIT	FIGHTING STRENGTH — This should *not* include details attached to unit, or personnel detailed to march with the Train, or any men unfit to go into action with unit											RATION STRENGTH — To include Fighting Strength, Personnel detailed to march with the Train, and all Personnel and animals attached for Rations and Forage										
	Personnel		Horses and Mules		Other Animals							Personnel	Horses and Mules		Other Animals		Mechanically Propelled Vehicles					
	Officers	Other Ranks	Riding	Draught and Pack			Guns and Ammunition Wagons (stating nature)	Machine Guns	Ambulances	Tool Carts, Technical Carts (stating nature)	Remarks	Total, all Ranks entitled to Rations.	Heavy Horses	Other Horses and Mules			Motor Cars	Motor Bicycles.	Lorries. 3 Ton	Lorries. 30 Cwt.	Tractors	Remarks
(1)	(2)	(3)	(4)	(5)	(6)	(7)	(8)	(9)	(10)	(11)	(12)	(13)	(14)	(15)	(16)	(17)	(18)	(19)	(20)	(21)	(22)	(23)
	32	916	11	44			8 Lewis	6		14 [?]		822		56								9 officers 129 OR detached from Batt
TOTALS ...	32	916	11	44				8		14 [?]		822		56								

Ammunition with Unit:—

·303 inch; approximate number of rounds per Man

·303 inch; „ „ „ per Machine Gun

Gun or Howitzer; approximate number of rounds per Gun or Howitzer

Supplies with Unit:—

Approximate number of days' rations for men of ration strength

„ „ „ forage for Animals „ „

„ „ „ fuel and lubricants for Mechanically Propelled Vehicles

P.T.O.

Signature of Commander Sd H. C. Butcher [?] [illegible] Major Comdg 1st Bn The Dorsetshire R[illegible]

(90988.) Wt.W. 5216—2140. 900,000 7/15. J. P. & Co. Ltd. Forms B 231/3

Lt W. A. Smellie. To Leave 9. 5. 16.
W. A. Fraser — " — 12. 5. 16
" A. C. Mainhood From Leave. 5. 5. 16
Capt W. B. Alger " 3. 5. 16
Capt R. W. Kestell Cornish To " 9. 5. 16

Unit 1st Bn Dorset Regt.
Place In the Field
Date 18 5 16

FIELD STATE.

Army Form B 231.

To be rendered in accordance with Field Service Regulations, Part II.

UNIT	FIGHTING STRENGTH — This should *not* include details attached to unit, or personnel detailed to march with the Train, or any men unfit to go into action with unit											RATION STRENGTH — To include Fighting Strength, Personnel detailed to march with the Train, and all Personnel and animals attached for Rations and Forage										
	Personnel		Horses and Mules		Other Animals		Guns and Ammunition Wagons (stating nature)	Machine Guns	Ambulances	Tool Carts, Technical Carts (stating nature)	Remarks	Personnel	Horses and Mules		Other Animals		Mechanically Propelled Vehicles					Remarks
	Officers	Other Ranks	Riding	Draught and Pack								Total, all Ranks entitled to Rations.	Heavy Horses	Other Horses and Mules			Motor Cars	Motor Bicycles.	Lorries. 3 Ton	Lorries. 30 Cwt.	Tractors	
(1)	(2)	(3)	(4)	(5)	(6)	(7)	(8)	(9)	(10)	(11)	(12)	(13)	(14)	(15)	(16)	(17)	(18)	(19)	(20)	(21)	(22)	(23)
	31	983	11	42			8 Lewis	8		17		901		54								11 Officers 114 OR detached from Battn
TOTALS ...	31	983	11	42				8		17		901		54								

Ammunition with Unit:—

·303 inch; approximate number of rounds per Man

·303 inch; " " " per Machine Gun

Gun or Howitzer; approximate number of rounds per Gun or Howitzer

Supplies with Unit:—

Approximate number of days' rations for men of ration strength

" " " forage for Animals " "

" " " fuel and lubricants for Mechanically Propelled Vehicles

(90988.) Wt.W. 5216—2140. 900,000 7/15. J. P. & Co. Ltd. Forms B 231 / 3

Signature of Commander [illegible] Major Comdg 1st Bn Dorset Regt

Unit 1st Bn Dorset Regt
Place In the Field
Date 25 5 16

FIELD STATE.

Army Form B 231.

To be rendered in accordance with Field Service Regulations, Part II.

UNIT	FIGHTING STRENGTH. This should *not* include details attached to unit, or personnel detailed to march with the Train, or any men unfit to go into action with unit											RATION STRENGTH. To include Fighting Strength, Personnel detailed to march with the Train, and all Personnel and animals attached for Rations and Forage										
	Personnel		Horses and Mules		Other Animals		Guns and Ammunition Wagons (stating nature)	Machine Guns	Ambulances	Tool Carts, Technical Carts (stating nature)	Remarks	Personnel	Horses and Mules		Other Animals		Mechanically Propelled Vehicles					Remarks
	Officers	Other Ranks	Riding	Draught and Pack								Total, all Ranks entitled to Rations.	Heavy Horses	Other Horses and Mules			Motor Cars	Motor Bicycles.	Lorries. 3 Ton	Lorries. 30 Cwt.	Tractors	
(1)	(2)	(3)	(4)	(5)	(6)	(7)	(8)	(9)	(10)	(11)	(12)	(13)	(14)	(15)	(16)	(17)	(18)	(19)	(20)	(21)	(22)	(23)
	27	996	11	44			8 Lewis	8		17		1001		56								2 Officers 32 Other Ranks detached from Batt.
Totals ...	27	996	11	44				8		17		1001		56								

Ammunition with Unit:—

·303 inch; approximate number of rounds per Man ____

·303 inch; " " " per Machine Gun ____

Gun or Howitzer; approximate number of rounds per Gun or Howitzer ____

Supplies with Unit:—

Approximate number of days' rations for men of ration strength ____

" " " forage for Animals " " ____

" " " fuel and lubricants for Mechanically Propelled Vehicles ____

Signature of Commander (Sd) A. C. Butcher Lieut. Major Comdg 1st Dorset Regt

(90988.) Wt.W. 5216—2140. 900,000 7/15. J. P. & Co. Ltd. Forms B 231 / 3

Situation Report to 4 pm. 8th Apl. 1916

1st Bn Dorset Regt

Patrols. 1. Standing patrols covering wiring parties were out early last night.

2. Lieut Mansel-Pleydell went up the curved road from trench K.25.2 at 3.15 pm and reconnoitred the wood through which it runs. Undergrowth reported dense. Single strands of wire are laid through the wood and across the road at short intervals. There appears to be an observation post in a tree near German trench by the edge of this wood. There is a listening post in the road which is not held by day.

Artillery. See separate report.

T.M. Batteries. do

Spring Guns & Catapults ~~do~~. NIL.

State of Trenches. Those held by the

Very little work was accomplished last night owing to the relief. Hammerhead Sap was repaired, and from R.31.4. to FOXBAR Street parts of the parapet were repaired where blown in, and the fire trenches were deepened.

State of Wire. A great deal of work still requires to be done and is being taken in hand at once.

1st Dorset Regt
7.5.16

H Cecil Butcher
Lieut & Adjt.

a wire entanglement.

See also separate report refce. raid made by enemy.

A. C. Butcher.
Lieut & adjt.

1st Dorset Rgt.
8.5.16

Situation Report to 5pm 9th Apl. 1916.
1st Dorset Regt.

Patrols. Patrols were out along the whole of this front covering wiring parties.
A patrol going up the curved road from THIEPVAL POINT NORTH at 3.30pm found 6 German hand grenades, a British rifle with fixed bayonet and a British Steel helmet.

Artillery. About 9am 20. 77mm shells fell around HAMILTON Avenue and GEMMEL St. No damage. Our 18 pounders retaliated on THIEPVAL.

T.M. Batteries. NIL.

Spring Guns NIL.

State of Trenches. Fair on the right. On the left a great deal of repairing needs to be done.
In Rs. 5/4 parapet and

two right companies are in good condition. The left centre company's trenches are badly damaged by shell fire and Minnenwerfer, while the trenches occupied by the left company (Q BUCHANAN Street) ~~and~~ are almost demolished.

A considerable amount of work has been done on these trenches though much of it was ruined by the bombardment last night. On the right fire trenches have been deepened. In R.31.4. a listening post was dug, the fire-step heightened and parados sandbagged; 15 yards of parapet revetted. In R.31.5. 12 yards of parapet was revetted.

State of Wire. Bad. During the short time available all companies had wiring parties at work.

Working Parties. A party of 1 offr. + 50 men of the 15th H.L.I. worked on fire steps in GEMMEL St. and commenced putting up

fire step have been improved.
In R25 6/5 listening post continued.
On the left all labour was employed making the trenches passable, revetting and making fire steps.

State of Wire. Fair. About 40 coils of barbed wire were put out along this front, & 3 or 4 coils of French wire. All companies had strong wiring parties out.

Working Parties. One offr. & 50 men of 15th H.L.I. assisted.

1st Dorset Rgt.
9.5.16

H. C. Butcher
Lieut & Adjt.

Situation report to 4pm 7th May 1916

1st Dorset Regt.

Patrols. Nil.

Artillery. Three or four 77mm shells were fired in direction of GEMMEL Street about 10.30am. doing no damage.

T.M. Batteries. Five or six MINNENWERFER bombs fell near GEMMEL Street between 12 and 1pm. doing little damage. Our 18 pounders retaliated on enemy second line with good effect, the shells bursting well in the trench.

A few light T.M. bombs fell around JOHNSTON Post about 1pm. doing no damage.

Spring Guns / Catapults. Nil.

State of Trenches. Somewhat sticky since the rain this afternoon. A great deal of repairing needs to be done.

Intelligence Report: 7-5-16

Artillery: No enemy shells have fallen in this subsector since the battalion arrived.

Mortars. also nil.

Machine Guns. MGs were active last night – our parapet was swept several times during the night and indirect fire was also directed against valley near JOHNSON'S POST.

Lights. No unusual lights were sent up.

General Extreme quietness prevails.

H Mansel Pleydell I.O.

1st Dorset

Thiepval Subsector.

PATROLS – Patrols were out all along the front of the subsector last night covering wiring parties – Nothing unusual to report.

A Patrol at 3·30 pm, going up the curved road from THIEPVAL POINT NORTH found 6 German hand grenades a British rifle with fixed bayonet & a British steel helmet – thus showing that the raiding party undoubtedly returned this way.

H Mansel Pleydell

10. DORSET

THIEPVAL SUB SECTOR

8-5-16. INTELLIGENCE

Artillery – At 12.55 pm ~~several~~ about 6 light mortars on the Stokes principle fell in valley round JOHNSTONE'S POST – no damage.

Between 12.30 & 1 pm Minenwerfer were thrown around ~~our~~ mortar position in GEMMEL STREET – no damage.

Between 2.15 pm and 5 pm the enemy sent about 30 10.5 cm around the same mortar position – no damage.

At 3.35 pm enemy sent 6 10.5 cm shells just behind our front line trench R25.6. At the same time he sent 2 10.5 cm shells into his own front line trench opposite this place. No damage was done to us.

Movements of hostile troops. At 11.50 last night the Germans raided our trenches with 3 parties strength 36, 25 and 25. They entered our lines to the right and left of HAMMERHEAD & remained in our trenches about 15 minutes. Several of them were killed in the trench & one, an Alsacian surrendered. The 50 minute preliminary bombardment was very intense. Our field guns opened up quickly, but the howitzers were very slow

INTELLIGENCE REPORT
THIEPVAL SUBSECTOR 9-5-16

Artillery has been very quiet the last 24 hours – at about 9 am enemy put about 20 shrapnel from a 77mm gun near GRANDCOURT over our trenches around HAMILTON AVENUE and GEMMEL STREET Our 18 pndrs put 12 rounds into THIEPVAL by way of retaliation. No damage was done

Enemy transport was heard EAST of THIEPVAL at 9.10 pm This was horse transport.

Enemy Working Parties – enemy wiring parties were located last night working at 11 pm opposite R25.4 – they were fired on by a Lewis gun & stopped work.

Movement of Hostile Troops – A German patrol is thought to have been covering the above wiring party and to have been withdrawn with it.

Machine Guns – Enemy machine guns were very active last night trying to stop our wiring and working parties – no casualties. One gun was firing from the wood opposite THIEPVAL POINT NORTH

Enemy's Lights and Signals

Enemy were sending up Red green and "Falling Rain" rockets during the bombardment yesterday from opposite MAISON GRIS SAP. These were sent up in no apparent system & seemed to be intending merely to confuse any signals sent up by us for the Artillery

Patrols LIEUT MANSEL-PLEYDELL went up the curved road from trench R25 12 at 3.15 pm and reconnoitred wood through which it runs. Reports Undergrowth dense. Single strands of wire are laid through the wood and across the road at short intervals. There appears to be an observing post in a tree near the German trench by the edge of this wood. Germans have an abattis across the road & a listening post behind it – this listening post is not held by day

H Mansel-Pleydell
1st Dorset. Thiepval Subsec. Lieut 3.10

Situation Report to 3pm 10 Apl 1916
1st Dorset Rgt.

Patrols. Lieut Mansel-Pleydell and one O.R. went out at 3pm from THIEPVAL point north to reconnoitre enemy lines behind the trees. They found a snipers post in the wood and brought back the portable snipers plate.

Artillery. Enemy artillery NIL. Our 8" Howitzers have been registering during the afternoon.

T.M. Batteries. Very occasional shots doing no damage.

Rifle Grenades & Catapults. NIL.

State of Trenches. Much improved. Quite dry under foot.
Much work was done on the left, the whole fire trench except the extreme left being now cleared and put in a state of defence again. Thirty yards of

Fire trench on the left has been deepened and ARTURLIE Street is almost cleared.

Sandbagging and revetting has been carried on on the right, and a Lewis gun emplacement made in R.25.8.

Two large sandbag traverses nearly completed at JOHNSTON POST. These are to protect from enemy machine gun fire down the valley.

State of Wire. Still requires a great deal of work. Parties were out wiring along the whole front last night and much work was carried on.

Working Parties. 1 off. + 50 men 15 H.L.I. worked in this subsector. GEMMEL street fire steps were improved and wire was put out there.

W. E. Butcher
Lieut & Adjt

1st/Dorset Rgt.
10.5.16

INTELLIGENCE 10-5-16

ARTILLERY. No artillery activity against this subsector since midday yesterday

MINENWERFE Also nil

MACHINE GUNS still very active – were sweeping our parapet last night intermittently. They did no damage.

MOVEMENTS OF HOSTILE TROOPS. A German with field glasses was observed looking from R 19 D 2·0 towards HAMMERHEAD SAP. He stayed there about a minute, was shot at twice and disappeared.

PATROLS. LIEUT MANSEL-PLEYDELL and L/CORP DENNER went out ~~from~~ at 3PM from THIEPVAL POINT NORTH to reconnoitre German line behind the trees – i.e. from R 25 A 9·0 to R 25 B 2·3.
They found a sniping post in the wood & brought back the plate – a portable one. For result see attached map.

J M Mansel-Pleydell I.O.

THIEPVAL SUBSECTOR DORSET

Supplement on Tar to 6 days's intelligence report

Plan of armoured plate taken from German Sniping Port

4'6"

2"

In section

A A Buckles for carrying-strap
B Handle
C "Support" on ~~handle~~ swivel
D Observation slit
E Clip for support staking when not in use
F Firing slit with movable shutter

The Plate is about ¼ of an inch thick

G F Mansel-Pleydell
10. Dorset
10.5.16.

Situation Report. 15 May 1916

1st Dorset Rgt.

Patrols. Nil owing to relief.

Artillery. During the morning the enemy has been shelling GEMMEL street intermittently with single 77mm shells, doing no damage.

About 4 H.E. shells fell at western end of PAISLEY ave. at 12.30 pm.

Trench Mortars. At 11 pm last night enemy sent over 3 oil-cans on to HAMMERHEAD sap. One of these buried a Lewis gun and team.

Spring Guns + Catapults. NIL.

State of Trenches. Not good. It was not possible to do much work last night owing to relief and rain though a certain amount of revetting and repairing was done on the left.

State of Wire. Much still requires to be done. None was put out last night.

H. C. Butcher
Lt + adjt

1st Dorset Rgt.
15.5.16

Intelligence Report:
15-5-16

Artillery – at 10:45 pm there was some artillery and mortar activity well away on our right – probably near LA BOISSELLE.
At 9:00 a.m. enemy started to put single 77 mm shells at intervals of two or three minutes in neighbourhood of GEMMEL STREET no damage. About 20 shells were fired.

Mortars. – At 11 pm enemy sent over 3 "oil cans" onto the head of the HAMMERHEAD SAP. One of these buried a Lewis ~~Gun~~ Automatic Rifle and team.

Machine Guns. Enemy appear to be very anxious to stop us repairing our wire. Last night he kept up bursts of M.G. fire continuously. Three or Four M.G. appear to be in DIAMOND WOOD. Suggest having a field gun laid on it.

Rifle Grenades. At 10.45 am a shower of rifle grenades (about 20) was directed against TRONGATE ST.

Rifle Grenades (cont) No damage was done.

Miscellaneous: There appears to be no change in the German trenches since we were last in the subsector except some timber thrown up where the Stokes gun destroyed a M.G. emplacement.

It is obvious from the behaviour of the enemy that a relief has taken place. The Germans now in trenches are more bloodthirsty than formerly.

The weather this morning has made observation practically impossible.

H Mansel Pleydell
Lieut & I.O.
1st Batt The Dorset Reg

[Thiepval Subsector]

Intelligence Report 16-5-16

Artillery: THIEPVAL SECTOR

At 10 AM yesterday four high explosive shrapnel shells were fired round HAMILTON AVENUE. No damage.

At 12.30 PM eight 10 cm shells were fired at the road at the bottom of HAMILTON AVENUE. No damage.

At 3.10 pm eight 77 mm shells were fired round GEMMEL STREET. No damage was done.

At 3.45 pm two heavy shrapnel were fired over SKINNER STREET. No damage.

At ~~6.30 pm~~ 7 pm 5 oil-cans were sent over round R25 i trench – one of these destroyed 10 yards of the trench. At the same time another "oil-can" was fired which dropped just in front of their own trench.

Between 8 & 9.30 a.m. this morning enemy were putting high explosive shrapnel and 77 mm occasionally on road to AUTHUILLE – They were apparently firing at working parties coming to trenches which they had spotted from their observation ballon

Enemy's New Work.

Enemy were seen carrying timber along their trench yesterday afternoon just south of OBLONG ~~[illegible]~~ WOOD.

An enemy working party was observed from head of FOXBAR STREET in front of trenches about 3 miles due North on crest of hill beyond river. A line of chalk has been turned up at this point during the day.

Transport Enemy transport was heard behind THIEPVAL between 9 & 9.30 pm.

Wiring Parties a wiring party was heard at 10 pm opposite R 25.3. trench. Our Lewis guns opened fire and wiring ceased.

Aircraft An enemy Observation Balloon (bearing 41° True from Johnstones post) was sent up at 6.30 a.m. Our aeroplanes approached and it was pulled down slightly. Our machines were heavily shelled. A German machine came over our lines at 7.10 AM but was driven off by our machines.

Between 11.15 and 11.30 pm an aeroplane travelling west and flying high, dropped a ~~light~~ red & a white light over GOSSET STREET – it circled NORTH over THIEPVAL WOOD and repeated the signal – after that it could no longer be traced.

General:

At 12.45 a.m there was great activity to the North. It appears that the enemy attempted to raid the 31st division. It is suggested that at the same time there was another raid still further away.

Machine Guns were again active against our wire last night – our Artillery fired at the M.G.s in DIAMOND WOOD – they appeared to change position and continued firing.

H Mansel-Pleydell
Lieut I.O.
1st Dorset

Thiepval Subsector.

Situation report to 3.30 pm 16/5/16
1st Dorset Rgt.

Patrols. Patrols covering wiring parties have nothing to report.

Artillery. About 3 pm yesterday eight 77 mm shells were fired near GEMMEL Pt. doing no damage.
At 7 pm 5 oil-cans were fired near R.25.1. One of these did considerable damage to the trench. Another enemy oil-can dropped just in front of their own trench.
Between 8 and 9.30 am this morning enemy fired 77 mm shells intermittently on road to AUTHUILLE.
There was great artillery activity in the direction of HAMEL last night.

Trench Mortar Batteries. Our T.M:

batteries have been searching for enemy machine guns this afternoon, with what success is unknown.

Spring Guns & Catapults. NIL.

State of Trenches. Good. The fine weather has improved conditions considerably.

On the left deepening, revetting with sandbags etc. has been carried on, and work continued improving the trenches on our extreme left – between our sector and the Battn. on our left.

In R25.1. the part of trench blown in is being repaired.

In R31.4. a traverse is nearly completed.

SAUCHIHALL St. near fire trench is being rebuilt.

State of wire. Fair. Some work was done last night.

16. 5. 16 H. C. Bytchey Lt + Adjt.

Situation Report to 3.30 pm 17/5/16

1st Dorset Rgt.

Patrols. A patrol reconnoitred the cross-roads in front of HAMMERHEAD SAP at 12.30 am and reported all clear.

The brightness of the moon prevented much patrolling.

Artillery. At 4.45 pm yesterday three 77mm shells were fired round THIEPVAL Avenue doing no damage.

About 5.30 am this morning 10. 10cm shells were fired (from direction of GRANDCOURT) around CAUSEWAY SIDE St doing no damage.

At 9.30 am 10 shells were fired at AUTHUILLE road — probably at a working party.

Our artillery fired at enemy support line trenches about midday in retaliation for several T.M. bombs that were fired near JOHNSTONE POST. The latter did very little damage.

Trench Mortars. Our trench mortars and STOKES guns fired at enemy machine gun emplacements in DIAMOND WOOD during the morning. Result not known.

Spring Guns & Catapults. NIL.

State of Trenches. Good. A considerable amount of work has been done.

Parados revetted for 10 yards with sandbags in R.25.1.

Fire-steps raised in R.36.2

Sandbag traverse built in R.31.5.

Ammunition store in GEMMEL St. commenced.

Fire steps & parapet repaired in R.31.3. and 4.

SAUCHIEHALL St. deepened one foot for 12 yds and sides of trench built up.

Observation post commenced

at head of FOXBAR St.
Sandbagging and general repairing carried on in the left sector.

State of Wire. Fair. A certain amount of wiring was done on the left but the moon prevented very much being done.

H. C. Butcher
Lieut + Adjt

1st Dorset Rgt.
17.5.16

17-5-16 Intelligence Report

Artillery:

At 12.45 p.m. yesterday four 77 mm shells were fired round GEMMEL STREET – no damage.

At 2.15 pm eight 10 cm shells were fired from direction of GRANDCOURT onto road leading into AUTHUILLE no damage was done.

At 4.45 pm three 77 mm were fired round THIEPVAL AVENUE, no damage.

At 5.30 a.m. enemy fired about 10 10 cm shells from direction of GRANDCOURT round ~~co~~ CAUSEWAY SIDE no damage.

At 9.30 a.m. the same gun fired at 10 shells at working parties coming from AUTHUILLE – One man was wounded.

Transport Abnormal horse transport was heard E of THIEPVAL between 9.30 and 10.30 pm. And at 12.45 a.m. steam transport which sounded like a tram k was heard which seemed to be going from THIEPVAL to GRANDCOURT

Lights and Signals Four red lights were sent up at 12 midnight from behind OBLONG WOOD. No results were noticed.

WORKING Parties

At 10.15 pm a party was heard in the German wire opposite the immediate right of DIAMOND WOOD. Our Lewis Guns opened fire & noise ceased.

Machine Guns

MGs were fairly quiet up to 11 pm, but active after that. The MG was again firing from DIAMOND WOOD.

Movements of Troops Owing to abnormal MG and Transport conditions it is suggested that a relief took place last night opposite this subsector.

Patrols

A patrol reconnoitred cross roads in front of HAMMERHEAD SAP at 12.30 AM & reported all clear. Moon was too bright for patrolling in the open.

General A hostile aeroplane crossed our line from E to W at 9.25 pm and returned at 10.10 pm — an aeroplane was also heard over THIEPVAL WOOD at 1 AM.

German Captive Balloons were taken down at 6PM yesterday & were up again at one at 5 a.m and

3 at 5·30 a.m round COURCELETTE
Apparently these were compelled to descend owing to MG fire from one of our aeroplanes.

A German machine came over our lines at 6·30 a.m. but was turned back by our A.A. Guns.

At 11·10 ~~p~~ a.m. Two "oil-cans" fell just behind JOHNSTONE'S POST no damage.

H Mansel-Pleydell
17-5-16 Lieut & I.O.
1st Dorset.
Thiepval Subsector

Situation report to 4 pm. 18.5.16.

1st Dorset Regt.

Patrols. A patrol consisting of Capt ALGEO & Lieut. MANSEL-PLEYDELL went out from HAMMERHEAD SAP yesterday morning and have not yet returned. Details have already been sent you.

Artillery. A salvo of shrapnel was fired at THIEPVAL Ave. at 6.30 pm. yesterday.

During the morning 5.9" shells have been fired intermittently near THIEPVAL Ave and GEMMEL TRENCH.

A few H.E. shells were fired close to JOHNSTON POST about midday. Our artillery retaliated.

The enemy shelling caused little damage.

Our artillery fired at an enemy working party in wood opposite HAMMERHEAD

SAP last night between 10 & 11 pm. The shooting was very accurate and the party ceased work.

Our artillery also fired at enemy transport behind THIEPVAL; great confusion was caused, and horses were heard to run away.

Trench Mortars. About 15 oil-cans fell near GEMMEL TRENCH at 6 pm last night but did little damage.

4 small T.M. bombs fell near JOHNSTON POST. and a part of R.25.2 trench was damaged at 8 pm by a T.M.

Our Stokes guns and T.M.'s have retaliated two or three times on enemy emplacements

Spring Guns. NIL.

State of Trenches. Good. A large amount of work has been done. 30 yds of THIEPVAL Ave. was cleared 10 yds of R.31.4 deepened.

Observation post in FOXBAR St. continued.

Revetting, sandbagging, rebuilding fire steps etc. has been continued all along the line.

<u>State of Wire</u>. Fair. Some wire was put up outside R.31.3. but moon prevented much work.

18. 5. 16. H. C. Butcher.
Lieut + adjt.

INTELLIGENCE REPORT.

THIEPVAL SUBSECTOR, 17–18th May 1916.

ARTILLERY.

At 1.40 P.M. 77mm. shells fell at intervals round lower end of PAISLEY AVENUE until 7.10 P.M. No damage.

At 3 P.M. eight small shrapnel shells fell near THIEPVAL AVENUE coming from direction left of OBLONG WOOD.

At 6.30 P.M. enemy shelled THIEPVAL AVENUE with a salvo of high shrapnel.

From 8 A.M. till 11 A.M. 5.9 inch shells fell at intervals near THIEPVAL AVENUE and behind GEMMEL TRENCH.

TRENCH MORTARS ETC:

At 6 P.M. fifteen "oil-can" bombs fell behind GEMMEL TRENCH. No damage.

At 7 P.M. four small Trench mortar bombs fell between CAUSEWAYSIDE ST: and JOHNSTON POST.

At 8 P.M. four small Trench mortar bombs fired from direction of THIEPVAL CHATEAU fell on right of R.25.2 trench, blowing in the trench in one place.

[illegible]

ENEMY TRANSPORT.

From 9.30 P.M. till 10.30 P.M. heavy transport was heard behind THIEPVAL, together with the sound of iron girders being unloaded. Our artillery opened, & horses were heard to run away.

WORKING PARTIES. [see end of Report].

From 9 P.M. to 10.45 P.M. an enemy working party was heard in the Wood in front of HAMMERHEAD SAP, apparently wiring. The sound of stakes being driven in was heard, and in the morning what appeared to be new strands of barbed wire was seen by the aid of glasses.

2 discs were fired at the party by a Lewis gun, and at 10.45 P.M. it was finally dispersed by our artillery.

At 4 A.M. a working party was heard in the same place as above, and was dispersed by a salvo from our artillery.

ENEMY AIRCRAFT. [See end of Report]

A captive balloon was seen in direction of COURCELETTE on the 17th. This was taken down at 4.30 P.M.

At 4 A.M. an enemy aeroplane passed over R.25.A trench. Owing to a thick mist its course could not be traced.

At 9.45 A.M. an enemy aeroplane circled over THIEPVAL WOOD.

LIGHTS & SIGNALS.

At 3 A.M. three green rockets were seen opposite the trenches held by the Battalion on our left.

PATROLS.

A patrol consisting of CAPTAIN ALGEO, LIEUT: MANSEL-PLEYDELL and SGT: GOODWILLIE went out at 11.30 A.M. on the 17th., details of which have already been reported.

MISCELLANEOUS.

About 8.30 P.M. a man was observed looking over German parapet opposite R.25.3 trench. Our Lewis gun opened fire and the man was seen to fall backwards.

J. Murray
2Lieut.
I.O., 1st Dorset Rgt.

THIEPVAL SUBSECTOR,
18th May, 1916.

P.T.O.

Since Reported:-

WORKING PARTIES.

German working party was observed about 1 A.M. opposite R.31.3 trench, and fired on with Lewis Gun. Screams were heard so it is assumed one of the party was hit.

ENEMY AIRCRAFT.

Between 11.30 P.M. and 12.30 A.M. an aeroplane flew over THIEPVAL WOOD towards POZIERES.

5 yards of trench has been blown in by an 'oil-can' bombe in R.25.1.

J. Mount Lieut:
I.O., 1st Dorset Rgt.

18/5/1916.

14th Brigade.

32nd Division.

1st BATTALION

DORSETSHIRE REGIMENT

J U N E 1 9 1 6:

Instructions regarding War Diaries and Intelligence Summaries are contained in F. S. Regs., Part II, and the Staff Manual respectively. Title pages will be prepared in manuscript.

Army Form C. 2118.

WAR DIARY
or
INTELLIGENCE SUMMARY.
(*Erase heading not required.*)

Place	Date	Hour	Summary of Events and Information	Remarks and references to Appendices
MIRVAUX	1st June		Battalion in billets in MIRVAUX training. All ranks re-inoculated	
"	2nd		In Billets in MIRVAUX	
"	3rd		" " "	
"	4		" " "	
			Continued overleaf.	

(A9475) Wt W2358/P360 600,000 12/17 D. D. & L. Sch. 52a. Forms/C2118/15.

Instructions regarding War Diaries and Intelligence Summaries are contained in F. S. Regs., Part II. and the Staff Manual respectively. Title pages will be prepared in manuscript.

WAR DIARY

or

~~INTELLIGENCE SUMMARY.~~

(*Erase heading not required.*)

Army Form C. 2118.

Hour, Date, Place		Summary of Events and Information	Remarks and references to Appendices
	1916		
MIRVAUX	June 5th	In billets in MIRVAUX, training. Held Battn. sports.	HB
do	" 6th	Do.	HB
do	" 7.	Do. At 7.25pm Battn. moved to bivouacs in BAVELINCOURT WOOD; Part of Divisional training scheme.	HB
do	" 8th	In billets in MIRVAUX, training.	HB
do	" 9th	Ditto.	HB
do	" 10th	Ditto	HB
do	" 11th	Ditto. At 8pm the Battalion moved to bivouacs in BAVELINCOURT WOOD.	HB
WARLOY	" 12th	Battn. moved to WARLOY at 4.30pm after training with Division in the BASIEUX - BAVELINCOURT area. One man accidentally wounded.	HB
"	" 13th	In billets in WARLOY.	HB
BLACKHORSE SHELTERS.	" 13/14th.	Night of 13/14th. May Battn. relieved 2nd Ryl. Inniskilling in dugouts at BLACKHORSE Bridge.	HB
do.	" 14th	Battn. in dugouts at BLACKHORSE Bridge (S. of AUTHUILLE) in Bde. reserve.	HB
do	" 15th	Ditto.	HB.

(73989) W4141—463. 400,000. 9/14. H.&J.Ltd. Forms/C. 2118/10.

Army Form C. 2118.

Instructions regarding War Diaries and Intelligence Summaries are contained in F.S. Regs., Part II. and the Staff Manual respectively. Title pages will be prepared in manuscript.

WAR DIARY
or
~~INTELLIGENCE SUMMARY.~~

(Erase heading not required.)

Hour, Date, Place 1916.	Summary of Events and Information	Remarks and references to Appendices
BLACKHORSE SHELTERS and THIEPVAL subsector. June 16/17.	Battalion moved from BLACKHORSE SHELTERS to THIEPVAL subsector, relieving 15th H.L.I. Relief complete at 4.10 am. June 17th.	HB
THIEPVAL subsector June 17th	Situation normal, with considerable machine gun fire. Casualties NIL.	HB
do. " 18th	Situation normal. Enemy T.M.'s active between 7 & 8 pm. A & C. Coys commence digging new advanced trench in left of subsector. This has to be finished at all cost. 5. O.R. wounded.	HB
do. June 19th	Considerable enemy activity with machine guns, T.M.'s and artillery. 2 other ranks killed, 14 wounded, majority of these in A. Coys party digging new advanced trench.	HB
do June 20th	Enemy T.M.'s still active. A. Coys. Hdqrs. hit by heavy T.M. One O.R. killed, one wounded.	HB
do. June 20/21st	Battn. relieved by 15th H.L.I. Enemy's MINNENWERFER very active. 3. O.R. killed, 14 O.R. wounded (3 later died of wounds)	HB
BLACKHORSE SHELTERS. June 22nd	Battn. in BLACKHORSE SHELTERS. Very large amount of work to be done. At 11 pm operation orders for the coming advance were received.	HB

(73989) W4141—463. 400,000. 9/14. H.&J.Ltd. Forms/C. 2118/10.

Instructions regarding War Diaries and Intelligence Summaries are contained in F. S. Regs., Part II. and the Staff Manual respectively. Title pages will be prepared in manuscript.

WAR DIARY
or
~~INTELLIGENCE~~ SUMMARY.
(Erase heading not required.)

Army Form C. 2118.

Hour, Date, Place 1916	Summary of Events and Information	Remarks and references to Appendices
June 23rd. BLACKHORSE SHELTERS.	Whole Battalion employed digging, carrying ammunition etc. Relieved by 2nd Royal Inniskilling Fusiliers on the night 23/24th June leaving 4 officers and 120 other ranks at AVELUY to carry ammunition.	
June 24th 3.15 am. Camp W. of SENLIS.	Arrived at point about one mile West of SENLIS (South of the SENLIS-WARLOY road) where camp had been pitched by advance party. Weather very wet and cold; troops very tired on arrival, partly owing to large amount of work done lately and partly owing to march across country to avoid main roads.	
June 25th Camp West of SENLIS.	Battalion – together with rest of the 14th Inf Bde – inspected by 32nd Divisional Commander.	
June 26th Ditto	In camp resting. Extra SAA. grenades, signalling equipment etc. required for forthcoming offensive operations were drawn & distributed.	
" 27th Ditto	In camp resting & bathing.	
" 28th Ditto	Ditto. (Battalion was ordered to move to ~~SAA~~ Assembly trenches in AVELUY Wood, but owing to postponement of operations this order was cancelled later.)	
" 29th Ditto.	In camp resting.	
30th 8.20 pm	Left camp and marched to BLACKHORSE SHELTERS (South of AUTHUILLE)	

(73989) W4141—463. 400,000. 9/14. H.&J.Ltd. Forms/C. 2118/10.

Unit 1st Bn Dorset Regt

Place In the field

Date 1. 6. 16.

FIELD STATE.

Army Form B 231.

To be rendered in accordance with Field Service Regulations, Part II.

UNIT	FIGHTING STRENGTH. This should *not* include details attached to unit, or personnel detailed to march with the Train, or any men unfit to go into action with unit											RATION STRENGTH. To include Fighting Strength, Personnel detailed to march with the Train, and all Personnel and animals attached for Rations and Forage										
	Personnel		Horses and Mules		Other Animals		Guns and Ammunition Wagons (stating nature)	Machine Guns	Ambulances	Tool Carts, Technical Carts (stating nature)	Remarks	Personnel	Horses and Mules		Other Animals		Mechanically Propelled Vehicles					Remarks
	Officers	Other Ranks	Riding	Draught and Pack								Total, all Ranks entitled to Rations.	Heavy Horses	Other Horses and Mules			Motor Cars	Motor Bicycles.	Lorries. 3 Ton	Lorries. 30 Cwt.	Tractors	
(1)	(2)	(3)	(4)	(5)	(6)	(7)	(8)	(9)	(10)	(11)	(12)	(13)	(14)	(15)	(16)	(17)	(18)	(19)	(20)	(21)	(22)	(23)
	36	1144	11	44			8 Lewis	8		17		1161		56								3 officers 28 O R detached from Ration
TOTALS ...	36	1144	11	44			[illegible]	8		17		1161		56								

Ammunition with Unit:—

·303 inch; approximate number of rounds per Man ____

·303 inch; " " " per Machine Gun ____

Gun or Howitzer; approximate number of rounds per Gun or Howitzer ____

Supplies with Unit:—

Approximate number of days' rations for men of ration strength ____

" " " forage for Animals " " ____

" " " fuel and lubricants for Mechanically Propelled Vehicles ____

Signature of Commander (Sd) [illegible] Lieut & A/Adjt [illegible] 1st Bn Dorset Regt

(90988.) Wt.W. 5216—2140. 900,000 7/15. J. P. & Co. Ltd. Forms B 231 / 3

Unit 1st Bn Dorset Regt

Place In the field

Date 8.6.16.

FIELD STATE.

Army Form B 231.

To be rendered in accordance with Field Service Regulations, Part II.

UNIT	FIGHTING STRENGTH — This should *not* include details attached to unit, or personnel detailed to march with the Train, or any men unfit to go into action with unit											RATION STRENGTH — To include Fighting Strength, Personnel detailed to march with the Train, and all Personnel and animals attached for Rations and Forage										
	Personnel		Horses and Mules		Other Animals		Guns and Ammunition Wagons (stating nature)	Machine Guns	Ambulances	Tool Carts, Technical Carts (stating nature)	Remarks	Personnel	Horses and Mules		Other Animals		Mechanically Propelled Vehicles					Remarks
	Officers	Other Ranks	Riding	Draught and Pack								Total, all Ranks entitled to Rations.	Heavy Horses	Other Horses and Mules			Motor Cars	Motor Bicycles.	Lorries. 3 Ton	Lorries. 30 Cwt.	Tractors	
(1)	(2)	(3)	(4)	(5)	(6)	(7)	(8)	(9)	(10)	(11)	(12)	(13)	(14)	(15)	(16)	(17)	(18)	(19)	(20)	(21)	(22)	(23)
	37	1149	11	43			8 Lewis	8		17		1166		55								1 Officer 31 O.R. detached from Battn.
TOTALS ...	37	1149	11	43				8		17		1166		55								

Ammunition with Unit:—

·303 inch; approximate number of rounds per Man

·303 inch; " " " per Machine Gun

Gun or Howitzer; approximate number of rounds per Gun or Howitzer

Supplies with Unit:—

Approximate number of days' rations for men of ration strength

" " " forage for Animals " "

" " " fuel and lubricants for Mechanically Propelled Vehicles

(90988.) Wt.W. 5216—2140. 900,000 7/15. J. P. & Co. Ltd. Forms B 231 / 3

Signature of Commander (Sd) H. C. Batchelor Lieut for Major Comdg 1st Bn Dorset Regt

Unit 1st Dorset Regt.
Place In the field
Date 15. 6. 16.

FIELD STATE.

Army Form B 231.

To be rendered in accordance with Field Service Regulations, Part II.

FIGHTING STRENGTH

This should *not* include details attached to unit, or personnel detailed to march with the Train, or any men unfit to go into action with unit

UNIT (1)	Personnel: Officers (2)	Personnel: Other Ranks (3)	Horses and Mules: Riding (4)	Horses and Mules: Draught and Pack (5)	Other Animals (6)	Other Animals (7)	Guns and Ammunition Wagons (stating nature) (8)	Machine Guns (9)	Ambulances (10)	Tool Carts, Technical Carts (stating nature) (11)	Remarks (12)
	39	1153	11	43			8 Lewis	8		17	
TOTALS ...	39	1153	11	43				8		17	

RATION STRENGTH

To include Fighting Strength, Personnel detailed to march with the Train, and all Personnel and animals attached for Rations and Forage

UNIT (1)	Personnel: Total, all Ranks entitled to Rations. (13)	Horses and Mules: Heavy Horses (14)	Horses and Mules: Other Horses and Mules (15)	Other Animals (16)	Other Animals (17)	Mechanically Propelled Vehicles: Motor Cars (18)	Motor Bicycles. (19)	Lorries. 3 Ton (20)	Lorries. 30 Cwt. (21)	Tractors (22)	Remarks (23)
	1172		55.								1 Officer & 31 OR attached from 1 Batt.
TOTALS ...	1172		55								

Ammunition with Unit:—

·303 inch; approximate number of rounds per Man

·303 inch; " " " per Machine Gun

Gun or Howitzer; approximate number of rounds per Gun or Howitzer

Supplies with Unit:—

Approximate number of days' rations for men of ration strength

" " " forage for Animals " "

" " " fuel and lubricants for Mechanically Propelled Vehicles

Signature of Commander (Sd) H C Butcher Lieut for Comdg 1st Dorset Regt.

(90988.) Wt.W. 5216—2140. 900,000 7/15. J. P. & Co. Ltd. Forms B 231 / 3

Unit 1st Bn Dorset Regt

Place In the field

Date 22.6.16.

FIELD STATE.

Army Form B 231.

To be rendered in accordance with Field Service Regulations, Part II.

UNIT	FIGHTING STRENGTH — This should *not* include details attached to unit, or personnel detailed to march with the Train, or any men unfit to go into action with unit											RATION STRENGTH — To include Fighting Strength, Personnel detailed to march with the Train, and all Personnel and animals attached for Rations and Forage										
	Personnel		Horses and Mules		Other Animals		Guns and Ammunition Wagons (stating nature)	Machine Guns	Ambulances	Tool Carts, Technical Carts (stating nature)	Remarks	Personnel	Horses and Mules		Other Animals		Mechanically Propelled Vehicles					Remarks
	Officers	Other Ranks	Riding	Draught and Pack								Total, all Ranks entitled to Rations.	Heavy Horses	Other Horses and Mules			Motor Cars	Motor Bicycles.	Lorries. 3 Ton	Lorries. 30 Cwt.	Tractors	
(1)	(2)	(3)	(4)	(5)	(6)	(7)	(8)	(9)	(10)	(11)	(12)	(13)	(14)	(15)	(16)	(17)	(18)	(19)	(20)	(21)	(22)	(23)
	39	1107	11	40			8 Lewis	8		17		1120		52								1 Officer + 35 OR detached from Battn
TOTALS ...	39	1107	11	40				8		17		1120		52								

Ammunition with Unit:—

·303 inch; approximate number of rounds per Man ___

·303 inch; ,, ,, ,, per Machine Gun ___

Gun or Howitzer; approximate number of rounds per Gun or Howitzer ___

Supplies with Unit:—

Approximate number of days' rations for men of ration strength ___

,, ,, ,, forage for Animals ,, ,, ___

,, ,, ,, fuel and lubricants for Mechanically Propelled Vehicles ___

(Sd) H. C. Butcher Lieut for Major

Signature of Commander Comdg 1st Bn Dorset Regt

(90988.) Wt.W. 5216—2140. 900,000 7/15. J. P. & Co. Ltd. Forms B 231 / 3

Unit 1st Bn Dorset Regt
Place In the Field
Date 29.6.16.

FIELD STATE.

Army Form B 231.

To be rendered in accordance with Field Service Regulations, Part II.

FIGHTING STRENGTH: This should *not* include details attached to unit, or personnel detailed to march with the Train, or any men unfit to go into action with unit (columns 2–12).

RATION STRENGTH: To include Fighting Strength, Personnel detailed to march with the Train, and all Personnel and animals attached for Rations and Forage (columns 13–23).

UNIT	Personnel: Officers	Personnel: Other Ranks	Horses and Mules: Riding	Horses and Mules: Draught and Pack	Other Animals	Other Animals	Guns and Ammunition Wagons (stating nature)	Machine Guns	Ambulances	Tool Carts, Technical Carts (stating nature)	Remarks	Personnel: Total, all Ranks entitled to Rations.	Horses and Mules: Heavy Horses	Horses and Mules: Other Horses and Mules	Other Animals	Other Animals	Mechanically Propelled Vehicles: Motor Cars	Mechanically Propelled Vehicles: Motor Bicycles.	Lorries: 3 Ton	Lorries: 30 Cwt.	Tractors	Remarks
(1)	(2)	(3)	(4)	(5)	(6)	(7)	(8)	(9)	(10)	(11)	(12)	(13)	(14)	(15)	(16)	(17)	(18)	(19)	(20)	(21)	(22)	(23)
	39	1107	11	41			8 Lewis	8		17		1112		53								3 officers & 39 OR detached from Battn
TOTALS ...	39	1107	11	41				8		17		1112		53								

Ammunition with Unit:—

·303 inch; approximate number of rounds per Man ________

·303 inch; " " " per Machine Gun ________

Gun or Howitzer; approximate number of rounds per Gun or Howitzer ________

Supplies with Unit:—

Approximate number of days' rations for men of ration strength ________

" " " forage for Animals " " ________

" " " fuel and lubricants for Mechanically Propelled Vehicles ________

Signature of Commander (Sd) H. C. Butcher Lieut for Major Comdg 1st Bn Dorset Regt

(90988.) Wt.W. 5216—2140. 900,000 7/15. J. P. & Co. Ltd. Forms B231/3

14th Bde.
32nd Div.

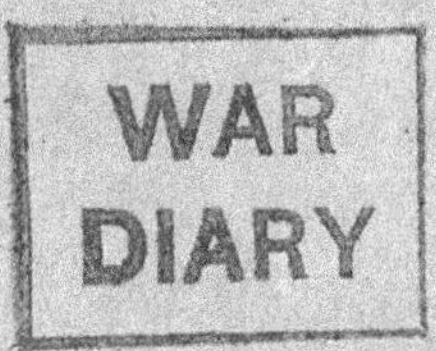

1st BATTALION.

THE DORSET REGIMENT.

JULY 1916.

Attached :- Operation Order.

Field State.

Instructions regarding War Diaries and Intelligence Summaries are contained in F. S. Regs., Part II. and the Staff Manual respectively. Title Pages will be prepared in manuscript.

WAR DIARY ~~or~~ ~~INTELLIGENCE~~ SUMMARY of 1st DORSET REGT.

(Erase heading not required.)

Army Form C. 2118.

Place	Date 1916.	Hour	Summary of Events and Information	Remarks and references to Appendices
Camp W. of SENLIS	June 30th		In camp resting.	HB Refce: Trench map Sheet 57 D. S.E. Edition B. 2.
	do	8.20pm.	Left camp and marched to BLACKHORSE SHELTERS (South of AUTHUILLE)	
	July 1st	12.50am.	Arrived at BLACKHORSE SHELTERS.	
	"	6.30am	Finished breakfasts. (Zero time for attack 7.30am)	HB
	"	7.10am	Started to leave BLACKHORSE SHELTERS by platoons at 100 yards interval, proceeding through AUTHUILLE WOOD along DUMBARTON TRACK in order to attack the enemy in accordance with orders. Capt. KESTELL-CORNISH and about ten other ranks were wounded by machine-gun fire as the Battalion was proceeding along DUMBARTON TRACK. After waiting about fifteen minutes in AUTHUILLE WOOD the O.C. "C" Coy (the leading Company) received information from our liason party attached to the 11th BORDER Regt (97th Inf. Bde) that the latter regiment had commenced its advance; 500 yards behind the rear platoon of 11th BORDER Regt. the leading platoon of 1st DORSET Regt. advanced from AUTHUILLE WOOD in accordance with orders previously received. The remainder of the Battalion followed by platoons or sections. [The 96th and 97th Infantry Brigades had attacked the hostile trenches just previous to the 1st DORSET Regt – the leading Battalion of the 14th Infantry Bde – leaving AUTHUILLE WOOD. They had not	

2449 Wt. W14957/M90 750,000 1/16 J.B.C. & A. Forms/C.2118/12.

Army Form C. 2118.

Instructions regarding War Diaries and Intelligence Summaries are contained in F. S. Regs., Part II. and the Staff Manual respectively. Title Pages will be prepared in manuscript.

WAR DIARY
or
~~INTELLIGENCE SUMMARY~~ of 1st Dorset Regt

(Erase heading not required.)

Place	Date	Hour	Summary of Events and Information	Remarks and references to Appendices
			however, been able to attain their objectives; this fact was not known until later although it was apparent that matters were not progressing quite as favourably as had been anticipated.]	
			Immediately the leading platoon left AUTHUILLE WOOD very heavy and extremely accurate machine-gun fire was opened by the enemy from some point on our right not definitely ascertained. As this fire concentrated mainly on the point at the edge of the wood where DUMBARTON TRACK ends – and past which the whole Battalion had to go – we endeavoured to find some other exit from the wood, but could not do so, barbed wire and other obstructions preventing.	
			The whole Battalion, therefore, advanced from this point by sections, and it was during the dash across country from AUTHUILLE WOOD to our own front line trench about 100yds ahead that at least half our total casualties were sustained. By the time half the Battalion had left the wood the end of DUMBARTON TRACK and the ground up to our front line trench was covered with our killed and wounded; yet the men continued	HB

Instructions regarding War Diaries and Intelligence Summaries are contained in F. S. Regs., Part II. and the Staff Manual respectively. Title Pages will be prepared in manuscript.

WAR DIARY ~~or~~ INTELLIGENCE SUMMARY of 1st DORSET. REGT

(Erase heading not required.)

Army Form C. 2118.

Place	Date	Hour	Summary of Events and Information	Remarks and references to Appendices
			to jump up and advance over their fallen comrades as the word to go was given. Four Lewis guns were lost here by the men being wounded; other men following who stopped in the endeavour to pick up the guns and take them forward, were also killed or wounded. On arrival in our front line trench we found it to be already occupied by the 11th BORDER Rgt. (numbering approximately 100 to 150 other ranks without any officers) Machine gunners, carrying parties and other details also occupied this trench and the shell craters in front and rear of it. Numbers of killed + wounded added to the congestion and lateral movement was practically impossible, except over the top, until we managed to organize matters somewhat and move the men further to the right. Six officers and about sixty men went forward almost at once into German front line trench. Part of this was found to be occupied by British troops and part by Germans. A few men of 11th Border Rgt. were already there with a considerable number of 17th H. L. I. on the left; some of the	ABP.

2449 Wt. W14957/M90 750,000 1/16 J.B.C. & A. Forms/C.2118/12.

Army Form C. 2118.

Instructions regarding War Diaries and Intelligence Summaries are contained in F. S. Regs., Part II. and the Staff Manual respectively. Title Pages will be prepared in manuscript.

WAR DIARY or INTELLIGENCE SUMMARY of 1st DORSET REGT

(Erase heading not required.)

Place	Date	Hour	Summary of Events and Information	Remarks and references to Appendices
			19th Lancashire Fusiliers reached the same place later. All these six officers were wounded – one very slightly who remained at duty –, and out of the sixty men who went forward to the German front line trench only about twenty-five actually reached there. Parties were organized to bomb down the enemy trenches to the right and when further advance became impossible barricades were built. The enemy made several attempts to bomb our troops out of their trenches and we lost some officers and men in this way, although the enemy were repulsed. Our bombs ran out and German grenades found in the captured trench were used.	
			Meanwhile the Dorsets, Borders + Lancashire Fusiliers in our front line trench had become organized. Major J.V. SHUTE had been wounded and Capt. LANCASTER being in the German trench (he had also been reported wounded) the Adjutant assumed command of both 1st Dorset and 11th Border Regt. Arrangements were made for a concerted attack upon the German position at a given signal; a patrol being first sent out to ascertain exactly	AB

2449 Wt. W14957/M90 750,000 1/16 J.B.C. & A. Forms/C.2118/12.

Army Form C. 2118.

Instructions regarding War Diaries and Intelligence Summaries are contained in F. S. Regs., Part II. and the Staff Manual respectively. Title Pages will be prepared in manuscript.

WAR DIARY or INTELLIGENCE SUMMARY of 1st DORSET REGT

(Erase heading not required.)

Place	Date	Hour	Summary of Events and Information	Remarks and references to Appendices
			which part of the German trench was in our hands and which was still held by the enemy. Also as our own guns were still firing on the German Trench it was necessary to wait till this barrage lifted before we advanced. Before this plan of attack could be carried out the Officer commanding the Right Column decided to withdraw the 19th Lancashire Fusiliers and 11th Border Regt from our front line trench, leaving the 1st Dorset Regt to hold the line. At that time we had – in addition to the Adjutant – three Lieutenants and eighty-five other ranks actually in the trench. Soon after them these men were sorted out into companies, a commander allotted to each company, sentries were posted, the two remaining Lewis guns in action, and we became again a definitely organized unit. We were unable to get into touch with anyone on our right or left. During the early part of the afternoon sixty more unwounded men rejoined – these having become detached in other parts of our trenches.	119B
			The enemy's artillery bombarded us continually all the afternoon and at 5pm his fire became so intense and accurate	

2449 Wt. W14957/M90 750,000 1/16 J.B.C. & A. Forms/C.2118/12.

Army Form C. 2118.

Instructions regarding War Diaries and Intelligence Summaries are contained in F. S. Regs., Part II. and the Staff Manual respectively. Title Pages will be prepared in manuscript.

WAR DIARY or INTELLIGENCE SUMMARY

(Erase heading not required.)

of 1st DORSET REGT

Place	Date 1916	Hour	Summary of Events and Information	Remarks and references to Appendices
			that our position became almost untenable. Thirty of the remaining men were either killed or wounded and the trench so damaged as to make communication very difficult. Soon after 3pm Major H.D. Thwaytes came up and took command; a message was received from Brigade saying that 12th H.L.I. would relieve 1st Dorset Regt and by 2am on the 2nd July we were clear of the front line trench. Party in German trench also ordered to withdraw.	HB
Outer defences of AUTHUILLE	July 2nd	4am	Battalion in KINTYRE trench (Northern outer defences of AUTHUILLE.) Carrying parties and detached men having rejoined the strength of Battalion was six officers (including M.O.) and 317 other ranks; this total does not include personnel left with transport. Casualties on July 1st/2nd were: 21 officers wounded, 18 other ranks killed, 94 other ranks missing, 368 other ranks wounded. During the day the Battalion rested; at night working parties of 1 off. + 105 other ranks carried ammunition. At 10pm	HB
	July 2/3		orders were received to occupy the front line from TYNDRUM Street to CHEQUERBENT Street and relief commenced about 12 midnight. Owing to the large amount of traffic in the trenches caused by a Battalion of 75th Inf Bde. coming in who did not know the trenches, relief was not complete till 5.50am July 3rd. With the assistance of	HB

2449 Wt. W14957/M90 750,000 1/16 J.B.C. & A. Forms/C.2118/12.

Army Form C. 2118.

Instructions regarding War Diaries and Intelligence Summaries are contained in F. S. Regs., Part II. and the Staff Manual respectively. Title Pages will be prepared in manuscript.

WAR DIARY or INTELLIGENCE SUMMARY of 1st DORSET REGT

(Erase heading not required.)

Place	Date 1916	Hour	Summary of Events and Information	Remarks and references to Appendices
	July 3rd		two machine guns of 14th Bde. M.G. Coy. the Battalion held the line from TYNDRUM St. to CHEQUERBENT St. till 11.35 pm when relieved by 1st WILTSHIRE Rgt. From 7am onwards all men that could be spared were employed carrying grenades TSAA to 15th H.L.I. who occupied German front trench opposite us and were carrying out bombing attacks. Regiments of 75th Inf Bde. also attacked the German position at 6.30 am.	HB
SENLIS.	" 4th	3.55 am	On completion of relief Battn. withdrew to billets in SENLIS arriving there at 3.55 am.	57D. S.E 1/20,000 HB
SENLIS and FORCEVILLE	" 5th	5.15 pm	Marched from SENLIS to billets in FORCEVILLE.	HB
FORCEVILLE	" 6th		In billets in FORCEVILLE.	HB
BOUZINCOURT	" 7th		Battalion marched from FORCEVILLE to billets in BOUZINCOURT, arriving there 7.20 a.m.	HB
BOUZINCOURT and OVILLERS	" 8th		Battalion relieved 9th Essex Rgt. in Western part of OVILLERS in the evening. Position difficult to take over owing to damaged state of trenches and the difficulty of locating points accurately on the map — all landmarks being demolished by our shell fire. Large numbers of our own & German dead & wounded, and the muddy state of the trenches delayed movement somewhat, and one company was sent back under Capt.	HB 15th H.L.I. on our right 2nd Manchesters on our left

2449 Wt. W14957/M90 750,000 1/16 J.B.C. & A. Forms/C.2118/12.

Army Form C. 2118.

WAR DIARY ~~or~~ INTELLIGENCE SUMMARY

of 1st DORSET REGT

Instructions regarding War Diaries and Intelligence Summaries are contained in F. S. Regs., Part II. and the Staff Manual respectively. Title Pages will be prepared in manuscript.

(Erase heading not required.)

Place	Date 1916	Hour	Summary of Events and Information	Remarks and references to Appendices
OVILLERS	July 8th		FENTON to remain in support in British original front line trench. This company was then employed carrying and evacuating wounded.	HB
do	" 9th		Concerted bombing attacks were carried out during the morning on the enemy positions. These were strongly held by machine-guns and manned by Guards regiments who stubbornly contested every yard. Our casualties were 2Lieut CAINES and 3 other ranks wounded. We advanced a short distance at a number of points and the positions were consolidated at night with the assistance of R.E. and the supporting company. Enemy snipers very active.	HB
do	" 10th		Strong bombing attacks again made on enemy's positions and some ground gained. Counter-sniping on our part made German snipers less active. Our casualties: 2Lieut SMELLIE, 2Lt. CARTMAN wounded; 2Lt. BENGER shell shock; 15 other ranks killed or wounded. A counter-attack by the enemy was repulsed. A large crater occupied by us was converted into a strong point.	HB
do	" 11th		Day spent consolidating positions.	HB
	" 11th	9 pm	Battalion relieved by 16th Lancashire Fusiliers.	
	" 11th	10.20 pm	Battalion in billets in BOUZINCOURT.	
BOUZINCOURT	" 12th		In billets in BOUZINCOURT.	HB

2449 Wt. W14957/M90 750,000 1/16 J.B.C. & A. Forms/C.2118/12.

Army Form C. 2118.

Instructions regarding War Diaries and Intelligence Summaries are contained in F. S. Regs., Part II. and the Staff Manual respectively. Title Pages will be prepared in manuscript.

WAR DIARY or ~~INTELLIGENCE~~ SUMMARY of 1st DORSET REGT.

(Erase heading not required.)

Place	Date 1916	Hour	Summary of Events and Information	Remarks and references to Appendices
BOUZINCOURT	July 13th		In billets in BOUZINCOURT.	RB
do	" 14th		Ditto	RB
	" 14th	8.15pm	Battalion relieved part of 96th Inf. Bde. in OVILLERS.	RB
OVILLERS	" 15	2.35am	7th Inf Bde. and Border Rgt. on our right commenced an attack on east of OVILLERS.	RB
	" 15	2.50am	One platoon of DORSETS attacked points 82 and 72 (refce. artillery map of OVILLERS) but were unable to gain their objectives. Casualties: Capt. FENTON killed, 2Lieut COLEY killed, 2 other ranks killed, 2 others missing, 1 other ~~rank~~ wounded.	
	" 15.	9.30pm.	Battalion relieved by 7th WORCESTER Rgt. and withdrew to billets in SENLIS.	
SENLIS.	" 16		In billets in SENLIS.	RB
SENLIS and HALLOY	" 17		Battalion marched from SENLIS to billets in HALLOY arriving latter place 3.50pm. Re-inforcement of 294 other ranks joined.	RB
HALLOY & BREVILLERS.	" 18		Battalion marched from HALLOY to billets in BREVILLERS, arriving there 4.25pm.	RB
BREVILLERS. & SIBIVILLE.	" 19th		Battalion marched from BREVILLERS to SIBIVILLE, arriving there 11.10am.	RB
SIBIVILLE & ORLENCOURT.	" 20th		Battalion marched from SIBIVILLE to ORLENCOURT, arriving there 11.50am. (Note: 99 years ago – in 1817 – the regiment was billetted in the same village. Mons. POITEVIN, at whose house the Commanding Officer stayed, informed us that Lieut-Col. STURT who commanded the 39th Rgt. in 1817, was billetted with his (Mons. Poitevin's) grandfather. A letter was produced which bears out this statement.) 14 officers joined.	RB

2449 Wt. W14957/M90 750,000 1/16 J.B.C. & A. Forms/C.2118/12.

Army Form C. 2118.

Instructions regarding War Diaries and Intelligence Summaries are contained in F. S. Regs., Part II. and the Staff Manual respectively. Title pages will be prepared in manuscript.

WAR DIARY
or
INTELLIGENCE SUMMARY.
(Erase heading not required.)

Place	Date 1916	Hour	Summary of Events and Information	Remarks and references to Appendices
ORLENCOURT & FLORINGHEM	July 21st	6.50am	Battalion moved from ORLENCOURT to FLORINGHEM.	A.R.B.
FLORINGHEM	" 22nd		Battalion in FLORINGHEM training.	A.R.B.
do	" 23rd		Ditto.	A.R.B.
do	" 24th		Ditto.	A.R.B.
do	" 25th		Ditto.	A.R.B.
FLORINGHEM & HOUCHIN.	" 26th		Battalion marched from FLORINGHEM to camp at HOUCHIN, arriving there 12.50pm.	A.R.B.
HOUCHIN.	" 27th		Battalion inspected by Bde. Commander at HOUCHIN.	A.R.B.
do	" 28th		Battalion inspected by 1st Army Commander near HESDIGNEUL.	A.R.B.
HOUCHIN & ANNEZIN.	" 29th		Battalion marched from HOUCHIN to ANNEZIN arriving there 11.50am.	A.R.B.
ANNEZIN	" 30th		In ANNEZIN training.	A.R.B.
do	" 31st		Ditto.	A.R.B.

A.R. Butcher.
Lieut & Adjutant.
1st Dorset Rgt.

2353 Wt. W2544/1454 700,000 5/15 D. D. & L. A.D.S.S./Forms/C. 2118.

SECRET

No. 15

Operation Orders
By Major J.V. Shute
Comdg 1st Bn Dorset Regt
25 - 6 - 1916

Reference Sheet 57 D. S.E. 1/20.000.

1. 1st Dorset Regt will take a principal part in an attack on the German positions.

2. Information. There is no increase in the strength of the enemy opposite us. Details of the enemy's strength and disposition, artillery etc, may be seen on application to the Adjutant.

3. Intention. The enemy must be attacked with the utmost vigour and determination.

4. Objective. The objective allotted to 1st Dorset Regt is the German second line from R. 34. a. 0. 9. to R. 27. b. 55. 15.
The objective of the 19th Lancs Fus. is from our left to R. 27. b. 20. 75. The 70th Bde 8th Divn will be on our right.

5. Time of the assault. The exact time of the assault will be fixed by higher authority. Zero will be the moment at which the artillery lifts off the enemy's front line trench.

6. Artillery. The attack will commence with a steady bombardment of the enemy's positions for 4 days & nights up to the moment of the Infantry assault on the 5th day (Z day).

7. Preliminary Moves. On the night X/Y the 1st Dorset Regt will concentrate in assembly trenches in AVELUY WOOD: and on the night Y/Z will move to BLACKHORSE SHELTERS.

8. Task. The Bde will attack in two columns:
1st Dorset Regt - leading the right column - will leave AUTHUILLE WOOD by track No. 1., and will follow the 11th Battn The Border Regt (the rear Battn of the 97th Infantry Bde) at 500 yards distance, marching on the gap

8 (contd) the gap in the trees just north of MOUQUET FARM.
The Battn will leave AVIHUILLE WOOD in artillery formation in following order: C. D. A. B. on company frontage, line of platoons in fours.
Very close touch must be kept between 11th BORDER Regt and 1st DORSET Regt. The intelligence officer with his runners will be responsible for this and for keeping Bn Hd. Qrs. informed of every detail possible with regard to the progress of the attack.
In addition to the Scouts already detailed, O.C. Coys will detail one runner per company to report to Intelligence Officer before the Battn moves from Blackhorse dugouts for keeping communication with 11th Border Regt.
When 11th Border Regt has captured MOQUET FARM these runners will rejoin their companies.
At 1.40 after zero - when the MOUQUET FARM has been taken by 97th Inf Bde - the 1st Dorset Regt will prepare to attack the German second line in accordance with time table and sketch attached. (Appendices A. A 1), at about point R. 27. d. 75. 50 under cover of a smoke barrage which will be thrown on the line to be attacked. The smoke barrage will last for 5 minutes during which time the Trench Mortar Battery will come into action and fire 30 rounds per gun. As soon as the stokes guns are in action a second smoke barrage will be thrown on the German line lasting for 5 minutes, under cover of which "C" Coy and Bangalore torpedo party of 1st Dorset Regt will advance as closely as possible to the point of attack. Three Bangalore torpedos will be carried and O.C. "C" Coy will make arrangements to ensure that in the event of casualties at least one party and torpedo is available to blow gaps in the wire.

8 (contd) A & D Coys will each detail one man trained in use of Bangalore torpedo to report to O.C. 'C' Coy for duty as soon as Battn arrives at Blackhorse dugouts.
3. 18 feet torpedoes will be drawn from Authuille wood magazine. Spare torpedoes if required are in Authuille village magazine. These torpedo men will rejoin their companies on completion of special duty.
At 2.10 after zero the artillery barrage will lift 200 yards and the 1st Dorset Regt will attack and capture the German trenches from R.34.a.0.9 to R27.b.55.15 subdivided as follows: 'C' Coy from R.34.a.0.8. to R27d.85.19.
'D' Coy from R27d.85.19 to R.27d.7.5.
'A' Coy from R27d.7.5. to R.27d.6.8.
'B' Coy from R27d.6.8. to R27b.50.17.
All positions captured will be held at all costs.
As soon as the German trenches are captured O.C. D Coy will establish a strong point at R.28.c.3.4. two platoons having been previously detailed to make and hold this strong point. Each of these platoons will carry 20 picks 20 shovels 2 hand axes 4 wire cutters 250 sandbags. The method of carrying these articles will be demonstrated by R.S.M.
One Lewis Gun team from 'D' Coy (in charge of Sgt SCOTT) will also assist in garrisoning this point assisted by 1 machine gun and team under Lieut BURTON detailed by Bde M.G. Coy. ½ section of the 206/Coy R.E. will accompany the Battn and assist in the consolidation of the position and especially the strong point.

9. Stokes Batteries. Four 4" Stokes Mortars and 3" Stokes battery will accompany the Battn for action as in Para. 8. The 4" Stokes mortars will meet the Battn as it leaves AUTHUILLE WOOD and both the 4" mortars and the 3" Stokes battery will advance in rear of 'C' Coy.

10. Bombers. Each Coy will detail 15 men as bombers, 3 for each platoon and 3 with Coy Commander (These men will carry 12 bombs in buckets and not the extra

10. (Contd). 2 bandoliers S.A.A.

11. Flanks. O.C. "C" & "B" Coys will be responsible for holding their flanks in the event of the Battn becoming isolated or the non success of the Regts on the right or left.

12. Offrs bomdg Coys will consolidate their line with the utmost speed as soon as they are in position, special parties being detailed to fill in all communication or other trenches leading to our line from the direction of the enemy. Communication trenches are not to be merely blocked but filled in for at least a distance of 10 yards. This to be carried out not less than 100 yards in front of our consolidated position.

13. Dress & Special Equipment. (a) Rifle & equipment (less pack) waterbottles full, 220 rds S.A.A. (2 bandoliers in addition to equipment) waterproof sheet, 2 sandbags tucked in belt, unexpended portion of days ration, 1 iron ration, 1 1lb tin of meat, and 4 biscuits, 4 sticks of chocolate. Mess tin with unexpended portion of days ration will be carried in the haversack. On X day all packs and greatcoats will be stored at BOUZINCOURT. (b) Each Offr N.C.O. and man will carry 2 fused mills grenades in his pocket excepting the case of bombers these grenades are not for the use of carriers; they are intended as a means of getting forward large numbers of grenades which will be collected when the objective is reached to replenish bombers stocks. OC Coys will arrange to collect these bombs when the consolidation has been completed and formed coy bomb stores. (C) Additional wire cutters will be carried as follows:-

	Mk V.	S.A. Decimals.	W. B.	L. H.
A Coy	5.	12.	15.	1.
B Coy	5.	12.	15.	1.
C Coy	12.	28.	35.	2.
D Coy	5.	12.	25.	2.

(d) Each coy and Bn HQrs will carry 9 red flares for communication with the contact patrol aeroplane.

13(d) These flares will be used only when the position has been (contd) captured. They will be fired in sets of 3 at ¼ minute interval between each single flare and at least 4 paces between each flare. (e). Rockets may or may not be issued, but if they are 6 red rockets is S.O.S. signal.

(f). A proportion of billhooks, axes, and hedging gloves will be carried by each coy

(g). Each platoon (with the exception of those of 'D' coy detailed for strong point) will carry 5 picks and 10 shovels.

14. Sgt UPSON will arrange to instruct all Str bearers by which trenches wounded are to be evacuated. Certain trenches are reserved for UP & DOWN traffic but lineman repairing lines may go in either direction. Special map may be procured by application to Adjutant.

15. Special instructions will be issued for the Transport and Qr Masters branch.

16. The authorized establishment of baggage and Stores including Offrs kits (35 lbs only) will be packed in baggage wagons on X day.

17. Rgt Sgt Major will ensure that Sgts. i/c ammunition and pack animal drivers know where the forward S.A.A. and grenade dumps are situated. Map shewing these together with First Aid posts water supply system etc may be seen on application to Adjutant. All coy commdrs and M.O. should take an opportunity of studying this.

18. There will be difficulty in getting up water to advanced troops. Great care must be taken to husband the supply in waterbottles.

19. Prisoners will be evacuated to BLACKHORSE BRIDGE and handed over to A.P.M. — 1 Guard to every 10 prisoners.

20. (a). All papers and orders are to be destroyed before the advance. No papers will be carried by Offrs & men in the attack except the 1/20,000 trench map shewing German trenches only, the 1/40,000 map sheet 57D & 57C and the LENS 1/100,000 series. All messages and reports

20(a) (Contd) will refer to one or the other of these maps.

(b) With the exception of the Str. Bearers, no offr, N.C.O or man in the Battn will fall out to bring back wounded, neither will they remain behind to assist wounded while their coys are advancing. Water and Field Dressings belonging to the wounded man himself must be used not those of unwounded men.

(c) Any guns captured which are in danger of being lost again must be rendered useless by damaging the sights and breech mechanism. Captured M.G^s to be collected.

(d) No Officer, N.C.O. or man will be allowed to collect souvenirs of any description.

(e) Each coy is responsible for establishing and keeping liaison with coys on its flanks. 'B' Coy will detail an intelligent L/Cpl to keep liaison with 19th L. Fus. and 'A' Coy will send similar N.C.O. to O.C. 'C' Coy at BLACKHORSE BDGE to assist them in keeping touch with Battn on our right.

(f) The following Offrs, N.C.O.s & men will report to Major THWAYTES immediately previous to the Battn marching away from WARLOY area, and will remain with him in BOUZINCOURT Huts till they receive orders to rejoin the Regt. after the attack:

CAPTAIN B.L. FENTON, 2/Lieut W.P. LIPSCOMB, Lt. R.J.D. FEW, 2/Lieut W. LINDSEY, 2/Lieut H.W. BORROUGH, Lt. F.R. BILLOT, 2/Lieut W.A. SMELLIE. Sgt SMITH (Signalling Sgt), C.S.M. COBB, Cpl BRYANT, (Bombing Cpl), Pte^s RUSH & WILSON (H.Q. Signallers) 1 Sgt, 1 Cpl, 1 L/C, 2 bombers and 2 Lewis Gunners from each coy

21. During the advance, Bn H.Qrs will be about the centre of the Battn, and may be distinguished by 4 or 5 orderlies carrying rifles with butt upwards.

22. Bde Battle H.Q. will be established at W. 12. a. 7. 7. on X/Y night. Probable line of advance of Bde H.Qrs will be up the valley through R. 32. central – R. 33. a. 5. 5.

23 (a) Appendix A shews the artillery barrages, lifts, and times.

(b) Appendix B (to be circulated later) shews number of men

23 (b) (contd) required from coys as carriers etc together with detail of times and places these men must report.

(c) Appendix C (to be circulated later) gives rough details with regard to maintenance of communication between coys, Bn HQrs, and Bde HQrs. Sgt Janaway and Cpl Hodge (Bn HQ Signallers) have been issued with detailed instructions which all coy signallers should take an opportunity of reading.

24. In the event of the enemy shewing the white flag, no attention whatever will be paid.

25. ACKNOWLEDGE.

H. C. Butcher
Lieut & Adjt
1st Bn Dorsetshire Regt

Copies Nos 1, 2, 3, 4, 5 to A Coy. 6, 7, 8, 9, 10 to B Coy
" " 11, 12, 13, 14, 15 to C Coy. 16, 17, 18, 19, 20 to D Coy
Copy No 21 to Qr Master. 22 to M.O. 23 to RSM. 24 to Adjt

Appendix 'A'

Table of Lifts for 18 Pdr Batteries

The barrage leaves [illegible] G	and moves to J' [illegible]	35
[illegible] I'	[illegible] J'	10
[illegible] I	[illegible] J	15
[illegible] J	[illegible] K'	20
[illegible] J	[illegible] K	30
[illegible] H'	[illegible] L	40
[illegible] H	[illegible] L	50

Army Form B 231.

FIELD STATE.

Unit 1st Bn Dorset Regt

Place In the Field

Date 6. 7. 16.

To be rendered in accordance with Field Service Regulations, Part II.

UNIT	FIGHTING STRENGTH — This should *not* include details attached to unit, or personnel detailed to march with the Train, or any men unfit to go into action with unit											RATION STRENGTH — To include Fighting Strength, Personnel detailed to march with the Train, and all Personnel and animals attached for Rations and Forage										
	Personnel		Horses and Mules		Other Animals		Guns and Ammunition Wagons (stating nature)	Machine Guns	Ambulances	Tool Carts, Technical Carts (stating nature)	Remarks	Personnel	Horses and Mules		Other Animals		Mechanically Propelled Vehicles					Remarks
	Officers	Other Ranks	Riding	Draught and Pack								Total, all Ranks entitled to Rations.	Heavy Horses	Other Horses and Mules			Motor Cars	Motor Bicycles.	Lorries. 3 Ton	Lorries. 30 Cwt.	Tractors	
(1)	(2)	(3)	(4)	(5)	(6)	(7)	(8)	(9)	(10)	(11)	(12)	(13)	(14)	(15)	(16)	(17)	(18)	(19)	(20)	(21)	(22)	(23)
	23	612	11.	41			4 Lewis	4		17		610.		53								4 Officers & 31 OR detached from Battn
Totals ...	23	612	11.	41				4		17		610		53								

Ammunition with Unit:—

·303 inch; approximate number of rounds per Man ______

·303 inch; " " " per Machine Gun ______

Gun or Howitzer; approximate number of rounds per Gun or Howitzer ______

Supplies with Unit:—

Approximate number of days' rations for men of ration strength ______

" " " forage for Animals " " ______

" " " fuel and lubricants for Mechanically Propelled Vehicles ______

Signature of Commander ______

(90988.) Wt. W. 5216—2140. 900,000 7/15. J. P. & Co. Ltd. Forms B231/3

Unit 1st Bn Dorset Regt

Place In the Field

Date 13. 7. 16.

FIELD STATE.

Army Form B 231.

To be rendered in accordance with Field Service Regulations, Part II.

UNIT	FIGHTING STRENGTH. This should *not* include details attached to unit, or personnel detailed to march with the Train, or any men unfit to go into action with unit											RATION STRENGTH. To include Fighting Strength, Personnel detailed to march with the Train, and all Personnel and animals attached for Rations and Forage										
	Personnel		Horses and Mules		Other Animals		Guns and Ammunition Wagons (stating nature)	Machine Guns	Ambulances	Tool Carts, Technical Carts (stating nature)	Remarks	Personnel	Horses and Mules		Other Animals		Mechanically Propelled Vehicles					Remarks
	Officers	Other Ranks	Riding	Draught and Pack								Total, all Ranks entitled to Rations.	Heavy Horses	Other Horses and Mules			Motor Cars	Motor Bicycles.	Lorries. 3 Ton	Lorries. 30 Cwt.	Tractors	
(1)	(2)	(3)	(4)	(5)	(6)	(7)	(8)	(9)	(10)	(11)	(12)	(13)	(14)	(15)	(16)	(17)	(18)	(19)	(20)	(21)	(22)	(23)
	16	556	11	39			10 Lewis	10		17		549		51								2 Officers & 31 OR detached from Battn
TOTALS ...	16	556	11	39				10		17		549		51								

Ammunition with Unit:—

·303 inch; approximate number of rounds per Man ______

·303 inch; " " " per Machine Gun ______

Gun or Howitzer; approximate number of rounds per Gun or Howitzer ______

Supplies with Unit:—

Approximate number of days' rations for men of ration strength ______

" " " forage for Animals " " ______

" " " fuel and lubricants for Mechanically Propelled Vehicles ______

Signature of Commander [illegible]

(90988.) Wt.W. 5216—2140. 900,000 7/15. J. P. & Co. Ltd. Forms B 231 / 3

Unit 1st Bn Dorset Regt

Place 20. 7. 16

Date In the field

FIELD STATE.

Army Form B 231.

To be rendered in accordance with Field Service Regulations, Part II.

UNIT	FIGHTING STRENGTH — This should *not* include details attached to unit, or personnel detailed to march with the Train, or any men unfit to go into action with unit											RATION STRENGTH — To include Fighting Strength, Personnel detailed to march with the Train, and all Personnel and animals attached for Rations and Forage										
	Personnel		Horses and Mules		Other Animals		Guns and Ammunition Wagons (stating nature)	Machine Guns	Ambulances	Tool Carts, Technical Carts (stating nature)	Remarks	Personnel	Horses and Mules		Other Animals		Mechanically Propelled Vehicles					Remarks
	Officers	Other Ranks	Riding	Draught and Pack								Total, all Ranks entitled to Rations.	Heavy Horses	Other Horses and Mules			Motor Cars	Motor Bicycles.	Lorries. 3 Ton	Lorries. 30 Cwt.	Tractors	
(1)	(2)	(3)	(4)	(5)	(6)	(7)	(8)	(9)	(10)	(11)	(12)	(13)	(14)	(15)	(16)	(17)	(18)	(19)	(20)	(21)	(22)	(23)
	30	840	11	41			8 Lewis	8		17		830		53								2 officers & 32 O.R. detached from Battn
TOTALS ...	30	840	11	41				8		17		830		53								

Ammunition with Unit:—

·303 inch; approximate number of rounds per Man ______

·303 inch; " " " per Machine Gun ______

Gun or Howitzer; approximate number of rounds per Gun or Howitzer ______

Supplies with Unit:—

Approximate number of days' rations for men of ration strength ______

" " " forage for Animals " " ______

" " " fuel and lubricants for Mechanically Propelled Vehicles ______

Signature of Commander [illegible]

(90988.) Wt.W. 5216—2140. 900,000 7/15. J. P. & Co. Ltd. Forms B 231/3

Lieut R. L. Faulkner 7 Borroll Jones Bn 17 7 16
" " Y. G. Berger R. Parker " " 16 7 16

Unit 1st Bn Dorset Regt

Place In the field

Date 27.7.16

FIELD STATE.

Army Form B 231.

To be rendered in accordance with Field Service Regulations, Part II.

FIGHTING STRENGTH

This should *not* include details attached to unit, or personnel detailed to march with the Train, or any men unfit to go into action with unit

UNIT	Personnel		Horses and Mules		Other Animals		Guns and Ammunition Wagons (stating nature)	Machine Guns	Ambulances	Tool Carts, Technical Carts (stating nature)	Remarks
	Officers	Other Ranks	Riding	Draught and Pack							
(1)	(2)	(3)	(4)	(5)	(6)	(7)	(8)	(9)	(10)	(11)	(12)
	29	854	11	43			8 Lewis	8		17	
TOTALS ...	29	854	11	43				8		17	

RATION STRENGTH

To include Fighting Strength, Personnel detailed to march with the Train, and all Personnel and animals attached for Rations and Forage

UNIT	Personnel	Horses and Mules		Other Animals		Mechanically Propelled Vehicles					Remarks
	Total, all Ranks entitled to Rations.	Heavy Horses	Other Horses and Mules			Motor Cars	Motor Bicycles.	Lorries. 3 Ton	Lorries. 30 Cwt.	Tractors	
(1)	(13)	(14)	(15)	(16)	(17)	(18)	(19)	(20)	(21)	(22)	(23)
	793		55								6 Officers 94 O.R. detached from Battn.
TOTALS ...	793		55								

Ammunition with Unit:—

·303 inch; approximate number of rounds per Man ______

·303 inch; " " " per Machine Gun ______

Gun or Howitzer; approximate number of rounds per Gun or Howitzer ______

Supplies with Unit:—

Approximate number of days' rations for men of ration strength ______

" " " forage for Animals " " ______

" " " fuel and lubricants for Mechanically Propelled Vehicles ______

Signature of Commander [illegible]

(90988.) Wt. W. 5216—2140. 900,000 7/15. J. P. & Co. Ltd. Forms B 231 / 3

Lieut. T.G. Denger R. Berks To F. Amb. 23-7-[illegible]

Lieut. F.R. Bellairs [illegible] 23 [illegible]

Lieut. T.A. Clarke R.A.M.C. To Leave [illegible]

14th Brigade.

32nd Division.

1st BATTALION

THE DORSET REGIMENT

AUGUST 1 9 1 6

Appendices attached:-

Field States.

SECRET.

A 341.

HQ 14th Bde

Herewith War Diary for 1st Bn The Dorsetshire Regt from 1-31.8.16

A. W. Bubb 2/Lt for Captain
Comdg 1st Bn The Dorsetshire Regt.

1. 9. 16

Instructions regarding War Diaries and Intelligence Summaries are contained in F. S. Regs., Part II. and the Staff Manual respectively. Title pages will be prepared in manuscript.

WAR DIARY
or
~~INTELLIGENCE SUMMARY.~~
(Erase heading not required.)

1st DORSET REGT.

Army Form C. 2118.

Place	Date 1916	Hour	Summary of Events and Information	Remarks and references to Appendices
ANNEZIN.	AUG. 1st	–	Battalion in billets in ANNEZIN training. (Division at rest) HCB	BETHUNE combined sheet 36.A.SE. 36.S.W. 36.B.N.E. 36.C.N.W. Edition 6.
Ditto.	" 2nd	–	Ditto. HCB	
Ditto.	" 3rd	–	Ditto. 1 officer & 50 other ranks sent to forward area for mining operations. HCB	
Ditto.	" 4th	–	Ditto. HCB	
		6.30pm	Battalion left ANNEZIN and marched to LE QUESNOY, arriving there 7.45 pm. Bivouacked in LE QUESNOY WOOD night of 4th/5th Aug.	
LE QUESNOY				
	" 5th		Battalion relieved 2nd EAST LANCASHIRE REGT. in CUINCHY RIGHT subsector (BOYAU 17 to BOYAU 31), marching from LE QUESNOY at 11.50 am at platoon intervals of 100 yards. Relief complete 3.05 pm. Situation quiet. HCB	AUCHY trench map.
CUINCHY Right subsector				
Ditto.	" 6th		In trenches - CUINCHY Right subsector. A.C. & D Coys front line; B. Coy in support. Situation normal. enemy active with snipers & rifle grenades. 1.O.R. killed 1.O.R. wounded. HCB	
Ditto.	" 7th		Ditto. HCB	
		8.31pm	We exploded a mine opposite right company's sector (A. Coy), troops having previously been withdrawn from vicinity. Enemy evidently unprepared and some casualties caused to him. Our bombers occupied near "lip" of crater while party was digging sap to consolidate position. Our artillery established a heavy barrage on enemy's lines for half-an-hour after explosion of the mine; enemy's retaliation was weak and without effect. Casualties: 1.O.R wounded and 2/Lieut SHADDICK killed.	
Ditto.	" 8th		Situation very quiet. A. Coy relieved by B. Coy. 1.O.R wounded. HCB	
Ditto.	" 9th		Ditto. Practise Gas Alarm carried out. 1.O.R. killed. 4.O.R. wounded. HCB	

Army Form C. 2118.

Instructions regarding War Diaries and Intelligence Summaries are contained in F. S. Regs., Part II. and the Staff Manual respectively. Title pages will be prepared in manuscript.

WAR DIARY
or
~~INTELLIGENCE SUMMARY.~~

(*Erase heading not required.*)

1st DORSETSHIRE Rgt.

Place	Date 1916	Hour	Summary of Events and Information	Remarks and references to Appendices
CUINCHY Right subsector	AUG. 10th	-	Situation normal. A. Coy. relieved D. Coy. Casualties. 1 O.R. died of wounds 3 O.R. wounded.	HB
do.	" 11th	-	Situation normal. Practise gas alarm carried out at 9.15 am.	HB
		6.30 pm	Battalion relieved by 15th H.L.I. and withdrew to close support in HARLEY St. VILLAGE LINE and KEEPS — taking over from 2nd Manchester Rgt. Two platoons of D. Coy. remained in TOWER RESERVE TRENCH to carry for 15th H.L.I.	
In close support to CUINCHY Sector.	" 12th		Battalion in Brigade close support, garrisoning KEEPS etc. and providing R.E. working parties.	HB
do	" 13th		Ditto.	HB
do.	" 14th		Ditto. A. Coy provided one platoon to garrison PARK LANE REDOUBT (A.21.b.6/2) and 'B' Coy. one platoon to garrison CABBAGE PATCH REDOUBT (A.15. d.6/0.) Re-inforcement 14 other ranks arrived.	HB
do.	" 15th		In Brigade close support and garrisoning KEEPS. A. Company's headquarters fired at by enemy 77 mm. guns. About 28 shells fired damaging building but causing no casualties. Capt. Hon. E.S. HEWITT. D.S.O. arrived and assumed command of Battalion.	HB
do.	" 16th		In Brigade close support and garrisoning KEEPS.	HB
do. and CUINCHY Right subsector	" 17th	4.05 pm.	Battalion relieved 15th H.L.I. in CUINCHY right subsection, and continued to garrison RUSSELL & PARK LANE REDOUBTS.	HB

2353 Wt. W2544/1454 700,000 5/15 D. D. & L. A.D.S.S./Forms/C. 2118.

Instructions regarding War Diaries and Intelligence Summaries are contained in F. S. Regs., Part II. and the Staff Manual respectively. Title pages will be prepared in manuscript.

WAR DIARY
or
INTELLIGENCE SUMMARY.
(Erase heading not required.)

Army Form C. 2118.

Place	Date 1916	Hour	Summary of Events and Information	Remarks and references to Appendices
CUINCHY Right subsection	AUG. 18th		Situation very quiet. 2/Lieut BURROUGHS. died of wounds. 1. O.R. wounded	HCB
Do.	" 19th		Situation normal. At 6.30 pm enemy blew a mine opposite Battn. on our right. No activity followed. Re-inforcement 31. O.R. arrived. 1. O.R. killed 4. O.R. wounded	HCB HCB
Do.	" 20th		Situation normal. Our stokes gun very active. 2. O.R. killed Reinforcement of 18. O.R. arrived.	HCB
Do.	" 21st		Situation normal. 3. O. R. wounded.	HCB
Do.	" 22nd		Situation quiet. till 3 pm when our artillery bombarded enemy saps and front line from A.21. d 83/15. to A.21. d. 88/88. for 10 minutes, our own saps being cleared of men previously. Enemy retaliation was not heavy. 2. O. R. wounded.	HCB
Do.	" 22nd		Draft of 8 OFFICERS arrived from 3rd Bn.	
Do.	25th		Battalion relieved by 15th H.L.I and marched to LE QUESNOY leaving 1 Officer & 20 O.R as a carrying party in B. ANNEQUIN. 1 OFFICER and 50 O.R in ANNEQUIN as carrying party. 2 OFFICERS and 1 PLATOON in CAMBRIN + BRADDELL KEEPS. ~~Bn arrived~~ Relief complete at 7.10 pm. Bn arrived in Billets 9.55 pm. 4 O.R. killed. 3 O.R wounded. Situation very quiet. Our artillery fairly active.	HCB HCB

H. C. Butcher Lieut & Adjutant

8353 Wt. W2544/1454 700,000 5/15 D. D. & L. A.D.S.S./Forms/C. 2118.

Instructions regarding War Diaries and Intelligence Summaries are contained in F. S. Regs., Part II. and the Staff Manual respectively. Title pages will be prepared in manuscript.

WAR DIARY
or
INTELLIGENCE SUMMARY.
(Erase heading not required.)

Army Form C. 2118.

Place	Date 1916	Hour	Summary of Events and Information	Remarks and references to Appendices
LE QUESNOY	24th Aug.		Battalion in Billets at LE QUESNOY training (Brigade reserve) 1 O.R. wounded	AHB
Do	25th ..		Do Do Draft of 11 OFFICERS arrived.	AHB
Do	26th ..		Do Do	AHB
Do	27th ..		Do Do	AHB
Do	28th ..		Do Do	AHB
Do	29th ..		Battalion relieved the 15th H.L.I. in CUINCHY right sub sector (BOYAU 17 to BOYAU 31) leaving LE QUESNOY at 1.00 p.m at platoon intervals of 3 minutes. Relief complete at 4.45 p.m. Situation quiet. Slight Artillery activity on our part.	AHB
CUINCHY right sub sector	30th ..		Owing to very bad weather conditions the night was occupied in the evacuation of water from the trenches & dug outs. Some trenches waist deep. Saps in very bad condition. COMPTON SAP fell in, but was cleared. 1 O.R. wounded & 1 Accidentally killed. Situation unusually quiet owing to weather. Slight activity on the part of our ARTILLERY & T.M's	AHB
Do	31st ..		Trenches, both communication & front line, still in very bad condition owing to more rain falling. The left Company are obliged to use some of the trenches of Bn on left for communication between Coy H.2 & front line. All saps are in very bad condition. COMPTON & SOUTH MIDNIGHT have been evacuated. 1 O.R. wounded	AHB

A G N Bull [?]
2/Lieut & adjt.

Unit 1st Bn The Dorsetshire Regt.
Place In the Field
Date 3. 8. 16

FIELD STATE.

Army Form B 231.

To be rendered in accordance with Field Service Regulations, Part II.

UNIT	FIGHTING STRENGTH — This should *not* include details attached to unit, or personnel detailed to march with the Train, or any men unfit to go into action with unit											RATION STRENGTH — To include Fighting Strength, Personnel detailed to march with the Train, and all Personnel and animals attached for Rations and Forage										
	Personnel		Horses and Mules		Other Animals		Guns and Ammunition Wagons (stating nature)	Machine Guns	Ambulances	Tool Carts, Technical Carts (stating nature)	Remarks	Personnel	Horses and Mules		Other Animals		Mechanically Propelled Vehicles					Remarks
	Officers	Other Ranks	Riding	Draught and Pack								Total, all Ranks entitled to Rations.	Heavy Horses	Other Horses and Mules			Motor Cars	Motor Bicycles.	Lorries. 3 Ton	Lorries. 30 Cwt.	Tractors	
(1)	(2)	(3)	(4)	(5)	(6)	(7)	(8)	(9)	(10)	(11)	(12)	(13)	(14)	(15)	(16)	(17)	(18)	(19)	(20)	(21)	(22)	(23)
1/Battalion The Dorsetshire Regiment	30	848.	11	43			8 Lewis Guns	8		14		795		56								detached Officers 6 Other Ranks 85.
TOTALS ...	30	848	11	43.				8		14		795		56								

Ammunition with Unit:—

·303 inch; approximate number of rounds per Man ______

·303 inch; „ „ „ per Machine Gun ______

Gun or Howitzer; approximate number of rounds per Gun or Howitzer ______

Supplies with Unit:—

Approximate number of days' rations for men of ration strength ______

„ „ „ forage for Animals „ „ ______

„ „ „ fuel and lubricants for Mechanically Propelled Vehicles ______

Signature of Commander Captain
Comdg 1st Bn Dorsetshire Regiment

(88762.) Wt.W. 2345—1438. 500,000 5/15. J. P. & Co. Ltd. Forms B 231/3

Unit 1st Bn The Dorsetshire Regiment
Place In the Field
Date 10. 8. 16

FIELD STATE.

Army Form B 231.

To be rendered in accordance with Field Service Regulations, Part II.

UNIT	FIGHTING STRENGTH — This should *not* include details attached to unit, or personnel detailed to march with the Train, or any men unfit to go into action with unit											RATION STRENGTH — To include Fighting Strength, Personnel detailed to march with the Train, and all Personnel and animals attached for Rations and Forage										
	Personnel		Horses and Mules		Other Animals		Guns and Ammunition Wagons (stating nature)	Machine Guns	Ambulances	Tool Carts, Technical Carts (stating nature)	Remarks	Personnel	Horses and Mules		Other Animals		Mechanically Propelled Vehicles					Remarks
	Officers	Other Ranks	Riding	Draught and Pack								Total, all Ranks entitled to Rations.	Heavy Horses	Other Horses and Mules			Motor Cars	Motor Bicycles.	Lorries. 3 Ton	Lorries. 30 Cwt.	Tractors	
(1)	(2)	(3)	(4)	(5)	(6)	(7)	(8)	(9)	(10)	(11)	(12)	(13)	(14)	(15)	(16)	(17)	(18)	(19)	(20)	(21)	(22)	(23)
1/Battalion The Dorsetshire Regiment.	28	830.	11	43			8 Lewis Guns	8		14		765		56								detached Officers 4 Other Ranks 105
TOTALS ...	28	830	11	43				8		14		765		56.								

Ammunition with Unit:—

·303 inch; approximate number of rounds per Man ______

·303 inch; " " " per Machine Gun ______

Gun or Howitzer; approximate number of rounds per Gun or Howitzer ______

Supplies with Unit:—

Approximate number of days' rations for men of ration strength ______

" " " forage for Animals " " ______

" " " fuel and lubricants for Mechanically Propelled Vehicles ______

(88762.) Wt.W. 2345—1438. 500,000 5/15. J. P. & Co. Ltd. Forms B 231 / 3

Signature of Commander Captain
Comdg 1st Bn The Dorsetshire Regt

Unit 1st Bn The Dorsetshire Regt
Place In the Field
Date 14. 8. 16

FIELD STATE.

Army Form B 231.

To be rendered in accordance with Field Service Regulations, Part II.

UNIT	FIGHTING STRENGTH — This should *not* include details attached to unit, or personnel detailed to march with the Train, or any men unfit to go into action with unit											RATION STRENGTH — To include Fighting Strength, Personnel detailed to march with the Train, and all Personnel and animals attached for Rations and Forage										
	Personnel		Horses and Mules		Other Animals		Guns and Ammunition Wagons (stating nature)	Machine Guns	Ambulances	Tool Carts, Technical Carts (stating nature)	Remarks	Personnel	Horses and Mules		Other Animals		Mechanically Propelled Vehicles					Remarks
	Officers	Other Ranks	Riding	Draught and Pack								Total, all Ranks entitled to Rations.	Heavy Horses	Other Horses and Mules			Motor Cars	Motor Bicycles	Lorries. 3 Ton	Lorries. 30 Cwt.	Tractors	
(1)	(2)	(3)	(4)	(5)	(6)	(7)	(8)	(9)	(10)	(11)	(12)	(13)	(14)	(15)	(16)	(17)	(18)	(19)	(20)	(21)	(22)	(23)
1/Battalion The Dorsetshire Regiment	29	842	11	44			9 Lewis Guns	9.		14		483		54.								detached Officers 5. Other Ranks 98
TOTALS ...	29	842	11	44				9		14		483		54								

Ammunition with Unit:—

·303 inch; approximate number of rounds per Man

·303 inch; " " " per Machine Gun

Gun or Howitzer; approximate number of rounds per Gun or Howitzer

Supplies with Unit:—

Approximate number of days' rations for men of ration strength

" " " forage for Animals " "

" " " fuel and lubricants for Mechanically Propelled Vehicles

(88762.) Wt. W. 2345—1438. 500,000 5/15. J. P. & Co. Ltd. Forms B 231 / 3

Signature of Commander Captain
1st Bn The Dorsetshire Regiment

Unit 1st Bn The Dorsetshire Regt.

Place In the Field

Date 24 8 16

FIELD STATE.

Army Form B 231.

To be rendered in accordance with Field Service Regulations, Part II.

UNIT	FIGHTING STRENGTH — This should *not* include details attached to unit, or personnel detailed to march with the Train, or any men unfit to go into action with unit											RATION STRENGTH — To include Fighting Strength, Personnel detailed to march with the Train, and all Personnel and animals attached for Rations and Forage										
	Personnel		Horses and Mules		Other Animals		Guns and Ammunition Wagons (stating nature)	Machine Guns	Ambulances	Tool Carts, Technical Carts (stating nature)	Remarks	Personnel	Horses and Mules		Other Animals		Mechanically Propelled Vehicles					Remarks
	Officers	Other Ranks	Riding	Draught and Pack								Total, all Ranks entitled to Rations.	Heavy Horses	Other Horses and Mules			Motor Cars	Motor Bicycles.	Lorries. 3 Ton	Lorries. 30 Cwt.	Tractors	
(1)	(2)	(3)	(4)	(5)	(6)	(7)	(8)	(9)	(10)	(11)	(12)	(13)	(14)	(15)	(16)	(17)	(18)	(19)	(20)	(21)	(22)	(23)
1/Battalion The Dorsetshire Regiment	40	840	11	44			9 Lewis Guns	9		14		831		54.								detached. Officers 5 Other Ranks 89
TOTALS ...	40	840	11	44.				9		14		831		54								

Ammunition with Unit:—

·303 inch; approximate number of rounds per Man ____

·303 inch; " " " per Machine Gun ____

Gun or Howitzer; approximate number of rounds per Gun or Howitzer ____

Supplies with Unit:—

Approximate number of days' rations for men of ration strength ____

" " " forage for Animals " " ____

" " " fuel and lubricants for Mechanically Propelled Vehicles ____

(88762.) Wt.W. 2345—1438. 500,000 5/15. J. P. & Co. Ltd. Forms B 231/3

Signature of Commander Captain

Comdg. 1st Bn The Dorsetshire Regt.

Unit 1st Bn. The Dorsetshire Regt.

Place In the Field

Date 31. 8. 16

FIELD STATE.

Army Form B 231.

To be rendered in accordance with Field Service Regulations, Part II.

UNIT	FIGHTING STRENGTH — This should *not* include details attached to unit, or personnel detailed to march with the Train, or any men unfit to go into action with unit											RATION STRENGTH — To include Fighting Strength, Personnel detailed to march with the Train, and all Personnel and animals attached for Rations and Forage										Remarks
	Personnel		Horses and Mules		Other Animals		Guns and Ammunition Wagons (stating nature)	Machine Guns	Ambulances	Tool Carts, Technical Carts (stating nature)	Remarks	Personnel	Horses and Mules		Other Animals		Mechanically Propelled Vehicles					
	Officers	Other Ranks	Riding	Draught and Pack								Total, all Ranks entitled to Rations.	Heavy Horses	Other Horses and Mules			Motor Cars	Motor Bicycles	Lorries. 3 Ton	Lorries. 30 Cwt.	Tractors	
(1)	(2)	(3)	(4)	(5)	(6)	(7)	(8)	(9)	(10)	(11)	(12)	(13)	(14)	(15)	(16)	(17)	(18)	(19)	(20)	(21)	(22)	(23)
	40	860	10	43			9 Lewis Guns	9		14		818		55								detached Officers 4 Other Ranks 88.
TOTALS ...	40	860	10	43				9		14		818		55								

Ammunition with Unit:—

·303 inch; approximate number of rounds per Man ______

·303 inch; " " " per Machine Gun ______

Gun or Howitzer; approximate number of rounds per Gun or Howitzer ______

Supplies with Unit:—

Approximate number of days' rations for men of ration strength ______

" " " forage for Animals " " ______

" " " fuel and lubricants for Mechanically Propelled Vehicles ______

Signature of Commander Captain

Comdg. 1st Bn. The Dorsetshire Regt.

(88762.) Wt.W. 2345—1438. 500,000 5/15. J. P. & Co. Ltd. Forms B 231 / 3

14th Brigade.

32nd Division.

1st BATTALION

THE DORSETSHIRE REGIMENT

SEPTEMBER 1 9 1 6

Appendices attached:-

Field States.

Army Form C. 2118.

WAR DIARY
or
~~INTELLIGENCE~~ SUMMARY
(Erase heading not required.)

1st Dorset Regt

Instructions regarding War Diaries and Intelligence Summaries are contained in F. S. Regs., Part II. and the Staff Manual respectively. Title Pages will be prepared in manuscript.

Place	Date 1916	Hour	Summary of Events and Information	Remarks and references to Appendices
CUINCHY Right subsection.	Sept. 1st	–	Situation quiet. Our Stokes guns and artillery somewhat active.	H.B.
"	" 2nd	–	Situation very quiet. Several patrols sent out at night to find a way across to enemy lines.	H.B.
"	" 3rd	–	Situation normal during the night, with artillery and Trench Mortar activity during the day. Test gas alarm carried out at 2.30 pm. Lieut. BARKER wounded, 1 O.R. killed, 1 O.R. wounded and 1 O.R. wounded and taken prisoner when on patrol.	H.B.
"	" 4th	–	Little activity during the day, except that our artillery bombarded enemy's line for 15 minutes about 11 am. Very little retaliation from enemy who fired a few MINNENWERFER bombs during the afternoon. Battalion relieved by 15th H.L.I. — relief complete at 5.35 pm. Withdrew to Brigade support with Hdqrs. in HARLEY Street, — two platoons remaining to work for 15th H.L.I.	
In Bde. support in KEEPS and HARLEY St.	" 5th	–	D. Coy. moved to LE QUESNOY to practise raid. Remainder of Battn. finding parties to work in trenches.	
	" 6th	-	Battalion finding parties to work in trenches. Preparations being made for carrying out raid. Hydraulic Pump & "Push Pipe" taken up to front line to clear a road through enemy wire. "Push Pipe" delayed & could not be used. Bangalore Torpedoes prepared instead. At 1.00 am night of 6th – 7th, owing to a misunderstanding, Artillery opened barrage fire. ZERO time was 1.15 am. Raid not carried out	H.B.

2449 Wt. W14957/M90 750,000 1/16 J.B.C. & A. Forms/C.2118/12.

Army Form C. 2118.

Instructions regarding War Diaries and Intelligence Summaries are contained in F. S. Regs., Part II. and the Staff Manual respectively. Title Pages will be prepared in manuscript.

WAR DIARY
or
~~INTELLIGENCE SUMMARY~~
(Erase heading not required.)

Place	Date	Hour	Summary of Events and Information	Remarks and references to Appendices
In Bde Support Keep + Harley St.	7.9.16		Battalion providing parties to work in trenches. Lieut H. C. BUTCHER rejoined from Special leave. Arrangements made for a small party to raid enemy trenches that night. "Push Pipe" in position at 1.30 am. Raiding party of 2nd Lieuts LAWES + FOSTER + 30 OR ready at 1.30 am. ZERO TIME 1.40 a.m. Explosion of pipe occurred at 1.40 a.m. Raiding party went forward after explosion, were heavily bombed by the enemy. No enemy actually encountered. Party returned at 2.00 am. 2nd Lieuts LAWES + FOSTER wounded 3 O.R. wounded 1. O.R. slightly wounded returned to duty. Raid in charge of CAPT. S. LANCASTER.	A.H.B.
	8th		Battalion relieved by the 2nd Bn K.O.Y.L.I. Regt. 14th Inf. Bde relieved by the 96th Inf. Bde + go into Divisional Reserve. Bn Relief complete at 5.50 pm. Bn went into billets in BETHUNE in TOBACCO FACTORY.	A.H.B.
BETHUNE	9th		Battalion in Billets in BETHUNE.	A.H.B.
	10th		" " "	A.H.B.
	11th		" " "	A.H.B.

2449 Wt. W14957/M90 750,000 1/16 J.B.C. & A. Forms/C.2118/12.

Army Form C. 2118.

Instructions regarding War Diaries and Intelligence Summaries are contained in F. S. Regs., Part II. and the Staff Manual respectively. Title Pages will be prepared in manuscript.

WAR DIARY
or
~~INTELLIGENCE~~ SUMMARY

(Erase heading not required.)

Place	Date	Hour	Summary of Events and Information	Remarks and references to Appendices
BETHUNE	11th Sept	-	Battalion in Billets in BETHUNE.	A.R.B.
	12th	-	" " " Battalion provided R.E. working party of 500 O.R. C.S.M. SHEPHARD left to join G.H.Q. Cadet School, BLENDEQUES.	A.R.B.
	13th		Battalion in Billets in BETHUNE.	A.R.B.
	14th		" " " 2 Officer Reinforcements 2/Lieut CHAMBERLAIN and YOUNG	A.R.B.
	15th		Battalion in Billets in BETHUNE	A.R.B.
	16th		" " " , Orders to do tour in trenches cancelled, + orders to be ready to move by rail or march route the following day, received. 2/Lieut. ALLBON & 50 O.R. MINING fatigue at ANNEQUIN rejoined Battalion	A.R.B.
	17th		Battalion moved to ECOIVRES by march route, starting 10 am + arriving at 4.30 pm.	A.R.B.
ECOIVRES	18th		Battalion in Huts at ECOIVRES.	
	19th		Two Companies moved into Dugouts in the Line. A Coy at MAISON BLANCHE + B. Coy at MOISSONEUSE for work under direction of 180th Bde. Work, being digging trenches, very difficult owing to heavy rainfall. C + D. Coys provide working parties under direction of 179th Bde.	A.R.B.

2449 Wt. W14957/M90 750,000 1/16 J.B.C. & A. Forms/C.2118/12.

Instructions regarding War Diaries and Intelligence Summaries are contained in F. S. Regs., Part II. and the Staff Manual respectively. Title Pages will be prepared in manuscript.

Army Form C. 2118.

WAR DIARY
or
~~INTELLIGENCE SUMMARY~~
(Erase heading not required.)

Place	Date	Hour	Summary of Events and Information	Remarks and references to Appendices
ECOIVRES	19 Sept	-	A & B. Coys return from forward area to Huts at ECOIVRES	AHB
	20th		Battalion marched out of ECOIVRES at 10 am & arrive ANNEQUIN at 4.00 pm	AHB
ANNEQUIN	21st		Battalion in Billets at ANNEQUIN. 1 Officer, 50 o.R. sent on permanent mining fatigue at ANNEQUIN	AHB
	22nd		Reinforcements 6 o.R. joined the Battalion. Battalion relieved the 2nd Manchester Regt in CAMBRIN right subsector. Relief complete at 4.20 pm. D Coy on right & C. Coy on left both in front line. A Coy in ARTHUR, SIMS & RAILWAY KEEPS & B. Coy in OLD BOOTS SUPPORT TRENCH. Trenches in bad condition, particularly front line between BOYAUX 4 & 5. Dugout accomodation poor.	AHB
CAMBRIN right sub. sector	23rd		Situation quiet. No retaliation by the enemy to our Rifle Grenade, Machine, & Stokes Gun Fire. Grenades in this sub sector in a rusty & uncared for condition. Work done on Front Line between BOYAUX 4 & 5. MAP POINT SAPS & RAILWAY SAPS in a very muddy & wet state owing to rain. Work of clearing these latter is proceeding. Dirty & rusty grenades are oiled & cleaned.	AHB

2449 Wt. W14957/M90 750,000 1/16 J.B.C. & A. Forms/C.2118/12.

Army Form C. 2118.

WAR DIARY
or
~~INTELLIGENCE SUMMARY~~

(Erase heading not required.)

Instructions regarding War Diaries and Intelligence Summaries are contained in F. S. Regs., Part II. and the Staff Manual respectively. Title Pages will be prepared in manuscript.

Place	Date	Hour	Summary of Events and Information	Remarks and references to Appendices
CAMBRIN right subsector	24th Sept	.	Situation very quiet. A few 4.2 enemy shells fell on our left front. doing no damage. T.M. fire intermittently all day. Our RIFLE GRENADE fire unanswered. Trenches gradually being improved, rain having stopped. Front line between BOYAUX 5 + 6 deepened. Duckboards relaid between BOYAU 6 + 9 in front line. A PATROL of 2 OR. reported our wire at A 27 d. 80.78 although only 2 feet high, to be thick & very good "A". Company moved to Billets in ANNEQUIN. "B" Company take over ARTHUR, SIMS & RAILWAY KEEPS	AHB
	25th		Situation quiet. No ARTILLERY activity. Our T M s cut enemy wire with slow fire & drew no retaliation. Trenches in a fair condition, as a result of continuous work. MAD POINT SAP had started to fall in, but was repaired. All SAPS are drained & fairly dry. 2nd Lieut DYASON & Sgt HALLINAN reconnoitred enemy wire & heard only 1 man walk along enemy trench during 2 hours listening. Sgt HANDS & Cpl HARPER left at 3. am & returned 4 am. reported enemy wire thick & good. Cpl WATTS + 3 OR left our trench ~~at~~ 11 pm to endeavour to surprise enemy working party in gap made in enemy wire by our T.M. after waiting 2 hours they withdrew - heard nothing of enemy. Cpl CARTER & 2 OR. reconnoitred enemy wire from 1 am to 2 am. Battalion held Test Gas Alarm at 2.00 pm. 2nd Lieut F. CHADWELL reported from Special leave.	AHB

2449 Wt. W14957/M90 750,000 1/16 J.B.C. & A. Forms/C.2118/12.

Army Form C. 2118.

Instructions regarding War Diaries and Intelligence Summaries are contained in F. S. Regs., Part II. and the Staff Manual respectively. Title Pages will be prepared in manuscript.

WAR DIARY
or
~~INTELLIGENCE SUMMARY~~
(Erase heading not required.)

Place	Date	Hour	Summary of Events and Information	Remarks and references to Appendices
CAMBRIN right sub sector	26th	-	Situation quiet. little ARTILLERY or T.M. activity, during morning. During the night Sally Ports were cleared. Snipers post has been constructed. Part of BOYAU 1 has been blown in by hostile T.M. Battalion, with the exception of 'B' Company who remained in KEEPS, were relieved by the 2nd Manchester Regt. Relief complete 3.15 pm. The Battalion relieved the 5/6 Royal Scots in the VILLAGE LINE & LEWIS KEEP. 2nd Lieut BILLOT reported from Hospital.	AHB
VILLAGE LINE in Bde Reserve	27th		Battalion in RESERVE in VILLAGE LINE. Supplying working parties & carrying parties for T.M. ammunition. "B" Coy, less one platoon in VILLAGE LINE, in KEEPS. "A" Coy still in Billets in ANNEQUIN. "A" Coy moved from ANNEQUIN to Dug outs in VILLAGE SUPPORT LINE. 1 O.R. wounded & subsequently died of wounds.	AHB
	28th		Battalion in Dug outs in VILLAGE LINE supplying working parties & carrying parties. Work of lifting duck boards & digging drains in VILLAGE LINE carried on. MAISON ROUGE ALLEY cleared of Sandbags & rubbish. 2nd Lieut G. N. WOOD joined the Battalion.	AHB
	29th		Battalion in VILLAGE LINE supplying working & carrying parties, & working on VILLAGE LINE	AHB
	30th	1.30 pm	Battalion in VILLAGE LINE finding working & carrying parties. Battalion, less one Company, relieve the 2nd Manchester Regiment in the CAMBRIN right sub sector.	AHB

2449 Wt. W14957/M90 750,000 1/16 J.B.C. & A. Forms/C.2118/12.

Instructions regarding War Diaries and Intelligence Summaries are contained in F. S. Regs., Part II. and the Staff Manual respectively. Title Pages will be prepared in manuscript.

WAR DIARY
or
~~INTELLIGENCE SUMMARY~~

(Erase heading not required.)

Army Form C. 2118.

Place	Date	Hour	Summary of Events and Information	Remarks and references to Appendices
VILLAGE LINE in Bde Reserve	30th Sept		"A" Company (attached to the 15th Bn Highland Light Infantry in the CAMBRIN left sub sector) relieved one Company of the 5/6th Royal Scots. Relief complete by 3.00 pm.	A.S.L.B.

A S L Bubb Lt a/Adjt
1st Dorset Regiment

2449 Wt. W14957/M90 750,000 1/16 J.B.C. & A. Forms/C.2118/12.

Unit 1st Bn. The Dorsetshire Regt

Place In the Field

Date 4. 9. 16

FIELD STATE.

Army Form B 231.

To be rendered in accordance with Field Service Regulations, Part II.

UNIT	FIGHTING STRENGTH — This should *not* include details attached to unit, or personnel detailed to march with the Train, or any men unfit to go into action with unit											RATION STRENGTH — To include Fighting Strength, Personnel detailed to march with the Train, and all Personnel and animals attached for Rations and Forage										
	Personnel		Horses and Mules		Other Animals		Guns and Ammunition Wagons (stating nature)	Machine Guns	Ambulances	Tool Carts, Technical Carts (stating nature)	Remarks	Personnel	Horses and Mules		Other Animals		Mechanically Propelled Vehicles					Remarks
	Officers	Other Ranks	Riding	Draught and Pack								Total, all Ranks entitled to Rations.	Heavy Horses	Other Horses and Mules			Motor Cars	Motor Bicycles.	Lorries. 3 Ton	Lorries. 30 Cwt.	Tractors	
(1)	(2)	(3)	(4)	(5)	(6)	(7)	(8)	(9)	(10)	(11)	(12)	(13)	(14)	(15)	(16)	(17)	(18)	(19)	(20)	(21)	(22)	(23)
1st Dorset Regt.	39	844	10	43			9 Lewis Guns	9		14		796		55								
TOTALS ...	39	844	10	43				9		14		796		55								

Ammunition with Unit:—

·303 inch; approximate number of rounds per Man ______

·303 inch; ,, ,, ,, per Machine Gun ______

Gun or Howitzer; approximate number of rounds per Gun or Howitzer ______

Supplies with Unit:—

Approximate number of days' rations for men of ration strength ______

,, ,, ,, forage for Animals ,, ,, ______

,, ,, ,, fuel and lubricants for Mechanically Propelled Vehicles ______

Signature of Commander Sd/ H. C. Butcher Lt/a Major
Comdg 1st Dorset Regiment

(88762.) Wt.W. 2345—1438. 500,000 5/15. J. P. & Co. Ltd. Forms B 231/3

Unit 1st Bn The Dorsetshire Regt

Place In the Field

Date 14. 9. 16

FIELD STATE.

Army Form B 231.

To be rendered in accordance with Field Service Regulations, Part II.

FIGHTING STRENGTH (columns 2–12): This should *not* include details attached to unit, or personnel detailed to march with the Train, or any men unfit to go into action with unit

RATION STRENGTH (columns 13–23): To include Fighting Strength, Personnel detailed to march with the Train, and all Personnel and animals attached for Rations and Forage

UNIT	Personnel		Horses and Mules		Other Animals		Guns and Ammunition Wagons (stating nature)	Machine Guns	Ambulances	Tool Carts, Technical Carts (stating nature)	Remarks	Personnel	Horses and Mules		Other Animals		Mechanically Propelled Vehicles					Remarks
	Officers	Other Ranks	Riding	Draught and Pack								Total, all Ranks entitled to Rations.	Heavy Horses	Other Horses and Mules			Motor Cars	Motor Bicycles.	Lorries. 3 Ton	Lorries. 30 Cwt.	Tractors	
(1)	(2)	(3)	(4)	(5)	(6)	(7)	(8)	(9)	(10)	(11)	(12)	(13)	(14)	(15)	(16)	(17)	(18)	(19)	(20)	(21)	(22)	(23)
	37	840	11	43			9 Lewis Guns	9		14		783	–	56								
TOTALS ...	37	840	11	43				9		14		783		56								

Ammunition with Unit:—

·303 inch; approximate number of rounds per Man______

·303 inch; „ „ „ per Machine Gun______

Gun or Howitzer; approximate number of rounds per Gun or Howitzer______

Supplies with Unit:—

Approximate number of days' rations for men of ration strength______

„ „ „ forage for Animals „ „______

„ „ „ fuel and lubricants for Mechanically Propelled Vehicles______

Signature of Commander (Sd) [illegible] for Major
Comdg 1st Dorset Regiment

(88762.) Wt.W. 2345—1438. 500,000 5/15. J. P. & Co. Ltd. Forms B 231 / 3

Army Form B 231.

FIELD STATE.

Unit 1st Bn Dorsetshire Regiment

Place In the Field

Date 21 — 9 — 16

To be rendered in accordance with Field Service Regulations, Part II.

FIGHTING STRENGTH — This should *not* include details attached to unit, or personnel detailed to march with the Train, or any men unfit to go into action with unit

RATION STRENGTH — To include Fighting Strength, Personnel detailed to march with the Train, and all Personnel and animals attached for Rations and Forage

UNIT	Fighting Strength: Personnel		Horses and Mules		Other Animals		Guns and Ammunition Wagons (stating nature)	Machine Guns	Ambulances	Tool Carts, Technical Carts (stating nature)	Remarks	Ration Strength: Personnel	Horses and Mules		Other Animals		Mechanically Propelled Vehicles					Remarks
	Officers	Other Ranks	Riding	Draught and Pack								Total, all Ranks entitled to Rations.	Heavy Horses	Other Horses and Mules			Motor Cars	Motor Bicycles.	Lorries. 3 Ton	Lorries. 30 Cwt.	Tractors	
(1)	(2)	(3)	(4)	(5)	(6)	(7)	(8)	(9)	(10)	(11)	(12)	(13)	(14)	(15)	(16)	(17)	(18)	(19)	(20)	(21)	(22)	(23)
	39	836	11	44			8 Lewis Guns	8		14		798		54								
TOTALS ...	39	836	11	44				8		14		798		54								

Ammunition with Unit:—

·303 inch; approximate number of rounds per Man ______

·303 inch; " " " per Machine Gun ______

Gun or Howitzer; approximate number of rounds per Gun or Howitzer ______

Supplies with Unit:—

Approximate number of days' rations for men of ration strength ______

" " " forage for Animals " " ______

" " " fuel and lubricants for Mechanically Propelled Vehicles ______

Signature of Commander [illegible] for Major

Comdg. 1st Dorset Regiment

(88762.) Wt. W. 2345—1438. 500,000 5/15. J. P. & Co. Ltd. Forms B 231 / 3

Unit: 1st Bn Dorsetshire Regt
Place: In the Field
Date: 25.9.16

FIELD STATE.

Army Form B 231.

To be rendered in accordance with Field Service Regulations, Part II.

UNIT	FIGHTING STRENGTH — This should *not* include details attached to unit, or personnel detailed to march with the Train, or any men unfit to go into action with unit											RATION STRENGTH — To include Fighting Strength, Personnel detailed to march with the Train, and all Personnel and animals attached for Rations and Forage										
	Personnel		Horses and Mules		Other Animals							Personnel	Horses and Mules		Other Animals		Mechanically Propelled Vehicles					
	Officers	Other Ranks	Riding	Draught and Pack			Guns and Ammunition Wagons (stating nature)	Machine Guns	Ambulances	Tool Carts, Technical Carts (stating nature)	Remarks	Total, all Ranks entitled to Rations.	Heavy Horses	Other Horses and Mules			Motor Cars	Motor Bicycles.	Lorries. 3 Ton	Lorries. 30 Cwt.	Tractors	Remarks
(1)	(2)	(3)	(4)	(5)	(6)	(7)	(8)	(9)	(10)	(11)	(12)	(13)	(14)	(15)	(16)	(17)	(18)	(19)	(20)	(21)	(22)	(23)
	40	843	11	44			5 Lewis Guns	5		17		789		56								9 officers 97 OR detached
TOTALS ...	40	843	11	44				5		17		789		56								

Ammunition with Unit:—

·303 inch; approximate number of rounds per Man ______

·303 inch; " " " per Machine Gun ______

Gun or Howitzer; approximate number of rounds per Gun or Howitzer ______

Supplies with Unit:—

Approximate number of days' rations for men of ration strength ______

" " " forage for Animals " " ______

" " " fuel and lubricants for Mechanically Propelled Vehicles ______

Signature of Commander (Sd) A L Bald Lt for Major
Cmdg 1/Dorsetshire Regt

(88762.) Wt.W. 2345—1438. 500,000 5/15. J. P. & Co. Ltd. Forms B 231 / 3

14th Brigade.

32nd Division.

1st BATTALION

THE DORSETSHIRE REGIMENT

OCTOBER 1 9 1 6

Appendices attached:-

Field States.

Instructions regarding War Diaries and Intelligence Summaries are contained in F. S. Regs., Part II. and the Staff Manual respectively. Title pages will be prepared in manuscript.

WAR DIARY
or
INTELLIGENCE SUMMARY.
(Erase heading not required.)

Army Form C. 2118.

Place	Date	Hour	Summary of Events and Information	Remarks and references to Appendices
CAMBRIN rt sub-section	1st Oct.		Battalion in front line trenches. Situation very quiet. No ARTILLERY or TRENCH MORTAR activity on either side. Weather wet & trenches in muddy condition. Reinforcements 4 OR arrived. Working parties at work day & night on trenches. Battalion has 2 Coys in front line, 1 Coy in SIMS, ARTHOR & RAILWAY KEEPS. One Coy lent to 15th H.L.I. for period in trenches.	AhB
"	2nd "	3 am.	Situation fairly quiet. Some T.M. fire by us, enemy retaliation with MINENWERFERS doing no damage. All possible men at work on trenches & SAPS cleaning out mud & water	AhB
"	"	3 pm.	T.M. bombardment of enemy front line & trenches generally by us for 1 hour between MINE POINT and RAILWAY SAP.	AhB
"	"	9 pm to 12 midnight	H.L.I. sent out patrols in front of our line. Parties at work in our trenches repairing floors & sides. Orders for move received.	AhB
	3rd "	3 am	Situation quiet. Our T.M. fire drew no hostile retaliation. Working parties improving trenches which are steadily getting dryer. Weather much improved but still wet. The 'A' Company with 15th H.L.I. relieved "D" Company in our front line. "C" Company proceeded to Billets at ANNEQUIN prior to going to Divisional School FERFAY. Relief of Coys complete 3.15 pm. 1 O.R. slightly wounded	AhB
	4th "	12 midnight to 4 am	15th H.L.I. send out patrols along our front between BOYAU 8 & RAILWAY SAP. Parties out wiring along the rest of our front. Situation very quiet. Trenches much dryer & weather a good deal improved.	AhB
	"	10 am	"C" Company proceeding to FERFAY by march route. 6 officers & 98 OR.	
	"	2.30 pm	Battalion (less C Company marching to FERFAY) relieved by 11th BORDER REGT.	
	"	3.00 pm	Battalion proceed to ANNEZIN by march route arriving at 5. pm.	AhB

#353 Wt. W2544/1454, 700,000 5/15 D. D. & L. A.D.S.S./Forms/C. 2118.

Instructions regarding War Diaries and Intelligence Summaries are contained in F. S. Regs., Part II. and the Staff Manual respectively. Title pages will be prepared in manuscript.

WAR DIARY
or
~~INTELLIGENCE~~ SUMMARY.
(Erase heading not required.)

Army Form C. 2118.

Place	Date	Hour	Summary of Events and Information	Remarks and references to Appendices
ANNEZIN	5th Oct		Battalion in Billets at ANNEZIN. Training	AHB
"	6th "		" " " " " "	AHB
"	7th "		" " " " " "	AHB
"	8th "		" " " " " Whole Battalion on fatigue	AHB
"	9th "		" " " " " Training	AHB
LA PERRIERE	10th "		" " LA PERRIERE. left ANNEZIN at 9 40 a m. arrived LA PERRIERE 12.50 pm	AHB
"	11th "		" " " " " " Training	AHB
"	12th "		" " " " " "	AHB
"	13th "		" " " " " "	AHB
"	14th "		" " " " " " "C" Company rejoined Battalion from Divisional School. FERFAY	AHB
"	15th "	9.00am	Battalion moved by March Route to FLORINGHEM arriving at 12 30 pm. Reinforcements 50 OR arrived.	AHB
FLORINGHEM	16th "	7.30am	Battalion moved by March Route to AVERDOINGT arriving at 12 30 pm.	AHB
AVERDOINGT	17th "	8.45am	" " " " " REBREUVIETTE carrying out a Brigade Tactical Scheme on the road, arriving in Billets at 12 30 pm.	AHB

2353 Wt. W2544/1454 700,000 5/15 D. D. & L. A.D.S.S./Forms/C. 2118.

Instructions regarding War Diaries and Intelligence Summaries are contained in F. S. Regs., Part II. and the Staff Manual respectively. Title Pages will be prepared in manuscript.

WAR DIARY
or
INTELLIGENCE SUMMARY

(Erase heading not required.)

Army Form C. 2118.

Place	Date	Hour	Summary of Events and Information	Remarks and references to Appendices
REBREUVIETTE	18th	7.15am	Battalion moved by March Route to BEAUVAL arriving at 1.45 pm. Reinforcements 2 OR arrived 5. pm.	AhB
BEAUVAL	19th	9.15am	Battalion started by March Route to WARLOY. Move cancelled on the way & Battalion returned to Billets at BEAUVAL arriving at 11.00 am.	AhB
"	20th		Battalion in Billets at ~~W~~ BEAUVAL Training	AhB
BEAUVAL	21st	9.10am	Battalion proceeded by march route to WARLOY. Weather condition good. Genl. GOUGH complimented Battalion on excellent march discipline displayed en route. Battalion arrived at WARLOY at 2.45 pm.	AhB
WARLOY	22nd		Battalion in Billets at WARLOY.	AhB
"	23rd	12.15pm	Battalion marched to BRICKFIELDS AREA between ALBERT and BOUZINCOURT and went into BIVOUACS at 3 pm.	AhB
ALBERT-BOUZINCOURT BRICKFIELDS AREA	24th		Battalion in Bivouacs. Weather conditions worse. Rain started falling.	AhB
"	25th		" " Weather still bad. rain continues. Battalion preparing to go into action	AhB

2449 Wt. W14957/M90 750,000 1/16 J.B.C. & A. Forms/C.2118/12.

Army Form C. 2118.

WAR DIARY
or
INTELLIGENCE SUMMARY
(Erase heading not required.)

Instructions regarding War Diaries and Intelligence Summaries are contained in F. S. Regs., Part II. and the Staff Manual respectively. Title Pages will be prepared in manuscript.

1st DORSET REGT

Place	Date	Hour	Summary of Events and Information	Remarks and references to Appendices
BRICKFIELDS AREA	26th Oct.	10.30am	BATTALION proceeded by march route to CONTAY WOOD, arriving at 2.45 pm.	A.L.B.
CONTAY WOOD	27th		Battalion in Huts in CONTAY WOOD training.	A.L.B.
"	28th		" " " " " " "	
"	29th		" " " " " " "	A.L.B.
"	30th		" " " " " " "	
"	31st		" " " " " ", BRIGADE training carried out.	A.L.B.

A.L. Bubb
Lt. & a/adjt

2449 Wt. W14957/M90 750,000 1/16 J.B.C. & A. Forms/C.2118/12.

Army Form B 231.

FIELD STATE.

Unit 1st Bn Dorset Regt.
Place In the Field
Date 5. 10. 16.

To be rendered in accordance with Field Service Regulations, Part II.

FIGHTING STRENGTH — This should *not* include details attached to unit, or personnel detailed to march with the Train, or any men unfit to go into action with unit

RATION STRENGTH — To include Fighting Strength, Personnel detailed to march with the Train, and all Personnel and animals attached for Rations and Forage

UNIT	Personnel: Officers	Personnel: Other Ranks	Horses and Mules: Riding	Horses and Mules: Draught and Pack	Other Animals	Other Animals	Guns and Ammunition Wagons (stating nature)	Machine Guns	Ambulances	Tool Carts, Technical Carts (stating nature)	Remarks	Personnel: Total, all Ranks entitled to Rations.	Horses and Mules: Heavy Horses	Horses and Mules: Other Horses and Mules	Other Animals	Other Animals	Mechanically Propelled Vehicles: Motor Cars	Motor Bicycles.	Lorries. 3 Ton	Lorries. 30 Cwt.	Tractors	Remarks
(1)	(2)	(3)	(4)	(5)	(6)	(7)	(8)	(9)	(10)	(11)	(12)	(13)	(14)	(15)	(16)	(17)	(18)	(19)	(20)	(21)	(22)	(23)
1st Bn Dorset Regt.	42	834	11	44			8 L. Guns	8				681.	8	47								15 Officers + 197 OR detached from Battn. 2 Offrs + 4 OR attached
TOTALS ...	42	834	11	44				8				681	8	47								

Ammunition with Unit:—

·303 inch; approximate number of rounds per Man ______

·303 inch; " " " per Machine Gun ______

Gun or Howitzer; approximate number of rounds per Gun or Howitzer ______

Supplies with Unit:—

Approximate number of days' rations for men of ration strength ______

" " " forage for Animals " " ______

" " " fuel and lubricants for Mechanically Propelled Vehicles ______

Signature of Commander [illegible] Lt for Major
[illegible]

(88762.) Wt.W. 2345—1438. 500,000 5/15. J. P. & Co. Ltd. Forms B 231 / 3

Unit 1st Bn Dorset Regt.
Place In the Field.
Date 12. 10. 16

FIELD STATE.

Army Form B 231.

To be rendered in accordance with Field Service Regulations, Part II.

UNIT	FIGHTING STRENGTH — This should *not* include details attached to unit, or personnel detailed to march with the Train, or any men unfit to go into action with unit											RATION STRENGTH — To include Fighting Strength, Personnel detailed to march with the Train, and all Personnel and animals attached for Rations and Forage										Remarks
	Personnel		Horses and Mules		Other Animals		Guns and Ammunition Wagons (stating nature)	Machine Guns	Ambulances	Tool Carts, Technical Carts (stating nature)	Remarks	Personnel	Horses and Mules		Other Animals		Mechanically Propelled Vehicles					
	Officers	Other Ranks	Riding	Draught and Pack								Total, all Ranks entitled to Rations.	Heavy Horses	Other Horses and Mules			Motor Cars	Motor Bicycles.	Lorries. 3 Ton	Lorries. 30 Cwt.	Tractors	
(1)	(2)	(3)	(4)	(5)	(6)	(7)	(8)	(9)	(10)	(11)	(12)	(13)	(14)	(15)	(16)	(17)	(18)	(19)	(20)	(21)	(22)	(23)
1st Bn Dorset Regt.	41	825	11	44			8 L. Guns	8				674	9	47								2 Officers and 189 O.R. detached from Battn. 2 Officers + 7 O.R. attached.
TOTALS ...	41	825	11	44				8				674	9	47								

Ammunition with Unit:—

·303 inch; approximate number of rounds per Man ______

·303 inch; „ „ „ per Machine Gun ______

Gun or Howitzer; approximate number of rounds per Gun or Howitzer ______

Supplies with Unit:—

Approximate number of days' rations for men of ration strength ______

„ „ „ forage for Animals „ „ ______

„ „ „ fuel and lubricants for Mechanically Propelled Vehicles ______

(88762.) Wt.W. 2345—1438. 500,000 5/15. J. P. & Co. Ltd. Forms B 231/3

Signature of Commander (Sd) A. S. Heale-Rubb [illegible]
Commanding 1st Bn Dorset Regt.

Unit 1st Bn The Dorsetshire Regt

Place In the Field

Date 19.10.16.

FIELD STATE.

Army Form B 231.

To be rendered in accordance with Field Service Regulations, Part II.

UNIT	FIGHTING STRENGTH — This should *not* include details attached to unit, or personnel detailed to march with the Train, or any men unfit to go into action with unit											RATION STRENGTH — To include Fighting Strength, Personnel detailed to march with the Train, and all Personnel and animals attached for Rations and Forage										
	Personnel		Horses and Mules		Other Animals		Guns and Ammunition Wagons (stating nature)	Machine Guns	Ambulances	Tool Carts, Technical Carts (stating nature)	Remarks	Personnel	Horses and Mules		Other Animals		Mechanically Propelled Vehicles					Remarks
	Officers	Other Ranks	Riding	Draught and Pack								Total, all Ranks entitled to Rations.	Heavy Horses	Other Horses and Mules			Motor Cars	Motor Bicycles.	Lorries. 3 Ton	Lorries. 30 Cwt.	Tractors	
(1)	(2)	(3)	(4)	(5)	(6)	(7)	(8)	(9)	(10)	(11)	(12)	(13)	(14)	(15)	(16)	(17)	(18)	(19)	(20)	(21)	(22)	(23)
1st Bn Dorset Regt.	41	860	11	44			8 L Guns	8				834	9	48								6 Officers and 18 O.R. detached from Battn. 2 Officers and 7 OR attached
TOTALS ...	41	860	11	44				8				834	9	48								

Ammunition with Unit:—

·303 inch; approximate number of rounds per Man ______

·303 inch; " " " per Machine Gun ______

Gun or Howitzer; approximate number of rounds per Gun or Howitzer ______

Supplies with Unit:—

Approximate number of days' rations for men of ration strength ______

" " " forage for Animals " " ______

" " " fuel and lubricants for Mechanically Propelled Vehicles ______

(88762.) Wt. W. 2345—1438. 500,000 5/15. J. P. & Co. Ltd. Forms B 231/3

Signature of Commander (Sd) A. L. Reade-Babb Lieut/for Major Comdg 1st Bn Dorset Regt.

Unit 1st Dorset Regt
Place In the Field
Date 26 10 16

FIELD STATE.

Army Form B 231.

To be rendered in accordance with Field Service Regulations, Part II.

UNIT	FIGHTING STRENGTH — This should *not* include details attached to unit, or personnel detailed to march with the Train, or any men unfit to go into action with unit											RATION STRENGTH — To include Fighting Strength, Personnel detailed to march with the Train, and all Personnel and animals attached for Rations and Forage										
	Personnel		Horses and Mules		Other Animals		Guns and Ammunition Wagons (stating nature)	Machine Guns	Ambulances	Tool Carts, Technical Carts (stating nature)	Remarks	Personnel	Horses and Mules		Other Animals		Mechanically Propelled Vehicles					Remarks
	Officers	Other Ranks	Riding	Draught and Pack								Total, all Ranks entitled to Rations.	Heavy Horses	Other Horses and Mules			Motor Cars	Motor Bicycles.	Lorries. 3 Ton	Lorries. 30 Cwt.	Tractors	
(1)	(2)	(3)	(4)	(5)	(6)	(7)	(8)	(9)	(10)	(11)	(12)	(13)	(14)	(15)	(16)	(17)	(18)	(19)	(20)	(21)	(22)	(23)
1st Dorset Regt	41	853	11	44			8 Lewis Guns	8				827	9	47								7 officers and 69 O.R. detached from Battn 2 officers and 7 O.R. attached
TOTALS ...	41	853	11	44				8				827	9	47								

Ammunition with Unit:—

·303 inch; approximate number of rounds per Man ______

·303 inch; " " " per Machine Gun ______

Gun or Howitzer; approximate number of rounds per Gun or Howitzer ______

Supplies with Unit:—

Approximate number of days' rations for men of ration strength ______

" " " forage for Animals " " ______

" " " fuel and lubricants for Mechanically Propelled Vehicles ______

Signature of Commander (Sd) H.C. Butcher [illegible]
Comdg 1st Dorset Regt

(88762.) Wt.W. 2345—1438. 500,000 5/15. J. P. & Co. Ltd. Forms B 231 / 3

14th Brigade.

32nd Division.

1st BATTALION

THE DORSETSHIRE REGIMENT

NOVEMBER 1 9 1 6

A ppendices attached:-

Lessons Learnt.

Field States.

Instructions regarding War Diaries and Intelligence Summaries are contained in F. S. Regs., Part II. and the Staff Manual respectively. Title Pages will be prepared in manuscript.

WAR DIARY
or
INTELLIGENCE SUMMARY

(Erase heading not required.)

Army Form C. 2118.

1 Dorset Regt REGT.

Vol 27

Place	Date 1916	Hour	Summary of Events and Information	Remarks and references to Appendices
CONTAY WOOD	1st Nov		Battalion in Billets Training Weather very wet. [illegible]	
	2nd		" " Brigade Tactical Scheme carried out [illegible]	
	3rd		" " [illegible]	
	4th		" " [illegible]	
	5th		" " [illegible]	
	6th		" " " Fatigue Party provided 600 strong for work at AVELUY [illegible]	
	7th		" " Training [illegible]	
	8th		" " " [illegible]	
	9th	10 am	Battalion moved by March Route to HARPONVILLE arriving at 12.30 pm [illegible]	
HARPONVILLE	10th		Battalion in Billets Training	
	11th		" 1 Officer & 60 OR sent to Ammunition Railhead CONTAY to [illegible]	[illegible]
	12th		" Fatigue 550 strong provided for work at AVELUY [illegible]	
	13th	8.15 am	Battalion moved by March Route to BOUZINCOURT arriving at 11.15 pm [illegible] 1 Officer & 66 OR rejoined from CONTAY.	
BOUZINCOURT	14th		In Billets in BOUZINCOURT Party of 500 sent to work in AVELUY [illegible]	
	15th		" " 250 [illegible]	

9.26

2449 Wt. W14957/M90 750,000 1/16 J.B.C. & A. Forms/C.2118/12.

Army Form C. 2118.

Instructions regarding War Diaries and Intelligence Summaries are contained in F. S. Regs., Part II. and the Staff Manual respectively. Title Pages will be prepared in manuscript.

WAR DIARY
or
INTELLIGENCE SUMMARY

(Erase heading not required.)

1st DORSET REGT

Place	Date 1916	Hour	Summary of Events and Information	Remarks and references to Appendices
MAILLY-MAILLET	NOV 15th		Battalion moved from BOUZINCOURT at 1.45pm and proceeded by march route to bivouacs in MAILLY-MAILLET. On the night of 15/16 Nov "C" Coy moved from bivouacs to take over part of the line about K35.c.2.5 [initials]	REDAN 1/5000 Trench map.
	16th	1.30pm	Remaining three companies moved to positions in captured German trenches about K35.c.2.5 & K35.c.4.7 with Battn HQ at K35.c.4.6. Capt I.A. CLARKE RAMC – Medical Officer – killed on the way up, the enemy having opened up a heavy barrage whilst the Battalion was proceeding along communication trenches. One other rank killed, eight other ranks wounded. [initials]	
	17th		Battalion in former German front line in close support to 2nd Manchester Regt and 15th H.L.I. who held advanced captured positions. At 5pm working parties sent out to dig communication trench to rear. Heavy enemy shelling. Work completed at midnight. [initials]	
	18th	6.10am	In conjunction with an attack of 97th Inf Bde on our right, the 2nd Manchester Regt & 15th Battn H.L.I. pushed forward to gain more advantageous positions [initials]	
		8.45am	"A" Coy sent to support 15th H.L.I. (our left front)	
		9.45am	"B" Coy sent to support 2nd Manchester Regt (our right front)	
		10.15am	"D" Coy sent to support 2nd Manchester Regt.	
		2.25pm	One Lewis Gun + team sent to 15th H.L.I.	

2449 Wt. W14957/M90 750,000 1/16 J.B.C. & A. Forms/C.2118/12.

Instructions regarding War Diaries and Intelligence Summaries are contained in F. S. Regs., Part II. and the Staff Manual respectively. Title Pages will be prepared in manuscript.

WAR DIARY
or
INTELLIGENCE SUMMARY

(Erase heading not required.)

Army Form C. 2118.

1st DORSET REGT

Place	Date	Hour	Summary of Events and Information	Remarks and references to Appendices
	1916 Nov. 18.	10 pm	40 men of "C" Coy relieved 40 men of "A" Coy holding advanced posts in H.L.I. line. All movements very badly hampered owing to trenches being almost impassable as result of mud and damage from shell fire. Most movements carried out across the open. Casualties: Lieut LYMES and SIMESTER wounded. Other ranks about 30 wounded. The combination of enemy artillery and an excess of mud made the bringing up of rations and water a task of considerable difficulty.	H.G.B.
	19th		"B" and "D" Coys under Capt KESTEL-CORNISH held most of original 2nd Manchester line i.e. SERRE Trench from points (89) to (95) and LAGER ALLEY from point (14) to pt (50) patrolling up to K.35 d. 9.5. "A" Coy assisting H.L.I. "C" Coy in close support at [illegible]. The night of 19/20 Nov being quiet, parties were organized and water was carried to front line. Considerable number of wounded (between 100 and 250) in dugouts in front & support lines. Lieut ORTON and BILLOT wounded.	H.G.B.
	20th		Situation quieter in the morning. Capt CAREW and Lieut FLEAR wounded by snipers when crossing the open with supplies for front line. Trenches still impassable. Lieut SPRAKE shell shock, Lieut BARKER killed. About 4.30 pm enemy opened heavy barrage, lasting about 2½ hours.	H.G.B.
	21st		Situation normal. Remainder of 2nd Manchester Regt (about 60) relieved at 10 pm by B & D Coys. Capt CAREW died of wounds. Trenches slightly improved.	H.G.B.

2449 Wt. W14957/M90 750,000 1/16 J.B.C. & A. Forms/C.2118/12.

Instructions regarding War Diaries and Intelligence Summaries are contained in F. S. Regs., Part II. and the Staff Manual respectively. Title Pages will be prepared in manuscript.

WAR DIARY
or
INTELLIGENCE SUMMARY
(Erase heading not required.)

Army Form C. 2118.

1st DORSET REGT

Place	Date	Hour	Summary of Events and Information	Remarks and references to Appendices
	1916 NOV 21st		Two Companies 16th Northumberland Fusiliers moved up to dug outs near Batt. Hd Qrs. in close support, coming under orders of OC 1st Dorset Regt. A Coy (with 15th HLI) returned to Battn Hd Qrs. Lt DICE wounded	HB
	22nd		Enemy very quiet. All wounded removed across the open during a fog which lasted till 3.30 pm. Two coys of 16th NF relieved B & D Coys in front line – relief complete 7 pm. Enemy observed relief taking place (owing to fog lifting) and opened heavy artillery fire, but caused no casualties. 2nd Manchester Regt relieved remainder of Battalion at 9.30 pm. Battalion withdrew to billets in MAILLY-MAILLET. Total casualties since 16th Nov 3 officers killed, 6 officers wounded, 10 other ranks killed, 66 other ranks wounded, 18 other ranks missing, 29 other ranks evacuated sick.	HB
MAILLY-MAILLET	23rd		In billets in MAILLY-MAILLET.	HB
"	24th		Battalion moved by march route to billets in TERRA-MESNIL	HB
TERRAMESNIL and DOULLENS	25th		Battalion moved by march route to billets in DOULLENS	HB
BERTEAUCOURT	26		BERTEAUCOURT.	HB

H. C. Butcher
Lieut & Adjutant
1st Dorset Regt

2449 Wt. W14957/M90 750,000 1/16 J.B.C. & A. Forms/C.2118/12.

Army Form C. 2118.

Instructions regarding War Diaries and Intelligence Summaries are contained in F. S. Regs., Part II. and the Staff Manual respectively. Title Pages will be prepared in manuscript.

WAR DIARY
or
INTELLIGENCE SUMMARY
(Erase heading not required.)

1st DORSET REGT.

Place	Date	Hour	Summary of Events and Information	Remarks and references to Appendices
BERTEAUCOURT	1916 Nov 27th		Battalion in billets in BERTEAUCOURT training. HCB	
	28th		Ditto HCB	
	29th		Ditto HCB	
	30		Ditto HCB	

H. C. Butcher
Lieut & Adjutant
1st Dorset Regt

2449 Wt. W14957/M90 750,000 1/16 J.B.C. & A. Forms/C.2118/12.

1 DORSET. REGT

The main lesson learnt from these operations is a very obvious and very important one, i.e.

(1) It is essential that Commanding Officers, company commanders and as many other officers as possible, should spend at least 24 hours in the trenches from which an attack is to be carried out, prior to the Battalion coming into the line. Otherwise under the present winter conditions, chaos is certain. So essential does it seem that the incoming troops should be given an opportunity of "getting their bearings" that it would appear sound tactics even to postpone the date of operations in order to allow of this being done.

In the operations under consideration 24 hours would not have been sufficiently long for even the most capable officers to have become well acquainted with the ground. Forward from the German old front line all trenches were a sea of impassable mud, choked also with debris and occasional dead bodies. Movement therefore must be carried out across the open – and consequently after dark.

Now to place a Battalion, a company or even a platoon in a trench they have never seen before and ask them to to take up a position in the dark, across country which is a sea of mud, covered entirely with shell holes + craters and barbed wire, and to expect that ~~expect~~ company to reach and occupy say MAIN TRENCH between points ① and ② – is merely asking for trouble. Guides – if available – almost invariably lose their way in the dark; – if provided, at least one officer and 8 men per company are required. But the only sure method of ensuring that troops will arrive at certain advanced points (the trenches are usually almost unrecognizable as such) is by having a certain proportion of the officers and men who are actually to carry out the task in hand, sent up beforehand to reconnoitre the ground for themselves. This has been proved a score of times. In the first week of last July a regiment ordered to attack through this Battalion failed dismally in its task chiefly because no one knew his way. And this despite the fact that twenty or thirty guides from this regiment where provided – though not asked for – every one of whom had lived in the sector for months and knew every inch of ground. These guides eventually managed to get two or three platoons to their positions, but the remainder of the Battalion had previously got so hopelessly lost that when zero hour arrived only a few of them attacked — and these in the wrong place.

(2). The necessity for every man going into action to take two complete days rations and filled water-bottle was again brought home. Under present conditions it may often happen that supplies cannot be brought up for nearly 48 hours. This, of course, is nothing new; but the point is that a Battalion has not sufficient preserved rations always on hand at a moments notice. Dumps of preserved meat and biscuit might be arranged near the line. In practise the "unexpended portion of the" "day's ration" becomes practically nothing — certainly not enough to fight on in winter. The reasons for this are obvious and well known and need no explanation here.

(3). It was found that a man cannot carry as heavy a load as is generally allotted to him when with an average carrying party. In dry weather a man can carry surprisingly heavy weights, but in very bad trenches it was found that

<u>one</u> petrol tin of water
or <u>one</u> sandbag of rations
or. <u>one</u> box of bombs

is quite suffient when the man has rifle and equipment. Two of any of the above is too much for one man over the knees in mud. Consequently he becomes exhausted and lost and nothing reaches its destination.

(4) Liaison. Each unit must send runners to the headquarters of every other near-by unit

at the earliest possible moment. Liaison officers between Battalions are not necessary in most cases. Visual signalling to the rear by lamp might be made more use of than at present. The result of pigeon messages was not known. Telephones and wire should always be taken by signallers. These were used for lateral communication over short distances very successfully. Rockets for signalling to the artillery were not used but should invariably be available in case of necessity. The enemy used them most successfully on three occasions.

(5). Bayonets should not be fixed until the last moment prior to an attack. They are seen by the enemy and give the show away.

(6) The evacuation of wounded is more important than

sometimes realized. It is not only the saving of the lives of the wounded men that has to be considered. On this occasion the wounded left by previous occupants of the trenches occupied about one third of our dugout accommodation, consumed large quantities of our rations and water, entailed a great amount of extra labour and possibly affected the morale of the others.

Stretcher bearers might possibly be available somewhat closer to the scene of operations, so that any opportunity of removing even one or two cases may be seized. One hundred bearers must have at least 3 officers with them. All parties sent to us had lost most of their men even before they reached Battalion headquarters. A larger percentage of officers would prevent this.

All ranks must have it impressed upon them that if they can possibly manage to walk (when wounded) – even though it occasions a great effort – they should do so in their own interests. Dozens of wounded men who had lain in dugouts for several days awaiting stretchers were persuaded to make the attempt to walk to Field Ambulance – and did so.

A.C. Butcher
Lieut & Adjutant.
for Lieut-Col.
Comdg. 1st Dorset Regt

1. 12. 16.

Unit 1st Dorset Regt

Place In the Field

Date 2 . 11 . 16

FIELD STATE.

Army Form B 231.

1st Dorset Regt

To be rendered in accordance with Field Service Regulations, Part II.

UNIT	FIGHTING STRENGTH — This should *not* include details attached to unit, or personnel detailed to march with the Train, or any men unfit to go into action with unit											RATION STRENGTH — To include Fighting Strength, Personnel detailed to march with the Train, and all Personnel and animals attached for Rations and Forage										
	Personnel		Horses and Mules		Other Animals		Guns and Ammunition Wagons (stating nature)	Machine Guns	Ambulances	Tool Carts, Technical Carts (stating nature)	Remarks	Personnel	Horses and Mules		Other Animals		Mechanically Propelled Vehicles					Remarks
	Officers	Other Ranks	Riding	Draught and Pack								Total, all Ranks entitled to Rations.	Heavy Horses	Other Horses and Mules			Motor Cars	Motor Bicycles.	Lorries. 3 Ton	Lorries. 30 Cwt.	Tractors	
(1)	(2)	(3)	(4)	(5)	(6)	(7)	(8)	(9)	(10)	(11)	(12)	(13)	(14)	(15)	(16)	(17)	(18)	(19)	(20)	(21)	(22)	(23)
1st Dorset Regt	39	840	11	44			10 L Guns	10		17		822	9	47								2 Officers & 7 OR attached to Bde 1 Officer & 10 OR detached from Bde
TOTALS ...	39	840	11	44				10		17		822	9	47								

Ammunition with Unit:—

·303 inch; approximate number of rounds per Man ______

·303 inch; " " " per Machine Gun ______

Gun or Howitzer; approximate number of rounds per Gun or Howitzer ______

Supplies with Unit:—

Approximate number of days' rations for men of ration strength ______

" " " forage for Animals " " ______

" " " fuel and lubricants for Mechanically Propelled Vehicles ______

Signature of Commander (Sd) H.H. Butler Lieut for Major Comdg 1 Dorset Regt

(88762.) Wt.W. 2345—1438. 500,000 5/15. J. P. & Co. Ltd. Forms B 231 / 3

Unit 1/Dorset Regt

Place In the Field

Date 9-11-16

FIELD STATE.

Army Form B 231.

To be rendered in accordance with Field Service Regulations, Part II.

FIGHTING STRENGTH — This should *not* include details attached to unit, or personnel detailed to march with the Train, or any men unfit to go into action with unit

RATION STRENGTH — To include Fighting Strength, Personnel detailed to march with the Train, and all Personnel and animals attached for Rations and Forage

UNIT	Fighting Strength: Personnel		Horses and Mules		Other Animals		Guns and Ammunition Wagons (stating nature)	Machine Guns	Ambulances	Tool Carts, Technical Carts (stating nature)	Remarks	Ration Strength: Personnel	Horses and Mules		Other Animals		Mechanically Propelled Vehicles					Remarks
	Officers	Other Ranks	Riding	Draught and Pack								Total, all Ranks entitled to Rations.	Heavy Horses	Other Horses and Mules			Motor Cars	Motor Bicycles.	Lorries. 3 Ton	Lorries. 30 Cwt.	Tractors	
(1)	(2)	(3)	(4)	(5)	(6)	(7)	(8)	(9)	(10)	(11)	(12)	(13)	(14)	(15)	(16)	(17)	(18)	(19)	(20)	(21)	(22)	(23)
1/Dorset Regt	41	834	11	44			16 L Guns	10		17		804	9	47								2 Officers & 8 Other Ranks attached to Bn; 7 Officers and 84 OR detached from Bn
TOTALS ...	41	834	11	44				10		17		804	9	47								

Ammunition with Unit:—

·303 inch; approximate number of rounds per Man

·303 inch; „ „ „ per Machine Gun

Gun or Howitzer; approximate number of rounds per Gun or Howitzer

Supplies with Unit:—

Approximate number of days' rations for men of ration strength

„ „ „ forage for Animals „ „

„ „ „ fuel and lubricants for Mechanically Propelled Vehicles

Signature of Commander (Sd) H.E. Butcher Lieut for Lt Col Comdg 1/Dorset Regt.

(88762.) Wt.W. 2345—1438. 500,000 5/15. J. P. & Co. Ltd. Forms B 231/3

Army Form B 251.

FIELD STATE.

Unit 1/Dorset Regt

Place In the Field

Date 16-11-16.

To be rendered in accordance with Field Service Regulations, Part II.

UNIT	FIGHTING STRENGTH — This should *not* include details attached to unit, or personnel detailed to march with the Train, or any men unfit to go into action with unit											RATION STRENGTH — To include Fighting Strength, Personnel detailed to march with the Train, and all Personnel and animals attached for Rations and Forage										
	Personnel		Horses and Mules		Other Animals		Guns and Ammunition Wagons (stating nature)	Machine Guns	Ambulances	Tool Carts, Technical Carts (stating nature)	Remarks	Personnel	Horses and Mules		Other Animals		Mechanically Propelled Vehicles					Remarks
	Officers	Other Ranks	Riding	Draught and Pack								Total, all Ranks entitled to Rations.	Heavy Horses	Other Horses and Mules			Motor Cars	Motor Bicycles.	Lorries. 3 Ton	Lorries. 30 Cwt.	Tractors	
(1)	(2)	(3)	(4)	(5)	(6)	(7)	(8)	(9)	(10)	(11)	(12)	(13)	(14)	(15)	(16)	(17)	(18)	(19)	(20)	(21)	(22)	(23)
1/Dorset Regt	41	840	11	44			10 L Guns	10		17		825	9	47								3 Offrs + 9 OR attached to Bde 5 Offrs + 73 OR detached from Battn
TOTALS ...	41	840	11	44				10		17		825	9	47								

Ammunition with Unit:—

·303 inch; approximate number of rounds per Man

·303 inch; " " " per Machine Gun

Gun or Howitzer; approximate number of rounds per Gun or Howitzer

Supplies with Unit:—

Approximate number of days' rations for men of ration strength

" " " forage for Animals " "

" " " fuel and lubricants for Mechanically Propelled Vehicles

Signature of Commander (Sd) A C Batcher Lieut for Lt. Col Comdg 1/Dorset Regt.

(88762.) Wt.W. 2345—1438. 500,000 5/15. J. P. & Co. Ltd. Forms B 231/3

Army Form B 231.

FIELD STATE.

Unit 1/Dorset Regt

Place In the Lines

Date 23. 11. 16.

To be rendered in accordance with Field Service Regulations, Part II.

UNIT	FIGHTING STRENGTH — This should *not* include details attached to unit, or personnel detailed to march with the Train, or any men unfit to go into action with unit: Personnel		Horses and Mules		Other Animals		Guns and Ammunition Wagons (stating nature)	Machine Guns	Ambulances	Tool Carts, Technical Carts (stating nature)	Remarks	RATION STRENGTH — To include Fighting Strength, Personnel detailed to march with the Train, and all Personnel and animals attached for Rations and Forage: Personnel	Horses and Mules		Other Animals		Mechanically Propelled Vehicles					Remarks
	Officers	Other Ranks	Riding	Draught and Pack								Total, all Ranks entitled to Rations.	Heavy Horses	Other Horses and Mules			Motor Cars	Motor Bicycles.	Lorries. 3 Ton	Lorries. 30 Cwt.	Tractors	
(1)	(2)	(3)	(4)	(5)	(6)	(7)	(8)	(9)	(10)	(11)	(12)	(13)	(14)	(15)	(16)	(17)	(18)	(19)	(20)	(21)	(22)	(23)
1/Dorset Regt	33	728	11	44			10 L Guns	10		17		700	9	47								3 Offrs + 19 OR attached to Bn. 9 Offrs + 76 OR detached from Bn
TOTALS ...	33	728	11	44				10		17		700	9	47	-							

Ammunition with Unit:—

·303 inch; approximate number of rounds per Man ________

·303 inch; „ „ „ per Machine Gun ________

Gun or Howitzer; approximate number of rounds per Gun or Howitzer ________

Supplies with Unit:—

Approximate number of days' rations for men of ration strength ________

„ „ „ forage for Animals „ „ ________

„ „ „ fuel and lubricants for Mechanically Propelled Vehicles ________

Signature of Commander C.W.A.C. Bates [illegible] Lt Col Comdg 1/Dorset Regt

(88762.) Wt.W. 2345—1438. 500,000 5/15. J. P. & Co. Ltd. Forms B 231/3

Unit 1/Dorset Regt

Place In the Field

Date 30. 11. 16.

FIELD STATE.

Army Form B 231.

To be rendered in accordance with Field Service Regulations, Part II.

UNIT	FIGHTING STRENGTH — This should *not* include details attached to unit, or personnel detailed to march with the Train, or any men unfit to go into action with unit											RATION STRENGTH — To include Fighting Strength, Personnel detailed to march with the Train, and all Personnel and animals attached for Rations and Forage										
	Personnel		Horses and Mules		Other Animals		Guns and Ammunition Wagons (stating nature)	Machine Guns	Ambulances	Tool Carts, Technical Carts (stating nature)	Remarks	Personnel	Horses and Mules		Other Animals		Mechanically Propelled Vehicles					Remarks
	Officers	Other Ranks	Riding	Draught and Pack								Total, all Ranks entitled to Rations.	Heavy Horses	Other Horses and Mules			Motor Cars	Motor Bicycles.	Lorries. 3 Ton	Lorries. 30 Cwt.	Tractors	
(1)	(2)	(3)	(4)	(5)	(6)	(7)	(8)	(9)	(10)	(11)	(12)	(13)	(14)	(15)	(16)	(17)	(18)	(19)	(20)	(21)	(22)	(23)
1/Dorset Regt	34	736	11	44			10 L. Guns [?]	10		17		714	9	47								3 Offrs 29 O.R. attached to Bde. 6 Off 72 O.R. attached from Battn [?]
TOTALS ...	34	736	11	44				10		17		714	9	47								

Ammunition with Unit:—

·303 inch; approximate number of rounds per Man __________

·303 inch; " " " per Machine Gun __________

Gun or Howitzer; approximate number of rounds per Gun or Howitzer __________

Supplies with Unit:—

Approximate number of days' rations for men of ration strength __________

" " " forage for Animals " " __________

" " " fuel and lubricants for Mechanically Propelled Vehicles __________

Signature of Commander (Sd) H. C. Butcher [?] Lieut for Lt Col Comdg 1/Dorset Regt

(88762.) Wt.W. 2345—1438. 500,000 5/15. J. P. & Co. Ltd. Forms B 231 / 3

14th Brigade.

32nd Division.

1st BATTALION

THE DORSETSHIRE REGIMENT

DECEMBER 1 9 1 6

Appendices attached:-

Field States.

WAR DIARY
or
~~INTELLIGENCE SUMMARY.~~
(Erase heading not required.)

Army Form C. 2118.

Instructions regarding War Diaries and Intelligence Summaries are contained in F. S. Regs., Part II. and the Staff Manual respectively. Title pages will be prepared in manuscript.

1st DORSET REGT.

Vol 28

Place	Date 1916	Hour	Summary of Events and Information	Remarks and references to Appendices
BERTEAUCOURT	Dec 1		Battalion in BERTEAUCOURT carrying out training	
	2		– Ditto – – Ditto –	
	3		– Ditto – – Ditto –	
	4		– Ditto – – Ditto –	
	5		– Ditto – – Ditto –	
	6		– Ditto – – Ditto –	
	7		– Ditto – – Ditto –	
	8		– Ditto – – Ditto –	
	9		– Ditto – – Ditto –	
	10		– Ditto – – Ditto Sporting Games carried out in afternoon	
	11		– Ditto – – Ditto –	
	12		– Ditto – – Ditto Tactical Scheme for Officers without troops in the afternoon	
	13		[illegible] Battalion attack scheme [illegible]	
	14		Battalion Route March	
	15		Battalion in BERTEAUCOURT training Sporting Games carried out in afternoon	
	16		– Ditto – Ditto	
	17		– Ditto – – Ditto –	
	18		2 Coys Brigade training 2 Coys firing on Range	
	19		Ditto Ditto	

G.27

Instructions regarding War Diaries and Intelligence Summaries are contained in F. S. Regs., Part II. and the Staff Manual respectively. Title pages will be prepared in manuscript.

WAR DIARY

or

INTELLIGENCE SUMMARY.

(Erase heading not required.)

Army Form C. 2118.

1st DORSET REGT

Place	Date	Hour	Summary of Events and Information	Remarks and references to Appendices
	1916			
BERTEAUCOURT	Dec 20		2 Coys Route March, 2 Coys Bombing Attack.	Cans 11
"	21st		Battalion in attack (M.G. Coy & T.M. Bty to co-operate)	
"	22nd		Battalion Outpost Scheme. Regtl ride for officers – officers to work out [illegible] and submit written solutions [illegible]	
"	23rd		Brigade Route March	
"	24		Battalion in BERTEAUCOURT [illegible]	
"	25		Christmas Day. Football Match & Concert held.	
"	26th		Battalion at BERTEAUCOURT [illegible]	
"	27th		[illegible]	
			[illegible] the advance.	
"	28		Tactical Scheme carried out.	
"	29		Brigade Training	
"	30th		Battalion Outpost [illegible]	
"	31st		Divisional [illegible] battalion [illegible]	

G. R. Wood 2nd Lt and Capt for Major
Cmdg 1st Bn Dorset Regt

2353 Wt. W2544/1454 700,000 5/15 D. D. & L. A.D.S.S./Forms/C. 2118.

Unit: 1st Dorset Regt.
Place: In the Field
Date: 8-12-16.

FIELD STATE.

Army Form B 231.

To be rendered in accordance with Field Service Regulations, Part II.

UNIT	FIGHTING STRENGTH. This should *not* include details attached to unit, or personnel detailed to march with the Train, or any men unfit to go into action with unit											RATION STRENGTH. To include Fighting Strength, Personnel detailed to march with the Train, and all Personnel and animals attached for Rations and Forage										
	Personnel		Horses and Mules		Other Animals		Guns and Ammunition Wagons (stating nature)	Machine Guns	Ambulances	Tool Carts, Technical Carts (stating nature)	Remarks	Personnel	Horses and Mules		Other Animals		Mechanically Propelled Vehicles					Remarks
	Officers	Other Ranks	Riding	Draught and Pack								Total, all Ranks entitled to Rations.	Heavy Horses	Other Horses and Mules			Motor Cars	Motor Bicycles.	Lorries. 3 Ton	Lorries. 30 Cwt.	Tractors	
(1)	(2)	(3)	(4)	(5)	(6)	(7)	(8)	(9)	(10)	(11)	(12)	(13)	(14)	(15)	(16)	(17)	(18)	(19)	(20)	(21)	(22)	(23)
1/Dorset Regt	32	812	12	42			10 L. Guns	10		17		776	9	45.								3 Offrs 9 OR attached. 6 Offrs + 74 OR detached.
TOTALS ...	32	812	12	42				10		17		776	9	45								

Ammunition with Unit:—

·303 inch; approximate number of rounds per Man ______

·303 inch; " " " per Machine Gun ______

Gun or Howitzer; approximate number of rounds per Gun or Howitzer ______

Supplies with Unit:—

Approximate number of days' rations for men of ration strength ______

" " " forage for Animals " " ______

" " " fuel and lubricants for Mechanically Propelled Vehicles ______

Signature of Commander (Sd) H. C Butcher Lieut for Major Comdg 1/Dorset Regt

(90988.) Wt.W. 5216—2140. 900,000 7/15. J. P. & Co. Ltd. Forms B 231/3

Unit 1st Dorset Regt.
Place In the Field.
Date 15 - 12 - 16

FIELD STATE.

Army Form B 231.

To be rendered in accordance with Field Service Regulations, Part II.

FIGHTING STRENGTH (columns 2–12): This should *not* include details attached to unit, or personnel detailed to march with the Train, or any men unfit to go into action with unit

RATION STRENGTH (columns 13–23): To include Fighting Strength, Personnel detailed to march with the Train, and all Personnel and animals attached for Rations and Forage

UNIT	Personnel		Horses and Mules		Other Animals		Guns and Ammunition Wagons (stating nature)	Machine Guns	Ambulances	Tool Carts, Technical Carts (stating nature)	Remarks	Personnel	Horses and Mules		Other Animals		Mechanically Propelled Vehicles					Remarks
	Officers	Other Ranks	Riding	Draught and Pack								Total, all Ranks entitled to Rations.	Heavy Horses	Other Horses and Mules			Motor Cars	Motor Bicycles	Lorries. 3 Ton	Lorries. 30 Cwt.	Tractors	
(1)	(2)	(3)	(4)	(5)	(6)	(7)	(8)	(9)	(10)	(11)	(12)	(13)	(14)	(15)	(16)	(17)	(18)	(19)	(20)	(21)	(22)	(23)
1/Dorset Regt.	33	926	12	42			10 L. Guns	10		17		868.	9	45.								2 Offrs + 8 O.R. attached.
																						4 Offrs + 97 O.R. detached.
TOTALS ...	33.	926.	12.	42				10		17		868	9	45								

Ammunition with Unit:—

·303 inch; approximate number of rounds per Man ________

·303 inch; " " " per Machine Gun ________

Gun or Howitzer; approximate number of rounds per Gun or Howitzer ________

Supplies with Unit:—

Approximate number of days' rations for men of ration strength ________

" " " forage for Animals " " ________

" " " fuel and lubricants for Mechanically Propelled Vehicles ________

(90988.) Wt.W. 5216—2140. 900,000 7/15. J. P. & Co. Ltd. Forms B 231 / 3

Signature of Commander (Sd) H.C. Butcher Lieut for Major
Comdg 1/Bn Dorset Regt

Army Form B 231.

FIELD STATE.

Unit 1st Dorset Regt

Place In the Field

Date 22-12-16.

To be rendered in accordance with Field Service Regulations, Part II.

UNIT	FIGHTING STRENGTH — This should *not* include details attached to unit, or personnel detailed to march with the Train, or any men unfit to go into action with unit											RATION STRENGTH — To include Fighting Strength, Personnel detailed to march with the Train, and all Personnel and animals attached for Rations and Forage										Remarks
	Personnel		Horses and Mules		Other Animals		Guns and Ammunition Wagons (stating nature)	Machine Guns	Ambulances	Tool Carts, Technical Carts (stating nature)	Remarks	Personnel	Horses and Mules		Other Animals		Mechanically Propelled Vehicles					
	Officers	Other Ranks	Riding	Draught and Pack								Total, all Ranks entitled to Rations.	Heavy Horses	Other Horses and Mules			Motor Cars	Motor Bicycles.	Lorries. 3 Ton	Lorries. 30 Cwt.	Tractors	
(1)	(2)	(3)	(4)	(5)	(6)	(7)	(8)	(9)	(10)	(11)	(12)	(13)	(14)	(15)	(16)	(17)	(18)	(19)	(20)	(21)	(22)	(23)
1/Dorset Rgt.	34	927	12	42			10 L. Guns	10		17		853	9	45								2 Offrs & 8 O.R. attached. 3 Offrs & 115 O.R. detached
TOTALS ...	34	927	12	42				10		17		853	9	45								

Ammunition with Unit:—

·303 inch; approximate number of rounds per Man ________

·303 inch; " " " per Machine Gun ________

Gun or Howitzer; approximate number of rounds per Gun or Howitzer ________

Supplies with Unit:—

Approximate number of days' rations for men of ration strength ________

" " " forage for Animals " " ________

" " " fuel and lubricants for Mechanically Propelled Vehicles ________

(88762.) Wt.W. 2345—1438. 500,000 5/15. J. P. & Co. Ltd. Forms B 231/3

Signature of Commander (Sd) H. C. Butcher Lieut for Major Comdg 1/Dorset Regt

Unit 1st Dorset Regt
Place In the Field
Date 29-12-16.

Army Form B 231.

FIELD STATE.

To be rendered in accordance with Field Service Regulations, Part II.

FIGHTING STRENGTH: This should *not* include details attached to unit, or personnel detailed to march with the Train, or any men unfit to go into action with unit

RATION STRENGTH: To include Fighting Strength, Personnel detailed to march with the Train, and all Personnel and animals attached for Rations and Forage

UNIT	Fighting Strength: Personnel		Horses and Mules		Other Animals		Guns and Ammunition Wagons (stating nature)	Machine Guns	Ambulances	Tool Carts, Technical Carts (stating nature)	Remarks	Ration Strength: Personnel	Horses and Mules		Other Animals		Mechanically Propelled Vehicles					Remarks
	Officers	Other Ranks	Riding	Draught and Pack								Total, all Ranks entitled to Rations.	Heavy Horses	Other Horses and Mules			Motor Cars	Motor Bicycles.	Lorries. 3 Ton	Lorries. 30 Cwt.	Tractors	
(1)	(2)	(3)	(4)	(5)	(6)	(7)	(8)	(9)	(10)	(11)	(12)	(13)	(14)	(15)	(16)	(17)	(18)	(19)	(20)	(21)	(22)	(23)
1/Dorset Regt.	32	939	12	42			12 L. Guns	12		17		863	9	45								2 offrs + 8 OR attached. 3 offrs + 115 OR detached.
TOTALS ...	32	939	12	42				12		17		863	9	45								

Ammunition with Unit:—
·303 inch; approximate number of rounds per Man ____
·303 inch; " " " per Machine Gun ____
Gun or Howitzer; approximate number of rounds per Gun or Howitzer ____

Supplies with Unit:—
Approximate number of days' rations for men of ration strength ____
" " " forage for Animals " " ____
" " " fuel and lubricants for Mechanically Propelled Vehicles ____

(88762.) Wt.W. 2345—1438. 500,000 5/15. J. P. & Co. Ltd. Forms B 231/3

Signature of Commander (Sd) G.N. Wood Lieut for Major Comdg 1/ Dorset Regt.

Instructions regarding War Diaries and Intelligence Summaries are contained in F. S. Regs., Part II. and the Staff Manual respectively. Title Pages will be prepared in manuscript.

WAR DIARY
or
INTELLIGENCE SUMMARY
(Erase heading not required.)

Army Form C. 2118.

14/32

1 Dorset Regt
DORSET REGT.
Vol 29

Place	Date 1917	Hour	Summary of Events and Information	Remarks and references to Appendices
BERTEAUCOURT	Jany 1st		Battalion in BERTEAUCOURT training	Ref a Map LENS 11.
"	2nd	8.30 a.m.	Tactical scheme under Brigade arrangements	
"	3rd		Battalion training	
"	4th		Battalion training	
"	5th		Battalion training	
"	6th		Route March	
"		9.20 a.m.	Battalion marched via FIEFFES - BONNEVILLE to BEHUVAL.	WD
			Arrived at BEHUVAL 1.45 p.m. distance 9½ miles.	
"	7th	7.20 a.m.	Embussed for BUS. Arrived at BUS - in reserve to 8th Bde	
BUS		3 p.m.	All mens feet rubbed with whale oil in preparation for move to trenches	
"	8th	11 a.m.	-do- -do- -do- -do- -do-	WD
"		1.45 p.m.	Battalion (less 1 Coy & Transport remaining at BUS) moved off to relieve 2nd Royal Scots (8th Bde) in trenches. 200 yards intervals between Coys. A & B Coy in front line C Coy and Bn HdQrs at WHITE CITY.	WD
Trenches	9th	4 p.m.	Reported to Bde "Our artillery active - very slight enemy retaliation. Casualties 1 OR. Wounded 2/Lt F.A. CHICK reported his arrival.	
"	10th		Intermittent shelling by enemy - Casualties 3 OR. Wounded	
"	11th		Quiet day Casualties 3 OR Wounded	
"	12th	5.45 p.m.	Relief by 5/6 Royal Scots commenced. Battn withdrew to huts in BUS. 1 OR Killed	
BUS.	13th		Battalion in huts in BUS.	
"	14th		Reinforcements 10 OR arrived.	WD
"	15th		Reinforcements 29 OR arrived.	

2449 Wt. W14957/M90 750,000 1/16 J.B.C. & A. Forms/C.2118/12.

Army Form C. 2118.

Instructions regarding War Diaries and Intelligence Summaries are contained in F. S. Regs., Part II. and the Staff Manual respectively. Title Pages will be prepared in manuscript.

WAR DIARY or ~~INTELLIGENCE SUMMARY~~

(Erase heading not required.)

1st DORSET REGT

Place	Date 1917.	Hour	Summary of Events and Information	Remarks and references to Appendices
BUS.	Aug 15th	3 p.m.	Battalion moved off to relieve 5/6 Royal Scots in trenches. D Coy Right C Coy Left front line	IRD.
			A Coy + Bn Hd Qrs at WHITE CITY B Coy. COURCELLES.	
Trenches.	" 16th		Very quiet day. C Coys "dugouts" slightly shelled	
"	" 17th		Water tanks at WHITE CITY destroyed by enemy shells. otherwise quiet day.	
			Battn withdrew to huts in BUS being relieved in trenches by 5/6 Royal Scots.	IRD.
BUS.	" 18th		In huts in BUS	
"	" 19th		-do- -do-	
"	" 20th	9.30 a.m.	Practiced the attack	
"	" 21st	9.30 a.m.	-do- -do-	
"	" 22nd		In huts in BUS.	
"	" 23rd	9.30 a.m.	Battn moved to huts in BERTRANCOURT.	IRD.
BERTRANCOURT.	" 24th	9.15 a.m.	Battn inspected by Generals of French Army in the attack. Divl Comdr. sent message to Battn saying how well all ranks played up and were a credit to Divn.	
"	" 25th	3.30 p.m.	Battn moved off to relieve 15th H.L.I. in trenches. C Coy Left D Coy Right in front line A + B Coys + Bn HQ at WHITE CITY.	
	" 26th		Quiet day 2 O.R. wounded.	
	" 27th	5 p.m.	Relief by 15th H.L.I. commenced. Bn withdrew to billets in MAILLY MAILLET.	IRD.
MAILLY-MAILLET.	" 28th		In billets in MAILLY MAILLET 435 men on fatigue	
"	" 29th	4.45 p.m.	Bn moved off to relieve 15th H.L.I. in trenches. Sector occupied as follows:- "A" left "B" right in front line "C" "D" + Bn HQ at WHITE CITY.	
Trenches.	" 30th		Quiet day	
"	" 31st	5 p.m.	Relief by 15th H.L.I. commenced. Battalion withdrew to billets in MAILLY MAILLET.	

2449 Wt. W14957/M90 750,000 1/16 J.B.C. & A. Forms/C.2118/12.

1.9.17. IRDyer. Lt & Adj. 1st Dorset Regiment

Unit 1st Dorset Regt.
Place In the Field
Date 5. 1. 17

FIELD STATE.

Army Form B 231.

To be rendered in accordance with Field Service Regulations, Part II.

UNIT	FIGHTING STRENGTH — This should *not* include details attached to unit, or personnel detailed to march with the Train, or any men unfit to go into action with unit											RATION STRENGTH — To include Fighting Strength, Personnel detailed to march with the Train, and all Personnel and animals attached for Rations and Forage										
	Personnel		Horses and Mules		Other Animals							Personnel	Horses and Mules		Other Animals		Mechanically Propelled Vehicles					
	Officers	Other Ranks	Riding	Draught and Pack			Guns and Ammunition Wagons (stating nature)	Machine Guns	Ambulances	Tool Carts, Technical Carts (stating nature)	Remarks	Total, all Ranks entitled to Rations.	Heavy Horses	Other Horses and Mules			Motor Cars	Motor Bicycles.	Lorries. 3 Ton	Lorries. 30 Cwt.	Tractors	Remarks
(1)	(2)	(3)	(4)	(5)	(6)	(7)	(8)	(9)	(10)	(11)	(12)	(13)	(14)	(15)	(16)	(17)	(18)	(19)	(20)	(21)	(22)	(23)
1st Dorset Regt.	34	993	11	42				12		14		927		54								Detached 3 Offrs 113 O.R.
TOTALS ...	34	993	11	42				12		14		927		54								

Ammunition with Unit:—

·303 inch; approximate number of rounds per Man

·303 inch; " " " per Machine Gun

Gun or Howitzer; approximate number of rounds per Gun or Howitzer

Supplies with Unit:—

Approximate number of days' rations for men of ration strength

" " " forage for Animals " "

" " " fuel and lubricants for Mechanically Propelled Vehicles

Signature of Commander (Sd) J.V. Shute Lt-Col.

(90988.) Wt.W. 5216—2140. 900,000 7/15. J. P. & Co. Ltd. Forms B 231/3

Unit 1st Dorset Regt.
Place In the Field
Date 12. 1. 17

FIELD STATE.

Army Form B 231.

To be rendered in accordance with Field Service Regulations, Part II.

UNIT	FIGHTING STRENGTH — This should *not* include details attached to unit, or personnel detailed to march with the Train, or any men unfit to go into action with unit											RATION STRENGTH — To include Fighting Strength, Personnel detailed to march with the Train, and all Personnel and animals attached for Rations and Forage										
	Personnel		Horses and Mules		Other Animals		Guns and Ammunition Wagons (stating nature)	Machine Guns	Ambulances	Tool Carts, Technical Carts (stating nature)	Remarks	Personnel	Horses and Mules		Other Animals		Mechanically Propelled Vehicles					Remarks
	Officers	Other Ranks	Riding	Draught and Pack								Total, all Ranks entitled to Rations.	Heavy Horses	Other Horses and Mules			Motor Cars	Motor Bicycles.	Lorries. 3 Ton	Lorries. 30 Cwt.	Tractors	
(1)	(2)	(3)	(4)	(5)	(6)	(7)	(8)	(9)	(10)	(11)	(12)	(13)	(14)	(15)	(16)	(17)	(18)	(19)	(20)	(21)	(22)	(23)
1st Dorset Regt.	38	998	11	42				12		14		953		54								Detached 5 Officers 83 O.R.
Totals ...	38	993	11	42.				12		14		953.		54								

Ammunition with Unit:—

·303 inch; approximate number of rounds per Man ______

·303 inch; „ „ „ per Machine Gun ______

Gun or Howitzer; approximate number of rounds per Gun or Howitzer ______

Supplies with Unit:—

Approximate number of days' rations for men of ration strength ______

„ „ „ forage for Animals „ „ ______

„ „ „ fuel and lubricants for Mechanically Propelled Vehicles ______

Signature of Commander (Sd) J.W. Shute Lt. Col.

(90988.) Wt.W. 5216—2140. 900,000 7/15. J. P. & Co. Ltd. Forms B 231 / 3

Unit 1st Dorset Regt.
Place In the Field.
Date 19. 1. 17.

FIELD STATE.

Army Form B 231.

To be rendered in accordance with Field Service Regulations, Part II.

FIGHTING STRENGTH

This should *not* include details attached to unit, or personnel detailed to march with the Train, or any men unfit to go into action with unit

UNIT	Personnel		Horses and Mules		Other Animals		Guns and Ammunition Wagons (stating nature)	Machine Guns	Ambulances	Tool Carts, Technical Carts (stating nature)	Remarks
	Officers	Other Ranks	Riding	Draught and Pack							
(1)	(2)	(3)	(4)	(5)	(6)	(7)	(8)	(9)	(10)	(11)	(12)
1st Dorset Regt.	41.	954	11	44				12.		14.	
TOTALS ...	41.	963.	11.	44.				12		14	

RATION STRENGTH

To include Fighting Strength, Personnel detailed to march with the Train, and all Personnel and animals attached for Rations and Forage

UNIT	Personnel	Horses and Mules		Other Animals		Mechanically Propelled Vehicles					Remarks
	Total, all Ranks entitled to Rations.	Heavy Horses	Other Horses and Mules			Motor Cars	Motor Bicycles.	Lorries. 3 Ton	Lorries. 30 Cwt.	Tractors	
(1)	(13)	(14)	(15)	(16)	(17)	(18)	(19)	(20)	(21)	(22)	(23)
1st Dorset Regt.	914		56.								Detached 7 offrs 92 O.R.
TOTALS ...	914.		56.								

Ammunition with Unit:—

·303 inch; approximate number of rounds per Man ______

·303 inch; „ „ „ per Machine Gun ______

Gun or Howitzer; approximate number of rounds per Gun or Howitzer ______

Supplies with Unit:—

Approximate number of days' rations for men of ration strength ______

„ „ „ forage for Animals „ „ ______

„ „ „ fuel and lubricants for Mechanically Propelled Vehicles ______

(90988.) Wt.W. 5216—2140. 900,000 7/15. J. P. & Co. Ltd. Forms B 231/3

Signature of Commander Sd. J V Shute Lt Col

Unit 1st Dorset Regt

Place In the Field

Date 26. 1. 14

FIELD STATE.

Army Form B 231.

To be rendered in accordance with Field Service Regulations, Part II.

UNIT	FIGHTING STRENGTH — This should *not* include details attached to unit, or personnel detailed to march with the Train, or any men unfit to go into action with unit											RATION STRENGTH — To include Fighting Strength, Personnel detailed to march with the Train, and all Personnel and animals attached for Rations and Forage										
	Personnel		Horses and Mules		Other Animals		Guns and Ammunition Wagons (stating nature)	Machine Guns	Ambulances	Tool Carts, Technical Carts (stating nature)	Remarks	Personnel	Horses and Mules		Other Animals		Mechanically Propelled Vehicles					Remarks
	Officers	Other Ranks	Riding	Draught and Pack								Total, all Ranks entitled to Rations.	Heavy Horses	Other Horses and Mules			Motor Cars	Motor Bicycles.	Lorries. 3 Ton	Lorries. 30 Cwt.	Tractors	
(1)	(2)	(3)	(4)	(5)	(6)	(7)	(8)	(9)	(10)	(11)	(12)	(13)	(14)	(15)	(16)	(17)	(18)	(19)	(20)	(21)	(22)	(23)
1st Dorset Regt	40	923	11	44				12		14		854		56								Detached 10 officers 114 O.R.
TOTALS ...	40	923	11	44				12		14		854		56								

Ammunition with Unit:—

·303 inch; approximate number of rounds per Man

·303 inch; „ „ „ per Machine Gun

Gun or Howitzer; approximate number of rounds per Gun or Howitzer

Supplies with Unit:—

Approximate number of days' rations for men of ration strength

„ „ „ forage for Animals „ „

„ „ „ fuel and lubricants for Mechanically Propelled Vehicles

Signature of Commander (Sd) J. V. Shute Lt Col

(90988.) Wt.W. 5216—2140. 900,000 7/15. J. P. & Co. Ltd. Forms B 231 / 3

Instructions regarding War Diaries and Intelligence Summaries are contained in F. S. Regs., Part II. and the Staff Manual respectively. Title pages will be prepared in manuscript.

Vol 30

Army Form C. 2118.

WAR DIARY
or
~~INTELLIGENCE SUMMARY.~~
(Erase heading not required.)

1st Dorset Regiment

Place	Date 1917	Hour	Summary of Events and Information	Remarks and references to Appendices
MAILLEY-MAILLET	Feb. 1st		Battn in billets in MAILLEY-MAILLET finding working parties.	Refer Map LENS. 11.
—do—	" 2nd		—do— —do—	Roche
—do—	" 3rd		—do— —do—	Roche
—do—	" 4th		—do— —do—	
Trenches.		5.15 p.m.	Bn. Moved off to relieve 15th H.L.I. in trenches. C Coy on left and D Coy on right in front line. "A" "B" Coys and Battn Hd Qrs at BURN WORK. 2/Lt J E SALMON + 9 OR wounded 2 OR Killed	Roche
—do—	" 5th		Quiet day. 2/Lt C.L. CHALLIS wounded. 1 OR Killed. 8 OR wounded.	
—do—	" 6th	3 a.m.	Reported considerable enemy artillery activity also short bursts of Machine Gun fire.	Roche
	" 7th		"A" Coy Relieved "C" on the left. "B" Coy relieved "D" on the right. – Quiet day after 6 p.m.	
—do—	" 7th		Casualties. Lt O.G. FOX + 2 OR Killed. 2/Lt H.L. TORR + 10 OR wounded. Situation normal.	Roche
—do—	" 8th	3.5 a.m.	Reported to Bde intermittent shelling and machine gun fire from enemy otherwise quiet day.	Roche
		5.15 p.m.	Relief by 2 Manchester Regt. commenced. Relief completed at 8.15 p.m. Bn withdrew to	
MAILLET-MAILLET		9.45 p.m.	billets in MAILLEY MAILLET. Casualties 3 OR wounded.	Roche
—do—	" 9th		Bn in Billets in MAILLET MAILLET training and finding working parties.	
—do—	" 10th		—do— —do— Bn ordered to be ready to move at ? notice.	
—do—	" 11th	4.30 p.m.	—do— —do— Bn moved to relieve 15th H.L.I. in the trenches	Roche
Trenches.			"C" on the left "D" on the right in the front line. "A+B" Coys + Bn H.Q. at BURN WORK.	
		9.25 p.m.	Relief complete.	
—do—	" 12.		Very quiet day.	Roche
—do—	" 13th		Little hostile shelling otherwise a quiet day. Relief by 1/5 D of Wellington W.R. Regt	
		5.15 p.m.	commenced. Bn withdrew to billets on the outskirts of MAILLEY MAILLET on FORCEVILLERS	Roche
MAILLEY MAILLET FORCEVILLERS	" 14th	4.25 p.m.	Battn in billets on MAILLEY-MAILLET-FORCEVILLERS	
	" 15th	11 a.m.	Moved to huts in BUS. Arrived at huts 12.50 p.m.	Roche

8353 Wt. W2544/1454 700,000 5/15 D. D. & L. A.D.S.S./Forms/C. 2118.

Instructions regarding War Diaries and Intelligence Summaries are contained in F. S. Regs., Part II. and the Staff Manual respectively. Title pages will be prepared in manuscript.

WAR DIARY
or
~~INTELLIGENCE~~ SUMMARY.
(Erase heading not required.)

Army Form C. 2118.

1st Dorset Regiment.

Place	Date 1917	Hour	Summary of Events and Information	Remarks and references to Appendices
BUS.	Feb. 16th	9.30 am	Bn marched via BUS – LOUVENCOURT – LEAAVILLERS – VARENNES to WARLOY.	LENS. 11.
WARLOY		1.50 pm	Bn in Billets in WARLOY Distance 9 miles.	
—do—	17th		—do—	
—do—	18th		—do—	
—do—	19th		—do— Training	
—do—	20th		—do— "	
—do—	21st	10.50 am	Batt. Moved to billets in MOLLIENS-AU-BOIS via BEAUCOURT. arrived at	AMIENS 17.
MOLLIENS-AU-BOIS		2 pm	MOLLIENS-AU-BOIS. Reinforcement of 49 OR joined. Distance marched 4½ miles	
—do—	22nd	10.35 am	Bn marched via RAINNEVILLE – AMIENS Rd to CAMON arriving there 2.30 pm. distance 10 miles	
CAMON.	23rd	9.20 am	Bn Moved via LONGEAU – DOMART to HANGARD Distance 11 miles arrived HANGARD 2 pm	
HANGARD.			Reinforcement of 35 OR joined	
—do—	24th	11.55 am	Moved via MAISON BLANCHE to LE QUESNEL arriving LE QUESNEL 3.30 pm Distance 5 miles	
LE QUESNEL	25th	12.30 pm	Batt. relieved French troops in trenches moving via WARVILLERS	
TRENCHES	26th		Quiet Day – The Commandant and company commanders of the Battalion of 75th French Infantry Regiment (whom we relieved) stayed up in the line till morning of 27th	
—do—	27th		Very quiet day – no casualties except that a Corporal committed suicide in a dugout	
—do—	28th		Very quiet.	

Capt & Adjt
1st Dorset Regiment.

Unit 1st Dorset Regt.
Place In the Field
Date 3. 2. 17

FIELD STATE.

Army Form B 231.

To be rendered in accordance with Field Service Regulations, Part II.

UNIT	FIGHTING STRENGTH — This should *not* include details attached to unit, or personnel detailed to march with the Train, or any men unfit to go into action with unit											RATION STRENGTH — To include Fighting Strength, Personnel detailed to march with the Train, and all Personnel and animals attached for Rations and Forage										Remarks
	Personnel		Horses and Mules		Other Animals		Guns and Ammunition Wagons (stating nature)	Machine Guns	Ambulances	Tool Carts, Technical Carts (stating nature)	Remarks	Personnel	Horses and Mules		Other Animals		Mechanically Propelled Vehicles					
	Officers	Other Ranks	Riding	Draught and Pack								Total, all Ranks entitled to Rations.	Heavy Horses	Other Horses and Mules			Motor Cars	Motor Bicycles.	Lorries. 3 Ton	Lorries. 30 Cwt.	Tractors	
(1)	(2)	(3)	(4)	(5)	(6)	(7)	(8)	(9)	(10)	(11)	(12)	(13)	(14)	(15)	(16)	(17)	(18)	(19)	(20)	(21)	(22)	(23)
	38	914	11	44				14		14		825			56							Detached 10 Officers 102 O.R.
TOTALS ...	36.	914	11	44				14		14		825.			56							

Ammunition with Unit:—

·303 inch; approximate number of rounds per Man ________

·303 inch; „ „ „ per Machine Gun ________

Gun or Howitzer; approximate number of rounds per Gun or Howitzer ________

Supplies with Unit:—

Approximate number of days' rations for men of ration strength ________

„ „ „ forage for Animals „ „ ________

„ „ „ fuel and lubricants for Mechanically Propelled Vehicles ________

(88762.) Wt.W. 2345—1438. 500,000 5/15. J. P. & Co. Ltd. Forms B 231 / 3

Signature of Commander (Sd) J V Shute Lt Col

Unit 1st Dorset Regt

Place In the Field

Date 10. 2. 14

FIELD STATE.

Army Form B 231.

To be rendered in accordance with Field Service Regulations, Part II.

UNIT	FIGHTING STRENGTH — This should *not* include details attached to unit, or personnel detailed to march with the Train, or any men unfit to go into action with unit											RATION STRENGTH — To include Fighting Strength, Personnel detailed to march with the Train, and all Personnel and animals attached for Rations and Forage										
	Personnel		Horses and Mules		Other Animals		Guns and Ammunition Wagons (stating nature)	Machine Guns	Ambulances	Tool Carts, Technical Carts (stating nature)	Remarks	Personnel	Horses and Mules		Other Animals		Mechanically Propelled Vehicles					Remarks
	Officers	Other Ranks	Riding	Draught and Pack								Total, all Ranks entitled to Rations.	Heavy Horses	Other Horses and Mules			Motor Cars	Motor Bicycles.	Lorries. 3 Ton	Lorries. 30 Cwt.	Tractors	
(1)	(2)	(3)	(4)	(5)	(6)	(7)	(8)	(9)	(10)	(11)	(12)	(13)	(14)	(15)	(16)	(17)	(18)	(19)	(20)	(21)	(22)	(23)
	34	902	11	43				14		14		813		55								Detached 9 Officers 102 O.R.
TOTALS ...	34	902	11	43				14		14		813		55								

Ammunition with Unit:—

·303 inch; approximate number of rounds per Man

·303 inch; ,, ,, ,, per Machine Gun

Gun or Howitzer; approximate number of rounds per Gun or Howitzer

Supplies with Unit:—

Approximate number of days' rations for men of ration strength

,, ,, ,, forage for Animals ,, ,,

,, ,, ,, fuel and lubricants for Mechanically Propelled Vehicles

Signature of Commander (Sd) J. V. Shute Lt Col

(88762.) Wt.W. 2345—1438. 500,000 5/15. J. P. & Co. Ltd. Forms B 231 / 3

2Lt. Foss. O.G. Killed in Action 5. 2. 17
Lt. Salmon J.E. Wounded 4. 2. 17
2 Lt Torr H.L. —do— 6. 2 17
Lt. Challis C.L. —do— 4 2 17

Unit 1st Dorset Regt.
Place In the Field
Date 17. 2. 17

FIELD STATE.

Army Form B 231.

To be rendered in accordance with Field Service Regulations, Part II.

UNIT	FIGHTING STRENGTH — This should *not* include details attached to unit, or personnel detailed to march with the Train, or any men unfit to go into action with unit											RATION STRENGTH — To include Fighting Strength, Personnel detailed to march with the Train, and all Personnel and animals attached for Rations and Forage										Remarks
	Personnel		Horses and Mules		Other Animals		Guns and Ammunition Wagons (stating nature)	Machine Guns	Ambulances	Tool Carts, Technical Carts (stating nature)	Remarks	Personnel	Horses and Mules		Other Animals		Mechanically Propelled Vehicles					
	Officers	Other Ranks	Riding	Draught and Pack								Total, all Ranks entitled to Rations.	Heavy Horses	Other Horses and Mules			Motor Cars	Motor Bicycles.	Lorries. 3 Ton	Lorries. 30 Cwt.	Tractors	
(1)	(2)	(3)	(4)	(5)	(6)	(7)	(8)	(9)	(10)	(11)	(12)	(13)	(14)	(15)	(16)	(17)	(18)	(19)	(20)	(21)	(22)	(23)
	34	845	11	43				14		14		803			55							Detached: 9 Officers 85 O.R.
TOTALS ...	34.	845.	11	43.						14		803			55							

Ammunition with Unit:—

·303 inch; approximate number of rounds per Man ______

·303 inch; " " " per Machine Gun ______

Gun or Howitzer; approximate number of rounds per Gun or Howitzer ______

Supplies with Unit:—

Approximate number of days' rations for men of ration strength ______

" " " forage for Animals " " ______

" " " fuel and lubricants for Mechanically Propelled Vehicles ______

Signature of Commander Sd) A. McG. Bald Lt Col
Comdg 1st Dorset Regt

(88762.) Wt.W. 2345—1438. 500,000 5/15. J. P. & Co. Ltd. Forms B 231/3

2/Lt Noble to England. 10. 2. 17.
Capt Kestell - Cornish R.F. Joined from England 14. 2. 17.

Unit 1st Dorset Regiment

Place In the Field

Date 24-2-17.

FIELD STATE.

Army Form B 231.

To be rendered in accordance with Field Service Regulations, Part II.

UNIT	FIGHTING STRENGTH. This should *not* include details attached to unit, or personnel detailed to march with the Train, or any men unfit to go into action with unit											RATION STRENGTH. To include Fighting Strength, Personnel detailed to march with the Train, and all Personnel and animals attached for Rations and Forage										
	Personnel		Horses and Mules		Other Animals		Guns and Ammunition Wagons (stating nature)	Machine Guns	Ambulances	Tool Carts, Technical Carts (stating nature)	Remarks	Personnel	Horses and Mules		Other Animals		Mechanically Propelled Vehicles					Remarks
	Officers	Other Ranks	Riding	Draught and Pack								Total, all Ranks entitled to Rations.	Heavy Horses	Other Horses and Mules			Motor Cars	Motor Bicycles.	Lorries. 3 Ton	Lorries. 30 Cwt.	Tractors	
(1)	(2)	(3)	(4)	(5)	(6)	(7)	(8)	(9)	(10)	(11)	(12)	(13)	(14)	(15)	(16)	(17)	(18)	(19)	(20)	(21)	(22)	(23)
	34	942	11	43.				14		17		891		55								9 Officers 91 O.Ranks detached
Totals ...	34	942	11	43.				14		17		891		55								

Ammunition with Unit:—

·303 inch; approximate number of rounds per Man______

·303 inch; " " " per Machine Gun______

Gun or Howitzer; approximate number of rounds per Gun or Howitzer______

Supplies with Unit:—

Approximate number of days' rations for men of ration strength______

" " " forage for Animals " "______

" " " fuel and lubricants for Mechanically Propelled Vehicles______

(88762.) Wt.W. 2345—1438. 500,000 5/15. J. P. & Co. Ltd. Forms B 231 / 3

Signature of Commander (Sd) R.A. Kestell-Cornish Capt-for Lt Col Comdg 1/Dorset Regt.

Instructions regarding War Diaries and Intelligence Summaries are contained in F. S. Regs., Part II. and the Staff Manual respectively. Title pages will be prepared in manuscript.

WAR DIARY
or
~~INTELLIGENCE SUMMARY.~~

(Erase heading not required.)

Army

1st Dorset Regiment.

Vol 31

Place	Date March	Hour	Summary of Events and Information	Remarks and references to Appendices
Trenches.	1st.		Quiet day - artillery (enemy) fairly active between 6 p.m. and 9 p.m.	Refce MAP LENS 11.
-do-	2nd.		Situation normal - Capt. R.S.D FEW wounded.	
-do-	3rd	6. a/m.	A few enemy shells fell near right Coys. H.Q. about 6 a.m. Otherwise the day was quiet.	RWC
-do-	4th.		Quiet day - slight activity on part of enemy "snipers." Lt GH WOOD wounded.	
-do-	5th.		Situation unchanged - Patrols were sent out during night but encountered nothing unusual.	RWC
-do-	6th.		Reported to Bde situation normal.	RWC
-do-	7th.		Slight enemy shelling - otherwise the day was very quiet.	RWC
-do-	8th.	5.30 p/m	Relief by 16th Lancashire Fusiliers commenced. Battalion withdrew to	RWC
LE QUESNEL			Billets in LE QUESNEL on relief. Batt. in billets in LE QUESNEL 11.40 p.m.	RWC
-do-	9th.		Batt. in BILLETS in LE QUESNEL cleaning up and refitting.	RWC
-do-	10th.	9.15 a/m	Batt. tactical scheme. Divl armourers inspected rifles of Bn.	RWC
-do-	11th.	9.15 a/m 10 a/m 11.15 a/m	Parade services for all C. of E.	RWC
-do-	12th.		Batt. in billets - Training and finding working parties	RWC
-do-	13th.		— do — — do —	RWC
-do-	14th.	5.35 p/m	Batt. moved to relieve 17th H.L.I. A & D Coys and Bn. Hd. Qrs. in dugouts in	RWC
ROUVROY. etc.			KOURPATKIN Trench B & C Coys. in ROUVROY. Relief complete 10 p.m.	RWC
	15th.		Batt. employed on improving KOUROPATKIN Trench and communications with the Front Line	RWC
	16th.		Ditto.	RWC

A5834 Wt. W4973 M687 750,000 8/16 D. D. & L. Ltd. Forms/C.2118/13.

Army Form C. 2118.

Instructions regarding War Diaries and Intelligence Summaries are contained in F. S. Regs., Part II. and the Staff Manual respectively. Title pages will be prepared in manuscript.

WAR DIARY
or
INTELLIGENCE SUMMARY.
(Erase heading not required.)

Place	Date	Hour	Summary of Events and Information	Remarks and references to Appendices
ROUVROY and KOUROPATKIN Trench	17th	6.30pm	Patrols of 2nd Manchester Regt and 15th HLI having ascertained that the Germans had evacuated their front line system of trenches, 14th Bde established themselves on the line DAMERY – FOUQUESCOURT, 1st Dorset Regt holding the ~~support~~ line old British line L 5 Central to L 16 D in support to 2nd Manchester Regt	Refce RWC 66D 1/40000
	18th	9am	The 2nd Manchester Regt and 15th HLI having continued the advance, the 1st Dorset Regt moved up into the line vacated by 15th HLI (from L 18 A 8 7 to L 5 D 4 4) + 4)	Trench Map 66 E.NE and 66D.NW
		11am	~~This on~~ The Battalion was in position at 11 am.	
		3pm	The Battalion marched from FOUQUESCOURT to LIANCOURT Wood via FRANSART, HATTENCOURT and LIANCOURT –	
		6.30pm	The Battalion bivouaced in LIANCOURT Wood in support to 15th HLI	RWC
	19th	8.30am	The Battalion marched from LIANCOURT Wood, crossing the SEPT – FOURS – ETALON Line	
		9.30am	at 9.30am (This line was held by 15th HLI ~~and~~. The Battalion passed through the 15th HLI) The enemy were reported on the line LIBERMONT – VOYENNES – QUIVIERES. The Battalion marched via ETALON – CURCHY – MESNIL le Petit [C Company marched via CURCHY – DRESLINCOURT – MESNIL le Petit ~~as~~ as Flank Guard] – MESNIL St Nicaise and took up an outpost line with the main line of resistance on high ground WEST of the canal, which runs from BREUIL via QUIQUERY to ROUY – le – GRAND – The right of the Battalion and the left of the 5/6th Royal Scots being I 10 D 8.4.	
		1pm	Battalion was in position	RWC

A5834 Wt. W4973 M687 750,000 8/16 D. D. & L. Ltd. Forms/C.2118/13.

Army Form C. 2118.

Instructions regarding War Diaries and Intelligence Summaries are contained in F. S. Regs., Part II. and the Staff Manual respectively. Title pages will be prepared in manuscript.

WAR DIARY
or
INTELLIGENCE SUMMARY.

(Erase heading not required.)

Place	Date	Hour	Summary of Events and Information	Remarks and references to Appendices
ROUY le Petit	19	1.45pm	The Battalion advanced across the Canal over temporary foot bridge at I 10 B 27 (where Bridge had been destroyed) and passing through ROUY le Petit ~~on~~ took up an outpost position on the ridge the Southern side of ROUY le Petit. Here the Battalion dug itself in – B Company remaining in support in ROUY le Petit.	Refce 66D 1/40,000
		3.30pm.	Battalion was in position about 3.30 pm.	R.W.C.
	20	9am.	Battalion withdrew to ROUY le Petit – The outpost line being held by one post per Company	
			During this day the Battalion rebuilt a bridge at I 10 B 27, that B Company had constructed on the night of 19th instant and over which all the Divisional Transport had passed. The Divisional General gave orders that this bridge was to be called DORSET Bridge.	R.W.C.
	21	11.30am	Battalion marched from ROUY le Petit via VOYENNES and BUNY to MATIGNY, where an outpost line was taken up from Cemetery D 15 c 51 to Cross roads D 22 C 09 thence to D 27 B 55 ~~and~~ with the Right of the Battalion on track at J 4 B 5.6. –	
			The 5/6th Royal Scots were responsible for our left Flank from the SOMME Canal to Cemetery D15c51 and 96th Brigade was on the right of the Battalion.	
		3pm	The Battalion was in position about 3pm. and started digging itself in and wiring the front.	R.W.C.

A5834 Wt. W4973 M687 750,000 8/16 D. D. & L. Ltd. Forms/C.2118/13.

Instructions regarding War Diaries and Intelligence Summaries are contained in F. S. Regs., Part II. and the Staff Manual respectively. Title pages will be prepared in manuscript.

Army Form C. 2118.

WAR DIARY
or
INTELLIGENCE SUMMARY.
(Erase heading not required.)

Place	Date	Hour	Summary of Events and Information	Remarks and references to Appendices
MATIGNY	22		Battalion ~~was~~ worked on filling in large crater at cross roads D 22 C 0 9 and half completed this task – still holding the outpost line as on 21st	Refce 66D 1/40000
	23		Crater at cross roads D 22 C 0 9 completed and ~~was~~ heavy transport passed over the crossroads	62C 1/40000
	24		The work of putting the village in a state of defence was continued.	R.W.H.C.
	25		Ditto	
	26		Ditto	
	27		Ditto.	R.W.H.C.
	28	5.30pm	The Battalion marched from MATIGNY ~~&~~ via UGNY ~~&~~ and occupied a position from W 30 A 53 to E 6 Central – (on the reverse slope of the ridge) with 2 Companies, 2 Companies being billeted in LANCHY. The 15th HLI were on the left of the Battalion and 97th Bde on the Right. This line was held by 7 strong points.	
	29		Line was held as on 28th instant with the addition of an Outpost Line from X 14 C 43 to X 20 D Central.	R.W.H.C. R.W.H.C.
	30 31	}	The line was held as on 29th instant	R.W.H.C. R.W.H.C.

A5834 Wt. W4973 M687 750,000 8/16 D. D. & L. Ltd. Forms/C.2118/13.

Unit 1st Dorset Regt

Place In the Field

Date 3 3 17

FIELD STATE.

Army Form B 231.

To be rendered in accordance with Field Service Regulations, Part II.

UNIT	FIGHTING STRENGTH — This should *not* include details attached to unit, or personnel detailed to march with the Train, or any men unfit to go into action with unit: Personnel		Horses and Mules		Other Animals		Guns and Ammunition Wagons (stating nature)	Machine Guns	Ambulances	Tool Carts, Technical Carts (stating nature)	Remarks	RATION STRENGTH — To include Fighting Strength, Personnel detailed to march with the Train, and all Personnel and animals attached for Rations and Forage: Personnel	Horses and Mules		Other Animals		Mechanically Propelled Vehicles					Remarks
	Officers	Other Ranks	Riding	Draught and Pack								Total, all Ranks entitled to Rations.	Heavy Horses	Other Horses and Mules			Motor Cars	Motor Bicycles.	Lorries. 3 Ton	Lorries. 30 Cwt.	Tractors	
(1)	(2)	(3)	(4)	(5)	(6)	(7)	(8)	(9)	(10)	(11)	(12)	(13)	(14)	(15)	(16)	(17)	(18)	(19)	(20)	(21)	(22)	(23)
1st Dorset Regt	34	941	11	43			14 L. Guns	14		17		902	—	55								7 officers & 80 OR detached from Bn. 2 officers & 7 OR attached to Bn.
TOTALS ...	34	941	11	43								902	—	55								

Ammunition with Unit:—

·303 inch; approximate number of rounds per Man

·303 inch; „ „ „ per Machine Gun

Gun or Howitzer; approximate number of rounds per Gun or Howitzer

Supplies with Unit:—

Approximate number of days' rations for men of ration strength

„ „ „ forage for Animals „ „

„ „ „ fuel and lubricants for Mechanically Propelled Vehicles

(88762.) Wt.W. 2345—1438. 500,000 5/15. J. P. & Co. Ltd. Forms B 231 / 3

Signature of Commander [illegible]

Lieut.	J. R. Walton	1st Dorset Regt.	To. S. A.	25/2/17
Captain	R. J. D. Lew	—	Wounded	2/3/17
Capt.	C. P. Whitaker	—	Joined Div.	26/2/17
Lieut.	A. J. Green	—	—	26/2/17

Unit 1st Dorset Regt
Place [illegible]
Date 10.3.17.

FIELD STATE.

Army Form B 231.

To be rendered in accordance with Field Service Regulations, Part II.

UNIT	FIGHTING STRENGTH — This should *not* include details attached to unit, or personnel detailed to march with the Train, or any men unfit to go into action with unit											RATION STRENGTH — To include Fighting Strength, Personnel detailed to march with the Train, and all Personnel and animals attached for Rations and Forage										
	Personnel		Horses and Mules		Other Animals		Guns and Ammunition Wagons (stating nature)	Machine Guns	Ambulances	Tool Carts, Technical Carts (stating nature)	Remarks	Personnel	Horses and Mules		Other Animals		Mechanically Propelled Vehicles					Remarks
	Officers	Other Ranks	Riding	Draught and Pack								Total, all Ranks entitled to Rations.	Heavy Horses	Other Horses and Mules			Motor Cars	Motor Bicycles.	Lorries. 3 Ton	Lorries. 30 Cwt.	Tractors	
(1)	(2)	(3)	(4)	(5)	(6)	(7)	(8)	(9)	(10)	(11)	(12)	(13)	(14)	(15)	(16)	(17)	(18)	(19)	(20)	(21)	(22)	(23)
1st Dorset Regt	32	933	11	43			14/Lewis	14		17		889	8	47								8 Offrs & 82 OR detached from Bn 2 Offrs & 7 OR attached to Bn
TOTALS ...	32	933	11	43				14		17		889	8	47								

Ammunition with Unit:—

·303 inch; approximate number of rounds per Man________

·303 inch; „ „ „ per Machine Gun________

Gun or Howitzer; approximate number of rounds per Gun or Howitzer________

Supplies with Unit:—

Approximate number of days' rations for men of ration strength________

„ „ „ forage for Animals „ „________

„ „ „ fuel and lubricants for Mechanically Propelled Vehicles________

Signature of Commander [illegible]

(88762.) Wt.W. 2345—1438. 500,000 5/15. J. P. & Co. Ltd. Forms B 231 / 3

Lieut. G. G. Wood 1st Dorset Regt. Wounded 4/3/17.

Unit 1st Dorset Regt

Place In the Field

Date 16/3/17

FIELD STATE.

Army Form B 231.

To be rendered in accordance with Field Service Regulations, Part II.

	FIGHTING STRENGTH — This should *not* include details attached to unit, or personnel detailed to march with the Train, or any men unfit to go into action with unit											RATION STRENGTH — To include Fighting Strength, Personnel detailed to march with the Train, and all Personnel and animals attached for Rations and Forage										
UNIT	Personnel		Horses and Mules		Other Animals		Guns and Ammunition Wagons (stating nature)	Machine Guns	Ambulances	Tool Carts, Technical Carts (stating nature)	Remarks	Personnel	Horses and Mules		Other Animals		Mechanically Propelled Vehicles					Remarks
	Officers	Other Ranks	Riding	Draught and Pack								Total, all Ranks entitled to Rations.	Heavy Horses	Other Horses and Mules			Motor Cars	Motor Bicycles.	Lorries. 3 Ton	Lorries. 30 Cwt.	Tractors	
(1)	(2)	(3)	(4)	(5)	(6)	(7)	(8)	(9)	(10)	(11)	(12)	(13)	(14)	(15)	(16)	(17)	(18)	(19)	(20)	(21)	(22)	(23)
1st Dorset Regt	35	919	11	43			M.G. Guns	14		17		839	8	47								1 offr + 12 O.R. attached from Bde; 2 offrs + 1 O.R. attached to Bde
TOTALS ...	35	919	11	43				14		17		839	8	47								

Ammunition with Unit:—

·303 inch; approximate number of rounds per Man

·303 inch; " " " per Machine Gun

Gun or Howitzer; approximate number of rounds per Gun or Howitzer

Supplies with Unit:—

Approximate number of days' rations for men of ration strength

" " " forage for Animals " "

" " " fuel and lubricants for Mechanically Propelled Vehicles

Signature of Commander [illegible]

(88762.) Wt.W. 2345—1438. 500,000 5/15. J. P. & Co. Ltd. Forms B 231 / 3

Lieut R. S. Faulkner 1st Dorset Regt Joined Bn. 12-3-17
" S. Wolferstan " " 12 3 17.
" L. Digby " " 12 3 17.
" A. S. Hands " " 12 3 17
Lieut P. J. Richmond.

Unit 1st Dorset Regt

Place In the Field

Date 23 3 17

FIELD STATE.

Army Form B 231.

To be rendered in accordance with Field Service Regulations, Part II.

UNIT	FIGHTING STRENGTH — This should *not* include details attached to unit, or personnel detailed to march with the Train, or any men unfit to go into action with unit											RATION STRENGTH — To include Fighting Strength, Personnel detailed to march with the Train, and all Personnel and animals attached for Rations and Forage										
	Personnel		Horses and Mules		Other Animals		Guns and Ammunition Wagons (stating nature)	Machine Guns	Ambulances	Tool Carts, Technical Carts (stating nature)	Remarks	Personnel	Horses and Mules		Other Animals		Mechanically Propelled Vehicles					Remarks
	Officers	Other Ranks	Riding	Draught and Pack								Total, all Ranks entitled to Rations.	Heavy Horses	Other Horses and Mules			Motor Cars	Motor Bicycles.	Lorries. 3 Ton	Lorries. 30 Cwt.	Tractors	
(1)	(2)	(3)	(4)	(5)	(6)	(7)	(8)	(9)	(10)	(11)	(12)	(13)	(14)	(15)	(16)	(17)	(18)	(19)	(20)	(21)	(22)	(23)
1st Dorset Regt	35	891	11	43			M.G. Guns	14		14		859	8	47								5 offrs & 7 OR attached from Bn. 2 offrs 2 OR attached to Bn
TOTALS ...	35	891	11	43				14		14		859	8	47								

Ammunition with Unit:—

·303 inch; approximate number of rounds per Man ______

·303 inch; „ „ „ per Machine Gun ______

Gun or Howitzer; approximate number of rounds per Gun or Howitzer ______

Supplies with Unit:—

Approximate number of days' rations for men of ration strength ______

„ „ „ forage for Animals „ „ ______

„ „ „ fuel and lubricants for Mechanically Propelled Vehicles ______

(88762.) Wt.W. 2345—1438. 500,000 5/15. J. P. & Co. Ltd. Forms B 231 / 3

Signature of Commander (Sd) [illegible] Major Comdg 1/Dorset Regt

Lieut. H. J. Green 1st Dorset Regt. To. S. A. 21. 3. 17

Unit 1st Devon Regt

Place In the Field

Date 30.3.17

FIELD STATE.

Army Form B 231.

To be rendered in accordance with Field Service Regulations, Part II.

UNIT	FIGHTING STRENGTH — This should not include details attached to unit, or personnel detailed to march with the Train, or any men unfit to go into action with unit											RATION STRENGTH — To include Fighting Strength, Personnel detailed to march with the Train, and all Personnel and animals attached for Rations and Forage											Remarks
	Personnel		Horses and Mules		Other Animals		Guns and Ammunition Wagons (stating nature)	Machine Guns	Ambulances	Tool Carts, Technical Carts (stating nature)	Remarks	Personnel	Horses and Mules		Other Animals		Mechanically Propelled Vehicles					
	Officers	Other Ranks	Riding	Draught and Pack								Total, all Ranks entitled to Rations.	Heavy Horses	Other Horses and Mules			Motor Cars	Motor Bicycles.	Lorries. 3 Ton	Lorries. 30 Cwt.	Tractors	
(1)	(2)	(3)	(4)	(5)	(6)	(7)	(8)	(9)	(10)	(11)	(12)	(13)	(14)	(15)	(16)	(17)	(18)	(19)	(20)	(21)	(22)	(23)
1st Devon Regt	40	891	11	42			14 L Guns	14		17		843	7	46								3 offrs + 100 OR attached from Bn [illegible] offrs / OR attached to Bn
TOTALS ...	40	891	11	42				14		17		843	7	46								

Ammunition with Unit:—

·303 inch; approximate number of rounds per Man

·303 inch; " " " per Machine Gun

Gun or Howitzer; approximate number of rounds per Gun or Howitzer

Supplies with Unit:—

Approximate number of days' rations for men of ration strength

" " " forage for Animals " "

" " " fuel and lubricants for Mechanically Propelled Vehicles

Signature of Commander

(88762.) Wt.W. 2345—1438. 500,000 5/15. J. P. & Co. Ltd. Forms B 231 / 3

Lieut. J. R. Walton	1st Dorset Regt	From F.A.	26/3/17.
C. E. Tye	-"-	Joined Bn	26/3/17.
S. L. Braddy	-"-	-"-	26/3/17.
S. H. Taylor	-"-	-"-	26/3/17.
W. C. Gosnell	-"-	-"-	26/3/17.
G. C. Seymour	-"-	-"-	27/3/17.

April

Instructions regarding War Diaries and Intelligence Summaries are contained in F. S. Regs., Part II. and the Staff Manual respectively. Title pages will be prepared in manuscript.

WAR DIARY
or
INTELLIGENCE SUMMARY.
(Erase heading not required.)

Army Form C. 2118.

1 Dorset Regt

Vol 32

Place	Date	Hour	Summary of Events and Information	Remarks and references to Appendices
LANCHY	1	9.30am	Battalion was ordered to proceed to FORESTE	Refs 66D 62B 62C
		11.30am	Battalion bivouaced in E16B FORESTE	
		5.30pm	Battalion marched to F9a near Chateau de POMMERY and remained there till	
		12 midnight	12 midnight. Battalion then moved via ROUPY and SAVY to a position on the Northern edge of SAVY Wood	1/40000
HOLNON	2	5am	Battalion advanced and attacked HOLNON under cover of our barrage (2nd Manchester Regt on our Right were attacking FRANCILLY and SELENCY)	RWhl
		6am	The village of HOLNON was entirely in our hands. Heavy enemy machine gun fire was being directed on the North East point of the village. At about 5.45am the enemy opened rapid rifle fire from the direction of Chateau in S3D. Battalion took up a line S3C 2.4 along the road to Cross Roads S2A thence Northwards to quarry in M32D.	
			Two Companies formed a defensive left flank from Cross Roads S2A along road to S7B07, thence along track to S7D78, thence along road to junction with Railway S13.0.0. Casualties. 2/Lt. P.J. RICHMOND wounded	
			The rest of the day was spent in consolidating our position. Co O.R. 1 killed 14 wounded	RWhl
		8.30pm	2 Coys moved from position on left flank and relieved 2nd KOYLI, taking up a line along the road from crossroads S2A to Mon de GARDE X35D85, joining up with C Company 1st Dorset Regt on the right and with the 61st Division on the left.	

A5834 Wt. W4973/M687 750,000 8/16 J. B. C. & A. Forms/C.2118/12.

Army Form C. 2118.

Instructions regarding War Diaries and Intelligence Summaries are contained in F. S. Regs., Part II. and the Staff Manual respectively. Title pages will be prepared in manuscript.

WAR DIARY
or
INTELLIGENCE SUMMARY.

(Erase heading not required.)

Place	Date	Hour	Summary of Events and Information	Remarks and references to Appendices
HOLNON	3		The work of consolidating our position carried on. 2nd Lieut S. WOLFERSTAN killed. Other ranks 1 killed – 8 wounded.	Ref. 62c. 62B.
		10pm.	The two Companies holding the line from M[in] de GARDE X35 D85 along the road to crossroads S2A. were relieved by 2/4 GLOUCESTER REGT. 61st DIVISION and retired to a support position at crater S7 D78.	RWhe
	4		The work of consolidating our position was carried on.	
		9pm.	Three Companies of the Battalion advanced to take up a new position running from M26 D1.1 – M33 B2.7 – M33 B8.0 thence due SOUTH to crater at S3 D7.7. The remaining Company took over the whole of the line – two platoons occupying the sunken road from S2a.72 to M32 d1.5 in order to cover the batteries expected in M32c. Strong enemy patrols were encountered by the right company, which delayed our advance for some time. On the left the enemy was found to be occupying a small copse NORTH of the WOOD in M33 Central, which commanded the whole of the valley running through M32 b and M33 a and b. Half a company attacked this copse and eventually forced the enemy to retire in the direction of FRESNOY. 2nd LIEUT S H TAYLOR was killed in this attack. The remainder of the line was occupied without opposition. Casualties 1 Other rank killed – 3 wounded.	
	5.	4am.	The line running from M26 D1.1 – M33 B2.7 – M33 B8.0 thence due SOUTH to crater at S3 D7.7. completely established. The work of consolidating our position was carried on until daylight.	RWhe
		7p.M.	Two platoons of the 5/6 ROYAL SCOTS occupied the sunken road in S2A ready to support the left company in case of emergency. Two platoons of the 5/6 ROYAL SCOTS also occupied the QUARRY at S3 D78. to support the right companies. Casualties 4 O.R. wounded	RWhe

A5834 Wt. W4973 M687 750,000 8/16 D. D. & L. Ltd. Forms/C.2118/13.

Instructions regarding War Diaries and Intelligence Summaries are contained in F. S. Regs., Part II. and the Staff Manual respectively. Title pages will be prepared in manuscript.

WAR DIARY
or
INTELLIGENCE SUMMARY.
(Erase heading not required.)

Army Form C. 2118.

Place	Date	Hour	Summary of Events and Information	Remarks and references to Appendices
HOLNON	6		The work of consolidating our position carried on until daylight.	62 B.
		9pm	The right company was relieved by 183rd Infantry Brigade who took over the line from M.33 B 8.0 – M33 B3.7 – M 26 D 3.1. The two companies of 5/6 ROYAL SCOTS attached to the 1st DORSET REGT were relieved by the 11th BORDER REGT. Casualties. 2 OR. killed 2 OR. missing.	[illegible]
	7	12.30am	The 2ND K.O.Y.L.I. relieved the two companies in the line from S 9 b.1.9 (exclusive) to M 33 b 8.0.	[illegible]
		4.30am	Relief reported complete. Battalion returned to GERMAINE.	
GERMAINE		7.30am	Battalion reported in Billets.	
	8		Battalion at rest in Billets at GERMAINE	[illegible]
	9		——— " ———	
	10		——— " ———	
	11		——— " ———	
	12	12.45am	2 Companies marched from GERMAINE and relieved 2 Companies 16th Lancashire Fusiliers in the line from Road Junction with Railway S 21 C 8.5 to Road Junction with Railway S 22 C 1.5, thence to Cross roads S 28 A 5.9. ~~whence the line~~ from which point to the right the line was held by the French	
		8am	Bn HQ and remaining 2 Companies relieved remainder of 16th Lancashire Fusiliers [illegible] line mentioned above.	[illegible]
		11.15am	Relief Complete. Casualties 2 O R wounded	

A5834 Wt. W4973 M687 750,000 8/16 D. D. & L. Ltd. Forms/C.2118/13.

Instructions regarding War Diaries and Intelligence Summaries are contained in F. S. Regs., Part II. and the Staff Manual respectively. Title pages will be prepared in manuscript.

WAR DIARY
or
INTELLIGENCE SUMMARY.
(Erase heading not required.)

Army Form C. 2118.

Place	Date	Hour	Summary of Events and Information	Remarks and references to Appendices
Near St QUENTIN	13	5am	In conjunction with a French attack on St QUENTIN, the Battalion pushed out strong patrols down the spurs to S23A55 – S17C52 – S16 Central and BOIS des ROSES.	Refce 62B
			Each patrol consisting of half a company and 2 Lewis Guns	
			The patrol at S23.A55 met with the greatest opposition, coming under heavy machine gun & artillery fire – The position in BOIS des ROSES was under machine gun and rifle fire from FAYET and was heavily shelled during the day from direction of St QUENTIN.	
			Battalion HQ were at S22 C2.3. 2 Companies were in support in strong points at S22C61 and S22C16. 2 Companies of French Infantry were entrenching in front of the left strong point and ~~along~~ the near Bn HQ. Casualties Capt L.G. HAMILTON wounded – O.R. 1 killed 11 wounded	RWHC
	14	6.30am	Received verbal orders to attack CEPY Farm at 7.30am – C Company delivered this attack, coming under heavy machine gun fire and considerable artillery fire. D Company being on C Company's right flank	
		9am	Battalion in position with its left on CEPY Farm and its right in S17C –	
			It is estimated from the number of Germans seen running away from CEPY Farm that the Farm was held by at least half a company at the time it was attacked – 5 prisoners were taken on the road about S5D03	RWHC

A5834 Wt. W4973/M687 750,000 8/16 D. D. & L. Ltd. Forms/C.2118/13.

Instructions regarding War Diaries and Intelligence Summaries are contained in F. S. Regs., Part II. and the Staff Manual respectively. Title pages will be prepared in manuscript.

WAR DIARY
or
INTELLIGENCE SUMMARY.
(Erase heading not required.)

Army Form C. 2118.

Place	Date	Hour	Summary of Events and Information	Remarks and references to Appendices
CEPY Farm	14	9am	and 2 prisoners were taken in CEPY Farm – The garrison of the Farm fired on the attacking force till within about 50 yards from the Farm and then fled. C Company took up a position along a hedge North East of the Farm with its post facing South East. – They were subjected to an intense Artillery bombardment during the day and the approaches to the Farm were swept by machine gun fire from St QUENTIN. D Company's left was on the FAYET – St QUENTIN Road in front of a small copse about S5 D 0 3 and their right on the cross roads S12 C. A Company's left was on the Anc^ne Voie Romaine about S17 B and their right in S17C. B Company was in support. Casualties 2/Lt W.C. GOSNELL wounded O.R. 7 killed 3 missing and 32 wounded	Info 62B
	14/15th		During the night of 14/15th C Company made 2 posts about 50 yards North East of the Farm and one post S.E. of the Farm with its right on the GRICOURT – St QUENTIN Road	RWhe
	15		~~At~~ Just before dawn these three posts were handed over to B Company who manned them with two platoons.	RWhe

A5834 Wt. W4973 M687 750,000 8/16 D. D. & L. Ltd. Forms/C.2118/13.

Instructions regarding War Diaries and Intelligence Summaries are contained in F. S. Regs., Part II. and the Staff Manual respectively. Title pages will be prepared in manuscript.

WAR DIARY
or
INTELLIGENCE SUMMARY.
(*Erase heading not required.*)

Army Form C. 2118.

Place	Date	Hour	Summary of Events and Information	Remarks and references to Appendices
CEPY Farm	15		CEPY Farm was subjected to a very heavy bombardment throughout the day which grew in intensity towards the evening –	Refce 66D. 62B 62C. 1/40,000
		3 pm	At the height of the bombardment Major H.C. BUTCHER DSO commanding the Battalion was wounded on the ATTICOURT – St QUENTIN Road as he was approaching CEPY Farm –	
			The garrison of the Farm suffered heavily. The casualties on this day were 2/Lt G.C. SEYMOUR and 2/Lt S.H. WITTY and 13 O.R. killed – Major H.C. BUTCHER DSO. Lieut R.S. FAULKNER 2/Lt C.V.M. SMART, 2/Lt H.S. WOODS and 22 other ranks wounded –	
		About 7 pm	As it grew dark the bombardment became more subdued –	
			During the night the Battalion was relieved by one company 16th Royal Scots and 3 Companies 15th HLI. –	
SAVY	16	6.30 am	Relief complete – Battalion withdrew to SAVY.	[illegible]
	17 18 19		Battalion remained in SAVY in bivouacs, cellars etc – On the 18th & 19th at about 4 pm the village was heavily shelled for two or three hours with 5.9 shells directed on a R.F.A. Battery – Casualties 2 men slightly wounded	[illegible]

A5834 Wt. W4973 M687 750,000 8/16 D. D. & L. Ltd. Forms/C.2118/13.

Instructions regarding War Diaries and Intelligence Summaries are contained in F. S. Regs., Part II. and the Staff Manual respectively. Title pages will be prepared in manuscript.

WAR DIARY
or
INTELLIGENCE SUMMARY.
(*Erase heading not required.*)

Army Form C. 2118.

Place	Date	Hour	Summary of Events and Information	Remarks and references to Appendices
SAVY	20	1.30pm	Battalion was relieved in SAVY by 6th Royal Warwick Regt and withdrew to UGNY and LANCHY. Bn HQ & 2 Companies at UGNY and 2 Companies at LANCHY	RWK AMIENS 17
	21 22 23 24 25 26 27 28 29		Battalion remained in UGNY and LANCHY. Training was carried out, special attention being paid to sectional formation – Each company cut down to two platoons to ensure having strong sections	RWK
	30		14th Brigade was inspected by Major General C.D. SHUTE. C.B. D.S.O Commanding 32nd Division, who congratulated the Brigade on the ~~work done~~ way in which they had carried out the recent operations	RWK
			Honours and Awards	
	D.R.O 2049 d/22/4/17		Captain C.P. WHITAKER. M.C. awarded a Bar to his Military Cross	RWK
	D.R.O 2043		8433 L/cpl W. BURT awarded Military Medal	
	MS R1849 21/4/17		7848 L/cpl R. DENNER awarded a Bar to his Military Medal	
	G 26/10/1-26/4/17		Hon. Lieut and QM. W. ALDERMAN awarded the Military Cross	

R.W. Walker Colonel
Lieut & Adjutant
15th ... Regt

A5834. Wt. W4373 M687 750,000 8/16 D. D. & L. Ltd. Forms/C.2118/13.

HEADQUARTERS
No. G.132/1
Date 17.4.17
14th INFANTRY BRIGADE

O.C., 1st Dorset Regt.

The attached confidential letter, 32nd Division G.S.1140/1/21 of 17th April, is forwarded for information and communication to all ranks.

It is highly gratifying to me to have been appointed to the Command of a Brigade which includes a Battalion capable of such gallant and sustained efforts as have been displayed by the 1st Battalion DORSET REGT.

The dash with which your Battalion attacked and the tenacity with which it has held on to CEPY FARM, under intense and continuous artillery bombardment, are not only object lessons to us all but are in accordance with the highest traditions of the British Army.

F.W. Lumsden

Brigadier General,
17th April 1917. Commanding 14th Infantry Brigade.

Confidential

G.O.C.
14th Bde

Please tell the O.C. 1st Dorset Regt how very distressed I am at the heavy losses his Battalion has incurred from shell fire in the neighbourhood of CEPY FARM & how much I appreciate the tenacity with which that important tactical point has been held.

I should like all the Battalion to be informed that every possible effort is being made to "counter-Battery" the enemy guns. The difficulty being that the weather & large number of enemy anti-aircraft guns makes it difficult for our planes to range our Heavies & also every available Heavy gun has gone to other parts of the line.

C. D. Shute, Maj. Genl.
Comm. 32nd Div.

17-4-17

O.C. B coy.

C coy A.S.K.

B coy JMS

A coy [illegible]

D coy

Unit 1st Dorset Regt.

Place In the Field

Date 6.4.17

FIELD STATE.

Army Form B 231.

To be rendered in accordance with Field Service Regulations, Part II.

UNIT	FIGHTING STRENGTH — This should *not* include details attached to unit, or personnel detailed to march with the Train, or any men unfit to go into action with unit											RATION STRENGTH — To include Fighting Strength, Personnel detailed to march with the Train, and all Personnel and animals attached for Rations and Forage										Remarks
	Personnel		Horses and Mules		Other Animals		Guns and Ammunition Wagons (stating nature)	Machine Guns	Ambulances	Tool Carts, Technical Carts (stating nature)	Remarks	Personnel	Horses and Mules		Other Animals		Mechanically Propelled Vehicles					
	Officers	Other Ranks	Riding	Draught and Pack								Total, all Ranks entitled to Rations.	Heavy Horses	Other Horses and Mules			Motor Cars	Motor Bicycles.	Lorries. 3 Ton	Lorries. 30 Cwt.	Tractors	
(1)	(2)	(3)	(4)	(5)	(6)	(7)	(8)	(9)	(10)	(11)	(12)	(13)	(14)	(15)	(16)	(17)	(18)	(19)	(20)	(21)	(22)	(23)
1st Dorset Regt.	40	841	11	42			16 L. Guns			1		824	7	46								3 offrs + 30 O.R. [illegible] / 2 offrs + 7 O.R. [illegible]
TOTALS ...	40	841	11	42				16		1		827	7	46								

Ammunition with Unit:—

·303 inch; approximate number of rounds per Man _____

·303 inch; " " " per Machine Gun _____

Gun or Howitzer; approximate number of rounds per Gun or Howitzer _____

Supplies with Unit:—

Approximate number of days' rations for men of ration strength _____

" " " forage for Animals " " _____

" " " fuel and lubricants for Mechanically Propelled Vehicles _____

Signature of Commander (Sd.) A. L. Butcher, Major, Comdg. 1/Dorset Regt.

(88762.) Wt.W. 2345—1438. 500,000 5/15. J. P. & Co. Ltd. Forms B 231 / 3

Lieut	P. J. Richmond	Dorset Regt	Wounded	2/4/17
"	S. Wolferstan	—"—	Killed in Action	3/4/17
"	S. H. Taylor	—"—	—"—	4/4/17
"	C. G. Miller	—"—	Joined Battn	2/4/17
"	J. T. Wylie	—"—	—"—	2/4/17
"	H. S. Wood	—"—	—"—	2/4/17

Unit 1st Dorset Regt

Place In the Field

Date 13. 4. 17

FIELD STATE.

Army Form B 231.

To be rendered in accordance with Field Service Regulations, Part II.

UNIT	FIGHTING STRENGTH — This should *not* include details attached to unit, or personnel detailed to march with the Train, or any men unfit to go into action with unit											RATION STRENGTH — To include Fighting Strength, Personnel detailed to march with the Train, and all Personnel and animals attached for Rations and Forage										
	Personnel		Horses and Mules		Other Animals		Guns and Ammunition Wagons (stating nature)	Machine Guns	Ambulances	Tool Carts, Technical Carts (stating nature)	Remarks	Personnel	Horses and Mules		Other Animals		Mechanically Propelled Vehicles					Remarks
	Officers	Other Ranks	Riding	Draught and Pack								Total, all Ranks entitled to Rations.	Heavy Horses	Other Horses and Mules			Motor Cars	Motor Bicycles.	Lorries. 3 Ton	Lorries. 30 Cwt.	Tractors	
(1)	(2)	(3)	(4)	(5)	(6)	(7)	(8)	(9)	(10)	(11)	(12)	(13)	(14)	(15)	(16)	(17)	(18)	(19)	(20)	(21)	(22)	(23)
1st Dorset Regt	39	827	11	42			16 L Guns	16		17		189	7	46								5 Offrs + 87 OR detached from Bn. 2 Offrs + 7 OR attached to Bn
TOTALS ...	39	824	11	42				16		17		189	7	46								

Ammunition with Unit:—

·303 inch; approximate number of rounds per Man ____

·303 inch; " " " per Machine Gun ____

Gun or Howitzer; approximate number of rounds per Gun or Howitzer ____

Supplies with Unit:—

Approximate number of days' rations for men of ration strength ____

" " " forage for Animals " " ____

" " " fuel and lubricants for Mechanically Propelled Vehicles ____

Signature of Commander [illegible]

(88762.) Wt.W. 2345—1438. 500,000 5/15. J. P. & Co. Ltd. Forms B 231 / 3

Capt.	L. G. Hamilton	1st Dorset Regt	Wounded	13/4/17
Lt. Col.	J. V. Shute	– " –	From Leave	8/4/17
Lt. Col.	J. V. Shute	– " –	To F. A.	9/4/17
Lieut.	H. K. L. Statham	– " –	Joined Battn	10/4/17
	B. C. J. Allbon	– " –	Struck off strength	10/4/17
	C. B. Stock	– " –	To F. A.	3/4/17

Unit 1st Dorset Regt

Place In the Field

Date 20-4-17.

FIELD STATE.

Army Form B 231.

To be rendered in accordance with Field Service Regulations, Part II.

UNIT	FIGHTING STRENGTH — This should *not* include details attached to unit, or personnel detailed to march with the Train, or any men unfit to go into action with unit											RATION STRENGTH — To include Fighting Strength, Personnel detailed to march with the Train, and all Personnel and animals attached for Rations and Forage										
	Personnel		Horses and Mules		Other Animals							Personnel	Horses and Mules		Other Animals		Mechanically Propelled Vehicles					
	Officers	Other Ranks	Riding	Draught and Pack			Guns and Ammunition Wagons (stating nature)	Machine Guns	Ambulances	Tool Carts, Technical Carts (stating nature)	Remarks	Total, all Ranks entitled to Rations.	Heavy Horses	Other Horses and Mules			Motor Cars	~~Motor~~ Bicycles.	Lorries. 3 Ton	Lorries. 30 Cwt.	Tractors	Remarks
(1)	(2)	(3)	(4)	(5)	(6)	(7)	(8)	(9)	(10)	(11)	(12)	(13)	(14)	(15)	(16)	(17)	(18)	(19)	(20)	(21)	(22)	(23)
1st Dorset Regt	33	721	9	40			16 L. Guns	16		17		649	7	43				9				7 Offrs + 114 OR. attached from Bn. 2 Offrs + 7 OR attached to Bn
TOTALS ...	33	721	9	40				16		17		649	7	43				9				

Ammunition with Unit:—

·303 inch; approximate number of rounds per Man ______

·303 inch; " " " per Machine Gun ______

Gun or Howitzer; approximate number of rounds per Gun or Howitzer ______

Supplies with Unit:—

Approximate number of days' rations for men of ration strength ______

" " " forage for Animals " " ______

" " " fuel and lubricants for Mechanically Propelled Vehicles ______

Signature of Commander (Sd) C P Whitaker Captain
Comdg 1st Dorset Regt

(88762.) Wt.W. 2345—1438. 500,000 5/15. J. P. & Co. Ltd. Forms B 231 / 3

Major H. C. Butcher DSO 1st Dorset Regt. Wounded 15/4/17.

Lieut C. V. M. Smart — " — — " — 15/4/17

— " — G. C. Seymour — " — Killed in Action 15/4/17

— " — H. S. Wood — " — Wounded 15/4/17.

— " — W. C. Gosnell — " — — " — 14/4/17.

— " — J. H. Witty — " — Killed in Action 15/4/17.

Unit 1st Dorset Regt.
Place In the Field
Date 27-4-17

FIELD STATE.

Army Form B 231.

To be rendered in accordance with Field Service Regulations, Part II.

UNIT	FIGHTING STRENGTH — This should *not* include details attached to unit, or personnel detailed to march with the Train, or any men unfit to go into action with unit											RATION STRENGTH — To include Fighting Strength, Personnel detailed to march with the Train, and all Personnel and animals attached for Rations and Forage										
	Personnel		Horses and Mules		Other Animals		Guns and Ammunition Wagons (stating nature)	Machine Guns	Ambulances	Tool Carts, Technical Carts (stating nature)	Remarks	Personnel	Horses and Mules		Other Animals		Mechanically Propelled Vehicles					Remarks
	Officers	Other Ranks	Riding	Draught and Pack								Total, all Ranks entitled to Rations.	Heavy Horses	Other Horses and Mules			Motor Cars	Motor Bicycles.	Lorries. 3 Ton	Lorries. 30 Cwt.	Tractors	
(1)	(2)	(3)	(4)	(5)	(6)	(7)	(8)	(9)	(10)	(11)	(12)	(13)	(14)	(15)	(16)	(17)	(18)	(19)	(20)	(21)	(22)	(23)
1st Dorset Regt	32	750	9	42			15 L. Guns	15		17		676	9	43				9				6 Offrs + 115 OR attached from Bn; 2 Offrs + 7 OR attached to Bn
TOTALS ...	32	750	9	42				15		17		679	9	43				9				

Ammunition with Unit:—

·303 inch; approximate number of rounds per Man

·303 inch; " " " per Machine Gun

Gun or Howitzer; approximate number of rounds per Gun or Howitzer

Supplies with Unit:—

Approximate number of days' rations for men of ration strength

" " " forage for Animals " "

" " " fuel and lubricants for Mechanically Propelled Vehicles

Signature of Commander (Sd) C. P. Whitaker Capt
Comdg. 1/Dorset Regt

(88762.) Wt.W. 2345—1438. 500,000 5/15. J. P. & Co. Ltd. Forms B 231 / 3

Lieut C B Stocks   1st Dorset Regt   Transferred to Ens

Instructions regarding War Diaries and Intelligence Summaries are contained in F. S. Regs., Part II. and the Staff Manual respectively. Title pages will be prepared in manuscript.

WAR DIARY
or
~~INTELLIGENCE SUMMARY~~.
(Erase heading not required.)

Army Form C. 2118.

1 Dorset Rgt
Vol 33

Place	Date MAY	Hour 1917.	Summary of Events and Information	Remarks and references to Appendices
UGNY and LANCHY	1st		Battalion in training at UGNY and LANCHY	RWHC
	2nd	9.30am	14th Brigade was inspected by Sir C. L. Woollcombe. K.C.B commanding 4th Corps.	RWHC
	3rd – 14th		Battalion in training at UGNY and LANCHY. The Attack was practised – especially the Trench to Trench Attack. The general principle being that three lines of trench would be allotted to a Battalion as its objective on a 400 yards frontage – The Method of attack being 4 waves – the first two waves being found by the leading two Companies – each on a two platoon frontage – and the rear two waves each being composed of a Company on a four platoon frontage – Sectional Training was continued, but the 4 platoon per Company organization was reverted to. A Range was built at UGNY and the whole Battalion fired an Application & Rapid Firing Practice	RWHC
OFFOY	15th		Battalion marched to OFFOY	RWHC
		7.35am	Battalion in billets in OFFOY –	
CURCHY & PUZEAUX	16th	5am	Battalion marched to CURCHY and PUZEAUX	RWHC
		9.45am	Battalion in billets. Two Coys at CURCHY and Bn HQ & 2 Coys at PUZEAUX. Major L.C. Hope joined the Battalion and assumed command	

A5834 Wt. W4973 M687 750,000 8/16 D. D. & L. Ltd. Forms/C.2118/13.

Army Form C. 2118.

WAR DIARY
or
INTELLIGENCE SUMMARY.
(*Erase heading not required.*)

[Instr]uctions regarding War Diaries and Intelligence Summaries are contained in F. S. Regs., Part II. and the Staff Manual respectively. Title pages will be prepared in manuscript.

Place	Date MAY 1917	Hour	Summary of Events and Information	Remarks and references to Appendices
[illegible]AY & PUZEAUX	17th	5.20am	Battalion marched to BEAUFORT via HATTENCOURT – FOUQUESCOURT & ROUVROY, thus crossing the trenches Battalion advanced from on March 18th 1917	
BEAUFORT		8.45am	Battalion in billets in BEAUFORT	
	18th, 19th, 20th, 21st, 22nd, 23rd, 24th, 25th, 26th, 27th, 28th, 29th		Battalion remained in Billets – Training was continued on the same lines as at UGNY and LANCHY. Practice attacks were made by the 14th Brigade on the old German front line system opposite FOUQUESCOURT	[signature]
				Honours and Awards
				Croix de Chevalier (Légion d'Honneur) Capt (Acting Major) C. F. WHITAKER M.C.
IGNAUCOURT	30th	6.40am	Battalion marched to IGNAUCOURT via CAIX and CAYEUX	Croix de Guerre
		9.35am	Battalion in billets in IGNAUCOURT	16803 PTE T. TRICKETT } * 9785 PTE J. LAMBETH }
	31st		Bn remained in billets in IGNAUCOURT	

[signature] Lieut Adjutant 1st Dorset Regt

* for action at CEPY Farm

A5834 Wt W4973/M687 750,000 8/16 D. D. & L. Ltd. Forms/C.2118/13.

Unit 1st Dorset Regiment

Place In the Field

Date 4/5/1917

FIELD STATE.

Army Form B 231.

To be rendered in accordance with Field Service Regulations, Part II.

UNIT	FIGHTING STRENGTH — This should *not* include details attached to unit, or personnel detailed to march with the Train, or any men unfit to go into action with unit											RATION STRENGTH — To include Fighting Strength, Personnel detailed to march with the Train, and all Personnel and animals attached for Rations and Forage										
	Personnel		Horses and Mules		Other Animals		Guns and Ammunition Wagons (stating nature)	Machine Guns	Ambulances	Tool Carts, Technical Carts (stating nature)	Remarks	Personnel	Horses and Mules		Other Animals		Mechanically Propelled Vehicles					Remarks
	Officers	Other Ranks	Riding	Draught and Pack								Total, all Ranks entitled to Rations.	Heavy Horses	Other Horses and Mules			Motor Cars	~~Motor~~ Bicycles.	Lorries. 3 Ton	Lorries. 30 Cwt.	Tractors	
(1)	(2)	(3)	(4)	(5)	(6)	(7)	(8)	(9)	(10)	(11)	(12)	(13)	(14)	(15)	(16)	(17)	(18)	(19)	(20)	(21)	(22)	(23)
1/Dorset Regt.	30.	776.	9.	42			Lewis Guns	16				684.	9	43.				9.				
TOTALS ...	30	776	9.	42				16				684	9.	43.				9.				

Ammunition with Unit:—

·303 inch; approximate number of rounds per Man

·303 inch; " " " per Machine Gun

Gun or Howitzer; approximate number of rounds per Gun or Howitzer

Supplies with Unit:—

Approximate number of days' rations for men of ration strength

" " " forage for Animals " "

" " " fuel and lubricants for Mechanically Propelled Vehicles

Signature of Commander Sd/ C. H. Whitaker. Captain

Comdg. 1/Dorset Regiment

(90988.) Wt.W. 5216—2140. 900,000 7/15. J. P. & Co. Ltd. Forms B 231 / 3

Capt G. C. K. Webb. F. Amb.

Unit 1st Dorset Regiment

Place In the Field

Date 11/5/17.

FIELD STATE.

Army Form B 231.

To be rendered in accordance with Field Service Regulations, Part II.

UNIT	FIGHTING STRENGTH — This should *not* include details attached to unit, or personnel detailed to march with the Train, or any men unfit to go into action with unit											RATION STRENGTH — To include Fighting Strength, Personnel detailed to march with the Train, and all Personnel and animals attached for Rations and Forage										
	Personnel		Horses and Mules		Other Animals		Guns and Ammunition Wagons (stating nature)	Machine Guns	Ambulances	Tool Carts, Technical Carts (stating nature)	Remarks	Personnel	Horses and Mules		Other Animals		Mechanically Propelled Vehicles					Remarks
	Officers	Other Ranks	Riding	Draught and Pack								Total, all Ranks entitled to Rations.	Heavy Horses	Other Horses and Mules			Motor Cars	~~Motor~~ Bicycles.	Lorries. 3 Ton	Lorries. 30 Cwt.	Tractors	
(1)	(2)	(3)	(4)	(5)	(6)	(7)	(8)	(9)	(10)	(11)	(12)	(13)	(14)	(15)	(16)	(17)	(18)	(19)	(20)	(21)	(22)	(23)
1/Dorset Regt.	30.	866	9	46			Lewis Guns	16.				448	9	47.				9				
TOTALS ...	30	866	9	46.				16				448.	9	47				9				

Ammunition with Unit:—

·303 inch; approximate number of rounds per Man ____

·303 inch; " " " per Machine Gun ____

Gun or Howitzer; approximate number of rounds per Gun or Howitzer ____

Supplies with Unit:—

Approximate number of days' rations for men of ration strength ____

" " " forage for Animals " " ____

" " " fuel and lubricants for Mechanically Propelled Vehicles ____

Signature of Commander (Sd) R.V. Kestell Cornish Lt for Major Comdg 1st Dorset Regiment

(90988.) Wt.W. 5216—2140. 900,000 7/15. J. P. & Co. Ltd. Forms B 231 / 3

Unit 1st Dorset Regiment

Place In the Field

Date 18/5/17

FIELD STATE.

Army Form B 231.

To be rendered in accordance with Field Service Regulations, Part II.

FIGHTING STRENGTH — This should *not* include details attached to unit, or personnel detailed to march with the Train, or any men unfit to go into action with unit

RATION STRENGTH — To include Fighting Strength, Personnel detailed to march with the Train, and all Personnel and animals attached for Rations and Forage

UNIT	Personnel		Horses and Mules		Other Animals		Guns and Ammunition Wagons (stating nature)	Machine Guns	Ambulances	Tool Carts, Technical Carts (stating nature)	Remarks	Personnel	Horses and Mules		Other Animals		Mechanically Propelled Vehicles					Remarks
	Officers	Other Ranks	Riding	Draught and Pack								Total, all Ranks entitled to Rations.	Heavy Horses	Other Horses and Mules			Motor Cars	~~Motor~~ Bicycles.	Lorries. 3 Ton	Lorries. 30 Cwt.	Tractors	
(1)	(2)	(3)	(4)	(5)	(6)	(7)	(8)	(9)	(10)	(11)	(12)	(13)	(14)	(15)	(16)	(17)	(18)	(19)	(20)	(21)	(22)	(23)
1/Dorset Regt	32	841	9	46	–	–		16	Lewis Guns.			483.	9.	47.				9.				
TOTALS ...	32	841	9	46				16				483	9	47.				9.				

Ammunition with Unit:—

·303 inch; approximate number of rounds per Man

·303 inch; " " " per Machine Gun

Gun or Howitzer; approximate number of rounds per Gun or Howitzer

Supplies with Unit:—

Approximate number of days' rations for men of ration strength

" " " forage for Animals " "

" " " fuel and lubricants for Mechanically Propelled Vehicles

Signature of Commander [illegible] Major
Comdg. 1st Dorset Regiment

(90988.) Wt.W. 5216—2140. 900,000 7/15. J. P. & Co. Ltd. Forms B 231/3

Lieut J. G. Coates F. Amb.
" C. E. Pye "

Unit 1st Dorset Regiment.
Place In the Field
Date 25. 5. 1917.

FIELD STATE.

Army Form B 231.

To be rendered in accordance with Field Service Regulations, Part II.

UNIT	FIGHTING STRENGTH This should *not* include details attached to unit, or personnel detailed to march with the Train, or any men unfit to go into action with unit											RATION STRENGTH To include Fighting Strength, Personnel detailed to march with the Train, and all Personnel and animals attached for Rations and Forage										
	Personnel		Horses and Mules		Other Animals		Guns and Ammunition Wagons (stating nature)	Machine Guns	Ambulances	Tool Carts, Technical Carts (stating nature)	Remarks	Personnel	Horses and Mules		Other Animals		Mechanically Propelled Vehicles					Remarks
	Officers	Other Ranks	Riding	Draught and Pack								Total, all Ranks entitled to Rations.	Heavy Horses	Other Horses and Mules			Motor Cars	~~Motor~~ Bicycles.	Lorries. 3 Ton	Lorries. 30 Cwt.	Tractors	
(1)	(2)	(3)	(4)	(5)	(6)	(7)	(8)	(9)	(10)	(11)	(12)	(13)	(14)	(15)	(16)	(17)	(18)	(19)	(20)	(21)	(22)	(23)
1st Dorset Regiment	31	845	10	44				16 Lewis Guns				812	9	46				9				
TOTALS ...	31	845	10	44				16 Lewis Guns				812	9	46				9				

Ammunition with Unit:—

·303 inch; approximate number of rounds per Man

·303 inch; " " " per Machine Gun

Gun or Howitzer; approximate number of rounds per Gun or Howitzer

Supplies with Unit:—

Approximate number of days' rations for men of ration strength

" " " forage for Animals " "

" " " fuel and lubricants for Mechanically Propelled Vehicles

Signature of Commander (Sd) R.V. [illegible] for Major Comdg 1st Dorset Regiment

(90988.) Wt. W. 5216—2140. 900,000 7/15. J. P. & Co. Ltd. Forms B 231 / 3

Lieut J.C. Coates To F. Amb
" C.E. Dep —,—

Instructions regarding War Diaries and Intelligence Summaries are contained in F. S. Regs., Part II. and the Staff Manual respectively. Title pages will be prepared in manuscript.

WAR DIARY
or
INTELLIGENCE SUMMARY.
(Erase heading not required.)

1 Dorset Regt
Vol 34

Army Form C. 2118.

Place	Date	Hour	Summary of Events and Information	Remarks and references to Appendices
IGNAUCOURT	1st June	1pm.	Battalion (less B Company) marched from IGNAUCOURT to MARCEL CAVE station and entrained. Train left MARCEL CAVE at 2.20 pm. and arrived at BAILLEUL at 1 a.m on the 2nd June.	[initials]
	2nd		From BAILLEUL the Battalion marched to billets in the STEENWERCK area.	
		3.55 am.	Battalion (less B Company) reported in billets. The remainder of the day was spent resting.	
STEENWERCK AREA.		3.30 pm.	"B" Company arrived at BAILLEUL and were in billets by 6 pm.	[initials]
	3rd 4th 5th 6th 7th 8th 9th 10th 11th 12th		Battalion in training. Officers and N.C.O's reconnoitred the tracks and trenches in case the Battalion was called upon to support the 3rd Australian Division during the MESSINES attack. On the 8th June Major J. H. Macdonell D.S.O. 1st Battalion H.L.I. joined the Battalion and assumed command.	[initials]
	13th	5a.m.	Battalion marched to EECKE area via DOULIEU, VIEUX BERQUIN, STRAZEELE and CAESTRE.	[initials]
EECKE		11.30am.	Battalion in billets.	

A5834 Wt. W4973/M687 750,000 8/16 D. D. & L. Ltd. Forms/C.2118/13.

WAR DIARY
or
~~INTELLIGENCE SUMMARY.~~
(Erase heading not required.)

Army Form C. 2118.

Instructions regarding War Diaries and Intelligence Summaries are contained in F. S. Regs., Part II. and the Staff Manual respectively. Title pages will be prepared in manuscript.

Place	Date	Hour	Summary of Events and Information	Remarks and references to Appendices
EECKE.	14th June		Devoted to training. The transport moved from EECKE to WORMHOUDT.	[initials]
	15th June	8 a.m.	Battalion moved by busses from EECKE to TETEGHEM via STEENVOORDE, WORMHOUDT, BERGUES and COODEKERQUE	
TETEGHEM.		11.55 a.m.	Battalion in billets. The transport rejoined the Battalion during the afternoon.	[initials]
	16th	7 a.m.	Battalion (less Transport) marched from TETEGHEM to DUNKERQUE and entrained ~~for COXYDE.~~ Battalion detrained at COXYDE and marched to JUNIAC CAMP	
JUNIAC CAMP OOST DUNKERQUE.			The transport proceeded by road and rejoined the Battalion in JUNIAC CAMP near OOST DUNKERQUE.	
		8 p.m.	The Battalion moved from JUNIAC CAMP to NIEUPORT and relieved a Battalion of the 3rd French Regt. who were in support to C Sub-sector.	[initials]
NIEUPORT.	17th	1.15 a.m.	Relief complete.	
		10 p.m.	Battalion ~~went~~ relieved a Battalion of the 3rd French Regt. in "C" Sub sector The order of the Companies in the line being ABCD "A" Coy on the right.	[initials]
	18th	3 a.m.	Relief complete Casualties – NIL. Battalion in the line Casualties 1. OR. wounded.	[initials]
	19th		Battalion in the line. Casualties 12 OR. wounded.	[initials]
	20th	2 p.m.	About 2 p.m. the gas alarm was sounded but the gas cloud was dispersed almost at once by rain. Casualties 1 OR killed. 1 OR. wounded. No casualties resulted from the gas cloud	[initials]

A5834 Wt. W4973/M687 750,000 8/16 D. D. & L. Ltd. Forms/C.2118/13.

Instructions regarding War Diaries and Intelligence Summaries are contained in F. S. Regs., Part II. and the Staff Manual respectively. Title pages will be prepared in manuscript.

WAR DIARY
or
INTELLIGENCE SUMMARY.
(Erase heading not required.)

Army Form C. 2118.

Place	Date	Hour	Summary of Events and Information	Remarks and references to Appendices
	21st June		Battalion in the line. The enemy was expected to raid our trenches during the night. The whole of the Battalion front was bombarded by shells & heavy trench mortars but no raid took place. Casualties 3 O.Rs killed. 30 O.Rs wounded	[illegible]
	22nd		Battalion was relieved by the 15th H.L.I and moved into the support position in NIEUPORT. The same precautions were taken for a raid as during the previous night. Casualties 3 O.Rs wounded.	[illegible]
	23rd	1.30am	Relief complete. Casualties 8 O.R. wounded.	[illegible]
	24th		Battalion in support in NIEUPORT. Casualties 3 O.Rs wounded.	[illegible]
	25th		Battalion in support in NIEUPORT Casualties 1 O.R. wounded. Battalion was relieved by the 14th H.L.I. and 2nd K.O.Y.L.I. and proceeded to GALLIMARD CAMP, OOST DUNKERQUE, in reserve.	[illegible]
	26th	2 a.m	Relief complete.	[illegible]
		4 30 a	Battalion reported in billets – GALLIMARD CAMP.	
	27th	12.30 pm	Battalion (less Transport) moved to RIBAILLET CAMP (2000 yds from GALLIMARD CAMP) in order to be nearer the Brigade. The transport did not move.	[illegible]
	28th		Battalion in RIBAILLET CAMP. Casualties 2nd LIEUT. P.L.C WALKER, 2nd LIEUT. E.M.F. LAW and 6 O.Rs were wounded while on a working party in E Sub sector	[illegible]
	29th 30th		Battalion in reserve in RIBAILLET Camp	[illegible]

1/7/17 [illegible] Lieut & Adjutant 1st Dorset Regt.

A5834 Wt. W4973 M687 750,000 8/16 D. D. & L. Ltd. Forms/C.2118/13.

Instructions regarding War Diaries and Intelligence Summaries are contained in F. S. Regs., Part II. and the Staff Manual respectively. Title pages will be prepared in manuscript.

WAR DIARY
or
INTELLIGENCE SUMMARY.
(Erase heading not required.)

1 Dorsets

Army Form C. 2118.

Vol 35

Place	Date	Hour	Summary of Events and Information	Remarks and references to Appendices
	JULY			
RIBAILLET CAMP	1		Battalion left RIBAILLET Camp and relieved 2nd Manchester Regt. in D. Subsector. Casualties Nil	Ref. BELGIUM FRANCE SHEET 11 [illegible] 12.S.W.
D Subsector	2.	2.15am	Relief complete – B and D Companies were in front line. Both left. A & C were in support – in NIEUPORT by day & in support trenches by night. Casualties 2.O.R. wounded.	
	3	12.35am	The enemy shelled the whole sector, especially NICE TRENCH & NICE SUPPORT – otherwise a quiet day. Casualties. 2.O.R. killed, 2.O.R. wounded	
	4.		Battalion in D. Subsector. Casualties 2.O.R.	
	5.		Battalion was relieved by 16th Lancashire Fusiliers and withdrew to JEANNIOT Camp. on the morning of 6th. – Relief was complete at 1.20am on 6th. Casualties on 5th inst. 1.O.R. killed. 5.O.R. wounded.	
	6		Major H.C. Lloyd. 2nd Welsh Regiment, assumed command of the Battalion.	

A5834 Wt. W4973 M687 750,000 8/16 D. D. & L. Ltd. Forms/C.2118/13.

Instructions regarding War Diaries and Intelligence Summaries are contained in F. S. Regs., Part II. and the Staff Manual respectively. Title pages will be prepared in manuscript.

WAR DIARY
or
INTELLIGENCE SUMMARY.
(*Erase heading not required.*)

Army Form C. 2118.

Place	Date	Hour	Summary of Events and Information	Remarks and references to Appendices
JEANNIOT Camp	6		Battalion moved from JEANNIOT Camp to Huts in GHYVELDE	Refce BELGIUM & FRANCE [illegible] Map Sheet 11 & 19
	7 8 9		Battalion in training at GHYVELDE. The normal Trench-to-Trench attack was practised.	
	10	11.20am	About Message received that Battalion was to be ready to move at half an hours notice, on account of heavy enemy shelling on our front	
		7.15pm	Battalion moved by busses in fighting order to JEAN BART Camp (near COXYDE)	
RIBAILLET Camp	11	9pm	Battalion remained in JEANBART Camp till 9pm on 11th inst, when they marched to RIBAILLET Camp. Casualties – NIL.	
	12.	10pm.	Battalion left RIBAILLET Camp for NIEUPORT. Battalion took over the Defence of NIEUPORT from 16th Northumberland Fusiliers.	
	13.	2am	Relief Complete	

A5834 Wt. W4973 M687 750,000 8/16 D. D. & L. Ltd. Forms/C.2118/13.

Instructions regarding War Diaries and Intelligence Summaries are contained in F. S. Regs., Part II. and the Staff Manual respectively. Title pages will be prepared in manuscript.

WAR DIARY
or
INTELLIGENCE SUMMARY.
(Erase heading not required.)

Army Form C. 2118.

Place	Date	Hour	Summary of Events and Information	Remarks and references to Appendices
NIEUPORT	13	Noon	8.15 pm – Heavy gas shell bombardment on the defences of NIEUPORT. – This continued throughout the night till about 2.30 am on 14th inst, when situation became quiet. – 2/Lt Braddy and 25 O.R. were officially diagnosed as having been gassed during the night – Other casualties Nil.	Ref. BELGIUM square map sheet 12 S.W.
	14		Battalion in Defences of NIEUPORT – Casualties NIL	
	15		Battalion relieved the 15th H.L.I. and 5/6th Royal Scots in that part of C. Subsector to the Left of the LOMBARTZYDE Road. Casualties. 10. O.R. wounded	
	16	5 am	Relief complete – Battalion in C. Subsector. Casualties 3. O. R. wounded.	
	17	7.30 pm	The junction of NOSE ALLEY and NOSE SUPPORT was attacked by two small parties – one (under 2/Lt F. C. DICE) working up NOSE ALLEY and the other (under 2/Lt W. V. RICHARDS) working along NOSE SUPPORT. Immediately these parties started to advance to the attack, the Germans sent up a rocket which was immediately answered by very heavy enemy shell fire, machine gun & rifle fire on the attacking parties	

A5834 Wt. W4973 M687 750,000 8/16 D. D. & L. Ltd. Forms/C.2118/13.

Instructions regarding War Diaries and Intelligence Summaries are contained in F. S. Regs., Part II. and the Staff Manual respectively. Title pages will be prepared in manuscript.

WAR DIARY
or
INTELLIGENCE SUMMARY.
(Erase heading not required.)

Army Form C. 2118.

Place	Date	Hour	Summary of Events and Information	Remarks and references to Appendices
C Subsector	17		At the same time Germans could be seen reinforcing the Objective (the junction of NOSE SUPPORT and NOSE ALLEY) – About 60 Germans were observed leaving NOSE TRENCH in the direction of the Objective – Each of our two attacking parties numbered 1 NCO + 8. O.R. – Owing to heavy casualties and the exposed approaches to the Objective the attacking parties failed to reach their objective.	Refer Map 28.N.W. 2 B.D.M. squared tracing Sheet 28.S.W.
			Casualties 2 Lt. F.C. DICE wounded. 3. O.R. killed 19. O.R. wounded 1. O.R. missing.	
			During the night the Battalion was relieved by 5th KOYLI.	
	18	2 am	Relief Complete – Battalion withdrew to JEAN BART Camp	
		5 am	arriving there at 5 am. – Casualties Lieut. T.C. COATES wounded 1. O.R. killed, 5. O.R. wounded.	
			In the evening Battalion moved to camp near ZUYDCOOTE	
		9.30 pm	at C.16.c arriving there at 9.30 pm	

A5834 Wt. W4973 M687 750,000 8/16 D. D. & L. Ltd. Forms/C.2118/13.

Instructions regarding War Diaries and Intelligence Summaries are contained in F. S. Regs., Part II. and the Staff Manual respectively. Title pages will be prepared in manuscript.

WAR DIARY
or
INTELLIGENCE SUMMARY.
(Erase heading not required.)

Army Form C. 2118.

Place	Date	Hour	Summary of Events and Information	Remarks and references to Appendices
C.16.C.	19 20 21 22 23 24 25 26 27 28 29 30 31		Battalion in Camp at C.16.C. – Training in Normal Trench-to-Trench Attack was carried out. On July 24th The Brigade was inspected by Major General SHUTE, Commdg 32nd Division and by Lieut. General. du CAINE, Commanding XV Corps.	Sheet 19 BELGIUM FRANCE Squared [initials]

[signature] Lieut
Adjt 1/ Dorset Regt.

A5834 Wt. W4973 M687 750,000 8/16 D. D. & L. Ltd. Forms/C.2118/13.

Army Form C. 2118.

1 Dorset Rgt

Vol 36

WAR DIARY
or
INTELLIGENCE SUMMARY.
(Erase heading not required.)

Instructions regarding War Diaries and Intelligence Summaries are contained in F. S. Regs., Part II. and the Staff Manual respectively. Title pages will be prepared in manuscript.

August

Place	Date	Hour	Summary of Events and Information	Remarks and references to Appendices
C.16.C.	1st		Battalion in Camp at C.16.C. Training in normal Trench to Trench Attack was carried out.	Sheet 19 Belgium France Special D.S.
	2nd	12.25pm	Battalion marched from Camp at C.16.C. via ZUYDCOOTE-ADINKERKE KERKE PANNE to COXYDE arriving COXYDE at 6.5 pm. Distance about 12 miles. Took over the billets of 1/4 West YORKS REGT. (T) 49th Divn. Very wet.	D.S.
COXYDE	3rd	5pm	Battalion marched from billets in COXYDE to billets in LAPANNE arrived at 6 pm. Distance about 3 miles.	D.S.
LAPANNE	4th		Battalion in Billets in LAPANNE. Training and cleaning up.	Sheet 11 S.E. D.S.
	5th		Church parade Service on Sea Shore.	D.S.
	6th		Battalion Training in Trench to Trench Attack	D.S.
	7th		Battalion Training in Open Warfare Attack	D.S.
	8th			D.S.
	9th			D.S.
	10th			D.S.
	11th			D.S.
	12th		Church Parade on Sea Shore. W 11. C.O.3.	D.S. Sheet 11 S.E.

A5834 Wt. W4973 M687 750,000 8/16 D. D. & L. Ltd. Forms/C.2118/13.

Instructions regarding War Diaries and Intelligence Summaries are contained in F. S. Regs., Part II. and the Staff Manual respectively. Title pages will be prepared in manuscript.

WAR DIARY
or
INTELLIGENCE SUMMARY.
(Erase heading not required.)

Army Form C. 2118.

Place	Date	Hour	Summary of Events and Information	Remarks and references to Appendices
LAPANNE	13th		In Billets LAPANNE. BATTALION TRAINING.	Sheet 11.SE DS
	14th		In Billets LAPANNE. A Company and 2 platoons of B. Coy Demonstration Drill Firing Practice for benefit of the Belgians.	DS
	15th		In Billets LAPANNE. Training. Outpost Scheme at night commencing at 12 (noon) 15th inst and finishing at 8 am 16th inst. Practice men cooking food in mess tins.	DS
	16th		In Billets LAPANNE. Training in the afternoon under O.C. Coys.	DS
	17th		Battalion in Billets LAPANNE. Short route march in the morning about 8 miles. Bathing parade in the afternoon.	DS
	18th		In Billets LAPANNE. Trench to Trench attack practice.	
	19th		Church parade in the grounds of Chateau OLLEVIER-LAPANNE. 1st BN 14 1st DORSET Regt play a football match against 6th Belgian Brigade. Result 3–1 in Belgians favour.	DS
	20th		In Billets LAPANNE. Open Warfare Attack practice.	
	21st		Battalion ~~with~~ DS. In Billets LAPANNE. Company Training and Battalion Training. Bathing Parade at close of morning's work.	DS W/19a DS
	22nd		Battalion in billets LAPANNE training. Battalion cinematographed marching past.	DS

A5834 Wt. W4973/M687 750,000 8/16 D. D. & L. Ltd. Forms/C.2118/13.

Instructions regarding War Diaries and Intelligence Summaries are contained in F. S. Regs., Part II. and the Staff Manual respectively. Title pages will be prepared in manuscript.

WAR DIARY
or
INTELLIGENCE SUMMARY.
(Erase heading not required.)

Army Form C. 2118.

Place	Date	Hour	Summary of Events and Information	Remarks and references to Appendices
LAPANNE	23rd		In Billets LAPANNE. BATTALION TRAINING in the morning. Aquatic Sports in the afternoon	D.S.
"	24th		In Billets LAPANNE Company and BATTALION TRAINING in the morning. Concert in the Chateau GLLEVIER in the evening.	D.S.
"	25th		In Billets LAPANNE Company and BATTALION TRAINING in the morning. French to Trench Attack at night returning at 5'30 am 26th inst.	D.S.
"	26th		In Billets LAPANNE. No Church Parade Service.	
LAPANNE	27th		Battalion marched from LAPANNE ~~Station~~ 8.16am arrived AUSTRALIA Camp (X.3.a.8.0) about 9.40 am. Marched from AUSTRALIA camp at 10.0 pm and relieved 20th Bn Royal Fusiliers in LOMBARTZYDE Sector ~~D.S.~~ Battalion in Support in REDAN M28.c.9.9. Relief Complete 3'30 am.	BELGIUM Sheet 11.S.E. 1/20000 D.S.
REDAN	28th		Battalion in Support in REDAN. VERY QUIET. WORKING PARTIES. Casualties Nil.	Sheet 12.S.W. 1/20000 D.S.
"	29th		Battalion in Support in REDAN: Working parties. Casualties 5. O.R wounded.	D.S.
"	30th		Battalion in Support in REDAN Working parties. Casualties 1, O.R wounded.	D.S.
"	31st		Battalion relieves 15th H.L.I. in the line Left Sub Sector of LOMBARTZYDE Sector. Relief Complete 2.30 am Casualties 2 O.R. Killed 11 O.R. wounded.	D.S.

D Stayner Capt. & Adjt
11 Dorset Regt.

A5834 Wt. W4973 M687 750,000 8/16 D. D. & L. Ltd. Forms/C.2118/13.

Instructions regarding War Diaries and Intelligence Summaries are contained in F. S. Regs., Part II. and the Staff Manual respectively. Title pages will be prepared in manuscript.

WAR DIARY
~~or~~
~~INTELLIGENCE SUMMARY.~~
(Erase heading not required.)

Army Form C. 2118.

1st Dorset Regt.

Vol 37

Place	Date SEPTEMBER	Hour	Summary of Events and Information	Remarks and references to Appendices
In the line	1st		Battalion in the line, Left Subsector of LOMBARTZYDE SECTOR. Casualties 1 OR killed 1 OR missing since reported killed.	D.S. D.S.
	2nd		Battalion in the line Casualties 1 OR killed.	D.S.
	3rd		Battalion in the line Casualties 6 OR wounded.	
	4th		Battalion in the line Casualties 1 OR wounded.	D.S.
	5th		Battalion relieved by 15th HLI and on relief withdrawn to the REDAN in support. 2/Lieut AKL STATHAM killed 16 OR wounded 2 OR missing.	D.S.
	6th		Battalion in support 4 OR's wounded.	D.S. D.S.
	7th		Battalion in support 4 OR's wounded	D.S.
	8th		Battalion in support 4 OR's wounded.	D.S.
	9th		Battalion relieved 15th HLI in the line Left Subsector LOMBARTZYDE SECTOR Casualties 2 OR's wounded.	D.S.
	10th		Battalion in the line 3 OR's wounded	
	11th		Battalion in the line. 2/Lieut AS WHEELER 2/Lieut RM WOODARD CAPT REV CORDUBANK C.F. wounded 1 OR killed 5 OR wounded.	D.S. D.S.
	12th		Battalion relieved by 15th LANCS FUSILIERS and withdrew to AUSTRALIA CAMP (COXYDE) relief complete 2.15 pm. 1 OR killed 1 OR wounded 1 OR missing.	D.S.
LA PANNE	13th		Battalion marched by Coys from AUSTRALIA Camp to LA PANNE.	D.S.
	14th		Battalion in Billets LA PANNE & parades time devoted to cleaning up.	D.S.
	15th		Battalion in Billets LA PANNE Coy parades refitting clothing etc.	D.S.

Instructions regarding War Diaries and Intelligence Summaries are contained in F. S. Regs., Part II. and the Staff Manual respectively. Title pages will be prepared in manuscript.

WAR DIARY
or
INTELLIGENCE SUMMARY.
(Erase heading not required.)

Army Form C. 2118.

1st DORSET REGT.

Place	Date	Hour	Summary of Events and Information	Remarks and references to Appendices
LA PANNE	16th		Battalion in billets LA PANNE Church parade on Sea Shore W13a	Sheet 11 S.E. D.S.
LA PANNE	17th		Battalion in billets LA PANNE Company and Section training	D.S.
LA PANNE	18th		Battalion in billets LA PANNE Company and Section training	D.S.
LA PANNE	19th		Battalion in billets LA PANNE Section training	D.S.
LA PANNE	20th		Battalion relieved 2 K.O.Y.L.I. in WULPEN Brigade Support. relief complete 9.0 pm.	
WULPEN	21st		Battalion in WULPEN working parties in Left Subsector of Right Sector working on NICE and NUN AVENUE. M.30. ref Trench map Sheet 12 S.W. 1/20000	D.S.
WULPEN	22nd		Battalion in WULPEN working parties in Left Subsector of Right Sector M.30	Trench Map Sheet 12 S.W. 1/20000 D.S.
WULPEN	23rd		Battalion in WULPEN working parties in Left Subsector of Right Sector M.30	D.S.
WULPEN	24th		Battalion relieved 15th H.L.I. in Right Subsector St. GEORGES relief complete 1.0 Am. Battalion moved from WULPEN in barges thence M 34 d 90 65 duck board track to HOOGE BRIDGE thence NORTH along RAMSCAPELLE Road to line.	Sheet 12 S.W. 1/20000 D.S.
In the line	25th		Battalion in the line very quiet.	D.S.
In the line	26th		Battalion in the line very quiet	D.S.
In the line	27th		Battalion in the line very quiet. Casualties 2nd Lieut W.D. RICHARDS wounded (at duty) 3 OR'S wounded	D.S.
In the line	28th		Battalion in the line very quiet	D.S.
In the line	29th		Battalion in the line very quiet. Enemy gas shelling [illegible]	D.S.
In the line	30th		Battalion in the line very quiet. Much aeroplane activity.	D.S.
In the line				D.S.

D. Stayner-Capt & Adj.
1/Dorset Regt.

A5834 Wt. W4973/M687 750,000 8/16 D. D. & L. Ltd. Forms/C.2118/13.

Army Form C. 2118.

Instructions regarding War Diaries and Intelligence Summaries are contained in F. S. Regs., Part II. and the Staff Manual respectively. Title pages will be prepared in manuscript.

WAR DIARY
or
~~INTELLIGENCE SUMMARY.~~

(*Erase heading not required.*)

1st DORSET Regt

Vol 38

Place	Date October	Hour	Summary of Events and Information	Remarks and references to Appendices
1st			Battalion in the line right subsector called St GEORGES. Very quiet 3. OR's wounded	Sheet 12 SW 1/20000 DS
2nd			Battalion in the line right subsector called St Georges. Very quiet 3 OR wounded much aeroplane activity several air fights	DS
3rd			Battalion in the line relieved by 15 H.L.I. relief complete by 11 o'clock. Withdrew to WULPEN divisional reserve.	DS
4th			Battalion in WULPEN. Cleaning up of men and equipment. No working parties	DS
5th			Battalion in WULPEN. Musketry parades in morning. No working parties	DS
6th			Battalion relieved by 4th East LANS. relief completed by 9.0 pm Withdrew to Australia Camp 1/4 mile from COXYDE. 2 ORS wounded by shell fire at WULPEN.	DS
7th			Battalion moved by ~~bus~~ Motor Bus to COUDEKERQUE-BRANCHE (suburb of DUNKERQUE). Billets good but very scattered.	DS
8th			Battalion in billets. Day devoted to cleaning up and making up any deficiencies	DS
9th 10th 11th			Battalion in billets. Parades in the morning. Drill Musketry etc.	DS DS DS
12th			Battalion in billets. Battalion Attack on full scale on ground G.6.a.	DS Belgium & France DS
13th 14th			Battalion in billets. Church parade in morning in B Company billets. Moved in afternoon to new Billets in St POL another suburb of DUNKERQUE. Town Major made no arrangements for billets	Sheet 19 1/40000 DS
15th 16th 17th 18th			Battalion in St POL. Training ~~by Coy~~ on Company firing.	DS DS DS DS

A5834 Wt. W4973 M687 750,000 8/16 D. D. & L. Ltd. Forms/C.2118/13.

WAR DIARY
or
INTELLIGENCE SUMMARY.
(*Erase heading not required.*)

Army Form C. 2118.

Instructions regarding War Diaries and Intelligence Summaries are contained in F. S. Regs., Part II. and the Staff Manual respectively. Title pages will be prepared in manuscript.

1st Dorset Regt.

Place	Date	Hour	Summary of Events and Information	Remarks and references to Appendices
St POL	19th		Company training. Attacking Strong Points	D.S.
..	20th			D.S.
..	21st		Church Parade in A Company Billet in St POL, otherwise no parades	D.S.
	22nd		Battalion Attack Practice	D.S.
	23rd		Battalion did Company parades. Very wet.	D.S.
	24th		Battalion inspection of Marching Order no training	
	25th		Battalion moved from St POL to ERINGHEM. Route St POL halte W19a 1.1. – cross roads N20d 9.6 – cross roads N26a 6.2 road junction T1bd 3.6. SPRENKWOT turn right Battalion Started at 8.30 am arrived 1.20 pm distance about 12 miles no men fell out. Packs carried in lorry	Ref map 1/40000 Sheets 19 & 27. D.S.
	26th		Battalion moved from ERINGHEM to ARNEKE route via VIOLON D'OR Battalion started 9.30 am arrived about 12 noon. Very wet. Two men fell out both sick. Distance of march about 7 miles.	Ref map 1/40000 Sheet 27
ARNEKE	27th		Battalion in Billets. Company Kit Inspection.	D.S.
	28th		Battalion in Billets. Church Parade in Scottish Church Hut. Billets good but very scattered.	D.S.
	29th		Battalion in Billets. Company training.	D.S.
	30th		Battalion in Billets. Company training. Attacking Strong points March Discipline etc. Very wet. Instruction in Billets. French treatment of men's feet. Prevention of Frost Bite.	D.S.
	31st		Battalion in Billets. Company training. Inter Platoon football matches.	D.S.

D Stayner capt & adj
1. Dorset Regt.

A5834 Wt. W4973 M687 750,000 8/16 D. D. & L. Ltd. Forms/C.2118/13.

Army Form C. 2118.

WAR DIARY
or
INTELLIGENCE SUMMARY.
(*Erase heading not required.*)

Instructions regarding War Diaries and Intelligence Summaries are contained in F. S. Regs., Part II. and the Staff Manual respectively. Title pages will be prepared in manuscript.

November 1st Dorset Regt.

Vol 39

Place	Date	Hour	Summary of Events and Information	Remarks and references to Appendices
ARNEKE	1st		Company and Battalion training.	DS
	2nd		Battalion route march.	DS
	3rd		Battalion training two companies did counter attack against 2nd Manchester Regt and 5/6th Royal Scots. Rugby football match 5/6th Royal Scots Dorset Regt won.	DS
	4th		Church Parade in Scottish Church Tent.	DS
	5th		Company training Battalion attack practice at 12 noon	DS
	6th		ditto ditto	DS
	7th		Cleaning up for Corps Commander Inspection	DS
	8th		Corps Commander Inspection Cancelled Battalion practice attack	DS
	9th		Brigade Attack practice. 1st Dorset Regt and HLI attacked 5/6th Royal Scots represented enemy	
	10th		No training day devoted to cleaning up.	DS
WINNEZEELE AREA.	11th		Battalion marched to WINNEZEELE Area via LEDRINGHEM - WORMHOUDT Road junction C17 b 0.5 - STEENVOORDE - BILLETS. Very wet remained for the night in tents.	Sheet 27 1/40000 DS
POPERINGHE	12th		Battalion marched to POPERINGHE via D21 d 0.0 D10 d 0.0 D10 c 8.5 - HOUTKERQUE - WATOU - Rd junction K4 b 5.6 - Cockwade? 30 c 4.5. St JAN-TER-BIEZEN Billets men's packs carried by lorries.	Sheet 27 1/40000

A5834 Wt. W4973 M687 750,000 8/16 D. D. & L. Ltd. Forms/C.2118/13.

Army Form C. 2118.

Instructions regarding War Diaries and Intelligence Summaries are contained in F. S. Regs., Part II. and the Staff Manual respectively. Title pages will be prepared in manuscript.

WAR DIARY
or
INTELLIGENCE SUMMARY.
(Erase heading not required.)

Place	Date	Hour	Summary of Events and Information	Remarks and references to Appendices
Poperinghe	13th		Battalion in Billets. Battalion parade at 12 noon otherwise bathing.	DS
	14		Battalion in Billets, Company training. Night Operations	DS
	15.		Company training, One Company on range	DS
	16		Company training	DS
	17		Company training Inspected by Divisional Gas Officer who reported Battalion very good.	DS
	18		Church Parade in YMCA hut Poperinghe.	DS
	19		Battalion Bathed Clean change of clothing	DS
	20		Battalion Training Brigade night operations practice on similar ground to that found on Corps front.	DS
	21.		Battalion practice attack in the morning.	DS
	22.		Battalion Blankets etc put through Delousing House in the morning. Battalion practice night attack, to barrage	DS
	23.		Battalion formed up with the Brigade and was given an address by the Divisional Commander	DS
	24.		Battalion moved by train from POPERINGHE to BRIELEN and thereby [illegible]	DS

A5834 Wt. W4973 M687 750,000 8/16 D. D. & L. Ltd. Forms/C2118/13.

Instructions regarding War Diaries and Intelligence Summaries are contained in F. S. Regs., Part II. and the Staff Manual respectively. Title pages will be prepared in manuscript.

WAR DIARY
or
INTELLIGENCE SUMMARY.
(Erase heading not required.)

Army Form C. 2118.

Place	Date	Hour	Summary of Events and Information	Remarks and references to Appendices
DAMBRE Camp.			to DAMBRE CAMP. B27a.5.5.	Sheet 28 [illegible] 1/20000. DS
IRISH Camp	25		Battalion moved ~~fr~~ to IRISH Camp. C27a 2.6	DS
	26		Battalion in IRISH Camp parties reconnoitred the line.	DS
	27		Battalion in IRISH Camp parties reconnoitred the line.	DS
BRAKE CAMP.	28		Battalion moved by train to Dirty Bucket siding thence to Brake Camp by road (Brake Camp. A30.a.1.9.)	DS
"	29		Battalion in BRAKE Camp.	DS
"	30		Battalion in BRAKE Camp. Battalion stood to but nothing happened. C.O. inspected Companies in fighting kit.	DS

30/11/17.

D Stayner
Capt cmdr
1 Dorset Regt.

A5834 Wt. W4973 M687 750,000 8/16 D. D. & L. Ltd. Forms/C.2118/13.

Instructions regarding War Diaries and Intelligence Summaries are contained in F. S. Regs., Part II. and the Staff Manual respectively. Title pages will be prepared in manuscript.

WAR DIARY
or
INTELLIGENCE SUMMARY.
(Erase heading not required.)

Army Form C. 2118.

December 1917

Vol 40

Place	Date	Hour	Summary of Events and Information	Remarks and references to Appendices
WURST Farm	1st		Battalion moved from BRAKE Camp to WURST Farm by train to St Jean thence by duckboards to WURST Farm. WURST Farm consisted of bivouacs the Battalion was at ¼ hrs notice to move.	Brake Camp A30 d 2.8 Wurst Farm D7 b 5.2 ref Sheet 28 1/40000 D.C.
	2nd		Battalion remained in WURST Farm. Officers and NCO's went to reconnoitre routes to the front line still at ¼ hrs notice to move. Reports from front line Battalion indicated situation bad	D.C.
	3rd		Battalion moved up to the ~~left~~ right subsector relieving the 16th N.F. Battalion Hd Qrs at VIRILE Farm V29 b 7.5 ref SPRIET 1/10000. Relief complete about 3.30 am	D.C.
	4th		Battalion in trenches. Very quiet. Casualties 2 killed 7 wounded.	D.C.
	5th		Battalion in trenches. Enemy snipers active. Much shelling of back areas and tracks to B.H.Q. 2 killed 5 wounded	D.C.
	6th		Battalion having pushed forward their posts about 50 yds in the early morning spent a quiet day in the front line. 4 killed 16 wounded ~~by~~ 1 DP not otherwise by M.G. & Rifle fire at night.	D.C.
	7th		Battalion in trenches 2 prisoners captured 1 killed the other (not) wounded they	D.C.

D. D. & L., London, E.C. (A7883) Wt. W809/M1672 350,000 4/17 Sch. 52a Forms/C/2118/14

Instructions regarding War Diaries and Intelligence Summaries are contained in F. S. Regs., Part II. and the Staff Manual respectively. Title pages will be prepared in manuscript.

WAR DIARY
or
INTELLIGENCE SUMMARY.
(*Erase heading not required.*)

Army Form C. 2118.

Place	Date	Hour	Summary of Events and Information	Remarks and references to Appendices
			to the 77th Hanoverian Reserve Regt. Day very quiet our Lewis	Map 28 1/40000
			Guns dispersed the enemy on entering their forward posts at dusk. 1 killed	
			6 wounded 2 missing.	
	8th		Battalion in the line B Company captured 3 prisoners (77th Hanoverian	D L
			Reserve Regt.) 1 wounded Prisoners were caught carrying bombs. Tapes	
			laid to posts to guide the way 2 killed 5 wounded 1 missing	
	9th		Battalion in the line, Boche sniper thought to be killed by O.C. A	
			Company. Casualties 3 wounded Remainder of the time normal.	D L
HILLTOP Farm	10th		Battalion relieved by 10 DLI and one company B Coy by One	
			Company 6th DCLI Battalion withdrew to HILLTOP Farm C21d 4.8.	Map 28 1/40000
			1 off. Lieut DAVIES (missing believed killed) 5 killed 9 wounded.	
			Battalion then moved to No. 5 SIEGE Camp. arriving about 3.0 pm.	Siege Camp B21d 5.8.
SIEGE Camp	11th		Battalion in No. 5 Siege Camp no training. men bathed.	D L
	12th		Battalion in No 5 Siege Camp.	D L
	13th		Battalion in No 5 Siege Camp. Battalion Drill and training under O.C.	
			Coys. Physical Drill training under Physical Drill Sgt Major att'd to Battalion.	

D. D. & L., London, E.C.
(A7883) Wt W809/M1672 350,000 4/17 Sch. 52a. Forms/C/2118/14

Instructions regarding War Diaries and Intelligence Summaries are contained in F. S. Regs., Part II, and the Staff Manual respectively. Title pages will be prepared in manuscript.

WAR DIARY
or
INTELLIGENCE SUMMARY.
(*Erase heading not required.*)

Army Form C. 2118.

Place	Date	Hour	Summary of Events and Information	Remarks and references to Appendices
SIEGE Camp	14th		Battalion Drill from 9–10 Company training remainder of the morning	[illegible]
	15th		Battalion Drill from 9–10. Company training, Physical Drill.	[illegible]
	16th		Battalion Church Parade (Service in the Open) Battalion visited by Col RANSOME (late Adjutant) who complimented the Battalion on its clean appearance	[illegible]
	17th		Battalion training under Coy Comdrs men's feet seen by M.O. Trench treatment carried out.	[illegible]
	18th		Battalion Drill from 9–10. Company training remainder of the morning.	[illegible]
	19th		Battalion training under Coy Comdrs	[illegible]
	20th		Battalion training. Physical Drill	[illegible]
	21st		Battalion training practicing for raid. Lt Col H.C.L. LLOYD left Batt sick Major C.P. WHITAKER M.C. takes command	[illegible]
	22nd		Battalion training for raid. Inspection of men in fighting kit. Batt ordered stand-to at 4.50 p.m. S.O.S. gone up. Stand down at 5.45 p.m.	[illegible]
	23rd		Battalion move from SIEGE CAMP for the front line by train from	

D. D. & L., London, E.C.
(A7883) Wt. W809/M1672 350,000 4/17 Sch. 52a Forms/C/2118/14

Instructions regarding War Diaries and Intelligence Summaries are contained in F. S. Regs., Part II. and the Staff Manual respectively. Title pages will be prepared in manuscript.

WAR DIARY
or
INTELLIGENCE SUMMARY.
(*Erase heading not required.*)

Army Form C. 2118.

December 1917

Place	Date	Hour	Summary of Events and Information	Remarks and references to Appendices
	23rd		TROIS TOURS to JULIET FARM, thence by track via ALBERTA & HUBNER FARM, Batt Hd Qrs. Relief complete 8.15pm. Three casualties going in. Coys work on strengthening line	[illegible]
	24th		Very misty, reconnoitring FISH post for the attack of same. Work carried on making new posts & wiring. Enemy very quiet no casualties.	[illegible]
	25th		Xmas day snow early in morning. Operations on FISH cancelled owing to clear. Enemy very quiet work carried on in the line & finishing an wiring of posts no casualties	[illegible]
	26th		More shelling to-day near Bn HdQrs. Enemy shelling at light railway night very clear owing to snow & full moon. SOS up on the right heavy fire from [illegible] SOS line, one casualty attack on FISH cancelled	[illegible]
	27th		Very quiet Bn relieved at 8.10 by 15th HLI one casualty Bn withdraw to HILL TOP FARM via ALBERTA TRACK all in by 10.5pm	[illegible]
Hill Top Fme	28th		Bn in Reserve inspection of rifles. Treatment for trench feet by M.O. working & carrying parties at night to the line	[illegible]

D. D. & L., London, E.C.
(A7883) Wt. W809/M1672 350,000 4/17 Sch. 52a Forms/C/2118/14

Instructions regarding War Diaries and Intelligence Summaries are contained in F. S. Regs., Part II. and the Staff Manual respectively. Title pages will be prepared in manuscript.

WAR DIARY
or
INTELLIGENCE SUMMARY.
(Erase heading not required.)

Army Form C. 2118.

December 1917.

Place	Date	Hour	Summary of Events and Information	Remarks and references to Appendices
	29th		Bn in Reserve. Cleaning up, inspections, rubbing feet. Carrying parties to front line	BEY
	30th		Battalion relieved. Bde in support. remain at HILLTOP FME cleaning up & feet rubbing.	BEY
	31st		Battalion in Brigade support	BEY

B E Young Lieut
A/Adjt
1st Dorset Regt

D. D. & L., London, E.C.
(A7883) Wt. W809/M1672 350,000 4/17 Sch. 52a Forms/C/2118/14

Instructions regarding War Diaries and Intelligence Summaries are contained in F. S. Regs., Part II, and the Staff Manual respectively. Title pages will be prepared in manuscript.

WAR DIARY
or
INTELLIGENCE SUMMARY.
(*Erase heading not required.*)

Army Form C. 2118.

1st Dorset Regt

Vol 41

Place	Date	Hour	Summary of Events and Information	Remarks and references to Appendices
	JANUARY 1918.			Map
Nielles les Ardres	1st		Battalion move from SIEGE CAMP to NIELLE les ARDRES for	DS Hazebrouck
			rest, by train via ST JEAN to AUDRUICQ then	DS 5A 1/100,000
			marched to billets	DS 3 A 15 2
	2nd		Battalion in billets, inspection of billets.	DS
	3rd		Battalion in billets training under Company Commanders	DS
	4th		Battalion in billets training under Company Commanders	DS
	5th		Battalion in billets. Whole Holiday Xmas day celebrated	DS
	6th		Battalion in billets Church parade in School Room at NIELLES-les-	DS
			ARDRES. Cleaning for Corps Commander's Inspection	DS
	7th		Battalion inspected by the Brigadier	DS
	8th		Battalion parade for inspection by C.O	DS
	9th		Battalion training	DS
	10th		Battalion firing on ranges	DS
	11th		Battalion training inspected by the Divisional Commander	DS
	12th		Battalion training	DS
	13th		Battalion Church Parade [illegible]	DS
			[illegible]	

D. D. & L., London, E.C. (A7883) Wt. W809/M1672 350,000 4/17 Sch. 52a Forms/C/2118/14

Instructions regarding War Diaries and Intelligence Summaries are contained in F. S. Regs., Part II. and the Staff Manual respectively. Title pages will be prepared in manuscript.

WAR DIARY
or
INTELLIGENCE SUMMARY.
(Erase heading not required.)

Army Form C. 2118.

Place	Date	Hour	Summary of Events and Information	Remarks and references to Appendices
Wattes-	14th		Battalion in Company training Lewis Gun Bombing Classes	[illegible]
les Ardres			etc	[illegible]
	15th		Battalion in Company training	[illegible]
	16th		Battalion Company training.	[illegible]
	17th		Battalion Company training	[illegible]
	18th		Battalion Company training	[illegible]
	19th		Battalion Open Warfare Attack.	[illegible]
	20th		Battalion Church Parade. Lt Col T W BULLOCK assumes	[illegible]
			Command	[illegible]
	21st		Battalion Transport marched for new area. Remainder of day	[illegible]
			devoted to cleaning up and preparing for move	[illegible]
			Capt H.D. Thwaytes rejoined and assumed duties O/C 2nd i/c.	[illegible]
DIRTY BUCKET	22nd		Battalion moved to Dirty Bucket Camp by train from	[illegible]
Camp.			AUDRUICQ to ELVERDINGHE thence by road arriving in	[illegible]
			new billets at 5.10 pm.	[illegible]
	23rd		A B C Coy inspected by C.O. in fighting kit. Other training under Coy	[illegible]

A6945 Wt. W11422/M1160 350,000 12/16 D. D. & L. Forms/C./2118/14.

Instructions regarding War Diaries and Intelligence Summaries are contained in F. S. Regs., Part II, and the Staff Manual respectively. Title pages will be prepared in manuscript.

WAR DIARY
or
INTELLIGENCE SUMMARY.
(Erase heading not required.)

Army Form C. 2118.

Place	Date	Hour	Summary of Events and Information	Remarks and references to Appendices
			Arrangements.	
[illegible] Camp	24		Company and Specialists Training	
	25		Company and Specialist Training. Battalion bathed at [illegible] Camp Baths	
	26		Company and Specialist Training. All men's gas helmets inspected by Bde Gas Officer.	
	27		Church Parade in Y.M.C.A. hut. Football match v 7th Buffs (Col Ransome's Battalion) score 3–3.	
	28		Company training.	
	29		Company training. Men put through French foot treatment	
[illegible] Camp	30		Battalion moved to [illegible] Camp B 5 d 2 4 [illegible] [illegible] [illegible] [illegible] [illegible] [illegible] at [illegible] Camp [illegible]	
	31		Battalion French foot treatment. Officers [illegible]	

[illegible signature]

A6945 Wt. W11422/M1160 350,000 12/16 D. D. & L. Forms/C./2118/14.

1st Dorset Regt

WAR DIARY
or
INTELLIGENCE SUMMARY.
(Erase heading not required.)

Instructions regarding War Diaries and Intelligence Summaries are contained in F. S. Regs., Part II, and the Staff Manual respectively. Title pages will be prepared in manuscript.

Army Form C. 2118.

February 1918.

Vol 42

Place	Date	Hour	Summary of Events and Information	Remarks and references to Appendices
February 1918				
BOESINGHE Camp	1st		Battalion moved into the left subsector leaving Boesinghe Camp at [illegible] pm. A and C Companies in the front line B and D Coys in Reserve. Battalion Hd Qrs at [illegible] U.4 C.15.95. Relief complete 8.5 pm.	Ref [illegible]
Left Subsector	2nd		Battalion in the line. Wiring squads used to erect wire on A Company front. C Company sent out patrols to reconnoitre the ground in NO MAN'S LAND round the CORVERBEEK U.3 b.2.7 Patrol [illegible]	DS
	3rd		Battalion in the line. Wiring squads used to erect wire. C Company sent a patrol across the CORVERBEEK to proceed up the [illegible] to find and capture a [illegible] post but no enemy were seen or found. The [illegible] on the Battalion left was of great assistance [illegible] patrols.	DS
BOESINGHE Camp	4th		Battalion withdrawn to BOESINGHE Camp being relieved by 11th [illegible]. Relief complete 8.20 pm.	DS
Right Subsector	5th		Battalion went through Trench Foot treatment in the morning & moved off at 4.15 pm to relieve the 15th [illegible] in the right subsector. B and D Companies in the line. C Company in support & A Company in reserve at VEEBEND. Bn Hd Qrs at AJAX HOUSE U.6 C.33.	DS

A6945 Wt. W11422/M1160 350,000 12/16 D. D. & L. Forms/C./2118/14.

Army Form C. 2118.

Instructions regarding War Diaries and Intelligence Summaries are contained in F. S. Regs., Part II. and the Staff Manual respectively. Title pages will be prepared in manuscript.

WAR DIARY
or
INTELLIGENCE SUMMARY.
(Erase heading not required.)

Place	Date	Hour	Summary of Events and Information	Remarks and references to Appendices
Right sub sector	6th		Battalion in the right subsector. [illegible] Patrol from D Coy saw German post	[illegible]
	7th		Battalion in the right subsector. Relieved by 2nd Manchester Regt 96th Inf Bde	
			and 15th HLI 14th Inf. Bde. Relief complete 10.30 pm. Battalion withdrawn	
			to support. Bn Hd Qrs at GRUYTERSZALE Farm. Patrol under Lieut	
			Fenton sent out to look for German post seen on night of 6/7th the post	
			was not discovered. Lieut J.R. Walton wounded and 1 OR.	
Support Battalion GRUYTERZALE Farm	8th		Battalion in support working parties.	
	9th		Battalion in support. Lieut Col. T W. Bullock assumed temporary	
			command of the Brigade. Major H.D. Thwaytes assuming command of the	
			Battalion	
	10th		Battalion relieved by 18 LANCS Fus. only 2 Companies relieving	
			the Battalion. Relief complete 8.0 pm. Battalion withdrew to Rugby	
			Dump C.1.a. Sheet 28 $\frac{1}{40000}$ thence by train to camp at T.25 b.d.	
			Sheet 20 $\frac{1}{40000}$. Battalion in camp 1.0 am.	
Camp T.25 b.d.	11th		Battalion in Camp. All men put through French foot treatment.	
	12th		Battalion [illegible] at ELVERDINGHE Chateau [illegible]	
			Lieut BARNETT U.S.R. Medical Officer [illegible]	

A6945 Wt. W11422/M1160 350,000 12/16 D. D. & L. Forms/C./2118/14.

Instructions regarding War Diaries and Intelligence Summaries are contained in F. S. Regs., Part II. and the Staff Manual respectively. Title pages will be prepared in manuscript.

WAR DIARY
or
INTELLIGENCE SUMMARY.
(Erase heading not required.)

Army Form C. 2118.

Place	Date	Hour	Summary of Events and Information	Remarks and references to Appendices
Camp [illegible]	12th		The Battalion to rejoin the Field Ambulance. The M.O. did most	DL
do			excellent work in stamping out Trench Feet	DL
do	13th		Battalion and Company training. Specialist Classes training	DL
do			under their leaders.	DL
do	14th		Battalion and Company training	DL
do	15th		Battalion working on Army line. Specialists left behind for [illegible]	DL
do	1[illegible]		Specialist training. Army line in U 19 a + c [illegible] of Brielen [illegible]	DL
do	16th		Battalion working on Army line. Specialists left behind under Specialist	DL
do			training	DL
do	17th		Battalion Church Parade. [illegible] B Company [illegible]. All officers	DL
do			seen by G.O.C. Battalion [illegible] foot treatment.	DL
do	18th		Battalion and Company training. All Companies practising Trench to	DL
do			Trench Attack. Lecture for all officers on Air Photos by Capt. [illegible]	DL
do			IV Army Intelligence in WOESTEN Area	DL
do	19th		Battalion relieved 11th Border Regt in Reserve [illegible]	DL
do			Two Companies on Canal Bank about T 29 a 9.6 and Company at Wood 14 T 30 d	DL

A6945 Wt. W11422/M1160 350,000 12/16 D. D. & L. Forms/C./2118/14.

Instructions regarding War Diaries and Intelligence Summaries are contained in F. S. Regs., Part II. and the Staff Manual respectively. Title pages will be prepared in manuscript.

WAR DIARY
or
INTELLIGENCE SUMMARY.
(*Erase heading not required.*)

Army Form C. 2118.

Place	Date	Hour	Summary of Events and Information	Remarks and references to Appendices
Left Subsector	19th		An Company at STATUETTE Farm U 19 c 1.2. Battn Hd Qrs at T.4.d.4.6.	DS
			Relief completed 5 pm Battalion moved by rail to Chapitre Cockerel.	DS
	20th		Companies working during the day time 3 hrs on improving billets	DS
			Work under RE in the evening in strengthening posts ISLAND VICTORY	DS
			CATINAT POSTS. Carrying material etc.	DS
	21st		Companies working during day 3 hrs on improving billets. C. Company	DS
			moved from WOOD 14 to TILLEUL WOOD.	DS
	22nd		Companies working during day 3 hrs improving and carrying material	DS
			working at [illegible] on Corps line. One O.R. killed.	DS
In the line	23rd		Battalion relieved 5/6th Royal Scots in the Left Subsector B. right	DS
			front Company A. centre front Co, C. left front Coy D Coy in support.	DS
			Relief completed 10.0 pm. Battn Hd Qrs at MONDOVI Wood.	DS
	24		Battalion in the line Capt Whitaker M.C. patrolling from right front Company	DS
	24		towards CORVER WOOD saw the enemy leaving their outpost line about 6.0 am	DS
	25		Battalion in the line. Casualties 1 OR wounded.	DS
	26		Battalion in the line. Casualties 1 OR Killed.	DS

A6945 Wt. W11422/M1160 350,000 12/16 D. D. & L. Forms/C./2118/14.

Instructions regarding War Diaries and Intelligence Summaries are contained in F. S. Regs., Part II. and the Staff Manual respectively. Title pages will be prepared in manuscript.

WAR DIARY
or
INTELLIGENCE SUMMARY.
(Erase heading not required.)

Army Form C. 2118.

Place	Date	Hour	Summary of Events and Information	Remarks and references to Appendices
In the line	27		Battalion in the line C and D Companies took part in a raid under Capt	D.S.
			WHITAKER MC in conjunction with 5/6th Royal Scots. [illegible] was used.	D.S.
			Raid was successful objective being the CASTLE O 3 d 1.2 3 2 1 0 was at	D.S.
			7.55 pm. Casualties 2/Lieut Ellicott wounded 3 O R ~~wounded~~ killed 2 D of	D.S.
			W. 2 O.R. missing 28 O R wounded.	D.S.
In the line	28		Battalion in the line. Cos C and D Coys which withdrew to the CORPS	D.S.
			line and came under command of OC 15th HLI. The other two Coys A & B	D.S.
			relieved by 15th HLI and withdrawn to CHAUME Pm and CAMBLAIN	D.S.
			[illegible] [illegible] [illegible] O.S.W.4. Relief Complete 9.30 pm	D.S.

H. B. [illegible] Major
Comdg 1st Dorset Regt.

A6945 Wt. W11422/M1160 350,000 12/16 D. D. & L. Forms/C./2118/14.

32nd Division.

14th Infantry Brigade

1st BATTALION

THE DORSET REGIMENT

MARCH 1 9 1 8

Instructions regarding War Diaries and Intelligence Summaries are contained in F. S. Regs., Part II. and the Staff Manual respectively. Title pages will be prepared in manuscript.

WAR DIARY or ~~INTELLIGENCE SUMMARY.~~ DS

(Erase heading not required.)

March 1918 — 1st Dorset Regt

Army Form C. 2118.

Vol 43

Place	Date	Hour	Summary of Events and Information	Remarks and references to Appendices
Battalion in Support line Subsector	1st		Battalion in Support C + D Coys working on CORPS line during the morning. A + B Coys	Sheet 28 DS
			working on Main line posts in the evening under R.E. Supervision.	1/10000 DS
	2nd		Battalion in Support work same as on the 1st	DS
	3rd		Battalion in Support work same as on the 2nd	DS
	4th		Battalion in Support C + D Coys working on CORPS line in the morning. Relieved by	DS
			15th H.L.I. in the evening relief complete 11.10pm. On relief, Battalion withdrew to	DS
			Corps reserve into billets vacated by 5/6th Royal Scots.	DS
			Battn H.d.Qrs BOSCHE Cross roads U 24 d 45 55 A Coy STATUETTE Farm U. 24 d. 90.15	DS
			B Coy T. 23 c 9.5 C Coy TILLEUL Wood U 24 d 8 8 D Coy T 29 d 4.1. In billets 1.0am	DS
Battalion in Reserve	5th		Battalion in Reserve. All Coys working in the morning under R.E. on the Army line.	DS
			B + C Coys bathed in the afternoon clean clothes, French foot treatment to the mens feet.	DS
			Lt.Col T.W. BULLOCK rejoined from leave and assumed command	DS
	6th		Battalion in Reserve All Coys working in the morning under R.E. on the Army line.	DS
			D Coy, Bn HQ bathed.	DS
	7th		Battn in Reserve. All Coys working in the morning under R.E. on the Army line	DS
			finishing work at 12.30pm. A Coy bathed in the afternoon. Battalion relieved	DS DS

D. D. & L., London, E.C.
(A7883) Wt. W809/M1672 350,000 4/17 Sch. 52a Forms/C/2118/14

Instructions regarding War Diaries and Intelligence Summaries are contained in F. S. Regs., Part II, and the Staff Manual respectively. Title pages will be prepared in manuscript.

WAR DIARY
or
INTELLIGENCE SUMMARY. DS
(Erase heading not required.)

Army Form C. 2118.

Place	Date	Hour	Summary of Events and Information	Remarks and references to Appendices
			5/6th Royal Scots in the front line D A C Coys in front line, B Coy in Support.	DS
			Relief complete 8.45pm Battn HQ at MONDOVI wood	DS
	8th		Battalion in the line, enemy very quiet until 4.0am when a heavy barrage started	DS
	9th		Enemy attacked Argyle + Sutherland Highlanders 97th Inf Bde and drove back six posts	DS
			of the battalion on our right U5a53 to U4b93. Our right post No 1 blown in	DS
			by a shell but garrison remained although Lewis Gun was blown up and two men	DS
			wounded. The NCO in charge Sgt CLARKE left the post at 9.30am and went to	DS
			No 2 post thence returning to Coy HQ for a Lewis gun in place of the one smashed	DS
			2 Coys K.O.Y.L.I. counter-attacked at 9.20am and retook the posts establishing the	DS
			original line of outposts again. Killed Lieut J T SHIEL, Wounded Lieut A R FENTON	DS
			2 O.R^s	DS
	9th		Battalion in the line, very quiet. Slight shelling round MANGELARE and main line	DS
			posts. Lieut FORD and two orderlies went out on the morning of the 9th at 5.0am and	DS
			got in touch with the Argyle and Sutherland Highlanders who had relieved the	DS
			2nd KOYLI who retook the posts on the night 8/9th.	DS
	10th		Battalion in the line, very quiet except for slight intermittent shelling on	DS

D. D. & L., London, E.C.
(A7883) Wt. W809/M1672 350,000 4/17 Sch. 52a Forms/C/2118/14

Instructions regarding War Diaries and Intelligence Summaries are contained in F. S. Regs., Part II. and the Staff Manual respectively. Title pages will be prepared in manuscript.

Army Form C. 2118.

WAR DIARY
or
~~INTELLIGENCE SUMMARY.~~ DS
(Erase heading not required.)

Place	Date	Hour	Summary of Events and Information	Remarks and references to Appendices
			main line and outposts.	DS
	11th		Battn relieved by 5/6th Royal Scots. Relief complete 10.10pm. On relief Battalion withdrew	DS
			to Support Bn H.Q MONDOVI Farm "A" Coy GOURBI Farm "B" Coy-STATUETTE "C" Coy CHAUME	DS
			"D" Coy-LANNES COPSE	DS
	12th		Battn in Support "A" & "D" Coys working on Corps line "B" Coy working on burial of signal	DS
			cable. Lieut A.O BIRKS wounded	DS
	13th		Battn in Support "A" & "D" Coys working on Corps line "B" Coy working on burial of	DS
			cable. Battalion relieved by 15th Lancs Fus. Relief complete 3.50pm withdrew to	DS
			Divisional Reserve in CANAL Bank vicinity of J.1 Bridge T.29 central	DS
	14th		Battn in Reserve CANAL BANK 400 ORs working on Army line.	DS
			Lieut A.O BIRKS died of wounds in 36th CCS	DS
	15th		Battalion in Divisional Reserve 400 ORs working on the Army line	DS
	16th		Battn in Divisional Reserve 400 ORs working on the Army line	DS
	17th		" " " " B Coy working on accommodation in CANAL Bank	DS
			A.C.D. HdQrs bathed, clean clothes and went through pediculine	DS
	18th		~~Battn in Divisional Reserve. 400 ORs working on the Army line.~~	
	19th		Battn in Divisional Reserve. Very Wet No training	DS

D. D. & L., London, E.C.
(A7883) Wt. W809/M1672 350,000 4/17 Sch. 52a Forms/C/2118/14

Instructions regarding War Diaries and Intelligence Summaries are contained in F. S. Regs., Part II. and the Staff Manual respectively. Title pages will be prepared in manuscript.

WAR DIARY
or
~~INTELLIGENCE SUMMARY.~~ DS

(*Erase heading not required.*)

Army Form C. 2118.

Place	Date	Hour	Summary of Events and Information	Remarks and references to Appendices
	20th		Battn in Divisional Reserve. Find the Army Interplatoon Association Rifle competition	DS
			No 12 platoon the winner.	DS
	21st		Battalion relieved the 2nd KOYLI in the left subsector on the right Brigade front.	DS
			Battn HQ at GRUYTERZALE Farm. A Coy D Coy in support at GRUYTERZALE Farm	DS
			B + C Coys in front line. Coy HQ AJAX House and FAIDHERBE Post. Relief	DS
			complete 10.40pm	DS
	22nd		Battalion in the line, day spent without any unusual event. 2 ORs Killed 14 ORs wnd.	DS
	23rd		Battalion in the line, artillery activity normal. Inter Coy reliefs	DS
	24th		"A + D Coys [struck through] take over front line. B + C become Brigade Reserve. Relief complete	DS
			12.30am Casualties 2 ORs wounded.	DS
	25th		Battn in the line, artillery activity normal. Two BOSCH seen in tree tops near	DS
			OWL'S WOOD. Artillery brought [struck through] to bear on these men who were made	DS
			to come down. Capt C P WHITAKER MC wounded. Lieut C G MILLER	DS
			wounded 1. OR Killed 2 wounded.	DS
	26th.		Battn in the line, artillery activity normal, change of dispositions in manner	DS
			of holding the line. D Coy took over the whole frontage less No1 and 2 post	DS

D. D. & L., London, E.C.
(A7883) Wt. W809/M1672 350,000 4/17 Sch. 52a. Forms/C/2118/14

Instructions regarding War Diaries and Intelligence Summaries are contained in F. S. Regs., Part II. and the Staff Manual respectively. Title pages will be prepared in manuscript.

WAR DIARY
or
~~INTELLIGENCE SUMMARY.~~ DS
(Erase heading not required.)

Army Form C. 2118.

Place	Date	Hour	Summary of Events and Information	Remarks and references to Appendices
			A Coy withdrew to NEY Shelter. B Coy to SIEGE Camp B.21.d the change in	DS
			dispositions made to facilitate handing over to the Belgians. Casualties	DS
			4 ORs wounded	DS
	27th		Battn in the line, no casualties, very quiet. D Coy relieved by	DS
			a coy of 3rd Bn 18th Regt d'Infanterie Belgium Army. C Coy by a coy of 3rd Bn	DS
			B.R.I. Belgium Army. Battn Hd Qrs by Bn HQ 3rd B.R.I. Very quiet relief	DS
			B and A Coys not relieved owing to change in dispositions. Relief	DS
			complete 12.45 am. Battn withdrew to SIEGE Camp.	DS
	28th		Battalion in SIEGE Camp. Fitting of clothing, grooming of Coys. Remainder	DS
			of day spent in rest. 100 men of B Coy sent to PESELHOEK to assist	DS
			loading at station	DS
	29		Battalion moved by train from PESELHOEK to TINQUES. Left SIEGE Camp	DS
			at 6.10 am. Left PESELHOEK 9.45 am arrived TINQUES 2.45 pm	DS
			B Coy 100 men had been sent in advance. Remainder of Battn in	[illegible]
			Billets HABARCQ 9.5 pm.	DS
	30th		Battn in Billets HABARCQ.	DS

D. D. & L., London, E.C.
(A7883) Wt. W809/M1672 350,000 4/17 Sch. 52a Forms/C/2118/14

Instructions regarding War Diaries and Intelligence Summaries are contained in F. S. Regs., Part II. and the Staff Manual respectively. Title pages will be prepared in manuscript.

WAR DIARY
or
~~INTELLIGENCE SUMMARY.~~ DS

(*Erase heading not required.*)

Army Form C. 2118.

Place	Date	Hour	Summary of Events and Information	Remarks and references to Appendices
			C.O., Adjt, 3 Coy Comdrs, I.O. Signalling Sgt reconnoitre new PURPLE line remainder of Battn practised rapid firing.	
	31st		Battalion in billets HABARCQ. Marched to the PURPLE line - Route - WANQUENTIN - Q 10 a 5 0 - BEAUMETZ - Les - LOGES - RANSART - MONCHY - PURPLE line F. 14 a 3 7 - F 2 d 2 2	
			All Coys in the line - relieved 11th East Lancs, 92nd Inf Bde. Relief complete 1.10 am.	DS

D Stayner Capt for Lieut Col Comdg [illegible] Regt

14th Inf.Bde.
32nd Div.

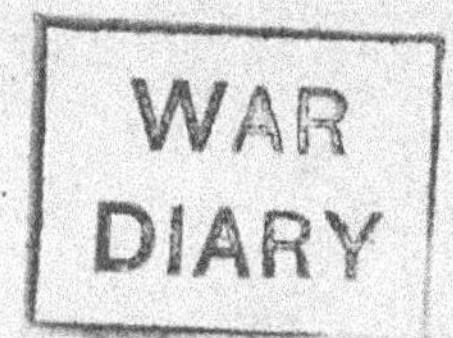

1st BATTN. THE DORSETSHIRE REGIMENT.

A P R I L

1 9 1 8

Instructions regarding War Diaries and Intelligence Summaries are contained in F. S. Regs., Part II. and the Staff Manual respectively. Title pages will be prepared in manuscript.

WAR DIARY
or
INTELLIGENCE SUMMARY.
(Erase heading not required.)

1 Dorset Regt

Army Form C. 2118.

14/32

95/44

Place	Date	Hour	Summary of Events and Information	Remarks and references to Appendices
	April 18			
	1st		Battalion in the PURPLE line very quiet.	
	2nd		Battalion in the PURPLE line. Bn Hd Qrs changed to F.26.85.25	
	3rd		Battalion in the PURPLE line 15th HLI took AYETTE. C Company lent to HLI to be in support. 3 O.R.s wounded.	
	4th		Battalion relieved 15th HLI in the left Battn Sector of the Bde front. Relief Complete 10am. Lieut ET JOHNS D of W received when leading his platoon in action. 1 O.R. killed. After 2 O.R.s wounded.	
	5th		Battalion in the line very quiet much material salvaged. 1 OR killed 3 OR's wounded.	
	6th		Battalion in the line very quiet. Wiring the front with German salvaged wire. C Company made Battle [illegible] and [illegible] in AYETTE. 3 OR's killed 7 OR's wounded	
	7th		Battalion in the line very quiet 4 OR's wounded.	
	8th		Battalion in the line very quiet usual work wiring etc. 3 OR's wounded	
	9th		Battalion in the line quiet. Wiring 5 OR's killed 3 OR's wounded.	
	10th		Battalion in the line Divisional Commander visited Battn Hd Qrs.	

D. D. & L., London, E.C.
(A7883) Wt. W809/M1672 350,000 4/17 Sch. 52a Forms/C/2118/14

WAR DIARY
or
INTELLIGENCE SUMMARY.
(Erase heading not required.)

Army Form C. 2118.

Instructions regarding War Diaries and Intelligence Summaries are contained in F. S. Regs., Part II, and the Staff Manual respectively. Title pages will be prepared in manuscript.

Place	Date	Hour	Summary of Events and Information	Remarks and references to Appendices
	11th		Battalion in the line. Quiet.	DS
	12th		Battalion in the line. Lt Col T W BULLOCK commanding the	DS
			Battalion killed. 2 OR killed 9 OR wounded.	DS
	13th		Battalion in the line. Battn Headquarters moved to 7 9a 70 25 1 OR wounded	DS
	14th		Battalion in the line relieved by 5/6th Royal Scots and withdrew	DS
			into Reserve with one Company in PURPLE line one in PURPLE RESERVE	DS
			line at MONCHY WOOD German front line. Lieut J R WALTON 2nd Lieut	DS
			R E C GOZZ. W.H.T. BARRETT 2 W. PEDGRIFT. L DIGBY & Capt	DS
			C.G. SKINNER M.O. 10 OR's diagnosed as gassed.	DS
	15th		C and B Companies bathed otherwise all quiet. 22 OR's diagnosed as gassed.	DS
	16th		D Company bathed	Map 17
	17th		A Company bathed and R.A.P.	DS
	18th		Battalion in Reserve. CAPT C J TERRARD Lieut J C ZEEDERBURG	DS
			diagnosed as gassed.	DS
	19th		Battalion relieved 15th HLI in right Subsector of Bde front. Relief	DS
			Complete 1.15 am. 4 OR's wounded	DS

D. D. & L., London, E.C.
(A7883) Wt. W809/M1672 350,000 4/17 Sch. 52a Forms/C/2118/14

Instructions regarding War Diaries and Intelligence Summaries are contained in F. S. Regs., Part II, and the Staff Manual respectively. Title pages will be prepared in manuscript.

WAR DIARY
or
INTELLIGENCE SUMMARY.
(*Erase heading not required.*)

Army Form C. 2118.

Place	Date	Hour	Summary of Events and Information	Remarks and references to Appendices
	20th		Battalion in the line heavy shelling 3 OR's wounded	
	21st		Battalion in the line very quiet	
	22nd		Battalion in the line very quiet. casualties nil.	
	23rd		Battalion in the line, slight shelling casualties 1 OR killed	
	&		3 O.R. wounded.	
	24th		Battalion in the line, Our artillery carried out burst of fire. One	
			prisoner 453 Regt captured by 'C' Coy. He was captured in shelter	
			in front of our wire. Casualties nil.	
		11pm.	Battalion relieved by 2nd Bn COLDSTREAM GUARDS.	
	25th		Relief complete 1.25 am. Bn embussed at MONCHY debussed	Reference map BUCQUOY 1/40,000
			at BAVINCOURT at 6 am. Bn in billets 6.30 am.	
			Battalion in Billets at BAVINCOURT resting, cleaning	
			up.	
	26th		Battalion in Billets. Bn Bathing, fitting clothing & cleaning	
			up.	
	27th		Battalion training. Major General C.D. SHUTE C.B. leaves Division	

D. D. & L., London, E.C.
(A7883) Wt. W809/M1672 350,000 4/17 Sch. 52a Forms/C/2118/14

Instructions regarding War Diaries and Intelligence Summaries are contained in F. S. Regs., Part II. and the Staff Manual respectively. Title pages will be prepared in manuscript.

WAR DIARY
or
INTELLIGENCE SUMMARY.
(*Erase heading not required.*)

Army Form C. 2118.

Place	Date	Hour	Summary of Events and Information	Remarks and references to Appendices
	27th contd		to command V Corps.	DS
	28.		Battalion in Billets - Divine Service in the morning Divisional Band played during service. C.O. Adjt Coy Comdrs made a reconnaissance of the forward Area	DS
	29th		Battalion training. A B & C Coys underwent French method in Foot Treatment. Draft of 99 other ranks joined.	DS
	30th		Battalion training. A & D Coys firing on Rifle Range. D Coy. Hd Qr Coy & 99 Draft underwent French method in Foot Treatment. Div Commander Major-General J. CAMPBELL C.B., C.M.G., DSO visited Battalion & saw B Coy in training.	DS

[illegible] Captain
[illegible] Adjt

D. D. & L., London, E.C.
(A7883) Wt. W809/M1672 350,000 4/17 Sch. 52a Forms/C/2118/14

Dorset Regt 1st Dorsets

Instructions regarding War Diaries and Intelligence Summaries are contained in F. S. Regs., Part II, and the Staff Manual respectively. Title pages will be prepared in manuscript.

WAR DIARY
or
INTELLIGENCE SUMMARY.
(Erase heading not required.)

MAY 1918

Army Form C. 2118.

Vol 45

Place	Date	Hour	Summary of Events and Information	Remarks and references to Appendices
	1st		Battalion carried out practice in Open Warfare Attack ref Sheet 51c S.E 1/20,000. W.11.b.1.3 to road running through W 10d and W11a inclusive	WtS
	2nd		Battalion in training. Message "Test MOVE to Alarm Posts" received at 6.15 pm. Assembly complete at 7.25 pm.	WtS
	3rd		Battalion in Training	WtS
	4th		Battalion in Training. Divisional General inspected the Battalion in practice Open Warfare Attack ref Sheet 51c S.E 1/20,000. W.11.b.1.3 to road running through W 10d and W11a inclusive	WtS
	5th		Battalion in Billets. Divine Service cancelled. Morning spent in cleaning of equipment and billets. CO and 2nd i/c attended conference at Bde Hd Qrs SAULTY. CO attended conference at SAULTY at 7.30 pm on New Organisation of Companies	WtS
	6th		Battalion in Billets. Reorganisation of Companies into 2 Riflemen Platoons and 2 L.G Platoons. "B" Coy carried out practice ATTACK in new formation under supervision of Brigadier General F.W. LUMSDEN V.C. D.S.O.	WtS

D. D. & L., London, E.C. (A7883) Wt. W809/M1672 350,000 4/17 Sch. 52a Forms/C/2118/14

1/Dorset Regt

Instructions regarding War Diaries and Intelligence Summaries are contained in F. S. Regs., Part II, and the Staff Manual respectively. Title pages will be prepared in manuscript.

WAR DIARY
or
INTELLIGENCE SUMMARY.
(Erase heading not required.)

Army Form C. 2118.

MAY 1918

Place	Date	Hour	Summary of Events and Information	Remarks and references to Appendices
	7th		Battalion in Training. Coys bathed.	WA
	8th.		Battalion training. Hd Qr Coy & Transport bathed. Bathing completed throughout Bn. Practice in Trench to Trench attack by Coys. A & D Coys on Range.	WA
	9th		Battalion practised Trench to Trench attack. Ref Sheet 57c S E area X 22 c (By day).	WA
	10th		Battalion in training. Men underwent French system of Foot Treatment. Battalion practised formation for Trench to Trench attack at 9.30 p.m.	WA
	11th.		Battalion in Billets. Moved into line during night. Relief complete at 3.40 A.M. 12.5.18. Casualties 1 Officer & 4 other ranks wounded.	WA
	12th.		Battalion in the line. Quiet day. All dark. Sunken road around B. H. Qr then shelled and also Reserve Line. Casualties 3 men wounded	WA
	13th		Battalion in the line. Much enemy shelling around vicinity of Battn. Hd. Qrs. during night.	WA
	14th.		Battalion in line. Relieved during night of 14th/15th by 2/R Scots. Battalion withdrew to Reserve position. Casualties 3 men wounded	WA
	15th.		Battalion in reserve. Resting. Fatigue party working on [illegible]	WA

D. D. & L., London, E.C.
(A7883) Wt W809/M1672 350,000 4/17 Sch. 52a Forms/C/2118/14

1/Dorset Regt.

WAR DIARY
or
INTELLIGENCE SUMMARY.
(Erase heading not required.)

Army Form C. 2118.

Instructions regarding War Diaries and Intelligence Summaries are contained in F. S. Regs., Part II. and the Staff Manual respectively. Title pages will be prepared in manuscript.

MAY 1918

Place	Date	Hour	Summary of Events and Information	Remarks and references to Appendices
	16		Battn in reserve. Specialists training during morning. Cleaning up of trenches. Much enemy shelling. Casualties two men wounded	WAS
	17		Battn in Reserve. Hd Qrs, A & C companies bathed at RANSART. B & D companies practise for raid. Casualties one man wounded	WAS
	18		Battn in Reserve. Day quiet, very little shelling. B & D Coys bathed at RANSART. Battn relieved 15th HLI in Right Sub Sector (centre Sector) No casualties. Relief completed at 12.20 AM.	WAS
	19		Battn in line. Little shelling, no casualties.	WAS
	20.		Battn in line. Reserve line shelled between 11 pm & 12 M.N. Casualties 1 NCO killed 3 O.R. wounded.	WAS
	21		Battn in line. RAID carried out on HAMLINCOURT at 3 am. RAID suc-cessful. 4 prisoners being taken & objective gained. Casualties heavy (7 officers & 79 O.R.). Owing to our barrage falling short a great number of these casualties were caused by our own artillery, it is to be noted that though the barrage fell on the raiding party before it had left the starting	WAS

D. D. & L., London, E.C.
(A7883) Wt. W809/M1672 350,000 4/17 Sch. 52a Forms/C/2118/14

1/Dorset Regt

Instructions regarding War Diaries and Intelligence Summaries are contained in F. S. Regs., Part II, and the Staff Manual respectively. Title pages will be prepared in manuscript.

WAR DIARY
or
INTELLIGENCE SUMMARY.
(Erase heading not required.)

Army Form C. 2118.

MAY 1918.

Place	Date	Hour	Summary of Events and Information	Remarks and references to Appendices
	21		point, the raid was carried through successfully (See letters attached commending party on its gallantry from G.O.C. 14th Bgde. G.O.C. 32nd Div. G.O.C. 3rd Army) The raid was carried out by B & D Companies. Little shelling during remainder of the day.	WA
	22		Battn in line. Little shelling one OR wounded. Day quiet.	WA
	23		Battn in line Bn HQ shelled 11.am no casualties during night 23/24 inter company relief.	WA
	24.		Battn in line. Little shelling casualties 1 OR wounded.	WA
	25		Battn in line. Little shelling casualties 1 OR wounded.	WA
	26		Battn in line. Bn relieved night 26/27 by 5/6 Royal Scots little shelling, one OR killed. Bn HQ shelled 11.p.m.	WA
	27		Battn in Reserve, relief completed, no shelling casualties nil.	WA
	28.		Battn in Reserve, Bn HQ ~~little~~ shelled wounded, 1 O.R.	WA
	29		Battn in Reserve. A & D Companies carried out tactical scheme little shelling casualties wounded 1 OR.	WA

D. D. & L., London, E.C.
(A7883) Wt. W809/M1672 350,000 4/17 Sch. 52a Forms/C/2118/14

1/Dorset Regt

Instructions regarding War Diaries and Intelligence Summaries are contained in F. S. Regs., Part II. and the Staff Manual respectively. Title pages will be prepared in manuscript.

WAR DIARY
or
INTELLIGENCE SUMMARY.
(Erase heading not required.)

Army Form C. 2118.

MAY 1918.

Place	Date	Hour	Summary of Events and Information	Remarks and references to Appendices
	30.		Batt in Reserve. Bn relieved 15th HLI in left sub sector (centre sector) relief completed 11.30. a.m. Little shelling wounded 1.O.R.	W.A.S
	31		Batt in line, little shelling around reserve line casualties Nil. Fighting patrol of 1 officer 2 NCOs & 11 men left our line at 11.30 pm arriving back at 1.AM with a prisoner.	W.A.S

H.K. Thwaytes Lt Colonel
2. 6. 18 Cmdg 1st Dorset Regt.

D. D. & L., London, E.C.
(A7883) Wt. W809/M1672 350,000 4/17 Sch. 52a Forms/C/2118/14

War Diary 1/Dorset Regt.

32nd Division. VI Corps No.G.S.50/45.

The following remarks of the Army Commander with reference to Raid carried out by 14th Infantry Brigade on the night 20/21st May are forwarded for your information:-

"I consider that this Raid bears testimony to a very high standard of dash and determination in the ranks of the Infantry of the 32nd Division. Nothing is more calculated to affect the ardour of the troops than the short shooting of their own artillery, and that this did not deter them from pushing the Raid through and inflicting considerable loss to the enemy is most commendable. Please convey my sincerest congratulations to the Battalion".

(Sgd) R.H.Kearsley,
B.G.G.S.

25th May, 1918.

1stnDorset Regiment. 14th Inf.Bde.No.G.176/7/8.

The G.O.C. has much pleasure in forwarding the above letter, He has already expressed his appreciation of the work done by the men of the 1st Dorset Regiment, but again takes this opportunity to say how much he values the courage and determination shown by all ranks who took part in the recent raid.

(Sgd) M.A.Green, Captain,
Brigade Major, 14th Infantry Brigade.

26th May, 1918.

COPY OF TELEGRAM.

To HOZA from QUHI 22nd May, 1918.

Following from Corps Commander begins:-

"Please convey my congratulations to HOZA in carrying through their raid so successfully this morning under most trying circumstances.

H.Q. 14th Infantry Brigade,
20/5/18.

My Dear Colonel,

As your men are in the line and I wont be able to get them together to tell them how much I appreciate the gallant manner in which they executed their attack today, I should be glad if you would pass it on to them.

To have carried out the operation and to have fought their way to their final objective in spite of heavy losses from shell fire before the start, is a splendid example of the courage, determination and fine fighting quqlities of all ranks of your Battalion.

It may not have been a showy operation, but it was a severe ordeal to which your men were subjected, and they faced and overcame it most gallantly.

I should like them to know how much I admire their fine soldierly qualities.

(Sgd) Yours sincerely,
F.W.Lumsden.

1 DORSET. REGT.

1 Dorset Rgt
Vol 46

Instructions regarding War Diaries and Intelligence Summaries are contained in F. S. Regs., Part II, and the Staff Manual respectively. Title pages will be prepared in manuscript.

WAR DIARY
or
INTELLIGENCE SUMMARY.
(Erase heading not required.)

Army Form C. 2118.

JUNE 1918

Place	Date	Hour	Summary of Events and Information	Remarks and references to Appendices
	1.		Battn in Line. Fighting patrol from B Coy did good work, opperation successful surprising a German post & capturing a Regt. Sergt. Major. Intermittent shelling during day casualties 1 O.R. Very quiet on front.	[illegible]
	2		Battn in Line. Little shelling till midnight. Back area gas shelled Blue X. B Coy in Defended Locality compelled to move. Bn Hd Qrs affected for 2 hours. All clear at 2.30 a.m. 3.6.18. 2 OR wounded.	[illegible]
	3		Battn in Line. Reserve Line shelled during morning. Work in Support Line stopped owing to shell fire. Casualties 1 Offr and 1 OR wounded. Brig. General F.W. LUMSDEN V.C., C.B., D.S.O. Killed.	[illegible]
	4.		Battn in Line. Day generally quiet. Little shelling around support line but casualties severe. O.C. "C" Coy & servant killed 2 other officers wounded and 3 O.R. Commanding Officer Lt Col. H.D THWAYTES represented the Battalion at the funeral of Brigadier General F.W. LUMSDEN V.C. C.B. DSO at RANSART.	[illegible]

D. D. & L., London, E.C.
(A7883) Wt. W809/M1672 350,000 4/17 Sch. 52a Forms/C/2118/14

1/Dorset Regt

Instructions regarding War Diaries and Intelligence Summaries are contained in F. S. Regs., Part II. and the Staff Manual respectively. Title pages will be prepared in manuscript.

WAR DIARY
or
INTELLIGENCE SUMMARY.
(Erase heading not required.)

Army Form C. 2118.

JUNE 1918

Place	Date	Hour	Summary of Events and Information	Remarks and references to Appendices
	5		Battalion in line. Little shelling except towards night when Reserve Line was shelled with 5.9 cm. Casualties 1 OR killed 2 Officers and 2 OR wounded.	WT
	6		Battalion in Line. Day quiet. Wiring party of A Coy attacked by enemy. Casualties 1 OR wounded.	WT
	7		Battalion in line. Shelling much below normal. During night of 7/8th June Battalion relieved by 5/6th ROYAL SCOTS. Battalion withdrew to Reserve Bn positions at HENDECOURT.	WT
	8		Battalion in Reserve. Very quiet day. Hd Qrs A and D COYS bathed all clothes ironed. 6 Officers and 200 men worked under R E at FINE CROSS ROADS from 10 pm to 2 A.M.	WT
	9		Battalion in Reserve. CHATEAU WOOD and PURPLE LINE shelled during morning. B & C COYS bathed All clothing ironed. Casualties 1 OR wounded	WT
	10		Battalion in Reserve. Quiet day. Capt. H.C. MORRIS M.C. MIDDLESEX REGT joined Bn and assumed duties of 2nd in Command. Draft of 2 Officers and 30 O.R. arrived from Depot Battalion.	WT

D. D. & L., London, E.C.
(A7883) Wt. W809/M1672 350,000 4/17 Sch. 52a Forms/C/2118/14

1/Dorset Regt.

Instructions regarding War Diaries and Intelligence Summaries are contained in F. S. Regs., Part II. and the Staff Manual respectively. Title pages will be prepared in manuscript.

WAR DIARY
or
INTELLIGENCE SUMMARY.
(*Erase heading not required.*)

Army Form C. 2118.

JUNE 1918.

Place	Date	Hour	Summary of Events and Information	Remarks and references to Appendices
	11		Battalion in Reserve. Brigadier-General L. P. Evans V.C., D.S.O. visited the Bn for the 1st time.	
	12		Battalion in Reserve. Very quiet day. During night of 12th/13th June Bn. relieved the 15th H.L.I. in the Right Subsector (Centre Sector).	
	13		Battalion in Line. Bn Hd Qrs and vicinity shelled during morning with 4.2s. Afternoon quiet. Hostile shelling of Front & Reserve Lines during night. Casualties. 2 Officers wounded. 3 O.R. killed 6 wounded.	
	14		Battalion in Line. Front Line bombarded otherwise little enemy shelling during the day. Casualties 1 Officer wounded. 1 OR killed.	
	15		Battalion in Line. Very quiet up to dusk. Enemy observation balloons in evidence throughout the day. No casualties.	
	16		Battalion in Line. Situation quiet. Enemy activity below normal. No casualties.	
	17		Battalion in Line. Enemy again quiet, but considerable aerial activity.	
	18		Battalion in Line. Quiet during day. At 2.30 a.m. night of 18th/19th June. False barrage put down by us. No retaliation by Boche.	

(A7092). Wt W12839/M1293 75,000. 1/17. D. D. & L., Ltd. Forms/C.2118/14.

1/4 Dorset Regt.

Instructions regarding War Diaries and Intelligence Summaries are contained in F. S. Regs., Part II. and the Staff Manual respectively. Title pages will be prepared in manuscript.

WAR DIARY
or
INTELLIGENCE SUMMARY.
(Erase heading not required.)

Army Form C. 2118.

JUNE 1918

Place	Date	Hour	Summary of Events and Information	Remarks and references to Appendices
	19		Battalion in Line. Little shelling during afternoon. From 8 to 11 pm Support Line subjected to continual shell bombardment. 1 man killed & 1 wounded. At 1 am night of 19/20th June small raid by 15th H.L.I. Enemy retaliated on Battery in COJEUL VALLEY. At 2 A.M. little gas shelling	[illegible]
	20		Battalion in line. Very quiet day. During night 20th/21st June the Battalion was relieved by the 5/6th ROYAL SCOTS	[illegible]
	21		Battalion in Reserve. No shelling. Battalion bathed at RANSART and BLAIREVILLE BATHS. All men's clothes were ironed	[illegible]
	22		Battalion in Reserve. Very quiet	[illegible]
	23		do do. Little shelling of HENDECOURT	[illegible]
	24		do Day quiet. Night 24th/25th June minor offensive on left. 1 officer 21 O.R. 6 M.Gs. + 1 T.M. captured	[illegible]
	25		do No shelling in vicinity. Our aeroplanes active	[illegible]
	26		do Day again quiet. No artillery activity	[illegible]
	27		do Again very quiet. Battalion bathed at RANSART and BLAIREVILLE BATHS. All clothes ironed	

(A7092). Wt W12839/M1293 75,000. 1/17. D. D. & L., Ltd. Forms/C.2118/14.

1/1 Dorset Regt.

Instructions regarding War Diaries and Intelligence Summaries are contained in F. S. Regs., Part II. and the Staff Manual respectively. Title pages will be prepared in manuscript.

WAR DIARY
or
INTELLIGENCE SUMMARY.
(Erase heading not required.)

Army Form C. 2118.

JUNE

Place	Date	Hour	Summary of Events and Information	Remarks and references to Appendices
	28		Batt. in Reserve. During night of 28/29th Bt relieved 5/6 Royal Scots in Centre Bgde Sector. Day quiet no casualties.	
	29		Battn in line. Day quiet no casualties.	
	30		Bn in line. Day quiet. Fighting Patrol went out under 2Lt PAIN and encountered strong resistance & much wire [illegible] a patrol not strong enough to take [illegible] & after reconnoitring the position, it returned. Casualties 2 ORs wounded.	

C. H. [illegible]
Major
Commanding 1/1 Dorset Regt.

(A7092). Wt. W12839/M1293. 75,000. 1/17. D. D. & L., Ltd. Forms/C.2118/14.

1/Dorset Regt.

1 Dorset Regt

Vol 47

Instructions regarding War Diaries and Intelligence Summaries are contained in F. S. Regs., Part II. and the Staff Manual respectively. Title pages will be prepared in manuscript.

JULY 1918

WAR DIARY
or
INTELLIGENCE SUMMARY.

(Erase heading not required.)

Army Form C. 2118.

Place	Date	Hour	Summary of Events and Information	Remarks and references to Appendices
	1.		Batt in line. Little shelling. Casualties 1 OR killed. Patrol under Lt PAIN went out to reconnoitre enemy's wire & a possible site with prisoners. No enemy met with.	SFC
	2		Batt in line. Day quiet. Casualties 3 OR wounded.	SFC
	3.		Batt in line. Little shelling. Casualties 3 OR wounded	SFC
	4.		Batt in line. Day quiet. Casualties Nil	SFC
	5.		Batt in line. Div. relief. Casualties Nil	SFC
	6.		Batt in Rest relieved ~~in~~ the line by 2nd Batt Coldstream Guards, morning 6th Batt bussed to BAVINCOURT	SFC
	7.		Batt in rest. Companies cleaning up.	SFC
	8.		Batt in rest. Companies training.	SFC
	9.		Batt in rest. Companies training. Heats of Regt. Sports run.	SFC
	10		Batt in rest. Companies training. Regt Band came 5th in VI Corps Band Competition.	SFC

(A7092). Wt W12839/M1293 75,000. 1/17. D. D. & L., Ltd. Forms/C.2118/14.

1/Dorset Regt.

Instructions regarding War Diaries and Intelligence Summaries are contained in F. S. Regs., Part II. and the Staff Manual respectively. Title pages will be prepared in manuscript.

WAR DIARY
or
INTELLIGENCE SUMMARY.
(Erase heading not required.)

Army Form C. 2118.

July 1918.

Place	Date	Hour	Summary of Events and Information	Remarks and references to Appendices
	11.		Battalion in rest. Company on range. Training. Heats run off for Bgde Sports entries.	W.T.S.
	12.		Battalion in rest. Company on range. Training. Test turn out. ~~to~~ Defence scheme.	W.T.S.
	13		Battalion in rest. Training remainder of heats for sports run off. Ceremonial parade for presentation of medals.	W.T.S.
	14.		Battalion in rest. Training.	W.T.S.
	15.		Battalion in rest. Training	W.T.S.
	16		Battalion in rest. Training	W.T.S.
	17		Battalion in rest. Training	W.T.S.
	18.		Battalion left BAYINCOURT & marched to MONDICOURT and entrained.	W.T.S.
	19.		Battalion detrained at WAYYENBURG & marched to OOST-CAPPELLE	
	20		Battalion in Army Reserve. Training. OOST-CAPPELLE	
	21.		Battalion in Army Reserve. Training. Officers reconnoitring trenches to front line	W.T.S.

(A7092). Wt. W12839/M1293 75,000. 1/17. D. D. & L., Ltd. Forms/C.2118/14.

1/Dorset Regt

Instructions regarding War Diaries and Intelligence Summaries are contained in F. S. Regs., Part II. and the Staff Manual respectively. Title pages will be prepared in manuscript.

WAR DIARY
or
INTELLIGENCE SUMMARY.
(Erase heading not required.)

Army Form C. 2118.

July 1918.

Place	Date	Hour	Summary of Events and Information	Remarks and references to Appendices
	22.		Battalion in Army Reserve, Training. Parties reconnoitring line	HS
	23.		Battalion in Army Reserve. Training. Parties reconnoitring line.	HS
	24.		Battalion in Army Reserve. Training. Parties reconnoitring line	HS
	25.		Battalion in Army Reserve. Training. Parties reconnoitring line	HS
	26.		Battalion in Army Reserve. Training Parties reconnoitring line	HS
	27.		Battalion in Army Reserve. Training Parties reconnoitring line	HS
	28.		Battalion in Army Reserve. Parties reconnoitring line.	HS
	29.		Battalion in Army Reserve. Training Bn on scheme (practice)	S.F.C
	30.		Battalion in Army Reserve Training Parties reconnoitring line. Battalion Concert at 5X Road. Brigadier General L. P. EVANS. V.C., D.S.O. present and presented prizes to winners of the Battalion Sports Events	S.F.C
	31.		Battalion in Army Reserve. Training during morning. 14th Infy Bde Sports from 1 p.m.	S.F.C.

H. Thwaytes
Lieut. Col.
Cmdg. 1st Dorset Regt

(A7092). Wt. W12839/M1293 75,0.0. 1/17. D. D. & L., Ltd. Forms/C.2118/14.

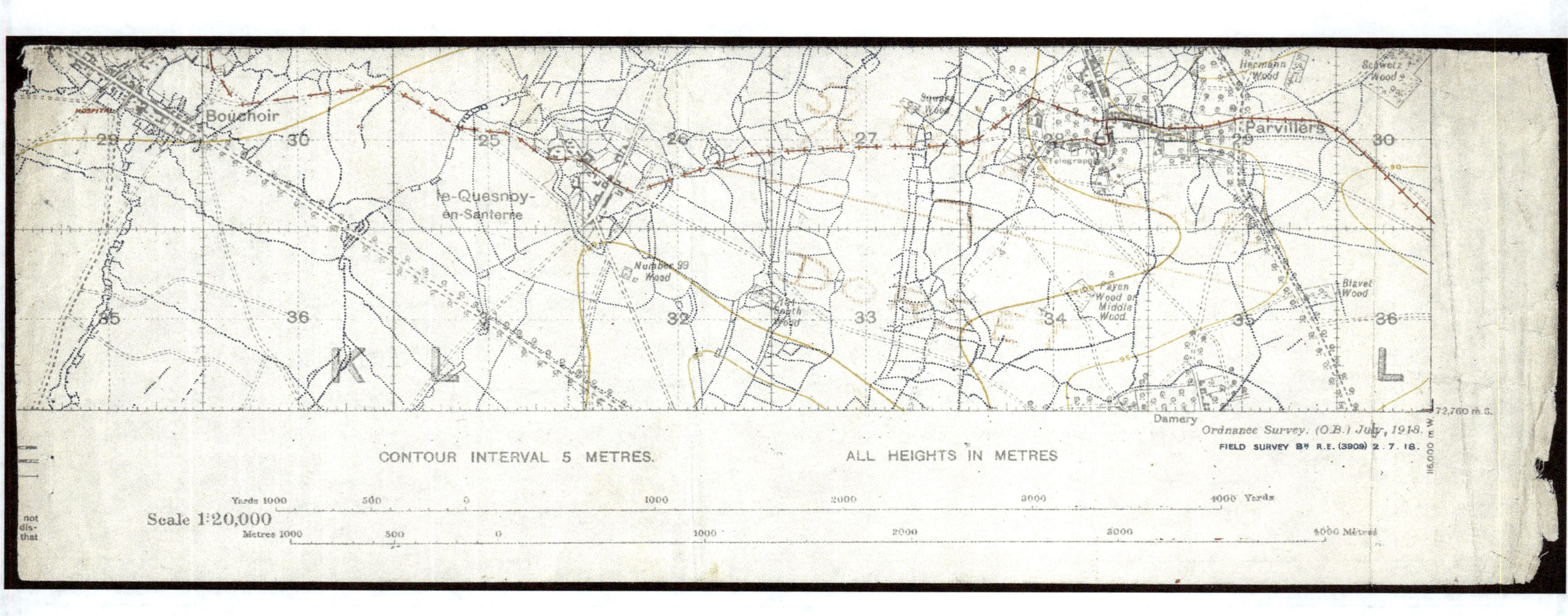

Bouchoir
HOSPITAL
le-Quesnoy-
en-Santerre
Parvillers
Hermann Wood
Schwetz Wood
Telegraph
Number 99 Wood
Payen Wood or Middle Wood
Blavet Wood
Damery
29
30
25
26
27
28
29
30
35
36
32
33
34
35
36
K
L
L
72,760 m. S.
116,000 m. W.
Ordnance Survey. (O.B.) July, 1918.
FIELD SURVEY Bn R.E. (3909) 2. 7. 18.
CONTOUR INTERVAL 5 METRES.
ALL HEIGHTS IN METRES
Scale 1:20,000
Yards 1000 500 0 1000 2000 3000 4000 Yards
Metres 1000 500 0 1000 2000 3000 4000 Metres

Instructions regarding War Diaries and Intelligence Summaries are contained in F. S. Regs., Part II. and the Staff Manual respectively. Title pages will be prepared in manuscript.

WAR DIARY
or
INTELLIGENCE SUMMARY.

(Erase heading not required.)

Army Form C. 2118.

14/32

AUGUST 1918 — 1st DORSET REGT.

Vol 4 8

Place	Date	Hour	Summary of Events and Information	Remarks and references to Appendices
	1.		Battalion in Army Reserve Training. Route March. Parties reconnoitring Line	S.F.C
	2.		Battalion in Army Reserve Training. Two Coys Tactical Exercise. 1 Coy on B.F.+P.T. Training Ground 1 Coy on Range	S.F.C
	3.		Battalion Route March 3 Coys. 1 Coy on B.F.+P.T. Training Ground	S.F.C
	4.		Battalion in Army Reserve. 4th Anniversary of the War. Brigade Service held at 11 A.M. Transport moved at 8.30 A.M. for Training Area CORMETTE CAMP. One Coy "C" proceeded to the new Area at 6.30 A.M. from ROUSBRUGGE	S.F.C
	5.		Move cancelled. "C" Coy & Transport returned to Battalion in Reserve	S.F.C
	6.		Battalion in Reserve Training	S.F.C
	7.		Battalion entrained at WATTENBURG at 9.30 A.M. Arrived [illegible]COURT at 9.[illegible] Marched to FORDRINOY and billeted	S.F.C
	8.		Battalion paraded for line of March at 2.15 p.m. Proceeded to [illegible] and embussed. Debussed at DOMA[illegible] [illegible]	S.F.C
	9.		Battalion moved at 4 p.m. [illegible] to [illegible]COURT Area. Camped for the night.	S.F.C

(A7092). Wt. W12839/M1293 75,000. 1/17. D. D. & L., Ltd. Forms/C.2118/14.

Army Form C. 2118.

Instructions regarding War Diaries and Intelligence Summaries are contained in F. S. Regs., Part II. and the Staff Manual respectively. Title pages will be prepared in manuscript.

WAR DIARY
or
INTELLIGENCE SUMMARY.
(Erase heading not required.)

AUGUST — 1st DORSET REGT

Place	Date	Hour	Summary of Events and Information	Remarks and references to Appendices
	10.		Battalion less details moved forward at 4.30 AM to Battle area. Transport parked at FOWES. Fighting portion of Battalion took up position in front of DAMERY. Details joined Transport during night 10th/11th Aug and were bombed (aircraft) in night. There were no casualties.	S.C.
	11.		REF. FRANCE Sheet 66E N.E. 1. The Battalion bivouaced on the night of 10/11th in L 24 central. 2. Orders were issued that the Battalion was to capture and hold DAMERY WOOD, DAMERY VILLAGE and join 5/6 ROYAL SCOTS at L 35 b 8.2 3. "D" Company was ordered to assemble in the British Front Line and capture the BOIS DAMERY. The remaining three companies were ordered to assemble behind the ridge at LE QUESNOY. On reconnaisance it was found possible to get forward to assembly positions in the old British Support Line EAST of BOIS 10: SUD under cover. C Company were ordered to attack DAMERY VILLAGE frontally. A Company were ordered to attack from the NORTH WEST. B Company were ordered to push through BOIS Pager MILIEU and establish communication with 5/6th ROYAL SCOTS at the wood in L 35 b	

(A7092). Wt W12839/M1293 75,0.0. 1/17. D. D. & L., Ltd. Forms/C.2118/14.

Instructions regarding War Diaries and Intelligence Summaries are contained in F. S. Regs., Part II. and the Staff Manual respectively. Title pages will be prepared in manuscript.

WAR DIARY
or
INTELLIGENCE SUMMARY.
(Erase heading not required.)

Army Form C. 2118.

AUGUST

1st DORSET REGT.

Place	Date	Hour	Summary of Events and Information	Remarks and references to Appendices
	11 (ctd)		4. At 9.20 AM the O.C. A. B and C Coys were pointed out their objectives by the Commanding Officer Lieut. Col H.D. THWAYTES.	
			5. At 9.30 AM the barrage opened and the companies went forward over the parapet.	
			6. As soon as the first man got over, very heavy machine gun fire opened from the direction of PARVILLERS and casualties were caused whilst going through dense wire in front of assembly position	
			7. "D" Company on preliminary reconnaissance found that BOIS EN EQUERRE (French) was occupied by the Lancashire Fusiliers and so pushed forward to a ~~wood~~ trench on the WESTERN side of the wood. At 10 AM the company moved forward through the wood, gained touch with the French in the wood just EAST of BOIS EN EQUERRE and proceeded forward, leaving one platoon in reserve in a Quarry in R 3 b. The Company then moved forward with two platoons in the Front line and one in support with orders to follow 100 yds in rear. About this time the Platoon commander of the support platoon was mortally wounded and the two leading platoons went forward without support.	

(A7092). Wt. W12839/M1293 75,0 0. 1/17. D. D. & L., Ltd. Forms/C.2118/14.

Army Form C. 2118.

Instructions regarding War Diaries and Intelligence Summaries are contained in F. S. Regs., Part II. and the Staff Manual respectively. Title pages will be prepared in manuscript.

WAR DIARY
or
INTELLIGENCE SUMMARY.
(*Erase heading not required.*)

AUGUST. 1st DORSET REGT.

Place	Date	Hour	Summary of Events and Information	Remarks and references to Appendices
	11 (ctd)		8. At 10.32 am when the barrage lifted, the Company was about 200x S.W. of the village and the enemy was seen to be running away from the wood. As touch could not be got with the left and as the right appeared to be clear the company changed direction N E and went direct for the village. About 10.40 am. two tanks came forward from BOIS en EQUERRE and with their assistance the Company was able to get within 100x of the village where they were held up by Machine Gun Fire from the flanks especially from the direction of BOIS Z and just N W of the village. At this time the support and reserve platoons were ordered forward to assist but it was found impossible to get into the village and it was decided to consolidate with two platoons in the front line in rifle pits and about 150x W of the village and two platoons in support in an old communication trench.	
			9. As soon as consolidation was complete, patrols were sent forward into the village and to try and find the company on the left.	

(A7092). Wt W12839/M1293. 75 ,0.0. 1/17. D. D. & L., Ltd. Forms/C.2118/14.

Instructions regarding War Diaries and Intelligence Summaries are contained in F. S. Regs., Part II. and the Staff Manual respectively. Title pages will be prepared in manuscript.

WAR DIARY
or
INTELLIGENCE SUMMARY.
(*Erase heading not required.*)

Army Form C. 2118.

1st DORSET REGT.

AUGUST

Place	Date	Hour	Summary of Events and Information	Remarks and references to Appendices
	11 (ctd)		The patrol in the village captured a heavy machine gun and four (4) prisoners but communication could not be established with the left owing to the heavy machine gun fire.	
			About 7.30 p.m. these dispositions had to be altered as the enemy pushed forward several machine guns S.W. of the village. The line occupied was roughly along the grid line from R4 central to L34 d.0.0 communicating with the French about R4 central. As events turned out during the night had this company attempted to hold its original position they would probably have been cut off.	
			About 10.30 pm the enemy counter attacked the French and part of the attack involved our right flank and was successfully beaten off by Lewis Guns and rifle fire	
	10.		'C' Company advanced from BOIS SUD and all Officers with the exception of one were casualties early on during the operations. This Officer lost direction and got towards BOIS MILIED. This Company had 100 casualties and the remainder of the Company joined A & B Companies on the left.	

(A7092). Wt W12839/M1293. 75 ,0 0. 1/17. D. D. & L., Ltd. Forms/C.2118/14.

Army Form C. 2118.

WAR DIARY
or
INTELLIGENCE SUMMARY.
(Erase heading not required.)

1st DORSET REGT.

Instructions regarding War Diaries and Intelligence Summaries are contained in F. S. Regs., Part II. and the Staff Manual respectively. Title pages will be prepared in manuscript.

AUGUST

Place	Date	Hour	Summary of Events and Information	Remarks and references to Appendices
	11 (ctd)		11. 'A' Coy advanced with their left flank on BOIS MILIEU and did not suffer many casualties until they were clear of the barbed wire when it was found necessary to reinforce with the two support platoons and reorganise as two platoons. The right platoon advanced towards DAMERY with their left on the track from BOIS MILIEU to DAMERY and the left platoon kept touch advancing on the right of this track. It was impossible to get in touch with the right and the company on the left were held up about 100 yards W of MILIEU WOOD. The enemy were attempting to envelope the right and there was heavy machine gun fire from BOIS MILIEU on the left. It was found impossible to move forward and it was decided to consolidate the trench about 100 yards W of BOIS MILIEU. Lewis Guns were pushed out on the flanks and withdrew to this line.	
			About 11.30 AM artillery support was called for on the right of BOIS MILIEU but was not forthcoming, the artillery firing into the village instead of the wood.	
			It is possible that had the artillery support been obtained the wood might have been taken	

(A7092). Wt W12839/M1293. 75,0 0. 1/17. D. D. & L., Ltd. Forms/C.2118/14.

7

Instructions regarding War Diaries and Intelligence Summaries are contained in F. S. Regs., Part II. and the Staff Manual respectively. Title pages will be prepared in manuscript.

AUGUST

WAR DIARY
or
INTELLIGENCE SUMMARY.
(Erase heading not required.)

Army Form C. 2118.

1st DORSET REGT.

Place	Date	Hour	Summary of Events and Information	Remarks and references to Appendices
	11 (cta)		12 'B' Coy got through the barbed wire with few casualties but suffered severely afterwards. The two leading platoons got right up to BOIS MILIEU when it was necessary to bring up the two supporting platoons.	
			It was decided to send half the company through the wood and half NORTH of it.	
			Rapid fire was opened by half the Company into the wood whilst the other half company advanced NORTH of it. They succeeded in getting to the North East edge of the wood without suffering very heavily.	
			The other half Company then advanced and succeeded in getting half way through the wood but were hung up by fire chiefly from PARVILLERS. As communication ~~[illegible]~~ could not be obtained with the flanks and casualties were heavy the company was withdrawn to trench about L34 d 9.2.	
			Here communication was established with 'A' Coy on the Right. About 11.15am as it was impossible to go forward and this trench was untenable the company was withdrawn	

Army Form C. 2118.

WAR DIARY
or
INTELLIGENCE SUMMARY.
(*Erase heading not required.*)

Instructions regarding War Diaries and Intelligence Summaries are contained in F. S. Regs., Part II. and the Staff Manual respectively. Title pages will be prepared in manuscript.

AUGUST

1st DORSET REGT.

Place	Date	Hour	Summary of Events and Information	Remarks and references to Appendices
	11 (Cd)		to a trench about 200 yards W of BOIS MILIEU (This must be the trench shown on the map as running through L 34 a but is shown as too far away from the wood.)	
			13. Reinforcements were asked for and 1 Coy of 2/Manchesters were sent up to get touch with 5/6th Royal Scots and our left flank. This was successfully carried out. 1 Coy of 15th H.L.I. was sent up to reinforce D Company and establish communication with the Companies about BOIS MILIEU but communication was not established.	
			14. On handing over, D Coy was in touch with the French on the road about R 4 b 0.2 and extended to about R 4 a 8.9 with two platoons in support behind this line. The H.L.I. were in a trench running N.E. from about R 34 d 3 3 for about 50 yards.	
			A Composite Coy 1/Dorset Regt held the trench from about L 34 a 1.8 to L 28 c 1 3	
			2/Manchester Regt joined from this point to the right of 5/6th Royal Scots	

(A7092). Wt W12839/M1293. 75 ,0 0. 1/17. D. D. & L., Ltd. Forms/C.2118/14.

9

Instructions regarding War Diaries and Intelligence Summaries are contained in F. S. Regs., Part II. and the Staff Manual respectively. Title pages will be prepared in manuscript.

WAR DIARY
or
INTELLIGENCE SUMMARY.
(Erase heading not required.)

Army Form C. 2118.

AUGUST — 1st. DORSET REGT.

Place	Date	Hour	Summary of Events and Information	Remarks and references to Appendices
	11 (ctd.)		The casualties in this battle were very heavy.	
			Officers Killed:- 2/Lt H A Ford M.C. Lieut E M F Law 2/Lt C J Tiddy Lieut H.S. Wood M.C. 2/Lt F A Andrews M.S.M. 2/Lt F J Blowley Lieut K. S. Courtenay.	
			Officers wounded:- a/Capt G L Baker* 2/Lt D R Oliver 2/Lt A J Gedye 2/Lt E A Cunningham 2/Lt J F Bain 2/Lt G Watt 2/Lt J A Airey D.C.M.	* Missing
			Other Ranks. Killed:- 26 Missing:- 42 Wounded:- 240 Wounded (Gas) 1	
			The following letters relating to the Battle were received from the Divisional and Brigade Generals respectively.	
			Copy	
			"32nd Div No. G.S. 1857/3/4 Addressed all branches of the Division (On conclusion of the first phase of the operations in which the Division had taken part during	

(A7092). Wt W12839/M1293 75 ,0 0. 1/17. D. D. & L., Ltd. Forms/C.2118/14.

Army Form C. 2118.

Instructions regarding War Diaries and Intelligence Summaries are contained in F. S. Regs., Part II. and the Staff Manual respectively. Title pages will be prepared in manuscript.

WAR DIARY
or
INTELLIGENCE SUMMARY.
(*Erase heading not required.*)

AUGUST 1918

1st Dorset Regt

Place	Date	Hour	Summary of Events and Information	Remarks and references to Appendices
	11th		the past few days, the Divisional Commander wishes to thank all ranks for the energy, endurance and courage shown both in the approach march to the battle front and in the two days hard fighting which followed. The Corps Commander Canadian Corps, has expressed his appreciation of the gallantry shown by all ranks in the difficult task which was given them. The fact that the strongly entrenched and heavily wired position was reached and entered all along the line and was broken through on at least half of the Divisional front may well be remembered with pride by all ranks of the Division.	
			The rapidity with which the Artillery was brought up and the boldness with which it was handled in action deserves the highest praise.	
			The collection and evacuation of the wounded was admirably carried out by the Medical Services and Stretcher bearers.	
			The work done by all branches of transport during the long marches and during the operation contributed largely to the success of the Division.	
			12th August 1918. (Sd) A. E. McNamara General Staff 32nd Division	Lt Col

11

Army Form C. 2118.

WAR DIARY
or
INTELLIGENCE SUMMARY.
(Erase heading not required.)

Instructions regarding War Diaries and Intelligence Summaries are contained in F. S. Regs., Part II. and the Staff Manual respectively. Title pages will be prepared in manuscript.

AUGUST 1918 — 1st DORSET REGT.

Place	Date	Hour	Summary of Events and Information	Remarks and references to Appendices
			14th Inf Bde No G 500. 12th August 1918 O.C. 1st Dorset Regt I wish to express my admiration of the gallantry and devotion to duty shown by the 5/6 Royal Scots, 1st Dorset Regt. and 'A' Coy 32nd Bn M.G.C. in the attack on the 11th. No time was available for reconnaissance, the frontage of attack was wide, and in view of the recent rapid advance the ammunition supply limited. The strength with which the position would be held could not be foretold, but the advantages to be gained by an immediate attack were that a large force of the enemy were in danger of being completely surrounded and the gaining of the ridges overlooking ROYE would probably have affected this. Although this object was not achieved, the result achieved was one to be proud of. The 14th Brigade attacking on a wide front, drove the enemy heavily reinforced with machine-guns back out of a considerable slice of carefully organised defences, and handed over intact to another Division a footing in the enemy defences clear of the thick wire of old "No man's land".	

(A7092). Wt W12839/M1293. 75,0 0. 1/17. D. D. & L., Ltd. Forms/C.2118/14.

Instructions regarding War Diaries and Intelligence Summaries are contained in F. S. Regs., Part II. and the Staff Manual respectively. Title pages will be prepared in manuscript.

WAR DIARY
or
INTELLIGENCE SUMMARY.
(Erase heading not required.)

Army Form C. 2118.

AUGUST 1918 — 1st Dorset Regt

Place	Date	Hour	Summary of Events and Information	Remarks and references to Appendices
			This result will materially achieve future operations. The loss of many valuable lives is deeply to be regretted but they have not been lost without result. The 5/6th Royal Scots, the 1st Dorset Regt. and A Coy. 32nd Bn. M.G.C. have good cause for pride in the action fought on 11th August, and the admiration of those f[illegible] in the Brigade who took no active share in the fighting is both deep and sincere. (Sd) J. P. Evans Brig Gen 14th Infy Bde	SFC
	12.		Battalion relieved at 6 A.M. moved to BEAUCOURT and bivouaced for the night.	SFC
	13.		The Divisional Commander Major General LAMBERT, C.B., C.M.G. visited the Battalion and complimented it on the splendid way the Battalion went over the top. At 4 pm the Battalion proceeded on the line of march to the DOMART area and bivouaced.	SFC
	14.		Battalion in rest. All men bathed, had hot foot-baths and received a clean change of clothing. Musketry carried out during the morning.	SFC

Army Form C. 2118.

WAR DIARY
or
INTELLIGENCE SUMMARY.
(Erase heading not required.)

Instructions regarding War Diaries and Intelligence Summaries are contained in F. S. Regs., Part II. and the Staff Manual respectively. Title pages will be prepared in manuscript.

AUGUST 1918 — 1st DORSET REGT

Place	Date	Hour	Summary of Events and Information	Remarks and references to Appendices
	15		Battalion in Reserve Training. Regtl Concert in evening.	JFC
	16		do. 14 OR reinforcements arrived	JFC
	17		do 15 O.R rejoined from Courses & F.A.	JFC
			292 O.R. reinforcements arrived	
	18		Divine Service for C of E at 10.30. RC at 11.30. At 9 A.M. Brigadier General L.P. EVANS V.C., D.S.O. addressed the Battalion less new draft and complimented the Officers & O.R on the splendid work they did in the attack on DAMERY on Aug. 11th 1918.	JFC
			At 9.30 AM the Br General inspected the new Draft and afterwards addressed them	
			At 9 p.m. the Battalion embussed and moved with Brigade & Division to HARBONNIERES Area in relief of 2nd Australian Division. 14th Infy Bde in Reserve in new position by 12.30 a.m. 19.8.18.	
	19		Battalion in Reserve Line of AMIENS DEFENCE.	JFC

(A7092). Wt W12839/M1293 75,000. 1/17. D. D. & L., Ltd. Forms/C.2118/14.

Instructions regarding War Diaries and Intelligence Summaries are contained in F. S. Regs., Part II. and the Staff Manual respectively. Title pages will be prepared in manuscript.

WAR DIARY
or
INTELLIGENCE SUMMARY.
(Erase heading not required.).

Army Form C. 2118.

AUGUST 1918 10th DORSET REGT.

Place	Date	Hour	Summary of Events and Information	Remarks and references to Appendices
	20		Battalion with Brigade in Reserve. Heavy shelling of LA FLAQUE Dump set on fire. HARBONNIERES also shelled. No shelling by enemy in ~~immediate~~ vicinity of Battalion. C Coy wiring	SFC
	21		Battalion with Brigade in Reserve. Day quiet excepting for shelling of neighbouring villages. A Coy continued wiring.	SFC
	22		Battalion with Brigade in Reserve. Little shelling as for 20th & 21st. D Coy continued wiring. A B + C Coys bathed & had change of clothing at HARBONNIERES.	SFC
	23		Battalion with Brigade in Reserve.	SFC
	24		Battalion with Brigade in Reserve. Bn relieved the K.O.Y.L.I and 16th Lancashire Fus in the left Sector (HERLEVILLE AREA) A & B Coys in Front Line. B Coy immediately after relief pushed forward and occupied trench at S.1.d of HERLEVILLE MESSAGE MAP.	SFC
	25		On right front A Coy pushed forward by bombing up trenches and occupied the trench system S 7 a 8.0 to S 7 a 3.8. 2/Lt SPICKERNELL and 4 O.R were wounded. HERLEVILLE and vicinity of B Coy Headquarters were heavily shelled at intervals during the day.	

(A7092). Wt. W12839/M1293. 75,000. 1/17. D. D. & L., Ltd. Forms/C.2118/14.

15

WAR DIARY
or
INTELLIGENCE SUMMARY.
(*Erase heading not required.*)

Army Form C. 2118.

Instructions regarding War Diaries and Intelligence Summaries are contained in F. S. Regs., Part II. and the Staff Manual respectively. Title pages will be prepared in manuscript.

AUGUST 1917 — 1st Dorset Regt

Place	Date	Hour	Summary of Events and Information	Remarks and references to Appendices
	26		During the early hours, heavy rain hindered progress, but from 8 A.M onwards, B. Coy on left front was engaged in bombing enemy blocks in SIRE ALLEY in order to occupy a more forward position and conform to the movements of A Coy. Considerable resistance was met and Capt D THIRLWELL was wounded. The Battalion on our right flank was subjected to gas and suffered heavy casualties. At 11.45pm a message was received from Brigade that the enemy was expected to retire the following morning.	[illegible]
	27		Hostile artillery was very active at 3.46 AM and continued shelling B Coy lines till 5 am. the Coy having 4 O.R wounded. At 8.30 AM information was received that the 96th Bde on right was advancing and our front Companies immediately endeavoured to go forward, but were held up by Field and Machine Gun Fire. To enable A and B Coys to conform to the movements of the 96th Bde, the support Coy "D" was ordered to work through STARRY WOOD from the SOUTH and brush away any opposition met by B Coy and to gain touch with BORDER REGT the left Bn of the 96th Bde. A and B Coys finally occupied a trench system N and E of STARRY WOOD and "C" Coy (Reserve) got into position in the old front line. At 3pm Bn Hd Qrs. moved forward to SORIEN ALLEY and at 5pm Major C.H MORRIS M.C. received orders from the Commanding Officer to take command	

(A7092). Wt W12839/M1293. 75,000. 1/17. D. D. & L., Ltd. Forms/C.2118/14.

Instructions regarding War Diaries and Intelligence Summaries are contained in F. S. Regs., Part II. and the Staff Manual respectively. Title pages will be prepared in manuscript.

WAR DIARY
or
INTELLIGENCE SUMMARY.
(Erase heading not required.)

Army Form C. 2118.

AUGUST 1918 — 1st DORSET REGT.

Place	Date	Hour	Summary of Events and Information	Remarks and references to Appendices
			of the 3 front companies and work up trench system with SOYECOURT as his objective. Severe shelling, from which A Coy suffered heavy casualties necessitated reorganisation but by 8.30 p.m. these Coys had pushed forward to the position S3c9.2 – S3c6.8 where they were held up by Machine and light Field Gun fire. Casualties: 2/Lt C. E. SALTER wounded. O.R. Killed 7 Wounded 13 Missing 3. At 11.50 p.m. orders were received that the Bn would continue to advance at 5 AM EAST of SOYECOURT and maintain touch with the enemy	SJC
	28.		At 5 AM the advance was resumed to the trench system in S5c ref. Sheet 62c S.W. Bn Hd Qrs and detached parties joined the Battn at this point and here the Bn reorganised. Touch was obtained with the 5/6th ROYAL SCOTS on left, but a big interval had been made between us and BORDER REGT on right. Orders were received that the 15th H.L.I. would pass through the 5/6th ROYAL SCOTS and that the advance would continue with 1st DORSET REGT on right and 15th H.L.I. on left with 5/6th ROYAL SCOTS in Bde reserve. The 1st DORSET REGT reached CERISES TRENCH and CHRISTOPHER ALLEY joining with 15th H.L.I. at BERNY WOOD and at this point touch was maintained with the enemy. Orders were received from the G.O.C. 14th Infy Bde to halt on this line and await further orders.	

(A7092). Wt. W12839/M1293 75,000. 1/17. D. D. & L., Ltd. Forms/C.2118/14.

17

Army Form C. 2118.

WAR DIARY
or
INTELLIGENCE SUMMARY.
(Erase heading not required.)

Instructions regarding War Diaries and Intelligence Summaries are contained in F. S. Regs., Part II. and the Staff Manual respectively. Title pages will be prepared in manuscript.

AUGUST 1918 — 1st DORSET REGT.

Place	Date	Hour	Summary of Events and Information	Remarks and references to Appendices
			Battalion Hd Qrs were established at TREMBLE COPSE. At 1.20pm we were ordered to continue our advance due EAST. The Bn now made good progress to FRESNES where it passed through an artillery barrage. Orders were now received to take up an Outpost line from T11 21.7 to T10 d 9.5. Casualties were very light 2 O.R only being wounded. Bn. Hd Qrs were established at the QUARRIES at T3 d 9.2. At this stage a BOCHE 8" HOWITZER and Machine pistol were secured.	JHC
	29.		The 5/6th ROYAL SCOTS leap-frogged the 1st Dorset Regt at 7 AM and the latter Battalion thus became Bde Reserve with Bn. Hd Qrs still at the QUARRIES. The day passed quietly there being very little shelling by the enemy and there were no casualties.	JHC
	30.		Battalion detailed to take over new front held by the 5th Australian Division from O 8c.0.0 to O 32 Central. This front was reconnoitred by the C.O and Adjutant and Coy Cmdrs of B, C and D Coys. The Bn was ordered to take over the whole of this front (about 3.500 yds) as an Outpost Battalion and to concentrate for this purpose at N 22 by 6 p.m. This latter order was cancelled and the Battalion moved off from Hd Qrs at 6.30 p.m direct, the relief being complete by 12.30 AM and without casualties.	

(A7092). Wt. W12839/M1293 75,0.0. 1/17. D. D. & L., Ltd. Forms/C.2118/14.

Instructions regarding War Diaries and Intelligence Summaries are contained in F. S. Regs., Part II. and the Staff Manual respectively. Title pages will be prepared in manuscript.

Army Form C. 2118.

WAR DIARY
or
INTELLIGENCE SUMMARY.

(Erase heading not required.)

AUGUST 1918 1st DORSET REGT.

Place	Date	Hour	Summary of Events and Information	Remarks and references to Appendices
			Between 9 and 11 pm the Transport Lines at ESTREES were bombed by aircraft, causing much damage. Capt W. ALDERMAN M.C. (QUARTERMASTER) was killed and one O.R. was wounded. Of the horses 10 were killed and 1 wounded.	[illegible]
	31		Quiet day. C. A. and D Coys in front line patrolled the SOMME VALLEY by day but saw no movement. A patrol of C Coy crossed the SOMME at dusk and located 4 enemy machine guns. During the night the pioneers of the 5/6th ROYAL SCOTS, 1st DORSET REGT and 15th H.L.I. were engaged in bridging the SOMME but without success.	[illegible]

September 1st 1918

[illegible] Lieut Colonel
Commanding 1st Dorset Regiment.

(A7092). Wt W12839/M1293 75,000. 1/17. D. D. & L., Ltd. Forms/C.2118/14.

1st Dorset Regiment 14/32 98149

Instructions regarding War Diaries and Intelligence Summaries are contained in F. S. Regs., Part II. and the Staff Manual respectively. Title pages will be prepared in manuscript.

WAR DIARY
~~or~~
~~INTELLIGENCE SUMMARY.~~
(Erase heading not required.)

Army Form C. 2118.

Place	Date	Hour	Summary of Events and Information	Remarks and references to Appendices
GABY TRENCH N 24d Sheet 62CSW	1/9/18		Lieuts. LAVOIE and REW Somerset Light Infantry reported themselves from the Divisional Depot Battalion and were posted to 'A' Coy. The day was quiet. About 6.30 P.M. the Commanding Officer ordered Lieut. CARTER commanding 'A' Coy. to establish and hold a post on the EASTERN bank of the SOMME Canal at O.21.B.3. This was carried out. The Officer Commanding 'D' Coy. was ordered to send scouts across BRIE bridge followed by an Officers patrol which was to work up to the outskirts of BRIE as soon as it was dusk. Lieut. FERRIS commanded the patrol which worked up into BRIE until sniped at seriously. TWO platoons 'D' Coy. were moved down to BRIE bridge ready to cross when the enemy put down a barrage on the bridge. The G.O.C. who was present ordered the patrol to withdraw and the TWO platoons returned to their original positions. ONE casualty was incurred during this minor operation.	
	2.9.18		The day was quiet. The O.C. 'A' Coy. was ordered to send out a patrol to find a track across the marsh. The patrol found a track but this ceased 50x from the enemy's side of the marsh, the patrol was fired on. The O.C. 'C' Coy. was ordered to find covering parties for the R.E. who were completing bridges in O.21.a and c. Patrols were also sent out by this Coy. The O.C. 'D' Coy. also sent out patrols to find tracks across the marsh.	

(A7092). Wt W12839/M1293 750,000. 1/17. D. D. & L., Ltd. Forms/C.2118/14.

Instructions regarding War Diaries and Intelligence Summaries are contained in F. S. Regs., Part II. and the Staff Manual respectively. Title pages will be prepared in manuscript.

WAR DIARY
or
INTELLIGENCE SUMMARY.

(Erase heading not required.)

Army Form C. 2118.

Place	Date	Hour	Summary of Events and Information	Remarks and references to Appendices
As for 2nd	3/9/18		Quiet morning. At midday a report was received from the G.O.C. that the enemy were burning villages behind their line and that aircraft had reported the enemy to be retiring. We were ordered to send out a patrol at dusk to occupy BRIE to be followed by TWO Companies. At 5 P.M. O.C. 'D' Coy. sent out a patrol under Sergt. ALLEN to reconnoitre the enemy trench system N.E. of BRIE. The patrol advanced along the road to a point 700x ~~from~~ on the EAST side of BRIE bridge when it was fired on. The Commanding Officer then went to see the situation and ordered 'D' Coy. to cross at dusk. About 8 P.M. 'D' Coy. commenced to cross but owing to heavy shell fire the operation was abandoned. At 11.10 P.M. the Bn. was relieved by TWO Companies 15th H.L.I. and TWO Companies 5/6 Royal Scots and marched to Brigade Reserve in trench system in N 29 a and c Sheet 62c S.W.	E.C.S.
Trench system N 29 a&c Sheet 62c S.W.	4/9/18		Quiet day, resting. The Bn. bathed.	E.C.S.
" " "	5/9/18	1.30 AM	The G.O.C. 14th Infantry Brigade sent for the Commanding Officer and informed him that the 15th H.L.I. had effected a crossing over the SOMME by a bridge in O 26 b, had had a fight in which they had killed a number of the enemy captured 30 prisoners and were then holding a position in GUTEMBERG trench with outposts in NASSAU trench. The 97th Bde. he said were held up SOUTH by St. CHRIST and he was sending the 5/6 Royal Scots down to assist them. The 1st Dorset Regt. were ordered to have their dinners issue rations and prepare to move as soon as possible to fill the gap between the 5/6 Royal Scots and the 15th H.L.I. with ATHIES WOOD as their objective. Information was to be sent back if BRIE bridge were passable	E.C.S.

(A7092). Wt W12839/M1293. 75,000. 1/17. D. D. & L., Ltd. Forms/C.2118/14.

Instructions regarding War Diaries and Intelligence Summaries are contained in F. S. Regs., Part II. and the Staff Manual respectively. Title pages will be prepared in manuscript.

WAR DIARY
or
INTELLIGENCE SUMMARY.
(Erase heading not required.)

Army Form C. 2118.

Place	Date	Hour	Summary of Events and Information	Remarks and references to Appendices
	5/9/18		Lt. BOILEAU and EIGHT Scouts were sent on to reconnoitre BRIE bridge. The Bn. moved off at 2.30 P.M. by platoons at 100x distance and 200x between Coys. Information was received that BRIE bridge was passable and orders were received for the Bn. to proceed by this road. The bridge was crossed without opposition and touch was gained with the Royal Scots and H.L.I. in NASSAU Trench in O.26d 55.40 at 3.45 P.M. Here it was ascertained that the 5/6 Royal Scots and 15th H.L.I. were holding the line along WURTZBERG and BINDEN trenches. The Bn. was ordered to attack the line running through P.25a 5.0 – P.31a 5.0 – V1a 5.0 and on reaching the line the 10th H.L.I. were to advance and occupy BADE trench. Orders were issued for 'B' Coy. to deploy S. of the road, 'A' Coy. N. of the road, 'D' Coy. in close support, and 'C' Coy. to remain in reserve N.W. ATHIES WOOD in O.29d. The Bn. moved forward about 4 P.M. as ordered. 'A' and 'B' Coys. were held up just EAST of ATHIES WOOD. Artillery support was obtained to fire on WOOD 5. at O.26b and TWO platoons 'D' Coy. were sent round the flank of 'A' Coy. to attack the QUARRY at P25c 00.45. As soon as these two Platoons commenced to attack MAJOR MORRIS, who was with 'A' Coy. saw some of the enemy retiring at once led forward a Platoon and captured 17 of the enemy. 'A' Coy having advanced, the enemy in front of 'B' Coy retired & the advance continued. ATHIES WOOD was heavily shelled and the reserve Coy & B.H.Q. were moved forward to trenches in O.30.c. The objective was reached at 6.45 p.m. Scouts were sent forward and reported the villages of PRUSLE and MONS-EN-CHAUSÉE unoccupied. The G.O.C. came forward to B.H.Q. & ordered the Battalion to advance & occupy the GREEN LINE. At 7.20 p.m. the BN moved forward, 'B' Coy on the right, 'D' Coy in the Centre, 'A' Coy on the left	X El.

(A7092). Wt. W12839/M1293. 750,000. 1/17. D. D. & L. Ltd. Forms/C.2118/14.

Army Form C. 2118.

WAR DIARY
or
~~INTELLIGENCE SUMMARY.~~

(*Erase heading not required.*)

Instructions regarding War Diaries and Intelligence Summaries are contained in F. S. Regs., Part II. and the Staff Manual respectively. Title pages will be prepared in manuscript.

Place	Date	Hour	Summary of Events and Information	Remarks and references to Appendices
			sending three Platoons through the villages of PROSLE & MONS-EN-CHAUSEE no resistance was met with until the BN reached the road in P 33 a, when they were fired on from about P27 d 5.3. & from the right flank. Lewis Guns and rifle fire were at once brought to bear on these points & the enemy fled leaving their prisoners in our hands. The line from P 33 b 7.4 – P 27 d 7.9 (GREEN LINE) was occupied at 9.15 p.m. but touch was not maintained with the 97th BDE on the right & the 15th H.L.I. on the left. It was afterwards ascertained that these UNITS had not advanced from the 1st Objective. Coys consolidated on the GREEN LINE. A, B & D Coys each with two Platoons in front & two Platoons in support. B & A Coys forming defensive flanks. "C" Coy were moved to P. 31 b & HQ. to the QUARRY at P. 25 c 00.45. Captured 22 prisoners & two M Gs	ECS
BN. Hq. Quarry at P31c00.45 Coys along the line P27b.6.0 – P27d6.0.	6.9.18	2.30 A.M.	Major GEDDES M.C. Commanding 31st BN Australian Infantry arrived at Headquarters and stated that his Battalion were relieving 1st Dorset Regt at dawn. Orders were received from 14th Infantry Bde. that if the Brigade were not relieved by 7 A.M. the BN would move forward and occupy the line P24d.0.0. – P29d.8.0 – P35 b.8.0. The BN waited for the 15th H.L.I. and 1/5 Border Regt. to reach the GREEN LINE and moved forward with them at 8 A.M. No opposition was met with and the objective was reached at 9 A.M. Patrols were at once sent forward to VRAIGNES and VALLEY Woods and reported NO enemy.	X ECS

(A7092). Wt. W12839/M1293 75,0:0. 1/17. D. D. & L., Ltd. Forms/C.2118/14.

Instructions regarding War Diaries and Intelligence Summaries are contained in F. S. Regs., Part II. and the Staff Manual respectively. Title pages will be prepared in manuscript.

WAR DIARY
or
INTELLIGENCE SUMMARY.
(Erase heading not required.)

Army Form C. 2118.

Place	Date	Hour	Summary of Events and Information	Remarks and references to Appendices
Sheet 62^c S.E.	6.9.18.		Orders were received that the Battalion would remain in their present location and that the 31st BN. A.I.F would advance at dawn on 7th. "C" Coy. and BN. Hqrs. moved to P29c 3.3.	ECl.
			Captures 7 Trench Mortars and 2 Heavy Minnenwerfers (one dismantled) Attached is a copy of a message received from the G.O.C. 14th Infantry Bde. 4 32nd Div. C.S. 1887/18/2	
	7.9.18	6.20 A.M.	Orders were received at 6.20 A.M. that the 31st BN. A.I.F. would advance from the GREEN Line at 6 A.M. and that when they had advanced 2000x through the BN. if no opposition were met the BN. would move to the trench system in Q32b.. The BN. moved at 8.30 A.M. Casualties 1 O.R. wounded by an air bomb	ECl.
Q 32 b.	8.9.18		32nd. Divisional Routine Orders were received containing the names of the following awarded gallantry cards 2253 Pte. Brooks, No. 14706 Pte. A SMITH, No. 7407 Pte. WEBSTER, No 6153 Pte. GOSLOF, No. 14666 Pte. Williams. Order attached. The night of 7/8 was spent in the trench system Q 32 b. The day was quiet and was spent in having rifle inspections and improving the trenches. Attached is a copy of a message received from the G.O.C. 32nd. Division.	ECl.
"	9.9.18		The day was quiet and was spent in cleaning up and inspections.	ECl.
"	10.9.18		Heavy rain fell during the night. A conference of C.O.s was held at Brigade Headquarters at 10 A.M.	ECl.
"	11.9.18	2.30 A.M.	An order was received that the Brigade Group would probably move to an area SOUTH of the ORMIGNON RIVER and that no move was probable before 9 A.M.	ECl.
"		10 A.M.	The BN. was ordered to move to Squares W 8 and 14 crossing the bridge at TERTRY by 11.30 A.M. At 10.50 A.M. the BN. moved and it was in billets at 2 P.M.	

(A7092). Wt W12839/M1293 75,000 1/17. D. D. & L., Ltd. Forms/C.2118/14.

Instructions regarding War Diaries and Intelligence Summaries are contained in F. S. Regs., Part II. and the Staff Manual respectively. Title pages will be prepared in manuscript.

WAR DIARY
or
INTELLIGENCE SUMMARY.
(Erase heading not required.)

Army Form C. 2118.

Place	Date	Hour	Summary of Events and Information	Remarks and references to Appendices
Squares W 8 and 14	12.9.18		The day was quiet and was spent in cleaning up and training. At 8.30 P.M. a warning order was received for the BN. to move on Sept. 14th to CORBIE.	E.C.S.
" " "	13.9.18		The day was quiet and was spent in training. 32nd Div G.S. 1882/18/3 attached.	E.C.S.
" " "	14.9.18	2.30 A.M.	Orders were received that the Bde. was being by the 16th Bde. on the 14th.	
			The BN. marched to MONTECOURT ~~where~~ and embussed. The BN. arrived at DAOURS at 5.50 and moved into billets. The transport marched by road in one stage and arrived at 9.30 P.M. Batt. G. 102 dd 14/9/18. 32nd Div. No G.S. 1882/18/4 dd 14/9/18 att.	E.C.S.
Sheet 62d. N6 d. 1/40000	15.9.18		The day was spent in cleaning up and refitting. All Companies were bathed and paid. The attached letter 32 Div. No. G.S. 1882/18/3. was received.	E.C.S.
DAOURS.	16.9.18		Orders were received that the Transport would move to the ATHIES - DEVISE area to-day and that the BN. would move by bus on 17th inst. The Transport marched at 3.45 P.M. The attached letter from the G.O.C. Australian Corps was received (32 Div. No: G.S. 1882/18/4).	E.C.S.
" "	17.9.18	2.15 A.M.	Orders were received to march to a point on the PONT-NOYELLES — DAOURS Road to embuss there and move to ENNEMAIN. The BN. paraded at 8.30 A.M. embussed and arrived at ATHIES at 1.30 P.M. The BN. was then allotted LEIGHTON PARK, TARRYTOWN, ENNEMAIN to billet in. The BN was in billets at 3.~~30~~ P.M. The Transport arrived at 5.30 P.M.	E.C.S.
Sheet 62c S.W. U23 b. "	18.9.18		The day was spent in cleaning up and training. 32nd Div. R.O. 3255, 3256, 3257 attached.	
LEIGHTON PARK. "	19.9.18		Day spent in Training.	
"	20.9.18		Training.	
" "	21.9.18		Training. Half the BN. bathed.	
	22.9.18		~~Training~~. Half the BN. bathed. DIVINE SERVICE held at 10.a.m.	
	23.9.18	8.30 A.M.	Orders were received for the BN. to be ready to move on receipt of orders to LARRIS Woods.	
		11.20 A.M.	The BN. paraded and marched to LARRIS WOODS. The BN. arrived at 2.3 P.M. 32ND DIV. joined IXth Corps.	

(A7092) Wt. W12839/M1293 750,000 1/17. D. D. & L., Ltd. Forms/C.2118/14.

Instructions regarding War Diaries and Intelligence Summaries are contained in F. S. Regs., Part II. and the Staff Manual respectively. Title pages will be prepared in manuscript.

WAR DIARY
or
INTELLIGENCE SUMMARY.
(Erase heading not required.)

Army Form C. 2118.

Place	Date	Hour	Summary of Events and Information	Remarks and references to Appendices
LARRIS WOOD 62C. S.E.	24.9.18		Day spent in Training.	X
	25.9.18		Day spent in Training at 4. p.m., a lecture on the subject of "Barrage" was given to Officers and N.C.O's by Bde. Major R.A.	E.L.S.
		10. am	C.O's Conference held at Bde. H.Q.	E.L.S.
	26.9.18		Morning spent in running off heats for Bn. Gymkhana. Lecture at 10.a.m. to Officers and N.C.O's, on the subject of "Contact Patrol"	
			The C.O's in the 14th Bde, with the Bde. Major reconnoitred the Trench System in forward area to be taken over by 14th Inf. Bde, on night of 28th Sept.	E.L.S.
		2 p.m.	Bn. Gymkhana held.	
	27.9.18	8 P.M.	Orders were received that the Brigade would move to the Trench system on LEVERGUIER Ridge on 28th.	E.L.S.
	28.9.18	6.30pm	Battalion paraded and marched to DEAN trench.	E.L.S.
	29.9.18	10.0am	Bn moved in artillery formation to trench system on LEHELENE ridge overlooking BELLENGLISE	E.L.S.
		3.15pm	Bn crossed the canal by two bridges at BELLENGLISE. A few casualties were incurred from shell fire. Bridges were also shelled with gas shells.	E.L.S.
			The Battalion formed up in artillery formation on the E. side of the canal and advanced with "C" + "D" Coys front line + B and A Coys in support. Number of casualties incurred from frontal and enfilade shell fire on the high ground E of BELLENGLISE	

(A7092). Wt. W12839/M1293 75,000. 1/17. D. D. & L., Ltd. Forms/C.2118/14.

Instructions regarding War Diaries and Intelligence Summaries are contained in F. S. Regs., Part II. and the Staff Manual respectively. Title pages will be prepared in manuscript.

WAR DIARY
or
INTELLIGENCE SUMMARY.
(Erase heading not required.)

Army Form C. 2118.

Place	Date	Hour	Summary of Events and Information	Remarks and references to Appendices
	29/9/18	3.15pm	Machine Guns & Snipers were also very active on the high ground from the right flank. GREEN LINE was reached by means of ECURIEL trench and thence through LEHAUCOURT. "A" and "C" Coys pushed through the GREEN line and attacked FLECHE WOOD in conjunction with 15th H.L.I. on the Right. "D" Coy reached the high ground South of LEVERGIES but was heavily fired on and forced to withdraw to the trench system in H 33 c to await daylight and to get into touch with the flanks.	Ref THE RIGHT map. E.L.S.
			"B" Coy remained in Reserve.	
			300 prisoners were captured in the neighbourhood of FLECHE WOOD together with 3 12" howitzers and 3 4.2 field guns.	
			Casualties Lieut L. Lonsdale killed, Lieut R.J.D. Few, Lieut E.J.G. Beagley, Lieut F.A. Rabino, Lieut A.R. Taylor and 16 OR wounded.	
	30/9/18	5.30am	The Commanding Officer (Major C.H. Morris M.C.) ordered "B" & "C" Coys to hold the line along the trench tramway in N.3.d with posts on the forward slope. "A" Coy was ordered to hold the trench in N.3.a and b. "D" Coy in Reserve in the trench in N.33.C. A message of congratulation was received from the G.O.C.	E.L.S.
		2pm	"A" Coy was ordered to work the ESCARBIN towards ECUME trench in conjunction	

D. D. & L., London, E.C.
(A7883) Wt. W593/M1672 350,000 4/17 Sch. 52a Forms/C/2118/14

Instructions regarding War Diaries and Intelligence Summaries are contained in F. S. Regs., Part II. and the Staff Manual respectively. Title pages will be prepared in manuscript.

WAR DIARY
or
~~INTELLIGENCE SUMMARY.~~
(*Erase heading not required.*)

Army Form C. 2118.

Place	Date	Hour	Summary of Events and Information	Remarks and references to Appendices
		2pm	with "D" Coy who were to work along ECUME trench from H. 33. c the object being to secure the high ground in H. 34. c. "A" Coy advanced but were held up by heavy machine Gun fire. "D" Coy advanced along ECUME trench and came into contact with the enemy at H. 33 d 4.7 where bombs were exchanged and a few casualties were incurred.	Ble
		6.25pm	Orders were received to attack LEVERGIES with 2 Coys in conjunction with the 97th Inf. Bde, the boundary line being the main road running E and W through the village. Barrage commenced at 6.30 pm and was due to cease at 7 pm. "D" Coy moved in Artillery formation towards LE VERGIES and on the barrage lifting went through the village and established a line on the high ground in H. 34 b with the left on the road running E and W. through the village. This objective was gained by 7.30pm. Touch was however not obtained with the 97th Inf Bde until 8.30 pm. "A" Coy worked along the sunken road in H. 34 c and took up a position on "D" Coy right. Enemy machine Guns were active from LE VERGIES and the high ground on the right. One Coy 15th H.L.I. moved up in support to the trench N. of FLECHE WOOD.	Ble

D. D. & L., London, E.C. (A7883) Wt. W809/M1672 350,000 4/17 Sch. 52a Forms/C/2118/14

Instructions regarding War Diaries and Intelligence Summaries are contained in F. S. Regs., Part II. and the Staff Manual respectively. Title pages will be prepared in manuscript.

WAR DIARY
or
~~INTELLIGENCE SUMMARY.~~

(*Erase heading not required.*)

Army Form C. 2118.

Place	Date	Hour	Summary of Events and Information	Remarks and references to Appendices
	30/9/18.	11 am.	The Commanding Officer ordered "B" + "C" Coys to push forward patrols to the line of exploitation.	
			"C" Coy established Lewis gun post in PONY COPSE.	ELS.
			"B" Coy made an attempt to establish a post in MULE COPSE but were heavily fired on and withdrew.	
		1 pm.	"B" Coy established a post in MULE COPSE by means of working through PONY COPSE.	
		2 pm.	The enemy counter attacked MULE and PONY COPSE capturing 4 of our wounded.	
			The artillery fired on an enemy concentration in FUME COPSE and dispersed them.	

E. L. Stephenson. Captain.
Adjutant 1st Dorset Regiment

[illegible] Lieut Col.
Comdg 1/Dorset Regt

D. D. & L., London, E.C.
(A10266) Wt W3300/P713 750,000 2/18 Sch. 52 Forms/C2118/16.

"A" Form.

Army Form C. 2121.
(In pads of 100.)

MESSAGES AND SIGNALS.

No. of Message..............

Prefix.......... Code.......... m	Words.	Charge.	This message is on a/c of:	Recd. at .... m.
Office of Origin and Service Instructions.	Sent		..........Service.	Date..........
	At..........m.			From ....
	To..........			
	By..........		(Signature of "Franking Officer.")	By..........

TO QOWA

* Sender's Number.	Day of Month.	In reply to Number.	AAA
~~A 70~~	6		

The	G.O.C.	congratulates	all
ranks	of	the	QOWA
Regt	on	their	fine
success	in	yesterdays	operations
~~AAA~~			

Certified true copy

E. K. Stephenson Capt.

a/Adgt. 1st Dorset Regt.

From BURI.

Place

Time

The above may be forwarded as now corrected. **(Z)**

Censor. Signature of Addressor or person authorised to telegraph in his name.

* This line should be erased if not required.

(5198.) Wt. W 12952/M1294. 375,000 Pads. 1/17. H. W. & V., Ld. (E. 818.)

W.D. 1st Dorsets 6 Copies / w Brigadier's Remarks

C.R.A.
C.R.E.
14th Inf.Bde.
96th Inf.Bde.
97th Inf.Bde.
32nd M.G.Battn.
16th H.L.I.(Pioneers).
A.D.M.S.
A.P.M.
Camp Comdt.
A. & Q.
21st Bde. R.G.A.)
23rd Army Bde.R.F.A.) through C.R.A.
6th Aust.F.A.Bde.)

32nd Div.No.G.S.1882/18/2.

The Divisional Commander congratulates the 14th and 97th Brigade Groups on the excellent work done yesterday. The surprise of the enemy opposite ETERPIGNY showed splemdid initiative by 15th H.L.I. The turning movements to encircle and clear BRIE and ST.CHRIST and the crossing of the party of K.O.Y.L.I. opposite CIZANCOURT were admirably carried out. The manner in which troops pushed on to the Green Line and the work of the Artillery were first class. The repair of the minor crossings and especially of the BRIE and ST.CHRIST bridges reflects the greatest credit on R.E. Companies and 16th H.L.I. Information of positions reached and of the situation was quickly and accurately transmitted.

The G.O.C. is sure that all ranks will make every endeavour to clear the country up to the objectives that have been given for to-day and to complete the success by harassing the enemy and destroying his organisation within reach of our Artillery. Troops must continue to be disposed in depth to meet possible counter-attacks, especially on the flanks, though the G.O.C. is convinced that these cannot be made in much strength. There must be no retirement from any position held even by a few men. To defend an exposed flank troops must be pushed up from the rear if necessary but existing flanks, however much exposed, must not be drawn back.

The high ground at BOUVINCOURT, Q.31.c., and East of MONCHY LAGACHE and DOUVIEUX will be invaluable for observation to cover deployment of our artillery. If this is gained Visual Signalling stations must be established there as soon as practicable. Assistance of artillery should be given freely to help the advance of the French and of the 5th Australian Division where required.

The French on our right are already reported on the line due South of DOUVIEUX.

E. Dillon
Lieut-Colonel,
General Staff,
32nd Division.

6th Septr. 1918.

The Brigadier heartily endorses all the Divisional Commander says & heartily congratulates all ranks of the Brigade on a real good days work, and especially the 15th HLI to whose enterprise is due the successful crossing of the Somme by the 32nd Division at least one day before the enemy had any intention of permitting it

R. Mary Bishopp

Capt.

8/9/18

A/Bde Major 14th I. Bde

32ND DIVISIONAL ROUTINE ORDERS.

6th Septr., 1918.

3236. GALLANTRY CARDS.

The Divisional Commander has much pleasure in awarding Gallantry Cards to the undermentioned :-

No: 22258	Private	A	A.J. BROOKS,	Dorset Regt. With D&B
No: 14706	"	C	A. SMITH,	-do- Runner
No: 7407	"	C	A.T.WEBSTER,	-do-
No: 6153	"	C	R. GOLLOP,	-do-
No: 14666	"	B	A. WILLIAMS,	-do- Runner
No: 41913	"		J.M. BEWS,	The Royal Scots.
No:358845	"		J.J. BOLTON,	-do-
No:302368	"		J.J. KENNY,	-do-
No:275167	"		W.R. TURNBULL,	-do-
No:250313	"		J.McG. BALLANTYNE,	-do-
No:331038	"		W. TAYLOR,	Lancs.Fusrs.(a)
No: 56965	"		H.J. CRANE,	-do-
No: 38197	"		F. TAYLOR,	-do-
No: 11490	Sergeant		J. FIELDHOUSE,	Lancs.Fusrs.(b)
No: 28475	Private		D. CROLLA,	Manchester Rgt.
No: 27513	"		A.J. COWPER,	-do-
No: 57278	"		R. DOVEY,	Divnl.M.G. Battn.
No: 8779	"		J. PAULINE,	A. & S. Highrs.
No:300574	"		W. LIVINGSTON,	-do-

3237. LEAVE.

The present leave allotment will cease on Septr. 10th and the following allotment will come into force on Septr. 11th (inclusive). All via BOULOGNE :-

(1) OFFICERS.

Date.	Unit, etc.	No.	Date.	Unit, etc.	No.
Sept.11th.	C. R. A.	2	Sept.26th.	H.L.I.(Pnrs.)	2
" 12th.	97th Inf.Bde.	2	" 27th.	C. R. A.	2
" 13th.	96th Inf.Bde.	2	" 28th.	96th Inf.Bde.	1
" 14th.	(14th Inf.Bde. (H.L.I.(Pnrs.)	1 1	" 29th.	97th Inf.Bde.	2
" 15th.	(Divnl.Train. (A.D.M.S.	1 1	" 30th.	C. R. A.	2
" 16th.	Camp Comdt.	1	Octr. 1st.	14th Inf.Bde.	2
" 17th.	C. R. A.	2	" 2nd.	(A.D.M.S. (Signal Coy.	1 1
" 18th.	M.G. Battn.	2	" 3rd.	C. R. A.	2
" 19th.	96th Inf.Bde.	2	" 4th.	Divnl.Train.	1
" 20th.	97th Inf.Bde.	2	" 5th.	C. R. A.	2
" 21st.	(Signal Coy. (Camp Comdt.	1 1	" 6th.	(Camp Comdt. (H.L.I.(Pnrs.)	1 1
" 22nd.	(14th Inf.Bde. (A.D.M.S.	1 1	" 7th.	96th Inf.Bde.	2
" 23rd.	C. R. A.	2	" 8th.	97th Inf.Bde.	2
" 24th.	97th Inf.Bde.	2	" 9th.	M.G. Battn.	2
" 25th.	(C. R. E. (Camp Comdt.	1 1	" 10th.	C. R. A.	2

---

(2) OTHER RANKS.

14th Inf.Bde.	4	daily.	Divnl.Train.	2	daily.
96th Inf.Bde.	3	"	A. D. M. S.	3	"
97th Inf.Bde.	6	"	H.L.I.(Pnrs.)	2	"
C. R. A.	10	"	M.G. Battn.	2	"
C. R. E.	3	"	Signal Co. &) Camp Comdt.)	2	" ø

ø. Notification of sub-allotment is made separately.

R.McGrant. Captn
for Lieut-Colonel,
A.A. & Q.M.G., 32nd Division.

The following remarks have been received by the Divisional Commander, & also the Brigadier General 14th Bde

---

The Divisional Commander congratulates the 14th and 97th Brigade Groups on the excellent work done yesterday. The surprise of the enemy opposite ETERPIGNY showed splendid initiative by the 15th H.L.I. The turning movements to encircle and clear BRIE and ST. CHRIST and the crossing of the party of K.O.Y.L.I. opposite CIZANCOURT were admirably carried out. The manner in which troops pushed on to the Green Line and the work of the Artillery were first class. The repair of the minor crossings and especially of the BRIE & ST CHRIST bridges reflects the greatest credit on R.E. Companies and 16th H.L.I. Information of positions reached and of the situation was quickly and accurately transmitted.

(Signed) E Dillon
Lieut Colonel. General Staff
32nd Division

Dated 6 Sept 1918

The Brigadier heartily endorses all the Divisional Commander says & heartily congratulates all ranks of the Brigade on a real good days work, and especially the 15th H.L.I. to whose enterprise is due the successful crossing of the SOMME by the 32nd Division at least 24 hours before the enemy had any intention of permitting it.

(Signed) R Massey-Westropp
a/Bde Major 14th Inf Bde

Dated 8/9/18

Certified true copy.

E. L. Stephenson Capt.
a/Adjt. 1st Dorset Regt.

1 Copy. A
1 " B
1 " C.

Office

C.R.A.,32nd Divn.
C.R.E.,32nd Divn.
14th Infantry Bde.
96th Infantry Bde.
97th Infantry Bde.
32nd M.G.Battn.
16th H.L.I.(Pioneers).
32nd Div.Signal Coy.
A. & Q.
A.D.M.S.

32nd Div.No.G.S.1882/18/3.

D.A.D.V.S.
D.A.D.O.S.
D.A.P.M.
Camp Comdt.
32nd Div.Train.
32nd Div.M.T.Coy.
32nd Div.Reception Camp.

1. The Divisional Commander desires to congratulate and to thank all ranks on the completion of the work which has been carried to such success during the past month.

Since the 7th August the Division has been engaged in continuous movement and in operations which will be always remembered with pride by those who took part in them and which have had a large share towards bringing the War to a successful conclusion. It has fought successful battles, it has advanced more than 20 miles in the face of the enemy, and it has forced the passage of the SOMME.

2. While the Division is at rest, the G.O.C. wishes the first two or three days to be devoted to cleaning up, refitting and resting. Transport must be brought up to its former standard in all respects, personal cleanliness and smartness insisted on and sanitation in its fullest sense made as perfect as possible in all camps, lines and billets.

3. The 17th and 18th September should be devoted to Platoon and Company training, including Musketry.
After the latter date the G.O.C. desires that units should be given a higher form of instruction under the direction or supervision of Brigade and Unit Commanders.

4. Simple schemes should be set for battalions and other units to encourage initiative on wide frontages and preferably such as may practice the employment of detachments of Artillery, Machine guns and Trench Mortars in conjunction with Infantry.

The rapid transmission of accurate information from the front, the quick consolidation of small posts, the maintenance of direction even in the dark, and many other subjects can be taught on what is possibly one of the best training grounds the Division has ever had.

5. The lessons to be taught at each exercise must be carefully thought out and all preparations made beforehand, even if the exercise is for a Company or a Platoon only.

Written orders should be reduced to a minimum, but practice given constantly in rapid issue of instructions on the ground, based on some general scheme which all can understand.

6. It is initiative and the desire to fool the enemy, to get round him, and to prove to him that we as individuals are the better men, that we must spare no pains to inculcate.

7./

7. Facilities for Musketry in order that all may attain a higher standard, the training of Lewis Gunners and other Specialists, the tactical use of observation and the transmission of information - these must all be included.

A careful study of the pamphlets and instructions issued by the Inspector of Training must be made by all officers and, the system of training therein laid down followed, special attention being paid to the training of each section, Platoon or higher formation by its own Commander.

8. The interior economy of some units requires much attention. The cleanliness of Cooks and cookhouses, the systems of messing among officers as well as men, and the instruction of recent drafts in the standard required to be maintained in the Division must not be forgotten.

9. The Division has a high reputation, which has been increased by the recent operations.

It can be maintained and raised even higher only if all ranks join in making it so.

[signature]
Lieut-Colonel,
General Staff,
32nd Division.

13th September 1918.

(Issued down to Batteries and Companies).

1st Dorset Regt.

HEADQUARTERS
G179
14 SEP 1918
14TH INFANTRY BRIGADE

The Brigadier wishes the substance of the attached letter to be read to the troops on parade, and that special attention be paid by all Unit Commanders to those points which deal with Training, Interior Economy and Sanitation.

R. Massy-Westropp
Major
a/Brigade Major
14th Infantry Brigade

14.9.18.

W.D.

C.R.A.,32nd Divn.
C.R.E.,32nd Divn.
14th Infantry Bde.
96th Infantry Bde.
97th Infantry Bde.
32nd M.G.Battn.
16th H.L.I.(Pioneers).
32nd Div.Signal Coy.
A. & Q.
A.D.M.S.

32nd Div.No.G.S.1882/18/3.

D.A.D.V.S.
D.A.D.O.S.
D.A.P.M.
Camp Comdt.
32nd Div.Train.
32nd Div.M.T.Coy.
32nd Div.Reception Camp.

1. The Divisional Commander desires to congratulate and to thank all ranks on the completion of the work which has been carried to such success during the past month.

Since the 7th August the Division has been engaged in continuous movement and in operations which will be always remembered with pride by those who took part in them and which have had a large share towards bringing the War to a successful conclusion. It has fought successful battles, it has advanced more than 20 miles in the face of the enemy, and it has forced the passage of the SOMME.

2. While the Division is at rest, the G.O.C. wishes the first two or three days to be devoted to cleaning up, refitting and resting. Transport must be brought up to its former standard in all respects, personal cleanliness and smartness insisted on and sanitation in its fullest sense made as perfect as possible in all camps, lines and billets.

3. The 17th and 18th September should be devoted to Platoon and Company training, including Musketry.
After the latter date the G.O.C. desires that units should be given a higher form of instruction under the direction or supervision of Brigade and Unit Commanders.

4. Simple schemes should be set for battalions and other units to encourage initiative on wide frontages and preferably such as may practice the employment of detachments of Artillery, Machine guns and Trench Mortars in conjunction with Infantry.

The rapid transmission of accurate information from the front, the quick consolidation of small posts, the maintenance of direction even in the dark, and many other subjects can be taught on what is possibly one of the best training grounds the Division has ever had.

5. The lessons to be taught at each exercise must be carefully thought out and all preparations made beforehand, even if the exercise is for a Company or a Platoon only.

Written orders should be reduced to a minimum, but practice given constantly in rapid issue of instructions on the ground, based on some general scheme which all can understand.

6. It is initiative and the desire to fool the enemy, to get round him, and to prove to him that we as individuals are the better men, that we must spare no pains to inculcate.

7./

7. Facilities for Musketry in order that all may attain a higher standard, the training of Lewis Gunners and other Specialists, the tactical use of observation and the transmission of information - these must all be included.

A careful study of the pamphlets and instructions issued by the Inspector of Training must be made by all officers and, the system of training therein laid down followed, special attention being paid to the training of each section, Platoon or higher formation by its own Commander.

8. The interior economy of some units requires much attention. The cleanliness of Cooks and cookhouses, the systems of messing among officers as well as men, and the instruction of recent drafts in the standard required to be maintained in the Division must not be forgotten.

9. The Division has a high reputation, which has been increased by the recent operations.

It can be maintained and raised even higher only if all ranks join in making it so.

Lieut-Colonel,
General Staff,
32nd Division.

13th September 1918.

(Issued down to Batteries and Companies).

Secret
W.D.

	At.....m.	..... Service.	Date.....
	To.....		From .....
	By.....	(Signature of "Franking Officer.")	By.....

TO
1. Commanding Officer
2. Adjutant
3 O.C. Hq. Coy.
4 O.C. A Coy.
5 " B "
6 " C "
7 " D "
8 R.S.M.
9 Office
10 War Diary

Sender's Number.	Day of Month.	In reply to Number.	AAA
* G 102	14		

1. The 14th Bde. is being relieved by the 16th Inf. Bde.

On relief the Battalion will move by march route and bus to the neighbourhood of CORBIE

2. Starting point — X Roads W8 b 5015.
Route — W8b 5015 – W2c06 – W1c00 – V11 b02.
Order of March — Headquarters B Coy. A Coy. C Coy. D Coy.
Time of passing the starting point — 10.30 A.M.
Intervals — 200x between Coys. 100x between platoons.

3. On arrival at the embussing point ~~about~~ V11 b 02 the Bn. will form up on the RIGHT of and off the road with Platoons in file and 20x interval between platoons.

4. Acknowledge.

From
Place
Time

E. L. Stephenson Capt.
Adjt. 1st Dorset Regt

The above may be forwarded as now corrected. (Z)

Censor. Signature of Addressor or person authorised to telegraph in his name.

* This line should be erased if not required.

(3796.) Wt. W 492/M1647. 650,000 Pads. 5/17. H.W. & V., Ld. (E. 1167.)

W.D.

Army Form C. 2121
(In pads of 100.)

"A" Form
MESSAGES AND SIGNALS.

No. of Message............

Prefix..........Code..........m.	Words	Charge.	*This message is on a/c of:*	Recd. at......m.
Office of Origin and Service Instructions	Sent		..........*Service.*	Date..........
[illegible]	At ....m.			From ....
	To			
	By		(Signature of "Franking Officer")	By..........

TO	[illegible]	[illegible]	[illegible]	

Sender's Number.	Day of Month.	In reply to Number.	AAA
* [illegible]	[illegible]		

[illegible] 10th Bde [illegible] being relieved by 16th [illegible] Bde [illegible] will move [illegible] neighbourhood of CORBIE [illegible] Point – X roads W8 b 50.15 [illegible] W8 b 50.05 – W2 c 05 [illegible] HQ B Coy A Coy C Coy D Coy [illegible] 10.30 [illegible] 100x [illegible]

20x [illegible]

From		[illegible]	
Place			
Time		[illegible]	

The above may be forwarded as now corrected. (Z) ....

.... *Censor.* Signature of Addressor or person authorised to telegraph in his name

* This line should be erased if not required.

Order No. 1625. Wt. W3253/ P 511. 27/4. H. & K., Ltd. (E. 2634).

Army Form C. 2121
(In pads of 100.)

"A" Form
MESSAGES AND SIGNALS.

No. of Message...........

Prefix..........Code..........m.	Words	Charge.	This message is on a/c of:	Recd. at......m.
Office of Origin and Service Instructions	Sent		..........Service.	Date..........
CRFT	At ....m.			From ....
	To			
	By		(Signature of "Franking Officer")	By..........

TO: 1 C.O. | 4 O.C. A Coy | 8 [illegible]
2 Adjutant | 5 O.C. B Coy | 9 [illegible]
3 O.C. H.Q. Coy | 6 O.C. C Coy | 11 [illegible]
7 O.C. D Coy

Sender's Number.	Day of Month.	In reply to Number.	AAA
[illegible]	[illegible]		

[illegible] Bde [illegible] Battalion [illegible]
[illegible]
2. [illegible] W 8 b 50 [illegible]
[illegible] W8b50.15 – W2 [illegible]
Order of march: H.Q. Coy, A Coy, C Coy, B Coy, D Coy
Time of passing starting point 10.30
[illegible]
3. [illegible]
W8b.0.2 [illegible]
RIGHT of [illegible]
[illegible]
[illegible]
4. ACKNOWLEDGE

From	[illegible]	[illegible]	
Place			
Time	[illegible]	[illegible]	

The above may be forwarded as now corrected. (Z)

..........*Censor.* Signature of Addressor or person authorised to telegraph in his name

* This line should be erased if not required.

Order No. 1625. Wt. W3253/ P 511. 27/2. H. & K., Ltd. (E. 2634).

(In pads of 100.)

MESSAGES AND SIGNALS.

No. of Message..............

Prefix.......... Code.......... m.	Words.	Charge.	This message is on a/c of:	Recd. at .... m.
Office of Origin and Service Instructions.	Sent		.... Service.	Date..............
	At.............. m.			From ....
	To..............			
	By..............		(Signature of "Franking Officer.")	By..............

TO { II

Sender's Number. *	Day of Month.	In reply to Number.	AAA

5 Cooking pots, mess boxes will be loaded in at Head Quarters at 8.15 AM

6 No unnecessary talking will take place on the embussing or debussing point

Signed H. G. Richardson Captain
adjt
1st [illegible] Regt

From			
Place			
Time			

The above may be forwarded as now corrected. (Z)

.... *Censor.* Signature of Addressor or person authorised to telegraph in his name.

* This line should be erased if not required.

(3796.) Wt. W 492/M1647. 650,000 Pads. 5/17. H.W. & V., Ld. (E. 1187.)

File + W.D.

32nd Div.No.G.S.1882/18/4.

C.R.A.
C.R.E.
14th Inf.Brigade.
96th Inf.Brigade.
97th Inf.Brigade.

32nd Bn.M.G.C.
16th H.L.I.(Pioneers).
32nd Divl.Signal Coy.
Q.
A.D.M.S.
D.A.D.O.S.

D.A.D.V.S.
D.A.P.M.
Camp Comdt.
Reception Camp
Divl.Train.
Divl.M.T.Coy.

Sir JOHN MONASH, K.C.B., commanding Australian Corps, has asked the Divisional Commander to express to all ranks his high appreciation of the services rendered by the Division while forming part of the Australian Corps during the recent operations.

The action of 23rd August, the advance, the forcing of the passage of the SOMME, and the pursuit up to the HOLNON WOOD inclusive were operations of which the Division may justly be proud.

Lieut-Colonel,
General Staff,
32nd Division.

14-9-18.

32ND DIVISIONAL ROUTINE ORDERS.

18th Septr., 1918.

3255. REWARDS.

The Field Marshal Commanding-in-Chief has, under authority granted by His Majesty the King, awarded the following decoration. (Fourth Army HR/32/533, dated 15/9/18).

THE DISTINGUISHED SERVICE ORDER.

Capt. (A/Lt.-Col.) H.D.THWAYTES, Dorsetshire Regiment.

The Corps Commander has awarded the following decorations. (Aust.Corps No:97/553, dated 16/9/18).

THE MILITARY MEDAL.

No:163828	Gnr.	F.BERRY,	'D' Bty., 168th Bde., RFA.
No: 19782	Dvr.	J.E.PEACOCK,	" " " " "
No:148369	Gnr.	F.C.KEENE,	" " " " "
No: 93640	Spr.	M.McCLYMONT,	219th Field Coy., R.E.
No: 83466	Dvr.	J.HUGHES,	" " " "
No:103274	L/Cpl.	J.H.A.HALLETT,	Div.Sig.Co.,att. 97 Bde.Sig.Sec.
No: 2069	Sgt.	E.TAYLOR,	Manchester Regiment.
No: 37181	L/Cpl.	F.BAKER,	" "
No: 510	L/Cpl.	A.CARTER,	" "
No: 29713	Pte.	F.THOMPSON,	" "
No:277790	"	C.MANN,	" "
No: 32594	"	H.DALE,	" "
No: 43671	"	A.CHAPPELL,	" "
No: 2856	"	T.V.JAMES,	" "
No: 51523	Sgt.	J.W.STAPLES,	K. O. Y. L. I.
No: 42964	Cpl.	B.McDERMOTT,	" "
No: 38654	Cpl.	J.WHALEY,	" "
No: 51558	"	T.C.PEACOCK,	" "
No:203028	L/Cpl.	E.HAYES,	" "
No: 26116	Pte.	E.JOHNSON,	" "
No: 13923	"	G.H.BATWRIGHT,	" "
No: 37134	"	C.F.CARTER,	" "
No: 23063	"	J.HINCHAN,	" "
No: 20101	"	A.HOLLINGSWORTH,	" "
No:241698	"	W.H.HORTON,	" "
No: 35291	"	F.STEPHENSON,	" "
No:S/2126	Sgt.	T.PATERSON,	Argyll & Suth. Highrs.
No:301216	"	D.McLAUGHLAN,	" " "
No: 7910	Cpl.	R.YOUNG,	" " "
No:S/13140	L/Cpl.	W.BOYD,	" " "
No: 4340	L/Cpl.	W.REID,	" " "
No:327328	Pte.	G.FOY,	" " "
No: 8518	"	G.McDOWALL,	" " "
No: 15803	"	J.ELLIOTT,	" " "
No: 16266	"	H.C.McINTOSH,	Bord.R. att. 97th Bde.Sig.Sec
No: 16447	Pte.(A/Cpl)	R.B.PATTINSON,	Bord.R. att. 97th T.M.Batter
No: 1490	Sgt.	S.B.MILLS,	A.V.C., att. 96th Inf.Bde.H.Q
No:M2/153797	Pte.	G.F.V.MARSH,	MT.A.S.C., att. 92nd Fld.Ambce.
No:M2/053889	"	W.J.BARRETT,	MT.A.S.C., att. 90th Fld.Ambce.

BAR TO THE MILITARY MEDAL.

No: 93350	Sgt.	R.AITKEN, M.M.,	219th Field Coy., R.E.
No: 1410	Pte.	H.STAPLETON, MM.,	Manchester Regiment.
No: 29333	Sgt.	C.E.WILSON, MM.,	K. O. Y. L. I.
No: 10103	L/Cpl.	W.WILKES, MM.,	A. & S. Hrs.

The Divisional Commander heartily congratulates the recipients of these honours, and thanks them for the credit brought to the Division.

P.T.O.

18th Septr., 1918.

3256. **DIVISIONAL MONTHLY CUP.**

The Divisional Monthly Cup for AUGUST has been won by the Argyll & Sutherland Highlanders.

The points gained are as follows :-

	Prisoners or Deserters (2 Points)	Identifications from killed (1 Point)	M.G's or T.M's (3 Pts.)	Aggregate for Month.
A. & S. Highrs.	200	-	12	436
K.O.Y.L.I.	95	-	20	250
Manchester Regt.	45	-	3	99
Lancs. Fusrs. (b)	3	-	8	30
Lancs. Fusrs. (a)	10	-	2	26
Dorset Regt.	8	-	2	22
Border Regt.	3	-	-	6
High. L.I. (a)	-	-	1	3
Royal Scots.	1	-	-	2
Total of Division for Month:-	365	-	48	

3257. **ORDNANCE . RENDERING OF BULK INDENTS TO D.A.D.O.S.**

C.O. Units will ensure that bulk Indents for Clothing, Boots, necessaries, etc., are rendered to D.A.D.O.S. weekly so as to reach him by 9 a.m. every Saturday morning at latest.

The practice of rendering Indents at irregular periods causes great delay in the supply of the Stores.

[signature]

Lieut.Colonel,
A.A. & Q.M.G.,
32nd Division.

N O T I C E.

LOST: Strayed from Transport Lines of 32nd Divisional Signal Coy., R.E., at DEVISE, on night of Septr. 13th, a MULE, description as under:-

Gelding; No:207; 15.1 hds; Dark Brown;
Markings:- On near hindquarter '26/8 △ C.';
on off hindquarters 'U.D.'

Information to O.C., 32nd Divisional Signal Coy., R.E.

14th Inf. Bde. No. G. 254/0/14.

5/6th Royal Scots.
1st Dorset Regt.
15th High. L. I.
14th T.M.Battery.

The attached letter from Australian Corps is forwarded for information and communication to all ranks.

W. Dean

Coy.

[signature]

Major,

24/9/1918. A/Brigade Major, 14th Infantry Brigade.

AUSTRALIAN CORPS.

Corps Headquarters,
12th September 1918.

My dear General,

As your Division has now passed out of my command, I want to send you a few lines to express to you & to your troops my very sincere thanks for their splendid co-operation with this Corps during the period that I have had the honour of having them with us.

No Commander could have received more loyal, more energetic and more efficient service. Your capture of HERLEVILLE and its environs, your energetic drive which hustled the enemy out of the bend of the SOMME, your forcing of the crossings at BRIE and ST.CHRIST by clever outflanking tactics, and your unremitting pursuit of the enemy to and through HOLNON WOOD were all feats of arms of which your Division can be justly proud.

I should like you also to accept and convey to all ranks an expression of the pride and pleasure which it has been to the Australian troops to be so closely associated with such a gallant Division of the Motherland.

Wishing you, your Staff, and the 32nd Divn. continued success.

Yours very sincerely,

(Sd) JOHN MONASH, Lieut-General,
Commdg. Australian Corps.

Maj-Gen. T.S.LAMBERT,
C.B.,C.M.G.
Commdg.32nd Division.

- 2 -

32nd Div. No. G.S. 1882/18/5.

C.R.A., 32nd Divn.	(11 copies)
C.R.E., 32nd Divn.	(4 ")
14th Inf.Bde.	(5 ")
96th Inf.Bde.	(5 ")
97th Inf.Bde.	(5 ")
16th H.L.I.	(1 ")
32nd Bn.M.G.C.	(5 ")
32nd Div.Signal Coy.	(1 ")
A. & Q.	(1 ")
A.D.M.S.	(4 ")
Divnl.Reception Camp.	(1 ")

D.A.D.V.S.	(1 copy)
D.A.D.O.S.	(1 ")
D.A.P.M.	(1 ")
Camp Comdt.	(1 ")
32nd Div.Train.	(5 copies)
32nd Div.M.T.Coy.	(1 copy)

For information and communication to all ranks.

E.S.Uso[illegible]

Lieut-Colonel,
General Staff,
32nd Division.

23rd September 1918.

A [illegible]

I Corp

HQ. [illegible]

32

Army Form C. 2118.

WAR DIARY
or
INTELLIGENCE SUMMARY.
(Erase heading not required.)

1st Dorsets

Vol. 50

Instructions regarding War Diaries and Intelligence Summaries are contained in F. S. Regs., Part II. and the Staff Manual respectively. Title pages will be prepared in manuscript.

Place	Date	Hour	Summary of Events and Information	Remarks and references to Appendices
FLECHE WOOD	1st Oct. 1918	3 A.M.	The Battalion was relieved by the LOYAL NORTH LANCASHIRE Regt. and moved back to INFANTS ALLEY near BELLINGLISE. The remainder of the day was spent in cleaning rifles and resting.	
INFANTS ALLEY	2nd Oct.	0200	Orders were received from 14th Infantry Brigade to move the 1st Dorset Regt. at 5 A.M. to the assembly positions occupied yesterday by the 15th H.L.I. The time of departure was afterwards altered to 4 A.M. The Battalion moved at 4 A.M. and occupied the trenches in H32 and H33. 5/6 Royal Scots attacked SEQUEHART supported by 15th BN. H.L.I.	
			'B' Coy. took up position along the bank running NORTH from H35 central	
			'C' Coy. took up position at SOUTH corner of LEVERGIES ready to support 5/6 Royal Scots. Later 'B' Coy. moved forward to assist Royal Scots and 'C' Coy. took up the position vacated by them.	THORIGNY MAP
H33d.			'A' Coy. was disposed in the trench in H33 c and d.	
			'D' Coy. remained in reserve in the trench in H32b – H33a	
		1115	5/6 Royal Scots were counter-attacked and forced to withdraw. 'A' Coy. reinforced the right of 'C' Coy.	
			At this time Lieut. W. A. WOOD was killed and Lieut. K. TARRANT wounded.	
		1600	Orders were received that the line held would be readjusted and that SEQUEHART would be bombarded at 10 P.M. The BN. was withdrawn accordingly to trenches in H34 c and d and H33d.	

D. D. & L., London, E.C.
(A10266) Wt W5300/P713 750,000 2/18 Sch. 52 Forms/C2118/16.

Army Form C. 2118.

Instructions regarding War Diaries and Intelligence Summaries are contained in F. S. Regs., Part II. and the Staff Manual respectively. Title pages will be prepared in manuscript.

WAR DIARY
or
INTELLIGENCE SUMMARY.
(Erase heading not required.)

Place	Date	Hour	Summary of Events and Information	Remarks and references to Appendices
H 33 d.	Oct. 3rd	0100	Orders were received (attached) for the BN. to attack SEQUEHART in conjunction with an attack by the 97th Bde. 46th Division and Australian Corps. A creeping barrage was put down on the high ground on the LEFT of SEQUEHART whilst a standing barrage played on the village. Officers Commanding Companies were taken forward by A/Major C.H. MORRIS M.C., Commanding the 1st Dorset Regt. whilst Lt. Col. H.D. Thwaytes D.S.O. was on leave, and the objectives were pointed out on the ground. Companies were in position by ~~6 a.m.~~ 0605 in the following order "A" Company on the RIGHT. "D" Company in the centre "B" Company on the LEFT "C" Company was in support. Zero was at 6.25 A.M. There was a slight ground mist and Companies worked up under the Barrage. The enemy replied but their barrage was put down in rear of the attacking Companies. A few shells however fell amongst the Companies chiefly on "C" Company where A/Capt. BRAIN and Lieut. E.W. BOILEAU, Hqs. Lewis Gun Officer who had been sent up to bring back information, were killed instantaneously. All objectives were gained by 0745. At 0800 the enemy counter attacked in great strength. All Companies were now very weak having suffered very heavy casualties from Machine Gun fire, which was very heavy from the village. "A" Company under Lieut. LONSDALE charged the enemy bayoneting 25 and driving a large number in front of them. About 250 Machine guns were found in the village which had caused our casualties. Further waves of the enemy attacked on both flanks and all Companies were forced to give ground. A line was formed along a ledge WEST of	BLS.

D. D. & L., London, E.C.
(A10266) Wt W5300/P713 750,000 2/18 Sch. 52 Forms/C21:8/16.

Instructions regarding War Diaries and Intelligence Summaries are contained in F. S. Regs., Part II. and the Staff Manual respectively. Title pages will be prepared in manuscript.

WAR DIARY
or
INTELLIGENCE SUMMARY.
(Erase heading not required.)

Army Form C. 2118.

Place	Date	Hour	Summary of Events and Information	Remarks and references to Appendices
	3.10.18		the village of SEQUEHART. Later all Companies went forward and occupied their previous position EAST of the village the situation being completely restored. TWO Companies 15th Highland Light Infantry then took up position EAST of the village with TWO Companies of 5/6. Royal Scots on their LEFT.	
			The 7th Dorset Regt. was then reorganized and took up an Outpost line on the RIGHT of the 15th. H.L.I. during this operation Lieut. W.A.A. COLLINGTON was wounded by a sniper. The night was spent in the same position.	ELS
			Captures 360 prisoners 250 Machine Guns	
			Casualties - Lieut. E.B.W. Boileau Killed	
			Lt. (a/Capt.) F.S. Brain -"-	
			2/Lieut. W.E. Edwards. D.C.M. Missing	
			" " H.B. Rathbone. Wndd. & P. of War.	
			" " E. Rew. Wounded	
			" " C.G. Radnedge Wounded.	
			" " K.F. Tarrant -"-	
			" " W.A.A. Collington -"-	
			and 307 O.R's. Killed, Wounded & Missing	

D. D. & L., London, E.C.
(A10266) Wt.W3300/P713 750,000 2/18 Sch. 52 Forms/C2118/16.

Army Form C. 2118.

Instructions regarding War Diaries and Intelligence Summaries are contained in F. S. Regs., Part II. and the Staff Manual respectively. Title pages will be prepared in manuscript.

WAR DIARY
or
INTELLIGENCE SUMMARY.

(Erase heading not required.)

Place	Date	Hour	Summary of Events and Information	Remarks and references to Appendices
SEQUEHART	4/10/15		The day was spent in reorganizing.	ELS
LEHAUCOURT	5.10.15		The 1st. Dorset Regt. remained in the same position until 19 00 when it was relieved by the Sherwood Foresters. The BN. then marched to LEHAUCOURT where it was billeted for the night.	ELS
VENDELLES	6.10.15		The 1st Dorset Regt marched to the VENDELLES area and were billeted in dugouts in the railway embankment.	ELS

D. D. & L., London, E.C.
(A10206) Wt W3300/P713 750,000 2/18 Sch. 52 Forms/C2118/16.

Instructions regarding War Diaries and Intelligence Summaries are contained in F. S. Regs., Part II. and the Staff Manual respectively. Title pages will be prepared in manuscript.

WAR DIARY
or
INTELLIGENCE SUMMARY.
(Erase heading not required.)

Army Form C. 2118.

Place	Date	Hour	Summary of Events and Information	Remarks and references to Appendices
BOUKINCOURT.	7/10/18		Batt. at rest. Day spent in cleaning up. Lt. Col. [illegible] rejoined Batt from leave. Batt addressed by the Div. Commander Maj Gen LAMBERT on the Batt's doings in recent operations outside SEQUEHART.	E.L.
	8/10/18		Batt at rest. Training. Games 2 PM – 4 PM. Baths.	E.L.
	9/10/18		Batt at rest. Training. Games 2 PM – 4 PM	E.L.
	10/10/18		Batt at rest. Training Games 2 PM – 4 PM	E.L.
	11/10/18		Batt at rest. Training Games 2 PM – 4 PM	E.L.
	12/10/18		Batt at rest. Church Parade.	E.L.
	13/10/18		Batt at rest Route March. Games 2 PM – 4 PM	E.L.
	14/10/18		Batt at rest. Training Route March. Games 2 PM – 4 PM	E.L.
	15/10/18		Batt at rest Route March. Games 2 PM – 4 PM.	E.L.
	16/10/18		Batt at rest. Tactical Exercise.	E.L.
	17/10/18		Batt moved to area in the vicinity of BELINGLISE G22 and 23	E.L.
	18/10/18		Batt at rest. Training.	E.L.
	19/10/18		Batt at rest ~~moved to BOHAIN~~ Training	E.L.
	20/10/18		Batt moved to BOHAIN.	E.L.
	21/10/18		Batt at rest. Presentation of medal ribbons by Maj Gen LAMBERT. [illegible]	E.L.
	22/10/18		Batt at rest. Tactical scheme	E.L.

D. D. & L., London, E.C.
(A10266) Wt W3300/P713 750,000 2/18 Sch. 52 Forms/C2118/16.

Army Form C. 2118.

Instructions regarding War Diaries and Intelligence Summaries are contained in F. S. Regs., Part II. and the Staff Manual respectively. Title pages will be prepared in manuscript.

WAR DIARY
or
INTELLIGENCE SUMMARY.
(Erase heading not required.)

Place	Date	Hour	Summary of Events and Information	Remarks and references to Appendices
Bohain	23/10/18		Batt at rest - Training	ELL
	24/10/18		Batt at rest - Training -	ELL
	25/10/18		Batt at rest - Training - Tactical scheme	ELL
	26/10/18		Batt at rest - Training -	ELL
	27/10/18		Batt at rest - Church Parade Service given by Senior Chaplain to the 32nd Division Rev. CROSS.	ELL
	28/10/18		Batt at rest - Training	ELL
	29/10/18		Batt at rest. Training - Route march	ELL
	30/10/18	1745	The 1st Dorset Regt. moved by March route to ST. SOUPLET Conference of C.O.s at 1900.	ELL
	31/10/18	1730	The 1st Dorset Regt relieved 2nd Bn. SHERWOOD FORESTERS in the line from ORS to the SOUTH along the SAMBRE-OISE canal. Battalion Headquarters in BAZEUL	ELS

1/11/1918

H.D. Thwaytes Lieut Col.
Commanding 1/Dorset Regt.

D. D. & L., London, E.C.
(A10266) Wt W5300/P713 750,000 2/18 **Sch. 52** Forms/C2118/16.

Instructions regarding War Diaries and Intelligence Summaries are contained in F. S. Regs., Part II. and the Staff Manual respectively. Title pages will be prepared in manuscript.

WAR DIARY
or
INTELLIGENCE SUMMARY.
(Erase heading not required.)

Army Form C. 2118.

1 Dorset Regt

Vol 51

Place	Date	Hour	Summary of Events and Information	Remarks and references to Appendices
ORS	1-11-18		Bn: holding line - Day quiet.	S.F.C
"	2-11-18		Bn: holding line - 3 O.R killed, 3 O.R wounded by shellfire	S.F.C
"	3-11-18		Bn holding line - 1 O.R killed, 4 O.R wounded by shellfire	S.F.C
"	4-11-18		During the night of the 3/4 the 5/6 R. Scots took over the front line from 1/Dorset Regt and 1/Dorset Regt took over from the right company of the 2nd Manchester in order to enable the 1/Dorset Regt to attack and force the passage of the SAMBRE CANAL at ORS.	S.F.C
			After the relief C Company and 2 platoons of D Company withdrew to cellars in ORS - B Company who were to cross the canal behind the 96th Bde on our left moved into railway cutting at L35 - A Company remained in their positions in close support.	Ref. Map BARZY [illegible]
			One 18 pounder gun was placed in position near ORS church from which it could fire point blank at the main Ors bridge if necessary.	
			4 Vickers guns were ordered to take up positions on canal bank N of ORS, and 4 Vickers guns were ordered [illegible] of ORS	

D. D. & L., London, E.C.
(A10206) Wt W3300/P713 750,000 2/18 Sch. 52 Forms/C2118/16.

Instructions regarding War Diaries and Intelligence Summaries are contained in F. S. Regs., Part II. and the Staff Manual respectively. Title pages will be prepared in manuscript.

WAR DIARY
or
INTELLIGENCE SUMMARY.
(Erase heading not required.)

Army Form C. 2118.

Place	Date	Hour	Summary of Events and Information	Remarks and references to Appendices
ORS	4-11-18		from which they could engage any enemy machine guns which opened fire at point blank range – Four Stokes guns were got into position about the church with orders to fire rapid from Zero to Zero + 3 on the Eastern side of the village – Before Zero the following alterations were made – Two platoons C Company were assembled behind a house 60x from the site 200x South of the main bridge where a floating bridge was to be erected by the R.E's – One platoon behind a house close up to the main bridge – 1 platoon on the canal bank North of Ors at the place selected for crossing – B Company assembled in an orchard in rear of 2/Manchester Regt. D Company assembled 2 platoons N. of Ors Church & 2 platoons South of ORS Church under cover ready to cross by whichever means was available –	

D. D. & L., London, E.C.
(A10266) Wt W5300/P713 750,000 2/18 Sch. 52 Forms/C2118/16.

Instructions regarding War Diaries and Intelligence Summaries are contained in F. S. Regs., Part II. and the Staff Manual respectively. Title pages will be prepared in manuscript.

WAR DIARY
or
INTELLIGENCE SUMMARY.
(*Erase heading not required.*)

Army Form C. 2118.

Place	Date	Hour	Summary of Events and Information	Remarks and references to Appendices
GRS	4-11-18	0545	Zero hour was at 0545 the ~~[illegible]~~ morning mist being made more intense by smoke shells being fired around the village.	
		0548	After the ~~[illegible]~~ barrage ceased the platoon at the main bridge rushed forward with the sappers & an improvised bridge to span the old bridge but were met with an intense enemy M.G. barrage and by a gun firing at point blank range. Several unsuccessful attempts were made and eventually the attempts were given up when a shell landed on the bridge & wounded the sapper officer. Seven O.R. were wounded in the attempt to get the bridge across.	
		0555	A message was received at B.H.Q. that it would be impossible to get the bridge across.	
		0550	Materials for the construction of a floating bridge was carried forward to the selected spot 200x S. of ORS & work was commenced under the covering fire of the two platoons detailed.	

D. D. & L., London, E.C.
(A10266) Wt W5300/P713 750,000 2/18 Sch. 52 Forms/C2118/16.

Instructions regarding War Diaries and Intelligence Summaries are contained in F. S. Regs., Part II. and the Staff Manual respectively. Title pages will be prepared in manuscript.

WAR DIARY
or
INTELLIGENCE SUMMARY.

(*Erase heading not required.*)

Army Form C. 2118.

Place	Date	Hour	Summary of Events and Information	Remarks and references to Appendices
ORS	4.11.18	0610	This bridge was completed & Headquarters informed & orders issued for the remainder of C Company & D Company to cross. At the same time orders were issued to A Company to move forward at once cross this bridge and mop up the village of ORS. North of ORS the platoon attached to cross by a collapsible boat though under heavy M.G. fire succeeded in launching the boat but were unable to cross as the boat capsized. Five casualties were caused here. Information was received that the 2 Manchester Regt had not managed to force a crossing and permission was asked for them to cross by the bridge S. of ORS, which they did followed by B Company 1/Dorset Regt. On crossing the canal companies at once worked forward to their positions on the "yellow" line, 2 platoons of D Coy. working along the canal southwards as far as RUE VERT taking over 70 prisoners.	

D. D. & L., London, E.C.
(A10266) Wt W3300/P713 750,000 2/18 Sch. 52 Forms/C2118/16.

Army Form C. 2118.

Instructions regarding War Diaries and Intelligence Summaries are contained in F. S. Regs., Part II. and the Staff Manual respectively. Title pages will be prepared in manuscript.

WAR DIARY
or
INTELLIGENCE SUMMARY.
(Erase heading not required.)

Place	Date	Hour	Summary of Events and Information	Remarks and references to Appendices
6 R S	4-11-18	0610	Two platoons D Coy advanced through the main street of the village capturing 80 prisoners –	
			On reaching the "yellow line" the companies received orders to reorganise and to consolidate as a temporary measure until the position was less obscure on the 96th Bde front.	
			The protective barrage 300× in front of the yellow line was called for and continued until it was considered safe for it to die down.	
			On reorganizing, the companies were in the following order – D company on the right in touch with 5/6 R. Scots at RUE VERT, C company Centre and B company on the left with A company in support.	
			Touch was maintained with the Manchester Regt. on the left.	
		1345	As there was very little enemy opposition no barrage was considered necessary to reach the "Blue dotted" line & the advance was continued, orders being given to the M.G. section who were co-operating to watch the left flank of the Bn.	

D. D. & L., London, E.C.
(10340) Wt W5300/P713 750,000 3/18 E 2688 Forms/C2118/16.

Army Form C. 2118.

Instructions regarding War Diaries and Intelligence Summaries are contained in F. S. Regs., Part II. and the Staff Manual respectively. Title pages will be prepared in manuscript.

WAR DIARY
or
INTELLIGENCE SUMMARY.
(Erase heading not required.)

Place	Date	Hour	Summary of Events and Information	Remarks and references to Appendices
6 R S	4-11-18	1345	Little opposition was met with on the advance and the "Dotted Blue Line" was reached and almost immediately the 15th H.L.I. passed through to their further objective.	
			The dotted blue line was consolidated with two companies and as the left flank was the weak spot, two companies were sent to consolidate on that flank & gain touch with the 2nd Manchester Regt who were reported to have their left about G 32 c 6.1	
			Companies were disposed as follows on the night Nov 4/5th	
			- D Coy: from M 14 c 9.0. to M 8 d 1.5. with 2 platoons in front and 2 in support.	
			C Coy: from M 8 d 1,5. to ROAD JUNCTION in M 3 c, 2 platoons in front, 2 in support.	
			B Coy: from X ROADS in M 3 c to M 2 d 9, 3.	
			A Coy: from M 2 d 9 3 to G 32 c 6 1 - These 2 Coys: each had 2 platoons in the front occupying the high ground & 2 in support.	

D. D. & L., London, E.C.
(10340) Wt W[illegible]/P713 750,000 3/18 E 2688 Forms/C2118/16.

Instructions regarding War Diaries and Intelligence Summaries are contained in F. S. Regs., Part II. and the Staff Manual respectively. Title pages will be prepared in manuscript.

WAR DIARY
or
INTELLIGENCE SUMMARY.
(Erase heading not required.)

Army Form C. 2118.

Place	Date	Hour	Summary of Events and Information	Remarks and references to Appendices
GRS	4.11.18		Shortly after touch was gained, the Manchesters went forward to the "Dotted Blue line" –	
			<u>Captures during Operations</u>	
			3 Officers 220 O.R.	
			30 Machine guns	
			3 4.2 Howitzers	
			<u>Casualties</u>	
			6-O.R killed	
			1 Officer 49 O.R Wounded	

D. D. & L., London, E.C.
(10340) Wt W5300/P713 750,000 3/18 E 2688 Forms/C2118/16.

Instructions regarding War Diaries and Intelligence Summaries are contained in F. S. Regs., Part II. and the Staff Manual respectively. Title pages will be prepared in manuscript.

WAR DIARY
or
INTELLIGENCE SUMMARY.
(Erase heading not required.)

Army Form C. 2118.

Place	Date	Hour	Summary of Events and Information	Remarks and references to Appendices
GRS	5-11-18	1030	Bn: assembled & marched to FAVRIL where they were billeted - Slight shelling but no casualties - 2 prisoners captured in a cellar -	S7C
FAVRIL	6-11-18		Bn: at rest, cleaning up etc -	S7C
FAVRIL	7-11-18	0915	Bn: marched to GRAND FAYT & went into billets -	S7C
GD: FAYT	8-11-18		Bn: at rest - Cleaning up etc -	S7C
GD: FAYT	9-11-18	0815	Bn: marched via AVESNES, where a halt was made for Dinners, to the	S7C Ref MAP
		1600	FLAUMONT sector, (K15 and 21) & relieved the outpost line of The BORDER Regt (97th BDE:) - The relief was carried out in daylight and the remainder of the day was quiet as Cavalry patrols were reported to be 8 kilometres ahead of the outpost line -	57A S7C
AVESNES	10-11-18		Two companies holding outpost line. Remainder of Battn in Billets. No shelling. Cavalry patrols still forward.	S7C
AVESNES	11-11-18		Outpost line pushed forward 2 kilom. B. Coy moved forward as Support & billeted at FLAUMONT. At 0700 news was received that hostilities would cease at 1100 hours French time. Outpost lines remained in position.	S7C
AVESNES	12-11-18		Day quiet [illegible]	S7C

D. D. & L., London, E.C.
(10340) Wt W5300/P713 750,000 3/18 E 2688 Forms/C2118/16.

Army Form C. 2118.

WAR DIARY
or
INTELLIGENCE SUMMARY.
(Erase heading not required.)

Instructions regarding War Diaries and Intelligence Summaries are contained in F. S. Regs., Part II. and the Staff Manual respectively. Title pages will be prepared in manuscript.

Place	Date	Hour	Summary of Events and Information	Remarks and references to Appendices
AVESNES	13.11.18	10.15	Battalion marched to and billeted at SAINS DU NORD	SJC
SAINS.	14.11.18		Battalion spent the day in cleaning [illegible]	SJC
SAINS	15.11.18		G.O.C. 14th Infy Bde (Brig. General J. P. EVANS V.C., D.S.O.,) inspected the Battalion and addressed them briefly on the cessation of hostilities and the "March to Germany".	SJC
SAINS.	16.11.18		14th Infy Bde parade for presentation of Meal Ribands and an address by G.O.C. 32nd Division (Major General T.S. LAMBERT C.B., C.M.G. C of E divine service for the Battalion. Lieut W.A.S. SMELLIE with Cpls CHARD and BLAKE proceeded to England to bring out the Colours	SJC
SAINS	17.11.18		Thanksgiving Service under 14th Brigade arrangements at 11.30 AM	SJC
SAINS	18.11.18		Battalion in billets. P.T. Games and Battalion Ceremonial parade during the morning. Football during afternoon.	SJC
SAINS	19.11.18		Commencement of the March to Germany. Orders that Battalion would pass Starting point at 0921 hours carried out. Midday halt for dinner from 1150 hours to 1300 hours. Battalion marched into SIVRY at 1515 hours. Bn billetted here for one night	SJC

D. D. & L., London, E.C.
(10340) Wt W5300/P713 750,000 3/18 E 2688 Forms/C2118/16.

Army Form C. 2118.

Instructions regarding War Diaries and Intelligence Summaries are contained in F. S. Regs., Part II. and the Staff Manual respectively. Title pages will be prepared in manuscript.

WAR DIARY
or
INTELLIGENCE SUMMARY.
(Erase heading not required.)

Place	Date	Hour	Summary of Events and Information	Remarks and references to Appendices
SIVRY	20.11.18		Bn passed starting point at 0830 hours and continued the March via RANCE to FROIDCHAPELLE which place was reached at 1235 hours. Billets in this place were very good. Information received that the Brigade Group would probably not move till 24. 11. 18.	SJC
FROIDCHAPELLE	21.11.18		Ceremonial parade from 1015 hours to 1115 hours. A and D Coys employed in cleaning portion of RANCE – FROIDCHAPELLE ROAD from 1300 hours to 1700 hours.	SJC
FROIDCHAPELLE	22.11.18		Ceremonial parade. Coy parades for Rifle Exercises also P.T. & Games included in the days programme of work. B and D Coys road cleaning from 1300 hours to 1700 hours on RANCE – FROIDCHAPELLE ROAD.	SJC
FROIDCHAPELLE	23.11.18		Battalion and Ceremonial parades during the morning. Sports and Amusements Committee met to arrange for Sports as soon as the Bn. became stationary. A list of Sports Outfit required was drawn up and forwarded to 14th. Infy. Bde. Orders received at 1600 hours that the March would be continued on 24-11-18. the 1st Bn. Dorset Regt to be billeted for one night at DAUSSOIS.	SJC

D. D. & L., London, E.C.
(10340) Wt W5300/P713 750,000 3/18 E 2688 Forms/C2118/16.

Instructions regarding War Diaries and Intelligence Summaries are contained in F. S. Regs., Part II. and the Staff Manual respectively. Title pages will be prepared in manuscript.

WAR DIARY
or
INTELLIGENCE SUMMARY.

(*Erase heading not required.*)

Army Form C. 2118.

Place	Date	Hour	Summary of Events and Information	Remarks and references to Appendices
FROIDCHAPELLE	24.11.18		Bn marched off at 0835 hours and passed starting point exactly at 0900 hours. The route was via CERFONTAINE and SOUMOY. DAUSSOIS was reached at 1205 hours. Information received at 1900 hours that the Brigade Group would not move on the 25. 11. 18.	SFC
DAUSSOIS	25.11.18		P.T. and Games. Ceremonial parade from 1000 hours to 1100 hours. Bn. informed that the 14th Infy Bde Group would not move from the present area for possibly a fortnight.	SFC
DAUSSOIS	26.11.18		Ceremonial parade. during morning	SFC
DAUSSOIS	27.11.18		Under Coy arrangements, the Battalion marched to VILLERS-deux-EGLISES and were in the new billets by 11 A.M. Excellent accommodation for the men was afforded in this village	SFC
VILLERS-deux-EGLISES	28.11.18		Ceremonial Drill during morning. Recreation Room established. Inter League Football Match. A Coy & C Coy Draw. No score.	SFC
VILLERS-deux-EGLISES.	29.11.18		P.T. & Games. Ceremonial Drill. 14th Infy Bde played 167 Bty R.F.A at association football. Result 14th Bde 9 goals R.F.A. 0. Four players from the Battn represented Bn in Bde team.	SFC

D. D. & L., London, E.C.
(10340) Wt W5300/P713 750,000 3/18 E 2688 Forms/C2118/16.

Army Form C. 2118.

WAR DIARY
or
INTELLIGENCE SUMMARY.

(*Erase heading not required.*)

Instructions regarding War Diaries and Intelligence Summaries are contained in F. S. Regs., Part II. and the Staff Manual respectively. Title pages will be prepared in manuscript.

Place	Date	Hour	Summary of Events and Information	Remarks and references to Appendices
VILLERS deux EGLISES.	30/11/18		Battalion Route March. Inter-Coy League Football during the afternoon. Results Hd. Qrs. 5 D Coy 1. Transport & Q.M. Stores 6 'C' Coy 3.	[illegible]

30/11/18.

[illegible signature] Major
Comdg 1 Dorset Regiment

D. D. & L., London, E.C.
(10340) Wt W5300/P713 750,000 3/18 E 2688 Forms/C2118/16.

Army Form C. 2118.

WAR DIARY
or
INTELLIGENCE SUMMARY.
(*Erase heading not required.*)

Instructions regarding War Diaries and Intelligence Summaries are contained in F. S. Regs., Part II. and the Staff Manual respectively. Title pages will be prepared in manuscript.

December 1918 — 1st Dorset Regt

Place	Date	Hour	Summary of Events and Information	Remarks and references to Appendices
VILLERS-deux-EGLISES.	1		Church Parade. Lieut W.A. Smellie, 2/Lieut E.S. Cousins, C.S.M. Gaylard, A/Sgt Chard & A/Sgt Blake arrived from England with the Kings and Regimental Colours. Football match against 5/6 R Scots lost 1-0	SRC
do.	2.		Battalion in training. P.T. Games & Ceremonial Drill during the morning. Organised games in the afternoon. Inter Coy League Football Matches resulted as follows. A Coy 6. C Coy 0. D Coy 3. B Coy 2.	SRC
do	3		Ceremonial Parade. Marching past with Colours. G.O.C. 14th Infy Bde - Brig General L. P. Evans V.C., D.S.O. in attendance. The King's Colours was carried by Lieut W.A. Smellie and the Regimental Colour by 2/Lt. A.H. Carter M.C., M.M. the remainder of Colour Party being Sgts Dodge, Chard and Blakely. The Battalion formed up in line and the Colours were then marched on. On arrival of the G.O.C. the General Salute was given and the General then inspected the Battalion including the Transport. After marching past in Column and Close Column the Battalion ~~reformed~~ the original line	SRC

D. D. & L., London, E.C. (10340) Wt W5300/P713 750,000 3/18 E 2688 Forms/C2118/16.

Army Form C. 2118.

WAR DIARY
or
INTELLIGENCE SUMMARY.
(Erase heading not required.)

Instructions regarding War Diaries and Intelligence Summaries are contained in F. S. Regs., Part II. and the Staff Manual respectively. Title pages will be prepared in manuscript.

December 1918

Place	Date	Hour	Summary of Events and Information	Remarks and references to Appendices
			After forming the 3 sides of a square the G. O. C addressed the Bn. speaking of the honours shown on the Regimental Colours, the splendid work the Bn had done during this war and what was intended during the months ahead. Line was again formed and the Colours marched away with "D" Coy as escort.	SOC
			During the afternoon a Gymkana was held, all events being very keenly contested.	
VILLERS-deux EGLISES.	4.		Training including P.T., B.F. Guard Mounting and Squad Drill. Practice Rugby game in the afternoon. French Class commenced under Lt. H A Rabino.	SOC
do	5		Training - Tactical Schemes. A Coy in attack. Inter. Coy League Football Bn Hd Qrs 1. Tpt & Q M Stores 4. Arithmetic Class under 2/Lt W S Journeaux M.C	SOC
do	6		Training - P.T. Coy Drill. B F and Musketry. Young Officers Class under Capt. E L Stephenson M.C. and N.C.Os Class under Major C. H. Morris D.S.O, M.C were started, the classes to be held daily. French & Arithmetic Classes also met. Inter Coy League Football results. A Coy 1 v D Coy 1. - B Coy 4 v C Coy 2.	SOC

(10340) Wt [illegible] P713 750,000 3/18 D. D. & L., London, E.C. E 2688 Forms/C2118/16.

Instructions regarding War Diaries and Intelligence Summaries are contained in F. S. Regs., Part II. and the Staff Manual respectively. Title pages will be prepared in manuscript.

WAR DIARY
or
INTELLIGENCE SUMMARY.
(Erase heading not required.)

Army Form C. 2118.

December 1918

Place	Date	Hour	Summary of Events and Information	Remarks and references to Appendices
VILLERS-deux-EGLISES	7		Training. Squad Drill without arms. Officers + N.C.O classes also French + Arithmetic.	SJC
do	8		Church Parade.	SJC
do	9.		Training. P.T. Musketry. Guards. All classes held during morning. Result of Football Match. 5/6 R. Scots 4. 1st Dorset R. 2	SJC
do	10.		Route March. All classes held.	SJC
do	11		Battalion Training	SJC
do	12.		Battalion marched to METTET and billeted for the night.	SJC
METTET	13		Battalion marched to ANHÈE on the MEUSE.	SJC
ANHÈE	14		Battalion resting and Cleaning up.	SJC
do	15.		Church parade cancelled. Commander-in-Chief passed through the village during the morning	SJC
do	16.		Battalion in Training. Class held for Young Officers. Other Ranks. Squad + Arm Drill	SJC

D. D. & L., London, E.C.
(A10266) Wt W5300/P713 750,000 2/18 Sch. 52 Forms/C2118/16

Army Form C. 2118.

WAR DIAR[Y]
or
INTELLIGENCE SUMMARY.
(Erase heading not required.)

Instructions regarding War Diaries and Intelligence Summaries are contained in F. S. Regs., Part II. and the Staff Manual respectively. Title pages will be prepared in manuscript.

December 1918 — 1st Dorset Regt.

Place	Date	Hour	Summary of Events and Information	Remarks and references to Appendices
ANHEE	17		Bn Route March.	SFC
do	18		Bn in training. Educational Classes in Mathematics, English, Geography, History & French commenced. 84 in attendance of 4 classes each subject.	SFC
do	19		Battalion in training. Organised games during the afternoon.	SFC
do	20.		Battalion training.	SFC
do	21		Battalion training.	SFC
do	22		Church Parade. 14 O.R dispatched for demobilization.	SFC
do.	23		Battalion in Training. Officers and N.C.Os classes held. 4OR. dispatched for demobilisation.	SFC
do.	24		Battalion parade. 19 O.Rs. dispatched for demobilization	SFC
do	25.		Xmas Day. Holiday. G.O.C. 14th Infy Bde. visited all Coy Mess Rooms. 1. OR dispatched for demobilisation. Church Parade. G.O.C 14th Infy Bde attended. Battalion Officers dinner at 8pm	SFC

D. D. & L., London, E.C.
(A10266) Wt W5300/P713 750,000 2/18 Sch. 52 Form[s C. 2118]

Army Form C. 2118.

WAR DIARY
or
INTELLIGENCE SUMMARY.
(*Erase heading not required.*)

Instructions regarding War Diaries and Intelligence Summaries are contained in F. S. Regs., Part II. and the Staff Manual respectively. Title pages will be prepared in manuscript.

December 1918

Place	Date	Hour	Summary of Events and Information	Remarks and references to Appendices
ANHEE	26		Holiday. Inter Bn Football Match. 1st Dorset Regt 1. 14th Bde HdQr 1. 4 OR despatched for demobilization	S.T.C.
do	27		Battalion in training	S.T.C.
do	28		Battalion in training. Inter Bn Football Match. 15th H.L.I. 1 1st Dorset Regt. 2.	S.T.C.
do	29		Church Parade	S.T.C.
do	30		Training as per syllabus.	S.T.C.
do	31		Training as per syllabus. 7 ORs despatched to England for duty in connection with demobilization. Watford Details.	S.T.C.

1st Jan. 1919.

H S Thwaytes Lieut Col
Commanding 1st Dorset Regiment

D. D. & L., L[illegible] (A10266) Wt W5300/P713 750,00[illegible] Forms/C2118/16

LANCASHIRE DIVISION
(LATE 32ND DIVN)

14TH INFY BDE (1ST LANCS INFY BDE)

1ST BN DORSET REGT.

JAN-~~FEB 1919~~ MAR

LCS

Army Form C. 2118.

WAR DIARY
or
INTELLIGENCE SUMMARY.
(Erase heading not required.)

Instructions regarding War Diaries and Intelligence Summaries are contained in F. S. Regs., Part II. and the Staff Manual respectively. Title pages will be prepared in manuscript.

January 1919 — 1st Dorset Regt

Place	Date	Hour	Summary of Events and Information	Remarks and references to Appendices
ANHÈE	1.		Holiday. Day observed as a holiday	[illegible]
do	2.		Battalion in training.	[illegible]
do	3.		Battalion Route March.	[illegible]
do	4.		Coy training during morning. Bde Cross Country Run held and won by 1st Dorset Regt.	[illegible]
do	5.		Divine Service. C Coy moved to Namur for the purpose of guarding bridges and Barges.	[illegible]
do	6.		Battalion in training.	[illegible]
do	7		Coys at Anhée bathed. Remainder of day spent in training	[illegible]
do	8.		Battalion Route March. 1 Pivotal man despatched for demobilization.	[illegible]
do	9.		Bn. Ceremonial Drill. 2 Long Service Men demobilized. 2 Watford Details proceed to England. 25 Serving Soldiers proceed on 28 days furlough.	[illegible]
do.	10.		Coy & Platoon Drill. B.F. & P.T. 4 officers and 3 O.R. demobilised.	[illegible]

D. D. & L., London, E.C.
(A10266) Wt W5300/P713 750,000 2/18 Sch. 52 Forms/C2118/16

Army Form C. 2118.

Instructions regarding War Diaries and Intelligence Summaries are contained in F. S. Regs., Part II. and the Staff Manual respectively. Title pages will be prepared in manuscript.

WAR DIARY
or
INTELLIGENCE SUMMARY.
(Erase heading not required.)

January 1919 — 1st Dorset Regt.

Place	Date	Hour	Summary of Events and Information	Remarks and references to Appendices
ANHEE	11.		Coys at disposal of O.C Coys.	JFC
do	12.		Divine Service. 34 O.R. despatched for demobilization.	JFC
do	13		Battalion in training.	JFC
do	14		Presentation of Medal Ribands for decorations. 1st Dorset Regt receive 23. 1st Dorset Regt. also presented with the 32nd Divisional Monthly Cup for prisoners & guns captured during November the last month of hostilities.	JFC
do.	15.		Battalion in training. Each of A B & D Coys drilled under an Army Gym Staff Instructor.	JFC
do.	16.		Route March for A. B & D Coys.	JFC
do.	17		D. Coy in training. 'A' Coy moved to WEPION and 'B' Coy to "ABBEY" for the purpose of taking over guards on barges. 1 officer & 35 O.R. despatched for demobilization.	JFC

D. D. & L., London, E.C.
(A10266) Wt W3300/P713 750,000 2/18 Sch. 52 Forms/C2118/16.

Instructions regarding War Diaries and Intelligence Summaries are contained in F. S. Regs., Part II. and the Staff Manual respectively. Title pages will be prepared in manuscript.

WAR DIARY
or
INTELLIGENCE SUMMARY.
(*Erase heading not required.*)

Army Form C. 2118.

January 1919 — 1st Dorset Regt

Place	Date	Hour	Summary of Events and Information	Remarks and references to Appendices
ANHEE	18		D Coy in training. A. B & C Coys on guard duty.	S.F.C
do	19.		D. Coy moved to WEPION to take over part of Guards found by A. Coy. One Officer and 43 O.R despatched for demobilisation.	S.F.C
NAMUR	20.		All Coys on Guard duty.	S.F.C
do	21		A. Coy relieved by a Coy of 5/6th Royal Scots and moved into NAMUR to provide Guards with "B" Coy. 2 Officers & 27 O.R. despatched for demobilisation. 13 OR re-engaged proceed on re-engagement furlough.	S.F.C
do.	22.		All Coys on Guard duty.	S.F.C
do	23.		do	S.F.C
do	24		do.	S.F.C
do	25		do.	S.F.C

D. D. & L., London, E.C.
(A10266) Wt W3300/P713 750,000 2/18 Sch. 52 Forms/C2118/10.

Instructions regarding War Diaries and Intelligence Summaries are contained in F. S. Regs., Part II. and the Staff Manual respectively. Title pages will be prepared in manuscript.

WAR DIARY
or
INTELLIGENCE SUMMARY.
(Erase heading not required.)

Army Form C. 2118.

January 1919 — 1st Dorset Regt

Place	Date	Hour	Summary of Events and Information	Remarks and references to Appendices
NAMUR	26		All Coys on Guard Duty	S.F.C.
do	27		All Coys on Guard Duty. Bn Hd Qrs moved from ANHEE to NAMUR. Coys relieved by 2nd Canadian Bn. Battalion staged for night at 32nd Divisional Reception Camp	S.F.C.
do	28.		Battalion entrained and left NAMUR for Germany at 6.40pm	S.F.C.
BEUEL	29		Battalion arrived at BEUEL at 3.20pm. Detrained and rested the night at the Cavalry Barracks at BONN. A Coy remained at BEUEL for detraining remaining units of 14th Infy Bde.	S.F.C.
BONN	30.		Battalion marched from BONN at 9.15 AM. and arrived OBERCASSEL at 11 AM. 1/4 Cheshire Regt relieved. C. Coy take over outpost line. "B." Coy furnish two Ferry Guards and 1 station Guard. "D." Coy find Inlying piquet for Billets. "A" Coy remain at BEUEL.	S.F.C.
OBERCASSEL	31.		B. C. & D Coys continue with duties taken over on 30th. "A" Coy rejoin Battalion.	S.F.C.

H.D. [illegible] Lieut Col
Cmdg 1st Dorset Regt
31/1/19

D. D. & L., London, E.C. (A10266) Wt W3300/P713 750,000 2/18 Sch. 52 Forms/C2118/16.

Instructions regarding War Diaries and Intelligence Summaries are contained in F. S. Regs., Part II. and the Staff Manual respectively. Title pages will be prepared in manuscript.

WAR DIARY
or
INTELLIGENCE SUMMARY.
(Erase heading not required.)

Army Form C. 2118.

February 1918 1st Dorset Regt. V8 54

Place	Date	Hour	Summary of Events and Information	Remarks and references to Appendices
OBERCASSEL	1		1 Coy on Outpost Duty. 1 Coy in training. 1 Coy furnishing Station and Ferry Guards and 1 Coy forming the Inlying Piquet.	S.Y.C.
do	2		Ferry Guards relieved by 4th T. M. Battery. Other duties continued.	S.Y.C.
			Church Parade Divine Service held in OBERCASSEL CHURCH.	
do	3		Inlying piquet taken off. Head Quarter Guard now made up to 2 NCOs. 6 men and 4 Lewis Gunners with 2 Lewis Guns.	S.Y.C.
			All available men in training as per weekly programme of training.	
do	4		Guards, Duties and Training.	S.Y.C.
do	5		Guards, Duties and training. Battalion baths at School Baths	S.Y.C.
			P.T. Class of 4 Officers and 16 men commenced	
do	6		Battalion less Guards and duties in training.	S.Y.C.
do	7		Battalion less Guards and duties in training	S.Y.C.
do	8		Coys at disposal of Coy Commanders.	S.Y.C.

D. D. & L., London, E.C.
(A10266) Wt W5300/P713 750,000 2/18 Sch. 52 Forms/C2118/16

Instructions regarding War Diaries and Intelligence Summaries are contained in F. S. Regs., Part II. and the Staff Manual respectively. Title pages will be prepared in manuscript.

WAR DIARY
or
INTELLIGENCE SUMMARY.
(Erase heading not required.)

Army Form C. 2118.

Place	Date	Hour	Summary of Events and Information	Remarks and references to Appendices
OBERCASSEL	9		Church Parade. Divine Service held in OBERCASSEL CHURCH.	SJC
do	10.		Parades + training as per weekly programme of training. Bn supplied Divisional Guard of 2 NCOs, 18 Ptes. + 1 Bugler.	SJC
do	11.		Divisional Guard increased by 1 Cpl. 1 Bugler and 9 Ptes. Baths allotted to Bn for the day. Battalion made a trip up the Rhine as far as COBLENZ.	SJC
do	12		Battalion in training. Station Guard relieved by M.G. Coy. Lewis gun class of 12 men commenced	SJC
do	13		Battalion parades as per programme. Instruction in use of Barr + Stroud Range Finder commenced.	SJC
do	14		Training as per programme. All Rifles + Guns of the Battalion inspected by Divisional Armourer	SJC
do	15.		Training as per programme	SJC
do	16.		Church Parade Divine Service in village Church	SJC

D. D. & L., London, E.C.
(A10266) Wt W5300/P713 750,000 2/18 Sch. 52 Forms/C2118/16

Army Form C. 2118.

Instructions regarding War Diaries and Intelligence Summaries are contained in F. S. Regs., Part II. and the Staff Manual respectively. Title pages will be prepared in manuscript.

WAR DIARY
or
INTELLIGENCE SUMMARY.

(*Erase heading not required.*)

Place	Date	Hour	Summary of Events and Information	Remarks and references to Appendices
OBERCASSEL	17		Parades as per programme. N.C.Os. Class of 4 NCOs per Coy commenced. Woodcutting party of 50 O.R. reported at VINXEL at 0900 hours. Brig. Gen. L.P. EVANS VC DSO, leaves 14th Inf Bde for ROTTERDAM.	SHC
do	18.		Training as per programme. Army Commander General Sir Herbert C.O. Plumer. G.C.B., G.C.M.G. G.C.V.O. A.D.C. visited 14th Bde Head Quarters. Lt. Col. H.D. Thwaytes D.S.O. with Bn. Commanders of other units in Bde interviewed. Army Commander complimented the Bn on the Divisional Guard.	SHC
do	19		Battalion in training.	SHC
do	20.		Battalion in training. Divisional Guard relieved.	SHC
do	21		Battalion in training. Lt Col H.D. Thwaytes DSO. proceeded to England on leave.	SHC
do	22		Parades as per programme. Bn training. Bn win Bde X Country run.	SHC
do	23		Divine Service held in OBERCASSEL CHURCH.	SHC
do	24		Bn in training. Lecture on Alsace Lorraine at 1730 hours by Mr C.P. Masterman Smith. 100 O.R. in attendance	SHC

D. D. & L., London, E.C.
(A10266) Wt W5300/P713 750,000 2/18 Sch. 52 Forms/C2118/16

Army Form C. 2118.

Instructions regarding War Diaries and Intelligence Summaries are contained in F. S. Regs., Part II. and the Staff Manual respectively. Title pages will be prepared in manuscript.

WAR DIARY
or
INTELLIGENCE SUMMARY.

(*Erase heading not required.*)

Place	Date	Hour	Summary of Events and Information	Remarks and references to Appendices
OBERCASSEL	25		Bn in training. Boys bathe at OBERCASSEL SCHOOLS.	JHC
do	26		Bn in training.	JHC
do	27		Bn in training	JHC
do	28		Bn in training. Divisional Cross Country Run. Bn get second place. Sgt Grey & Pte Gostling win the 1st & 2nd Individual prizes respectively.	JHC

March 1st 1919

J. S. Pearson Capt.
Commanding 1st Dorset Regt.

D. D. & L., London, E.C.
(A10266) Wt W5300/P713 750,000 2/18 Sch. 52 Forms/C2118/16

Instructions regarding War Diaries and Intelligence Summaries are contained in F. S. Regs., Part II. and the Staff Manual respectively. Title pages will be prepared in manuscript.

WAR DIARY
or
INTELLIGENCE SUMMARY.
(Erase heading not required.)

Army Form C. 2118.

MARCH 1919 — 1st DORSET REGT. — Vol 55

Place	Date	Hour	Summary of Events and Information	Remarks and references to Appendices
OBERCASSEL	1		Training during the morning "C" Coy on Outpost Duty. "Farewell Concert" by the Pedlars to the Regular Battalions of the Division, in the Stadt Theatre. 1st Dorset Regt represented by 20 Officers and 224 O.R.	WC
	2.		Divine Service. Summer time came into operation	WC
	3.		Training. Specialist classes for Lewis Gunners & NCOs commenced.	WC
	4.		Training. Coys bathed	WC
	5.		Training during morning	WC
	6.		Ditto	WC
	7		Training. Special instruction in use of the Barr and Stroud Rangefinder. The 1st Bn Band arrived from England.	WC
	8		Training	WC

D. D. & L., London, E.C.
(A10266) Wt W5300/P713 750,000 2/18 Sch. 52 Forms/C2118/16

Instructions regarding War Diaries and Intelligence Summaries are contained in F. S. Regs., Part II. and the Staff Manual respectively. Title pages will be prepared in manuscript.

WAR DIARY
or
INTELLIGENCE SUMMARY.
(Erase heading not required.)

Army Form C. 2118.

Place	Date	Hour	Summary of Events and Information	Remarks and references to Appendices
OBERCASSEL	9		~~Training~~ Divine Service	S.F.C.
	10.		Training. 'B' Coy beat 'D' in Inter-half coy Football knock out 4-0	S.F.C.
	11.		Training and Bathing.	S.F.C.
	12.		Training	S.F.C.
	13.		Training.	S.F.C.
	14.		G.O.C. 32nd Division inspected the Battalion, Transport included, prior to leaving Division.	S.F.C.
	15		Training.	S.F.C.
	16		Divine Service. ~~Division~~ G.O.C. Lancashire Division visited the Bn and inspected Billets.	S.F.C.
	17		Training	S.F.C.
	18.		Bathing. 5 officers and 137 O.R transferred to 15th Hampshire Bn. (for Army of occupation)	S.F.C.
ROMLINGHOVEN	19.		Remainder of Bn. closed into ROMLINGHOVEN, 53rd KING'S LIVERPOOL Battn arrived to relieve 1st DORSET REGT. 'C' Coy still on Outpost Duty.	S.F.C.

D. D. & L., London, E.C.
(A10266) Wt W5300/P713 750,000 2/18 Sch. 52 Forms/C2118/16

Instructions regarding War Diaries and Intelligence Summaries are contained in F. S. Regs., Part II. and the Staff Manual respectively. Title pages will be prepared in manuscript.

WAR DIARY
or
INTELLIGENCE SUMMARY.
(Erase heading not required.)

Army Form C. 2118.

Place	Date	Hour	Summary of Events and Information	Remarks and references to Appendices
ROMLINGHOVEN	20.		Bn supplying Outpost Coy.	SJC
	21.		2 officers and 42 O.R. leave for demobilization.	SJC
	22.		28 O.R. who left on 21st return from Concentration Camp & demobilization stopped on account of pending strikes in England.	SJC
	23.		Divine Service in OBERCASSEL CHURCH.	SJC
GRENAU	24.		Battalion relieved by 52nd KINGS LIVERPOOL REGT in Outpost Line at ROMLINGHOVEN. Battalion marched to GRENAU (BONN) and billeted at STADT HALLE.	SJC
	25		Arranging and cleaning of billet.	SJC
	26.		Bn continues reduction to Cadre. 81 O.R. proceed on demobilization.	SJC
	27		2 Officers & 17 OR proceed on demobilization.	SJC
	28		7 Officer Ranks proceed ~~to~~ demobilization. 41 O.R. join the 15th Hampshire Bn.	SJC

D. D. & L., London, E.C.
(A10266) Wt W5300/P713 750,000 2/18 Sch. 52 Forms/C2118/16

Army Form C. 2118.

WAR DIARY
or
INTELLIGENCE SUMMARY.
(Erase heading not required.)

Instructions regarding War Diaries and Intelligence Summaries are contained in F. S. Regs., Part II. and the Staff Manual respectively. Title pages will be prepared in manuscript.

Place	Date	Hour	Summary of Events and Information	Remarks and references to Appendices
GRENAU	29		1 Officer + 4 O.R. proceeded on demobilization.	[illegible]
	30.		18 O.R. proceed on demobilization	[illegible]
	31.		Bn in Billets.	[illegible]
			[illegible signature] Lieut Colonel	
			1. 4. 19. Cmdg 1st Bn Dorset Regiment	

D. D. & L., London, E.C.
(A10266) Wt W5300/P713 750,000 2/18 Sch. 52 Forms/C2118/16

www.ingramcontent.com/pod-product-compliance
Lightning Source LLC
Chambersburg PA
CBHW081422300426
44108CB00016BA/2282